Volume 1
Understanding
Cisco® Networking Technologies
Exam 200-301

Volume 1
Understanding
Cisco® Networking Technologies
Exam 200-301

Todd Lammle

SYBEX®
A Wiley Brand

Acknowledgments

There were many people that helped me build these new CCNA books. First, Kenyon Brown helped me put together the direction for the books and managed the internal editing at Wiley, so thank you, Ken, for working diligently for many months keeping these books moving along. The editors that I personally used in this first book in the CCNA series were Troy McMillan, who read each chapter in the full series multiple times, making amazing discoveries both technically and editorially and Todd Montgomery who also read through every chapter and helped with the technical edits with a sharp detailed eye. Also, Monica Lammle read and re-read each chapter and really helped me keep the voicing in place throughout the editorial process, which isn't an easy thing to do! Thanks also to Christine O'Connor, my production editor at Wiley for well over a decade now, and Louise Watson, proofreader at Word One.

About the Author

Todd Lammle is the authority on Cisco certification and internetworking and is Cisco certified in most Cisco certification categories. He is a world-renowned author, speaker, trainer, and consultant. Todd has three decades of experience working with LANs, WANs, and large enterprise licensed and unlicensed wireless networks, and lately he's been implementing large Cisco Security networks using Firepower/FTD and ISE.

His years of real-world experience are evident in his writing; he is not just an author but an experienced networking engineer with very practical experience from working on the largest networks in the world at such companies as Xerox, Hughes Aircraft, Texaco, AAA, Cisco, and Toshiba, among many others.

Todd has published over 90 books, including the very popular *CCNA: Cisco Certified Network Associate Study Guide, CCNA Wireless Study Guide, CCNA Data Center Study Guide, SSFIPS (Firepower)*, and *CCNP Security*, all from Sybex. He runs an international consulting and training company based in Colorado, where he spends his free time in the mountains playing with his golden retrievers.

You can reach Todd through his website at `www.lammle.com`.

Contents at a Glance

Contents

Introduction

Welcome to the exciting world of internetworking and your path towards Cisco certification. If you've picked up this book because you want to improve yourself and your life with a better, more satisfying, and secure job, you've chosen well!

Whether you're striving to enter the thriving, dynamic IT sector or seeking to enhance your skill set and advance your position within it, being Cisco certified can seriously stack the odds in your favor to help you attain your goals. This book is a great start.

Cisco certifications are powerful instruments of success that also markedly improve your grasp of all things internetworking. As you progress through this book, you'll gain a strong, foundational understanding of networking that reaches far beyond Cisco devices. And when you finish this book, you'll be ready to tackle the next step toward Cisco certification.

Essentially, by beginning your journey towards becoming Cisco certified, you're proudly announcing that you want to become an unrivaled networking expert, a goal that this book will help get you underway to achieving. Congratulations in advance for taking the first step towards your brilliant future!

 To find your included bonus material, as well as Todd Lammle videos, practice questions and hands-on labs, please see www.lammle.com/ccna.

Cisco's Network Certifications

It used to be that to secure the holy grail of Cisco certifications—the CCIE—you passed only one written test before being faced with a grueling, formidable hands-on lab. This intensely daunting, all-or-nothing approach made it nearly impossible to succeed and predictably didn't work out too well for most people.

Cisco responded to this issue by creating a series of new certifications, which not only created a sensible, stepping-stone-path to the highly coveted CCIE prize, it gave employers a way to accurately rate and measure the skill levels of prospective and current employees. This exciting paradigm shift in Cisco's certification path truly opened doors that few were allowed through before!

Way back in 1998, obtaining the Cisco Certified Network Associate (CCNA) certification was the first pitch in the Cisco certification climb. It was also the official prerequisite to each of the more advanced levels. But that changed in 2007, when Cisco announced the Cisco Certified Entry Network Technician (CCENT) certification. Then again, in May 2016, Cisco proclaimed new updates to the CCENT and CCNA Routing and Switching (R/S) tests. Today, things have changed dramatically again.

In July of 2019, Cisco switched up the certification process more than they have in the preceding 20 years! They've announced all new certifications that began in February 2020, and probably the reason you are reading this book!

For starters, the CCENT course and exam (or ICND1 and ICND2) are no more, plus there are no prerequisites for any of the certifications at all now, meaning for example, that you can go straight to CCNP without having to take the new CCNA exams.

The new Cisco certification process will look like Figure I.1.

FIGURE I.1   The Cisco certification path

Entry	Associate	Professional	Expert	Architect
Starting point for individuals interested in starting a career as a networking professional.	Master the essentials needed to launch a rewarding career and expand your job possibilities with the latest technologies.	Select a core technology track and a focused concentration exam to customize your professional-level certification.	This certification is accepted worldwide as the most prestigious certification in the technology industry.	The highest level of accreditation achievable and recognizes the architectural expertise of network designers.
CCT	DevNet Associate	DevNet Professional	CCDE	CCAr
	CCNA	CCNP Enterprise	CCIE Enterprise Infrastructure CCIE Enterprise Wireless	
		CCNP Collaboration	CCIE Collaboration	
		CCNP Data Center	CCIE Data Center	
		CCNP Security	CCIE Security	
		CCNP Service Provider	CCIE Service Provider	

First, the listed entry certification of CCT is just not worth your time. Instead, you'll want to head directly to CCNA after this foundational book, and then straight to the CCNP of your choice.

This book is a powerful tool to get you started in your CCNA studies, and it's vital to understand that material in it before you go on to conquer any other certifications!

What Does This Book Cover?

This book covers everything you need to know to solidly prepare you for getting into your CCNA studies. Be advised that just because much of the material in this book won't be official Cisco CCNA objectives in the future doesn't mean you won't be tested on it. Understanding the foundational, real-world networking information, and skills offered in this book is critical to your certifications and your career!

So as you move through this book, here's a snapshot of what you'll learn chapter by chapter:

Chapter 1: Internetworking   In Chapter 1, you'll learn the basics of the Open Systems Interconnection (OSI) model the way Cisco wants you to learn it.

Chapter 2: Ethernet Networking and Data Encapsulation   This chapter will provide you with the Ethernet foundation you need in order to understand the CCNA and CCNP material. Data encapsulation is discussed in detail in this chapter as well.

Chapter 3: Introduction to TCP/IP   Chapter 3 provides you with the background necessary for success on the CCNA/NP exams, as well as in the real world, with a thorough presentation of TCP/IP. It's an in-depth chapter that covers the very beginnings of the Internet Protocol stack and moves all the way to IP addressing. You'll gain an understanding of the difference between a network address and a broadcast address before finally ending with valuable network troubleshooting tips.

Chapter 4: Easy Subnetting   Believe it or not, you'll actually be able to subnet a network in your head after reading this chapter! Success will take a little determination, but you'll find plenty of help in this chapter as well as at: www.lammle.com/ccna.

Chapter 5: Troubleshooting IP Addressing   Here, we'll continue on from Chapters 3 & 4 and begin covering how to troubleshoot basic IP issues. You'll also test your understanding of the previous two chapters.

Chapter 6: Cisco's Internetworking Operating System (IOS)   Chapter 6 introduces you to the Cisco Internetworking Operating System (IOS) and command-line interface (CLI). In it, you'll learn how to turn on a router and configure the basics of the IOS, including setting passwords, banners, and more.

Chapter 7: Managing a Cisco Internetwork   This chapter provides you with the management skills needed to run a Cisco IOS network. Backing up and restoring the IOS and key router configuration skills are covered, as are the troubleshooting tools necessary to keep a network up and running well.

Chapter 8: Managing Cisco Devices   This chapter describes the boot process of Cisco routers, the configuration register, and how to manage Cisco IOS files. It wraps up with a section on Cisco's new licensing strategy for IOS.

Chapter 9: IP Routing   This is a super fun chapter because in it, we'll begin building a Cisco network and actually adding IP addresses and route data between routers. You also learn about static, default, and dynamic routing. The fundamentals covered in this chapter are probably the most important in the book because understanding the IP Routing process is what Cisco is all about! It's actually assumed that you solidly possess this knowledge when you get into the CCNA & CCNP studies.

Chapter 10: Wide Area Networks   This is the last chapter in the book. It covers multiple protocols in depth, especially HDLC and PPP for serial connections. We'll also discuss many other technologies such as cellular, MPLS T1/E1, and cable. I'll guide you through strategic troubleshooting examples in the configuration sections—don't even think of skipping them!

Chapter

1

Internetworking

Welcome to the exciting world of internetworking! This chapter is essentially an internetworking review, focusing on how to connect networks together using Cisco routers and switches. As a heads up, I've written it with the assumption that you have at least some basic networking knowledge.

Let's start by defining exactly what an internetwork is: You create an internetwork when you connect two or more networks via a router and configure a logical network addressing scheme with a protocol such as IP or IPv6.

I'm also going to dissect the Open Systems Interconnection (OSI) model and describe each part of it to you in detail because you really need comprehensive knowledge of it. Understanding the OSI model is key to the solid foundation you'll need to build upon with the more advanced Cisco networking knowledge gained down the line.

The OSI model has seven hierarchical layers that were developed to enable different networks to communicate reliably between disparate systems. Since this book is centering upon all things CCNA, it's crucial for you to understand the OSI model as Cisco sees it, so that's how I'll be presenting the seven layers to you.

> To find your included bonus material, as well as Todd Lammle videos, practice questions and hands-on labs, please see www.lammle.com/ccna.

Internetworking Basics

Before exploring internetworking models and the OSI model's specifications, you need to grasp the big picture and the answer to this burning question: Why is it so important to learn Cisco internetworking anyway?

Networks and networking have grown exponentially over the past 20 years, and understandably so. They've had to evolve at light speed just to keep up with huge increases in basic, mission-critical user needs (e.g., the simple sharing of data and printers) as well as greater burdens like multimedia remote presentations, conferencing, and the like. Unless everyone who needs to share network resources is located in the same office space, which is increasingly rare, the challenge is to connect relevant networks so all users can share the wealth of whatever services and resources are required, on site or remotely.

Figure 1.1 shows a basic *local area network (LAN)* that's connected using a *hub*, which is basically just an antiquated device that connects wires together. Keep in mind that a simple network like this would be considered one collision domain and one broadcast domain. No worries if you have no idea what I mean by that because we'll go over that soon. I'm going to talk about collision and broadcast domains enough to make you dream about them!

FIGURE 1.1   A very basic network

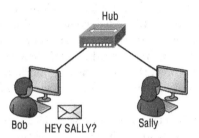

Things really can't get much simpler than this. And yes, though you can still find this configuration in some home networks, even many of those as well as the smallest business networks are more complicated today. As we move through this book, I'll just keep building upon this tiny network a bit at a time until we arrive at some really nice, robust, and current network designs—the types that will help you get your certification and a job!

But as I said, we'll get there one step at a time, so let's get back to the network shown in Figure 1.1 with this scenario: Bob wants to send Sally a file, and to complete that goal in this kind of network, he'll simply broadcast that he's looking for her, which is basically just shouting out over the network. Think of it like this: Bob walks out of his house and yells down a street called Chaos Court in order to contact Sally. This might work if Bob and Sally were the only ones living there, but not so much if it's crammed with homes and all the others living there are always hollering up and down the street to their neighbors just like Bob. Nope, Chaos Court would absolutely live up to its name, with all those residents going off whenever they felt like it—and believe it or not, our networks actually still work this way to a degree! So, given a choice, would you stay in Chaos Court, or would you pull up stakes and move on over to a nice new modern community called Broadway Lanes, which offers plenty of amenities and room for your home plus future additions all on nice, wide streets that can easily handle all present and future traffic? If you chose the latter, good choice...so did Sally, and she now lives a much quieter life, getting letters (packets) from Bob instead of a headache!

The scenario I just described brings me to the basic point of what this book and the Cisco certification objectives are really all about. My goal of showing you how to create efficient networks and segment them correctly in order to minimize all the chaotic yelling and screaming going on in them is a universal theme throughout my Cisco series books. It's just inevitable that you'll have to break up a large network into a bunch of smaller ones at some point to match a network's equally inevitable growth, and as that expansion occurs, user response time simultaneously dwindles to a frustrating crawl. But if you master the vital technology and skills I have in store for you in this series, you'll be well equipped to rescue your network and its users by creating an efficient new network neighborhood to give them key amenities like the bandwidth they need to meet evolving demands.

And this is no joke; most of us think of growth as good and it can be. But as many experience daily when commuting to work, school, etc., it can also mean your LAN's traffic congestion can reach critical mass and grind to a halt! Again, the solution to this problem begins with breaking up a massive network into a number of smaller ones—something called *network segmentation*. This concept is a lot like planning a new community or modernizing an existing one. More streets are added, complete with new intersections and traffic signals, plus post offices are built with official maps documenting all those street names and directions on how to get to each. You'll need to effect new laws to keep order to it all and provide a police station to protect this nice new neighborhood as well. In a networking neighborhood environment, all of this infrastructure is managed using devices like *routers*, *switches*, and *bridges*.

So let's take a look at our new neighborhood now.... Because the word has gotten out, many more hosts have moved into it, so it's time to upgrade that new high-capacity infrastructure that we promised to handle the increase in population. Figure 1.2 shows a network that's been segmented with a switch, making each network segment that connects to the switch its own separate collision domain. Doing this results in a lot less yelling!

FIGURE 1.2 A switch can break up collision domains.

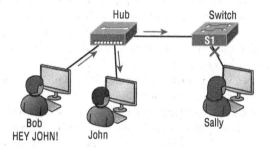

This is a great start, but I really want you to make note of the fact that this network is still one, single broadcast domain, meaning that we've really only decreased our screaming and yelling—not eliminated it. For example, if there's some sort of vital announcement that everyone in our neighborhood needs to hear about, it will definitely still get loud! You can see that the hub used in Figure 1.2 just extended the one collision domain from the switch port. The result is that John received the data from Bob but, happily, Sally did not, which is good because Bob intended to talk with John directly. If he had needed to send a broadcast instead, everyone, including Sally, would have received it, possibly causing unnecessary congestion.

Here's a list of some of the things that commonly cause LAN traffic congestion:

▪ Too many hosts in a collision or broadcast domain

▪ Broadcast storms

▪ Too much multicast traffic

- Low bandwidth
- Adding hubs for connectivity to the network
- A bunch of ARP broadcasts

Take another look at Figure 1.2 and make sure you see that I extended the main hub from Figure 1.1 to a switch in Figure 1.2. I did that because hubs don't segment a network; they just connect network segments. Basically, it's an inexpensive way to connect a couple of PCs, and again, that's great for home use and troubleshooting, but that's about it!

As our planned community starts to grow, we'll need to add more streets along with traffic control and even some basic security. We'll achieve this by adding routers because these convenient devices are used to connect networks and route packets of data from one network to another. Cisco became the de facto standard for routers because of its unparalleled selection of high-quality router products and fantastic service. So never forget that by default, routers are basically employed to efficiently break up a *broadcast domain*—the set of all devices on a network segment, which are allowed to "hear" all broadcasts sent out on that specific segment.

Figure 1.3 depicts a router in our growing network, creating an internetwork and breaking up broadcast domains.

FIGURE 1.3   Routers create an internetwork.

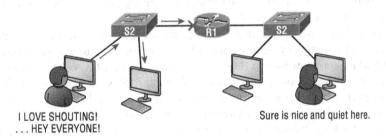

The network in Figure 1.3 is actually a pretty cool little network. Each host is connected to its own collision domain because of the switch, and the router has created two broadcast domains. So now Sally is happily living in peace in a completely different neighborhood, no longer subjected to Bob's incessant shouting! If Bob wants to talk with Sally, he has to send a packet with a destination address using her IP address—he cannot broadcast for her!

But there's more... Routers provide connections to *wide area network (WAN)* services as well via a serial interface for WAN connections—specifically, a V.35 physical interface on a Cisco router.

Let me make sure you understand why breaking up a broadcast domain is so important. When a host or server sends a network broadcast, every device on the network must read and process that broadcast—unless you have a router. When the router's interface receives this broadcast, it can respond by basically saying, "no thanks," and discard the broadcast without forwarding it on to other networks. Even though routers are known for breaking up broadcast domains by default, it's important to remember that they break up collision domains as well.

There are two advantages to using routers in your network:

- They don't forward broadcasts by default.
- They can filter the network based on layer 3 (Network layer) information such as an IP address.

Here are four ways a router functions in your network:

- Packet switching
- Packet filtering
- Internetwork communication
- Path selection

I'll tell you all about the various layers later in this chapter, but for now, it's helpful to think of routers as layer 3 switches. Unlike plain-vanilla layer 2 switches, which forward or filter frames, routers (layer 3 switches) use logical addressing and provide an important capacity called *packet switching*. Routers can also provide packet filtering via access lists, and when routers connect two or more networks together and use logical addressing (IP or IPv6), you then have an *internetwork*. Finally, routers use a routing table, essentially a map of the internetwork, to make best path selections for getting data to its proper destination and properly forward packets to remote networks.

Conversely, we don't use layer 2 switches to create internetworks because they don't break up broadcast domains by default. Instead, they're employed to add functionality to a network LAN. The main purpose of these switches is to make a LAN work better—to optimize its performance—providing more bandwidth for the LAN's users. Also, these switches don't forward packets to other networks like routers do. Instead, they only "switch" frames from one port to another within the switched network. And don't worry, even though you're probably thinking, "Wait—what are frames and packets?" I promise to completely fill you in later in this chapter. For now, think of a packet as a package containing data.

Okay, so by default, switches break up collision domains, but what are these things? *Collision domain* is an Ethernet term used to describe a network scenario in which one device sends a packet out on a network segment and every other device on that same segment is forced to pay attention no matter what. This isn't very efficient because if a different device tries to transmit at the same time, a collision will occur, requiring both devices to retransmit, one at a time—not good! This happens a lot in a hub environment, where each host segment connects to a hub that represents only one collision domain and a single broadcast domain. By contrast, each and every port on a switch represents its own collision domain, allowing network traffic to flow much more smoothly.

 Switches create separate collision domains within a single broadcast domain. Routers provide a separate broadcast domain for each interface. Don't let this confuse you.

The term *bridging* was introduced before routers and switches were implemented, so it's pretty common to hear people referring to switches as bridges. That's because bridges and switches basically do the same thing—break up collision domains on a LAN. Of note is that you cannot buy a physical bridge these days, only LAN switches that use bridging technologies. This does not mean that you won't still hear Cisco and others refer to LAN switches as multiport bridges now and then.

But does this mean that a switch is really just a multiple-port bridge with more brain-power? Actually, pretty much, but there are still some key differences. Switches do provide a bridging function, but they do it with greatly enhanced management ability and features. Plus, most bridges had only two or four ports, which is severely limiting. Of course, it was possible to get your hands on a bridge with up to 16 ports, but that's nothing compared to the hundreds of ports available on some.

Figure 1.4 shows how a network would look with all these internetwork devices in place. Remember, a router doesn't just break up broadcast domains for every LAN inter-face, it breaks up collision domains too.

FIGURE 1.4   Internetworking devices

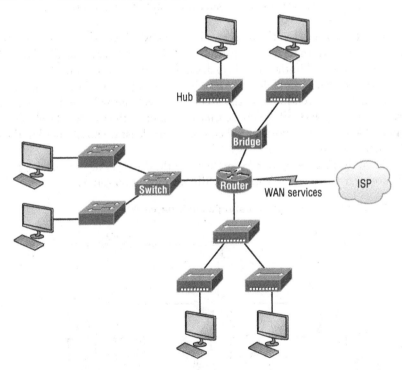

Looking at Figure 1.4, did you notice that the router has the center stage position and connects each physical network together? I'm stuck with using this layout because of the ancient bridges and hubs involved. I really hope you don't run across a network like this, but it's still really important to understand the strategic ideas that this figure represents.

See that bridge up at the top of our internetwork shown in Figure 1.4? It's there to connect the hubs to a router. The bridge breaks up collision domains, but all the hosts connected to both hubs are still crammed into the same broadcast domain. That bridge also created only three collision domains, one for each port, which means that each device connected to a hub is in the same collision domain as every other device connected to that same hub. This is really lame and to be avoided if possible, but it's still better than having one collision domain for all hosts! So don't do this at home...it's a great museum piece and a wonderful example of what not to do, but this inefficient design would be terrible for use in today's networks. It does show us how far we've come though, and again, the foundational concepts it illustrates are really important for you to get.

And I want you to notice something else: The three interconnected hubs at the bottom of the figure also connect to the router. This setup creates one collision domain and one broadcast domain and makes that bridged network, with its two collision domains, look much better by contrast!

> **NOTE** Don't misunderstand... Bridges/switches are used to segment networks, but they will not isolate broadcast or multicast packets.

The best network connected to the router is the LAN switched network on the left. Why? Because each port on that switch effectively breaks up collision domains. But it's not all good—all devices are still in the same broadcast domain. Do you remember why this can be really bad? One, because all devices must listen to all broadcasts transmitted. Two, if your broadcast domains are too large, the users have less bandwidth and are required to process more broadcasts. Network response time eventually will slow to a level that may cause riots and strikes, so it's important to keep your broadcast domains small in the vast majority of networks today.

Once there are only switches in our example network, things really change a lot. Figure 1.5 demonstrates a network you'll typically stumble upon today.

FIGURE 1.5 Switched networks creating an internetwork

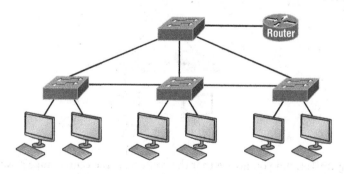

Here I've placed the LAN switches at the center of this network world, with the router connecting the logical networks. If I went ahead and implemented this design, I'll have created something called virtual LANs, or VLANs, which are used when you logically break up broadcast domains in a layer 2, switched network. It's really important to understand that even in a switched network environment, you still need a router to provide communication between VLANs. Don't forget that!

Still, clearly the best network design is the one that's perfectly configured to meet the business requirements of the specific company or client it serves, and it's usually one in which LAN switches exist in harmony with routers strategically placed in the network. It's my hope that this book will help you understand the basics of routers and switches so you can make solid, informed decisions on a case-by-case basis and be able to achieve that goal! But I digress....

So let's go back to Figure 1.4 now for a minute and really scrutinize it because you need to be able to answer this question correctly: How many collision domains and broadcast domains are really there in this internetwork? I hope you answered nine collision domains and three broadcast domains! The broadcast domains are definitely the easiest to spot because only routers break up broadcast domains by default, and since there are three interface connections, that gives you three broadcast domains. But do you see the nine collision domains? Just in case that's a "no," I'll explain: The all-hub network at the bottom is one collision domain; the bridge network on top equals three collision domains. Add in the switch network of five collision domains—one for each switch port—and you get a total of nine.

While we're at this, in Figure 1.5, each port on the switch is a separate collision domain, and each VLAN would be a separate broadcast domain. So how many collision domains do you see here? I'm counting 12. Remember that connections between the switches are considered a collision domain. Since the figure doesn't show any VLAN information, we can assume the default of one broadcast domain is in place.

Before we move on to Internetworking Models, let's take a look at a few more network devices that we'll find in pretty much every network today as shown in Figure 1.6.

FIGURE 1.6 Other devices typically found in our internetworks today

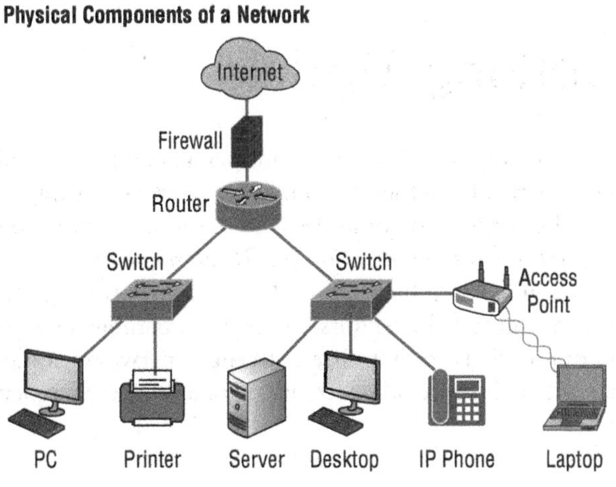

Physical Components of a Network

Taking off from the switched network in Figure 1.5, you'll find WLAN devices, including AP's, wireless controllers and firewalls. You'd be seriously hard pressed not to find these devices in your networks today. Let's look closer at these devices starting with WLAN devices: These devices connect wireless devices such as computers, printers, and tablets to the network. Since pretty much every device manufactured today has a wireless NIC, you just need to configure a basic access point (AP) to connect to a traditional wired network.

Access Points or APs: These devices allow wireless devices to connect to a wired network and extend a collision domain from a switch. They're typically in their own broadcast domain or what we'll refer to as a Virtual LAN (VLAN). An AP can be a simple stand-alone device, but today they're usually managed by wireless controllers, either in house or through the internet.

WLAN Controllers: These are the devices that network administrators or network operations centers use to manage access points in medium to large to extremely large quantities. The WLAN controller automatically handles the configuration of wireless access points and was typically used only in larger enterprise systems. However, with Cisco's acquisition of Meraki systems, you can easily manage a small to medium-sized wireless network via the cloud using their simple-to-configure web controller system.

Firewalls: These devices are network security systems that monitor and control incoming and outgoing network traffic based on predetermined security rules—usually an Intrusion Protection System (IPS). Cisco Adaptive Security Appliance (ASA) firewall typically establishes a barrier between a trusted, secure internal network and the Internet, which is not secure nor trusted. Cisco's acquisition of Sourcefire put them in the top of the market with Next Generation Firewalls (NGFW) and Next Generation IPS (NGIPS), which Cisco calls "Firepower." Firepower runs on dedicated appliances: Cisco's ASA's, ISR routers and even on Meraki products.

Okay, so now that you've gotten a pretty thorough introduction to internetworking and the various devices that populate an internetwork, it's time to head into exploring the internetworking models.

Internetworking Models

First a little history: When networks first came into being, computers could typically communicate only with computers from the same manufacturer. For example, companies ran either a complete DECnet solution or an IBM solution, never both together. In the late 1970s, the *Open Systems Interconnection (OSI) reference model* was created by the International Organization for Standardization (ISO) to break through this barrier.

The OSI model was meant to help vendors create interoperable network devices and software in the form of protocols so that different vendor networks could work in peaceable accord with each other. Like world peace, it'll probably never happen completely, but it's still a great goal.

Anyway, the OSI model is the primary architectural model for networks. It describes how data and network information are communicated from an application on one computer through the network media to an application on another computer. The OSI reference model breaks this approach into layers.

Coming up, I'll explain the layered approach to you plus how to use it when troubleshooting our internetworks.

 ISO, OSI, and soon you'll hear about IOS—confusing, right? Just remember that the ISO created the OSI and that Cisco created the IOS (Internetworking Operating System). All better now.

The Layered Approach

Understand that a *reference model* is a conceptual blueprint of how communications should take place. It addresses all the processes required for effective communication and divides them into logical groupings called *layers*. When a communication system is designed in this manner, it's known as a hierarchical or *layered architecture*.

Think of it like this: You and some friends want to start a company. One of the first things you'll do is sort out every task that must be done and decide who will do what. You would move on to determine the order in which you would like everything to be done with careful consideration of how all your specific operations relate to each other. You would then organize everything into departments (e.g., sales, inventory, and shipping), with each department dealing with its specific responsibilities and keeping its own staff busy enough to focus on their own particular area of the enterprise.

In this scenario, departments are a metaphor for the layers in a communication system. For things to run smoothly, the staff of each department has to trust in and rely heavily upon those in the others to do their jobs well. During planning sessions, you would take notes, recording the entire process to guide later discussions and clarify standards of operation, thereby creating your business blueprint—your own reference model.

And once your business is launched, your department heads, each armed with the part of the blueprint relevant to their own department, will develop practical ways to implement their distinct tasks. These practical methods, or protocols, will then be compiled into a standard operating procedures manual and followed closely because each procedure will have been included for different reasons, delimiting their various degrees of importance and implementation. All of this will become vital if you form a partnership or acquire another company because then it will be really important that the new company's business model is compatible with yours!

Models happen to be really important to software developers too. They often use a reference model to understand computer communication processes so they can determine which functions should be accomplished on a given layer. This means that if someone is creating a protocol for a certain layer, they only need to be concerned with their target layer's function. Software that maps to another layer's protocols and is specifically designed to be deployed there will handle additional functions. The technical term for this idea is *binding.* The communication processes that are related to each other are bound, or grouped together, at a particular layer.

Advantages of Reference Models

The OSI model is hierarchical, and there are many advantages that can be applied to any layered model. But as I said, the OSI model's primary purpose is to allow different vendors' networks to interoperate.

Here's a list of some of the more important benefits of using the OSI layered model:

- It divides the network communication process into smaller and simpler components, facilitating component development, design, and troubleshooting.
- It allows multiple-vendor development through the standardization of network components.
- It encourages industry standardization by clearly defining what functions occur at each layer of the model.
- It allows various types of network hardware and software to communicate.
- It prevents changes in one layer from affecting other layers to expedite development.

The OSI Reference Model

One of best gifts the OSI specifications give us is paving the way for the data transfer between disparate hosts running different operating systems, like Unix hosts, Windows machines, Macs, smartphones, and so on.

And remember, the OSI is a logical model, not a physical one. It's essentially a set of guidelines that developers can use to create and implement applications to run on a network. It also provides a framework for creating and implementing networking standards, devices, and internetworking schemes.

The OSI has seven different layers, divided into two groups. The top three layers define how the applications within the end stations will communicate with each other as well as with users. The bottom four layers define how data is transmitted end to end.

Figure 1.7 shows the three upper layers and their functions.

FIGURE 1.7 The upper layers

Application	• Provides a user interface
Presentation	• Presents data in the proper format • Handles processing such as encryption
Session	• Keeps different applications' data separate

When looking at Figure 1.7, understand that users interact with the computer at the Application layer and also that the upper layers are responsible for applications communicating between hosts. None of the upper layers knows anything about networking or network addresses because that's the responsibility of the four bottom layers.

In Figure 1.8, which shows the four lower layers and their functions, you can see that it's these four bottom layers that define how data is transferred through physical media like wire, cable, fiber optics, switches, and routers.

FIGURE 1.8   The lower layers

Transport	• Provides reliable or unreliable delivery • Performs error correction before retransmit
Network	• Provides logical addressing, which routers use for path determination
Data Link	• Combines packets into bytes and bytes into frames • Provides access to media using MAC address • Performs error detection not correction
Physical	• Moves bits between devices • Specifies voltage, wire speed, and pinout of cables

These bottom layers also determine how to rebuild a data stream from a transmitting host to a destination host's application.

The following network devices operate at all seven layers of the OSI model:

- *Network management stations (NMSs)*

- Web and application servers

- Gateways (not default gateways)

- Servers

- Network hosts

Basically, the ISO is pretty much the Emily Post of the network protocol world. Just as Ms. Post wrote the book setting the standards—or protocols—for human social interaction, the ISO developed the OSI reference model as the precedent and guide for an open network protocol set. Defining the etiquette of communication models, it remains the most popular means of comparison for protocol suites today.

The OSI reference model has the following seven layers:

- Application layer (layer 7)

- Presentation layer (layer 6)

- Session layer (layer 5)

- Transport layer (layer 4)

- Network layer (layer 3)

- Data Link layer (layer 2)
- Physical layer (layer 1)

Some people like to use a mnemonic to remember the seven layers, such as **All People Seem To Need Data Processing**. Figure 1.9 shows a summary of the functions defined at each layer of the OSI model.

FIGURE 1.9   OSI layer functions

Application	• File, print, message, database, and application services
Presentation	• Data encryption, compression, and translation services
Session	• Dialog control

Transport	• End-to-end connection
Network	• Routing

Data Link	• Framing
Physical	• Physical topology

I've separated the seven-layer model into three different functions: the upper layers, the middle layers, and the bottom layers. The upper layers communicate with the user interface and application, the middle layers handle reliable communication and routing to a remote network, and the bottom layers communicate to the local network.

With this in mind, you're now ready to explore each layer's function in detail.

The Application Layer

The *Application layer* of the OSI model marks the spot where users actually communicate to the computer and comes into play only when it's clear that access to the network will be needed soon. Take the case of Internet Explorer (IE). You could actually uninstall every trace of networking components like TCP/IP, the NIC card, and so on and still use IE to view a local HTML document. But things would get ugly if you tried to do things like view a remote HTML document that must be retrieved because IE and other browsers act on these types of requests by attempting to access the Application layer. So basically, the Application layer is working as the interface between the actual application program and the next layer down by providing ways for the application to send information down through the protocol stack. This isn't actually part of the layered structure, because browsers don't live in the Application layer, but they interface with it as well as the relevant protocols when asked to access remote resources.

Identifying and confirming the communication partner's availability and verifying the required resources to permit the specified type of communication to take place also occurs at the Application layer. This is important because, like the lion's share of browser functions, computer applications sometimes need more than desktop resources. It's more typical than you would think for the communicating components of several network applications to come together to carry out a requested function. Here are a few good examples of these kinds of events:

- Web Browsing
- File transfers
- Email
- Enabling remote access
- Network management activities
- Client/server processes
- Information location

Many network applications provide services for communication over enterprise networks, but for present and future internetworking, the need is fast developing to reach beyond the limits of current physical networking.

> The Application layer works as the interface between actual application programs. This means end-user programs like Microsoft Word don't reside at the Application layer, they interface with the Application layer protocols. Later, in Chapter 3, "Introduction to TCP/IP," I'll talk in detail about a few important programs that actually reside at the Application layer, like Telnet, FTP, and TFTP.

The Presentation Layer

The *Presentation layer* gets its name from its purpose: It presents data to the Application layer and is responsible for data translation and code formatting. Think of it as the OSI model's translator, providing coding and conversion services. One very effective way of ensuring a successful data transfer is to convert the data into a standard format before transmission. Computers are configured to receive this generically formatted data and then reformat it back into its native state to read it. An example of this type of translation service occurs when translating old Extended Binary Coded Decimal Interchange Code (EBCDIC) data to ASCII, the American Standard Code for Information Interchange (often pronounced "askee"). So just remember that by providing translation services, the Presentation layer ensures that data transferred from the Application layer of one system can be read by the Application layer of another one.

With this in mind, it follows that the OSI would include protocols that define how standard data should be formatted, so key functions like data compression, decompression, encryption, and decryption are also associated with this layer. Some Presentation layer standards are involved in multimedia operations as well.

The Session Layer

The *Session layer* is responsible for setting up, managing, and dismantling sessions between Presentation layer entities and keeping user data separate. Dialog control between devices also occurs at this layer.

Communication between hosts' various applications at the Session layer, as from a client to a server, is coordinated and organized via three different modes: *simplex, half-duplex,* and *full-duplex.* Simplex is simple one-way communication, kind of like saying something and not getting a reply. Half-duplex is actual two-way communication, but it can take place in only one direction at a time, preventing the interruption of the transmitting device. It's like when pilots and ship captains communicate over their radios, or even a walkie-talkie. But full-duplex is exactly like a real conversation where devices can transmit and receive at the same time, much like two people arguing or interrupting each other during a telephone conversation.

The Transport Layer

The *Transport layer* segments and reassembles data into a single data stream. Services located at this layer take all the various data received from upper-layer applications, then combine it into the same, concise data stream. These protocols provide end-to-end data transport services and can establish a logical connection between the sending host and destination host on an internetwork.

A pair of well-known protocols called TCP and UDP are integral to this layer, but no worries if you're not already familiar with them because I'll bring you up to speed later, in Chapter 3. For now, understand that although both work at the Transport layer, TCP is known as a reliable service but UDP is not. This distinction gives application developers more options because they have a choice between the two protocols when they are designing products for this layer.

The Transport layer is responsible for providing mechanisms for multiplexing upper-layer applications, establishing sessions, and tearing down virtual circuits. It can also hide the details of network-dependent information from the higher layers as well as provide transparent data transfer.

The term *reliable networking* can be used at the Transport layer. Reliable networking requires that acknowledgments, sequencing, and flow control will all be used.

The Transport layer can be either connectionless or connection-oriented, but because Cisco really wants you to understand the connection-oriented function of the Transport layer, I'm going to go into that in more detail here.

Connection-Oriented Communication

For reliable transport to occur, a device that wants to transmit must first establish a connection-oriented communication session with a remote device—its peer system—known as a *call setup* or a *three-way handshake*. Once this process is complete, the data transfer occurs, and when it's finished, a call termination takes place to tear down the virtual circuit.

Figure 1.10 depicts a typical reliable session taking place between sending and receiving systems. In it, you can see that both hosts' application programs begin by notifying their individual operating systems that a connection is about to be initiated. The two operating systems communicate by sending messages over the network confirming that the transfer is approved and that both sides are ready for it to take place. After all of this required synchronization takes place, a connection is fully established and the data transfer begins. And by the way, it's really helpful to understand that this virtual circuit setup is often referred to as overhead!

FIGURE 1.10   Establishing a connection-oriented session

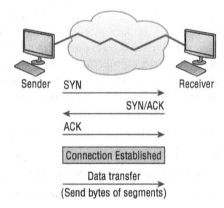

Okay, now while the information is being transferred between hosts, the two machines periodically check in with each other, communicating through their protocol software to ensure that all is going well and that the data is being received properly.

Here's a summary of the steps in the connection-oriented session—that three-way handshake—pictured in Figure 1.9:

- The first "connection agreement" segment is a request for *synchronization (SYN)*.

- The next segments *acknowledge (ACK)* the request and establish connection parameters—the rules—between hosts. These segments request that the receiver's sequencing is synchronized here as well so that a bidirectional connection can be formed.

- The final segment is also an acknowledgment, which notifies the destination host that the connection agreement has been accepted and that the actual connection has been established. Data transfer can now begin.

Sounds pretty simple, but things don't always flow so smoothly. Sometimes during a transfer, congestion can occur because a high-speed computer is generating data traffic a lot faster than the network itself can process it. And a whole bunch of computers simultaneously sending datagrams through a single gateway or destination can also jam things up pretty badly. In the latter case, a gateway or destination can become congested even though no single source caused the problem. Either way, the problem is basically akin to a freeway bottleneck—too much traffic for too small a capacity. It's not usually one car that's the problem; it's just that there are way too many cars on that freeway at once!

But what actually happens when a machine receives a flood of datagrams too quickly for it to process? It stores them in a memory section called a *buffer*. Sounds great; it's just that this buffering action can solve the problem only if the datagrams are part of a small burst. If the datagram deluge continues, eventually exhausting the device's memory, its flood capacity will be exceeded and it will dump any and all additional datagrams it receives like an overflowing bucket!

Flow Control

Since floods and losing data can both be tragic, we have a fail-safe solution in place known as *flow control*. Its job is to ensure data integrity at the Transport layer by allowing applications to request reliable data transport between systems. Flow control prevents a sending host on one side of the connection from overflowing the buffers in the receiving host. Reliable data transport employs a connection-oriented communications session between systems, and the protocols involved ensure that the following will be achieved:

- The segments delivered are acknowledged back to the sender upon their reception.

- Any segments not acknowledged are retransmitted.

- Segments are sequenced back into their proper order upon arrival at their destination.

- A manageable data flow is maintained in order to avoid congestion, overloading, or worse, data loss.

 The purpose of flow control is to provide a way for the receiving device to control the amount of data sent by the sender.

Because of the transport function, network flood control systems really work well. Instead of dumping and losing data, the Transport layer can issue a "not ready" indicator to the sender, or potential source of the flood. This mechanism works kind of like a stoplight, signaling the sending device to stop transmitting segment traffic to its overwhelmed peer. After the peer receiver processes the segments already in its memory reservoir, (its buffer), it sends out a "ready" transport indicator. When the machine waiting to transmit the rest of its datagrams receives this "go" indicator, it resumes its transmission. This process is pictured in Figure 1.11.

In a reliable, connection-oriented data transfer, datagrams are delivered to the receiving host hopefully in the same sequence they're transmitted. A failure will occur if any data segments are lost, duplicated, or damaged along the way—a problem solved by having the receiving host acknowledge that it has received each and every data segment.

FIGURE 1.11   Transmitting segments with flow control

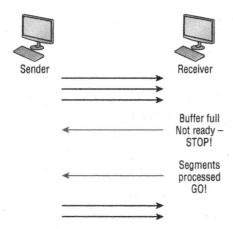

A service is considered connection-oriented if it has the following characteristics:

- A virtual circuit, or "three-way handshake," is set up.
- It uses sequencing.
- It uses acknowledgments.
- It uses flow control.

 The types of flow control are buffering, windowing, and congestion avoidance.

Windowing

Ideally, data throughput happens quickly and efficiently. And as you can imagine, it would be painfully slow if the transmitting machine had to actually wait for an acknowledgment after sending each and every segment! The quantity of data segments, measured in bytes, that the transmitting machine is allowed to send without receiving an acknowledgment is called a *window*.

 Windows are used to control the amount of outstanding, unacknowledged data segments.

The size of the window controls how much information is transferred from one end to the other before an acknowledgment is required. While some protocols quantify information depending on the number of packets, TCP/IP measures it by counting the number of bytes.

As you can see in Figure 1.12, there are two window sizes—one set to 1 and one set to 3.

FIGURE 1.12   Windowing

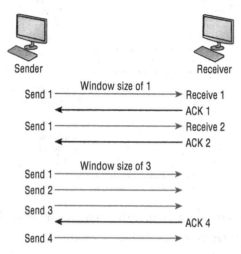

If you've configured a window size of 1, the sending machine will wait for an acknowledgment for each data segment it transmits before transmitting another one. A window set to 3 allows three to be transmitted before receiving an acknowledgment. In this simplified example, both the sending and receiving machines are workstations. Remember that in reality, the transmission isn't based on simple numbers but on the amount of bytes that can be sent.

If a receiving host fails to receive all the bytes that it should acknowledge, the host can improve the communication session by decreasing the window size.

Acknowledgments

Reliable data delivery ensures the integrity of a stream of data sent from one machine to the other through a fully functional data link. It guarantees that the data won't be duplicated or lost. This is achieved through something called *positive acknowledgment with retransmission*—a technique that requires a receiving machine to communicate with the transmitting source by sending an acknowledgment message back to the sender when it receives data. The sender documents each segment measured in bytes, then sends and waits for this acknowledgment before sending the next segment. Also important is that when it sends a segment, the transmitting machine starts a timer and will retransmit if the timer expires before it gets an acknowledgment back from the receiving end. Figure 1.13 pictures the process I just described.

FIGURE 1.13   Transport layer reliable delivery

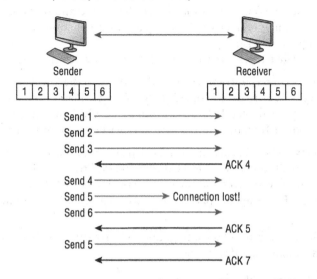

In the figure, the sending machine transmits segments 1, 2, and 3. The receiving node acknowledges that it has received them by requesting segment 4 (what it is expecting next). When it receives the acknowledgment, the sender then transmits segments 4, 5, and 6. If segment 5 doesn't make it to the destination, the receiving node acknowledges the event with a request for the segment to be re-sent. The sending machine will then resend the lost segment and wait for an acknowledgment, which it must receive in order to move on to the transmission of segment 7.

The Transport layer, working in tandem with the Session layer, also separates the data from different applications, an activity known as *session multiplexing*, and it happens when a client connects to a server with multiple browser sessions open. This is exactly what's taking place when you go someplace online like Amazon and click multiple links, opening them simultaneously to get information when comparison shopping. The client data from each browser session must be separate when the server application receives it, which is pretty slick technologically speaking, and it's the Transport layer that performs the juggling act.

The Network Layer

The *Network layer*, or layer 3, manages device addressing, tracks the location of devices on the network, and determines the best way to move data. This means that it's up to the Network layer to transport traffic between devices that aren't locally attached. Routers, which are layer 3 devices, are specified at this layer and provide the routing services within an internetwork.

Here's how that works: First, when a packet is received on a router interface, the destination IP address is checked. If the packet isn't destined for that particular router, it will look up the destination network address in the routing table. Once the router chooses an exit interface, the packet will be sent to that interface to be framed and sent out on the local network. If the router can't find an entry for the packet's destination network in the routing table, the router drops the packet.

Data and route update packets are the two types of packets used at the Network layer:

Data Packets   These are used to transport user data through the internetwork. Protocols used to support data traffic are called routed protocols, and IP and IPv6 are key examples. I'll cover IP addressing in Chapter 3, "Introduction to TCP/IP," and Chapter 4, "Easy Subnetting," and I'll cover IPv6 in Chapter 14, "Internet Protocol Version 6 (IPv6)."

Route Update Packets   These packets are used to update neighboring routers about the networks connected to all routers within the internetwork. Protocols that send route update packets are called routing protocols and the most critical ones for CCNA are Static Routing and OSPF Single Area. Route update packets are used to help build and maintain routing tables.

Figure 1.14 shows an example of a routing table. The routing table each router keeps and refers to includes the following information:

FIGURE 1.14   Routing table used in a router

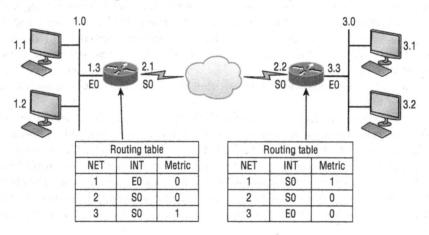

Network Addresses   Protocol-specific network addresses. A router must maintain a routing table for individual routing protocols because each routed protocol keeps track of a network with a different addressing scheme. For example, the routing tables for IP and IPv6 are completely different, so the router keeps a table for each one. Think of it as a street sign in each of the different languages spoken by the American, Spanish, and French people living on a street; the street sign would read Cat/Gato/Chat.

Interface   The exit interface a packet will take when destined for a specific network.

Metric   The distance to the remote network. Different routing protocols use different ways of computing this distance. I'm going to cover routing protocols thoroughly in Chapter 9,

"IP Routing." For now, know that some routing protocols like the Routing Information Protocol, or RIP, use hop count, which refers to the number of routers a packet passes through en route to a remote network. Others use bandwidth, delay of the line, or even tick count (1/18 of a second) to determine the best path for data to get to a given destination.

And as I mentioned earlier, routers break up broadcast domains, which means that by default, broadcasts aren't forwarded through a router. Do you remember why this is a good thing? Routers also break up collision domains, but you can also do this with layer 2, (Data Link layer), switches. Because each interface in a router represents a separate network, it must be assigned unique network identification numbers, and each host on the network connected to that router must use the same network number. Figure 1.15 shows how a router works in an internetwork:

FIGURE 1.15   A router in an internetwork. Each router LAN interface is a broadcast domain. Routers break up broadcast domains by default and provide WAN services.

Here are some router characteristics that you should never forget:

- Routers, by default, will not forward any broadcast or multicast packets.
- Routers use the logical address in a Network layer header to determine the next-hop router to forward the packet to.
- Routers can use access lists, created by an administrator, to control security based on the types of packets allowed to enter or exit an interface.
- Routers can provide layer 2 bridging functions if needed and can simultaneously route through the same interface.
- Layer 3 devices—in this case, routers—provide connections between *virtual LANs (VLANs)*.
- Routers can provide *quality of service (QoS)* for specific types of network traffic.

The Data Link Layer

The *Data Link layer* provides for the physical transmission of data and handles error notification, network topology, and flow control. This means that the Data Link layer will ensure that messages are delivered to the proper device on a LAN using hardware addresses and will translate messages from the Network layer into bits for the Physical layer to transmit.

The Data Link layer formats the messages, each called a *data frame*, and adds a customized header containing the hardware destination and source address. This added information forms a sort of capsule that surrounds the original message in much the same way that engines, navigational devices, and other tools were attached to the lunar modules of the Apollo project. These various pieces of equipment were useful only during certain stages of space flight and were stripped off the module and discarded when their designated stage was completed. The process of data traveling through networks is similar.

Figure 1.16 shows the Data Link layer with the Ethernet and IEEE specifications. When you check it out, notice that the IEEE 802.2 standard is used in conjunction with and adds functionality to the other IEEE standards. (You'll read more about the important IEEE 802 standards used with the Cisco objectives in Chapter 2, "Ethernet Networking and Data Encapsulation.")

FIGURE 1.16 Data Link layer

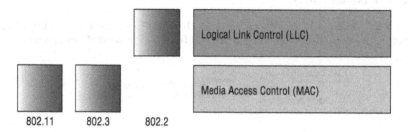

It's important for you to understand that routers, which work at the Network layer, don't care at all about where a particular host is located. They're only concerned about where networks are located and the best way to reach them—including remote ones. Routers are totally obsessive when it comes to networks, which in this case is a good thing. It's the Data Link layer that's responsible for the actual unique identification of each device that resides on a local network.

For a host to send packets to individual hosts on a local network as well as transmit packets between routers, the Data Link layer uses hardware addressing. Each time a packet is sent between routers, it's framed with control information at the Data Link layer, but that information is stripped off at the receiving router and only the original packet is left completely intact. This framing of the packet continues for each hop until the packet is finally delivered to the correct receiving host. It's also really important to understand that the packet itself is never altered along the route; it's only encapsulated with the type of control information required for it to be properly passed on to the different media types.

The IEEE Ethernet Data Link layer has two sublayers:

Media Access Control (MAC) Defines how packets are placed on the media. Contention for media access is "first come/first served" access where everyone shares the same bandwidth—hence the name. Physical addressing is defined here as well as logical topologies. What's a logical topology? It's the signal path through a physical topology. Line discipline, error notification (but not correction), the ordered delivery of frames, and optional flow control can also be used at this sublayer.

Logical Link Control (LLC) Responsible for identifying Network layer protocols and then encapsulating them. An LLC header tells the Data Link layer what to do with a packet once a frame is received. It works like this: A host receives a frame and looks in the LLC header to find out where the packet is destined—for instance, the IP protocol at the Network layer. The LLC can also provide flow control and sequencing of control bits.

The switches and bridges I talked about near the beginning of the chapter both work at the Data Link layer and filter the network using hardware (MAC) addresses. We'll talk about these next.

As data is encoded with control information at each layer of the OSI model, the data is named with something called a protocol data unit (PDU). At the Transport layer, the PDU is called a segment, at the Network layer it's a packet, at the Data Link a frame, and at the Physical layer it's called bits. This method of naming the data at each layer is covered thoroughly in Chapter 2.

Switches and Bridges at the Data Link Layer

Layer 2 switching is considered hardware-based bridging because it uses specialized hardware called an *application-specific integrated circuit (ASIC)*. ASICs can run up to high gigabit speeds with very low latency rates.

Latency is the time measured from when a frame enters a port to when it exits a port.

Bridges and switches read each frame as it passes through the network. The layer 2 device then puts the source hardware address in a filter table and keeps track of which port the frame was received on. This information—logged in the bridge's or switch's filter table—is what helps the machine determine the location of the specific sending device. Figure 1.17 shows a switch in an internetwork and demonstrates John sending packets to the Internet. Sally doesn't hear his frames because she's in a different collision domain.

FIGURE 1.17   A switch in an internetwork

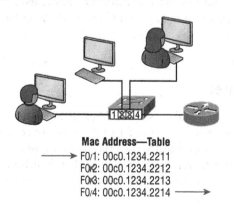

Mac Address—Table
F0/1: 00c0.1234.2211
F0/2: 00c0.1234.2212
F0/3: 00c0.1234.2213
F0/4: 00c0.1234.2214

The destination frame goes directly to the default gateway router, and Sally doesn't see John's traffic, much to her relief.

The real estate business is all about location, location, location, and it's the same way for both layer 2 and layer 3 devices. Though both need to be able to negotiate the network, it's crucial to remember that they're concerned with very different parts of it. Primarily, layer 3 machines (such as routers) need to locate specific networks, whereas layer 2 machines (switches and bridges) need to eventually locate specific devices. So, networks are to routers as individual devices are to switches and bridges. Similarly, routing tables that "map" the internetwork are for routers, as filter tables that "map" individual devices are for switches and bridges.

After a filter table is built on the layer 2 device, it will forward frames only to the segment where the destination hardware address is located. If the destination device is on the same segment as the frame, the layer 2 device will block the frame from going to any other segments. If the destination is on a different segment, the frame can be transmitted only to that segment. This is called *transparent bridging*.

When a switch interface receives a frame with a destination hardware address that isn't found in the device's filter table, it will forward the frame to all connected segments. If the unknown device that was sent the "mystery frame" replies to this forwarding action, the switch updates its filter table regarding that device's location. But in the event the destination address of the transmitting frame is a broadcast address, the switch will forward all broadcasts to every connected segment by default.

All devices that the broadcast is forwarded to are considered to be in the same broadcast domain. This can be a problem because layer 2 devices propagate layer 2 broadcast storms that can seriously choke performance. The only way to stop a broadcast storm from propagating through an internetwork is with a layer 3 device—a router.

The biggest benefit of using switches instead of hubs in your internetwork is that each switch port is actually its own collision domain. Remember that a hub creates one large collision domain, which is not a good thing! But even armed with a switch, you still don't get to just break up broadcast domains by default because neither switches nor bridges will do that. They'll simply forward all broadcasts instead.

Another benefit of LAN switching over hub-centered implementations is that each device on every segment plugged into a switch can transmit simultaneously. Well, at least they can as long as there's only one host on each port and there isn't a hub plugged into a switch port. As you probably guessed, this is because hubs allow only one device per network segment to communicate at a time.

The Physical Layer

Finally arriving at the bottom, we find that the *Physical layer* does two things: it sends bits and receives bits. Bits come only in values of 1 or 0—a Morse code with numerical values. The Physical layer communicates directly with the various types of actual communication media. Different kinds of media represent these bit values in different ways. Some use audio tones, while others employ *state transitions*—changes in voltage from high to low and low to high. Specific protocols are needed for each type of media to describe the proper bit patterns to be used, how data is encoded into media signals, and the various qualities of the physical media's attachment interface.

The Physical layer specifies the electrical, mechanical, procedural, and functional requirements for activating, maintaining, and deactivating a physical link between end systems. This layer is also where you identify the interface between the *data terminal equipment (DTE)* and the *data communication equipment (DCE)*. (Some old phone-company employees still call DCE "data circuit-terminating equipment.") The DCE is usually located at the service provider, while the DTE is the attached device. The services available to the DTE are most often accessed via a modem or *channel service unit/data service unit (CSU/DSU)*.

The Physical layer's connectors and different physical topologies are defined by the OSI as standards, allowing disparate systems to communicate. The Cisco exam objectives are interested only in the IEEE Ethernet standards.

Hubs at the Physical Layer

A hub is really a multiple-port repeater. A repeater receives a digital signal, reamplifies or regenerates that signal, then forwards the signal out the other port without looking at any data. A hub does the same thing across all active ports: any digital signal received from a segment on a hub port is regenerated or reamplified and transmitted out all other ports on the hub. This means all devices plugged into a hub are in the same collision domain as well as in the same broadcast domain. Figure 1.18 shows a hub in a network and how when one host transmits, all other hosts must stop and listen.

FIGURE 1.18   A hub in a network

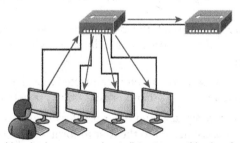

I love it when everyone has to listen to everything I say!

Hubs, like repeaters, don't examine any of the traffic as it enters or before it's transmitted out to the other parts of the physical media. And every device connected to the hub, or hubs, must listen if a device transmits. A physical star network, where the hub is a central device and cables extend in all directions out from it, is the type of topology a hub creates. Visually, the design really does resemble a star, whereas Ethernet networks run a logical bus topology, meaning that the signal has to run through the network from end to end.

Hubs and repeaters can be used to enlarge the area covered by a single LAN segment, but I really do not recommend going with this configuration! LAN switches are affordable for almost every situation and will make you much happier.

Topologies at the Physical layer

One last thing I want to discuss at the Physical layer is topologies, both physical and logical. Understand that every type of network has both a physical and a logical topology.

- The physical topology of a network refers to the physical layout of the devices, but mostly the cabling and cabling layout.

- The logical topology defines the logical path on which the signal will travel on the physical topology.

Figure 1.19 shows the four types of topologies.

FIGURE 1.19   Physical vs. Logical Topolgies

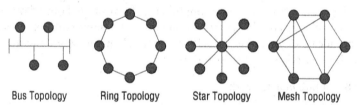

- Physical topology is the physical layout of the devices and cabling.
- The primary physical topology categories are bus, ring, star, and mesh.

Bus Topology   Ring Topology   Star Topology   Mesh Topology

Here are the topology types, although the most common, and pretty much the only network we use today is a physical star, logical bus technology, which is considered a hybrid topology (think Ethernet):

- Bus: In a bus topology, every workstation is connected to a single cable, meaning every host is directly connected to every other workstation in the network.

- Ring: In a ring topology, computers and other network devices are cabled together in a way that the last device is connected to the first to form a circle or ring.

- Star: The most common physical topology is a star topology, which is your Ethernet switching physical layout. A central cabling device (switch) connects the computers and other network devices together. This category includes star and extended star topologies. Physical connection is commonly made using twisted-pair wiring.

- Mesh: In a mesh topology, every network device is cabled together with connection to each other. Redundant links increase reliability and self-healing. The physical connection is commonly made using fiber or twisted-pair wiring.

- Hybrid: Ethernet uses a physical star layout (cables come from all directions), and the signal travels end-to-end, like a bus route.

Summary

Phew! I know this seemed like the chapter that wouldn't end, but it did—and you made it through! You're now armed with a ton of fundamental information; you're ready to build upon it and are well on your way to certification.

I started by discussing simple, basic networking and the differences between collision and broadcast domains.

I then discussed the OSI model—the seven-layer model used to help application developers design applications that can run on any type of system or network. Each layer has its special jobs and select responsibilities within the model to ensure that solid, effective communications do, in fact, occur. I provided you with complete details of each layer and discussed how Cisco views the specifications of the OSI model.

In addition, each layer in the OSI model specifies different types of devices, and I described the different devices used at each layer.

Remember that hubs are Physical layer devices and repeat the digital signal to all segments except the one from which it was received. Switches segment the network using hardware addresses and break up collision domains. Routers break up broadcast domains as well as collision domains and use logical addressing to send packets through an internetwork.

Chapter

2

Ethernet Networking and Data Encapsulation

Before we begin exploring a set of key foundational topics like the TCP/IP DoD model, IP addressing, subnetting, and routing in the upcoming chapters, I really want you to grasp the big picture of LANs conceptually. The role Ethernet plays in today's networks as well as what Media Access Control (MAC) addresses are and how they are used are two more critical networking basics you'll want a solid understanding of as well.

We'll cover these important subjects and more in this chapter, beginning with Ethernet basics and the way MAC addresses are used on an Ethernet LAN, and then we'll focus in on the actual protocols used with Ethernet at the Data Link layer. To round out this discussion, you'll also learn about some very important Ethernet specifications.

You know by now that there are a whole bunch of different devices specified at the various layers of the OSI model and that it's essential to be really familiar with the many types of cables and connectors employed to hook them up to the network correctly. I'll review the types of cabling used with Cisco devices in this chapter, demonstrate how to connect to a router or switch, plus show you how to connect a router or switch via a console connection.

I'll also introduce you to a vital process of encoding data as it makes its way down the OSI stack, known as encapsulation.

To find your included bonus material, as well as Todd Lammle videos, practice questions, and hands-on labs, please see www.lammle.com/ccna.

Ethernet Networks in Review

Ethernet is a contention-based media access method that allows all hosts on a network to share the same link's bandwidth. Some reasons it's so popular are that Ethernet is pretty simple to implement and it makes troubleshooting fairly straightforward as well. Ethernet is also readily scalable, meaning that it eases the process of integrating new technologies into an existing network infrastructure, like upgrading from Fast Ethernet to Gigabit Ethernet.

Ethernet uses both Data Link and Physical layer specifications, so you'll be presented with information relative to both layers, which you'll need to effectively implement, troubleshoot, and maintain an Ethernet network.

Collision Domain

In Chapter 1, "Internetworking," you learned that the Ethernet term *collision domain* refers to a network scenario wherein one device sends a frame out on a physical network segment forcing every other device on the same segment to pay attention to it. This is bad because if two devices on a single physical segment just happen to transmit simultaneously, it will cause a collision and require these devices to retransmit. Think of a collision event as a situation where each device's digital signals totally interfere with one another on the wire. Figure 2.1 shows an old, legacy network that's a single collision domain where only one host can transmit at a time.

FIGURE 2.1   Legacy collision domain design

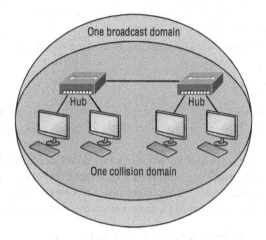

The hosts connected to each hub are in the same collision domain, so if one of them transmits, all the others must take the time to listen for and read the digital signal. It is easy to see how collisions can be a serious drag on network performance, so I'll show you how to strategically avoid them soon!

Okay—take another look at the network pictured in Figure 2.1. True, it has only one collision domain, but worse, it's also a single broadcast domain—what a mess! Let's check out an example, in Figure 2.2, of a typical network design still used today and see if it's any better.

FIGURE 2.2   A typical network you'd see today

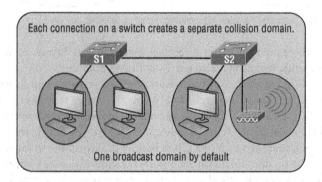

Because each port off a switch is a single collision domain, we gain more bandwidth for users, which is a great start. But switches don't break up broadcast domains by default, so this is still only one broadcast domain, which is not so good. This can work in a really small network, but to expand it at all, we would need to break up the network into smaller broadcast domains or our users won't get enough bandwidth. And you're probably wondering about that device in the lower-right corner, right? That's a *wireless access point*, sometimes referred to as an AP, which stands for access point. It's a wireless device that allows hosts to connect wirelessly using the IEEE 802.11 specification and I added it to the figure to demonstrate how these devices can be used to extend a collision domain. But still, understand that APs don't actually segment the network, they only extend them, meaning our LAN just got a lot bigger, with an unknown amount of hosts that are all still part of one measly broadcast domain! This clearly demonstrates why it's so important to understand exactly what a broadcast domain is, and now is a great time to talk about them in detail.

Broadcast Domain

Let me start by giving you the formal definition: *broadcast domain* refers to a group of devices on a specific network segment that hear all the broadcasts sent out on that specific network segment.

But even though a broadcast domain is usually a boundary delimited by physical media like switches and routers, the term can also refer to a logical division of a network segment, where all hosts can communicate via a Data Link layer, hardware address broadcast.

Figure 2.3 shows how a router would create a broadcast domain boundary.

FIGURE 2.3   A router creates broadcast domain boundaries.

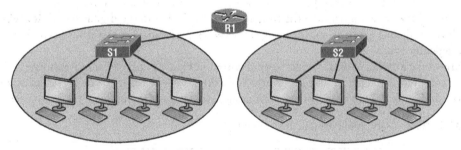

Two broadcast domains. How many collision domains do you see?

Here you can see there are two router interfaces giving us two broadcast domains, and I count 10 switch segments, meaning we've got 10 collision domains.

The design depicted in Figure 2.3 is still in use today, and routers will be around for a long time, but in the latest, modern switched networks, it's important to create small broadcast domains. We achieve this by building virtual LANs (VLANs) within our switched networks, which I'll demonstrate shortly. Without employing VLANs in today's switched environments, there wouldn't be much bandwidth available to individual users. Switches break up collision domains with each port, which is awesome, but they're still only one broadcast domain by default. It's also one more reason why it's extremely important to design networks very carefully.

And key to carefully planning your network design is to never allow broadcast domains to grow too large and get out of control. Both collision and broadcast domains can easily be controlled with routers and VLANs, so there's just no excuse to allow user bandwidth to slow to a pitiful crawl when there are plenty of tools in your arsenal to prevent the suffering.

An important reason for this book's existence is to ensure that you really get the foundational basics of Cisco networks nailed down so you can effectively design, implement, configure, troubleshoot, and even dazzle colleagues and superiors with elegant designs that lavish your users with all the bandwidth their hearts could possibly desire.

To make it to the top of that mountain, you need more than just the basic story, so let's move on to explore the collision detection mechanism used in half-duplex Ethernet.

CSMA/CD

Ethernet networking uses a protocol called *Carrier Sense Multiple Access with Collision Detection (CSMA/CD)*, which helps devices share the bandwidth evenly while preventing two devices from transmitting simultaneously on the same network medium. CSMA/CD was actually created to overcome the problem of the collisions that occur when packets are transmitted from different nodes at the same time. And trust me—good collision management is crucial, because when a node transmits in a CSMA/CD network, all the other nodes on the network receive and examine that transmission. It's only switches and routers that can effectively prevent a transmission from propagating throughout the entire network!

So, how does the CSMA/CD protocol work? Let's start by taking a look at Figure 2.4.

FIGURE 2.4 CSMA/CD

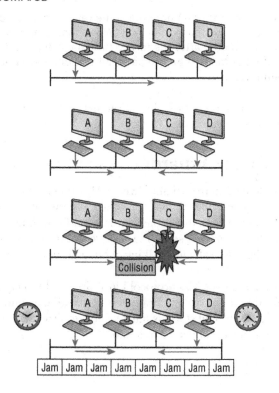

When a host wants to transmit over the network, it first checks for the presence of a digital signal on the wire. If all is clear and no other host is transmitting, the host will then proceed with its transmission.

But it doesn't stop there. The transmitting host constantly monitors the wire to make sure no other hosts begin transmitting. If the host detects another signal on the wire, it sends out an extended jam signal that causes all nodes on the segment to stop sending data—think busy signal.

The nodes respond to that jam signal by waiting a bit before attempting to transmit again. Backoff algorithms determine when the colliding stations can retransmit. If collisions keep occurring after 15 tries, the nodes attempting to transmit will then time out. Half-duplex can be pretty messy!

When a collision occurs on an Ethernet LAN, the following happens:

1. A jam signal informs all devices that a collision occurred.

2. The collision invokes a random backoff algorithm.

3. Each device on the Ethernet segment stops transmitting for a short time until its back-off timer expires.

4. All hosts have equal priority to transmit after the timers have expired.

The ugly effects of having a CSMA/CD network sustain heavy collisions are delay, low throughput, and congestion.

> Backoff on an Ethernet network is the retransmission delay that's enforced when a collision occurs. When that happens, a host will resume transmission only after the forced time delay has expired. Keep in mind that after the backoff has elapsed, all stations have equal priority to transmit data.

At this point, let's take a minute to talk about Ethernet in detail at both the Data Link layer (layer 2) and the Physical layer (layer 1).

Half- and Full-Duplex Ethernet

Half-duplex Ethernet is defined in the original IEEE 802.3 Ethernet specification, which differs a bit from how Cisco describes things. Cisco says Ethernet uses only one wire pair with a digital signal running in both directions on the wire. Even though the IEEE specifications discuss the half-duplex process somewhat differently, it's not actually a full-blown technical disagreement. Cisco is really just talking about a general sense of what's happening with Ethernet.

Half-duplex also uses the CSMA/CD protocol I just discussed to help prevent collisions and to permit retransmitting if one occurs. If a hub is attached to a switch, it must operate in half-duplex mode because the end stations must be able to detect collisions. Figure 2.5 shows a network with four hosts connected to a hub.

FIGURE 2.5   Half-duplex example

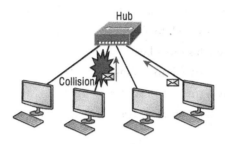

The problem here is that we can only run half-duplex, so if two hosts communicate at the same time there will be a collision. Also, half-duplex Ethernet is only about 30 to 40 percent efficient because a large 100Base-T network will usually only give you 30 to 40 Mbps, at most, due to overhead.

But full-duplex Ethernet uses two pairs of wires at the same time instead of a single wire pair like half-duplex. And full-duplex uses a point-to-point connection between the transmitter of the transmitting device and the receiver of the receiving device. This means that full-duplex data transfers happen a lot faster when compared to half-duplex transfers. Also, because the transmitted data is sent on a different set of wires than the received data, collisions won't happen. Figure 2.6 shows four hosts connected to a switch, plus a hub. Definitely avoid using hubs, so this is just for an example to differentiate them from a switch.

FIGURE 2.6   Full-duplex example

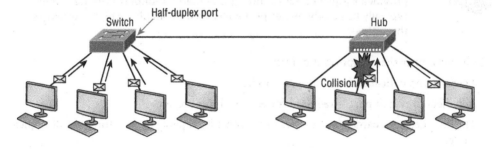

Theoretically all hosts connected to the switch in Figure 2.6 can communicate at the same time because they can run full-duplex. Just keep in mind that the switch port connecting to the hub, as well as the hosts connecting to that hub, must run at half-duplex.

The reason you don't need to worry about collisions is because now it's like a freeway with multiple lanes instead of the single-lane road provided by half-duplex. Full-duplex Ethernet is supposed to offer 100 percent efficiency in both directions—for example, you can get 20 Mbps with a 10 Mbps Ethernet running full-duplex, or 200 Mbps for Fast Ethernet. But this rate is known as an aggregate rate, which translates as "you're supposed to get" 100 percent efficiency. No guarantees, in networking as in life!

You can use full-duplex Ethernet in at least the following six situations:

- With a connection from a switch to a host
- With a connection from a switch to a switch
- With a connection from a host to a host
- With a connection from a switch to a router
- With a connection from a router to a router
- With a connection from a router to a host

 Full-duplex Ethernet requires a point-to-point connection when only two nodes are present. You can run full-duplex with just about any device except a hub.

Now this may be a little confusing...because if it's capable of all that speed, why wouldn't it actually deliver? Well, when a full-duplex Ethernet port is powered on, it first connects to the remote end and then negotiates with the other end of the Fast Ethernet link. This is called an *auto-detect mechanism*. This mechanism first decides on the exchange capability, which means it checks to see if it can run at 10, 100, or even 1000 Mbps or more. It then checks to see if it can run full-duplex, and if it can't, it will run half-duplex.

 Remember that half-duplex Ethernet shares a collision domain and provides a lower effective throughput than full-duplex Ethernet, which typically has a private per-port collision domain plus a higher effective throughput.

Last, remember these important points:

- There are no collisions in full-duplex mode.
- A dedicated switch port is required for each full-duplex node.
- The host network card and the switch port must be capable of operating in full-duplex mode.
- The default behavior of 10Base-T and 100Base-T hosts is 10 Mbps half-duplex if the autodetect mechanism fails, so it is always good practice to set the speed and duplex of each port on a switch if you can.

Now let's take a look at how Ethernet works at the Data Link layer.

Ethernet at the Data Link Layer

Ethernet at the Data Link layer is responsible for Ethernet addressing, commonly referred to as MAC or hardware addressing. Ethernet is also responsible for framing packets received from the Network layer and preparing them for transmission on the local network through the Ethernet contention-based media access method.

Ethernet Addressing

Here's where we get into how Ethernet addressing works. It uses the *Media Access Control (MAC)* address burned into each and every Ethernet network interface card (NIC). The MAC, or hardware, address is a 48-bit (6-byte) address written in a hexadecimal format.

Figure 2.7 shows the 48-bit MAC addresses and how the bits are divided:

FIGURE 2.7   Ethernet addressing using MAC addresses

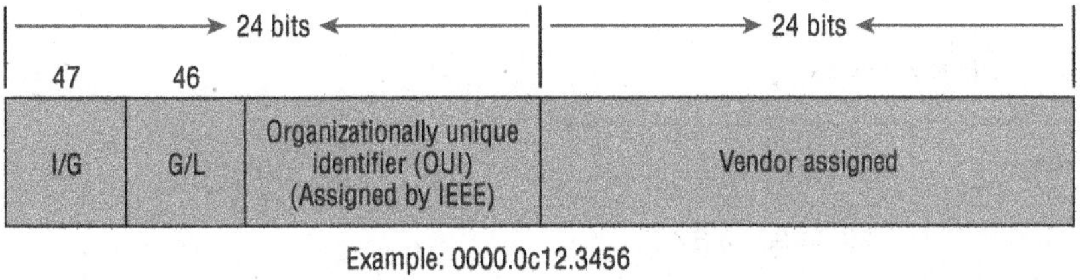

Example: 0000.0c12.3456

The *organizationally unique identifier (OUI)* is assigned by the IEEE to an organization. It's composed of 24 bits, or 3 bytes, and it in turn assigns a globally administered address also made up of 24 bits, or 3 bytes, that's supposedly unique to each and every adapter an organization manufactures. (Surprisingly, there's no guarantee when it comes to that unique claim!) Okay, now look closely at the figure. The high-order bit is the Individual/Group (I/G) bit. When it has a value of 0, we can assume that the address is the MAC address of a device and that it may well appear in the source portion of the MAC header. When it's a 1, we can assume that the address represents either a broadcast or multicast address in Ethernet.

The next bit is the Global/Local bit, sometimes called the G/L bit or U/L bit, where *U* means *universal*. When set to 0, this bit represents a globally administered address, as assigned by the IEEE, but when it's a 1, it represents a locally governed and administered address. The low-order 24 bits of an Ethernet address represent a locally administered or manufacturer-assigned code. This portion commonly starts with 24 0s for the first card made and continues in order until there are 24 1s for the last (16,777,216th) card made. You'll find that many manufacturers use these same six hex digits as the last six characters of their serial number on the same card.

Let's stop for a minute and go over some addressing schemes important in the Ethernet world.

Binary to Decimal and Hexadecimal Conversion

Before we get into working with the TCP/IP protocol and IP addressing, which we'll do in Chapter 3, "Introduction to TCP/IP," it's really important for you to get the differences between binary, decimal, and hexadecimal numbers and how to convert one format into the other.

We'll start with binary numbering, which is really pretty simple. The digits used are limited to either a 1 or a 0, and each digit is called a *bit*, which is short for *binary digit*. Typically, you group either 4 or 8 bits together, with these being referred to as a nibble and a byte, respectively.

The interesting thing about binary numbering is how the value is represented in a decimal format—the typical decimal format being the base-10 number scheme that we've all used since kindergarten. The binary numbers are placed in a value spot, starting at the right and moving left, with each spot having double the value of the previous spot.

Table 2.1 shows the decimal values of each bit location in a nibble and a byte. Remember, a nibble is 4 bits and a byte is 8 bits.

TABLE 2.1 Binary values

Nibble Values	Byte Values
8 4 2 1	128 64 32 16 8 4 2 1

What all this means is that if a one digit (1) is placed in a value spot, then the nibble or byte takes on that decimal value and adds it to any other value spots that have a 1. If a zero (0) is placed in a bit spot, you don't count that value.

Let me clarify this a little. If we have a 1 placed in each spot of our nibble, we would then add up 8 + 4 + 2 + 1 to give us a maximum value of 15. Another example for our nibble values would be 1001, meaning that the 8 bit and the 1 bit are turned on, which equals a decimal value of 9. If we have a nibble binary value of 0110, then our decimal value would be 6, because the 4 and 2 bits are turned on.

But the *byte* decimal values can add up to a number that's significantly higher than 15. This is how: If we counted every bit as a one (1), then the byte binary value would look like the following example because, remember, 8 bits equal a byte:

11111111

We would then count up every bit spot because each is turned on. It would look like this, which demonstrates the maximum value of a byte:

128 + 64 + 32 + 16 + 8 + 4 + 2 + 1 = 255

There are plenty of other decimal values that a binary number can equal. Let's work through a few examples:

10010110

Which bits are on? The 128, 16, 4, and 2 bits are on, so we'll just add them up: 128 + 16 + 4 + 2 = 150.

01101100

Which bits are on? The 64, 32, 8, and 4 bits are on, so we just need to add them up: 64 + 32 + 8 + 4 = 108.

11101000

Which bits are on? The 128, 64, 32, and 8 bits are on, so just add the values up: 128 + 64 + 32 + 8 = 232.

I highly recommend that you memorize Table 2.2 before you start studying subnetting in Chapter 4.

TABLE 2.2   Binary to decimal memorization chart

Binary Value	Decimal Value
10000000	128
11000000	192
11100000	224
11110000	240
11111000	248
11111100	252
11111110	254
11111111	255

Hexadecimal addressing is completely different than binary or decimal—it's converted by reading nibbles, not bytes. By using a nibble, we can convert these bits to hex pretty simply. First, understand that the hexadecimal addressing scheme uses only the characters 0 through 9. Because the numbers 10, 11, 12, and so on can't be used (because they are two-digit numbers), the letters A, B, C, D, E, and F are used instead to represent 10, 11, 12, 13, 14, and 15, respectively.

Hex is short for *hexadecimal*, which is a numbering system that uses the first six letters of the alphabet, A through F, to extend beyond the available 10 characters in the decimal system. These values are not case sensitive.

Table 2.3 shows both the binary value and the decimal value for each hexadecimal digit.

TABLE 2.3 Hex to binary to decimal chart

Hexadecimal Value	Binary Value	Decimal Value
0	0000	0
1	0001	1
2	0010	2
3	0011	3
4	0100	4
5	0101	5
6	0110	6
7	0111	7
8	1000	8
9	1001	9
A	1010	10
B	1011	11
C	1100	12
D	1101	13
E	1110	14
F	1111	15

Did you notice that the first 10 hexadecimal digits (0–9) are the same value as the decimal values? If not, look again because this handy fact makes those values super easy to convert!

Now suppose you have something like this: 0x6A. This is important because sometimes Cisco likes to put *0x* in front of characters so you know that they are a hex value. It doesn't have any other special meaning. So what are the binary and decimal values? All you have to remember is that each hex character is one nibble and that two hex characters joined together make a byte. To figure out the binary value, put the hex characters into two nibbles and then join them together into a byte. Six equals 0110, and A, which is 10 in hex, equals 1010, so the complete byte would be 01101010.

To convert from binary to hex, just take the byte and break it into nibbles. Let me clarify this.

Say you have the binary number 01010101. First, break it into nibbles—0101 and 0101—with the value of each nibble being 5 since the 1 and 4 bits are on. This makes the hex answer 0x55. And in decimal format, the binary number is 01010101, which converts to $64 + 16 + 4 + 1 = 85$.

Here's another binary number:

11001100

Your answer would be 1100 = 12 and 1100 = 12, so therefore, it's converted to CC in hex. The decimal conversion answer would be $128 + 64 + 8 + 4 = 204$.

One more example, then we need to get working on the Physical layer. Suppose you had the following binary number:

10110101

The hex answer would be 0xB5, since 1011 converts to B and 0101 converts to 5 in hex value. The decimal equivalent is $128 + 32 + 16 + 4 + 1 = 181$.

Ethernet Frames

The Data Link layer is responsible for combining bits into bytes and bytes into frames. Frames are used at the Data Link layer to encapsulate packets handed down from the Network layer for transmission on a type of media access.

The function of Ethernet stations is to pass data frames between each other using a group of bits known as a MAC frame format. This provides error detection from a *cyclic redundancy check (CRC)*. But remember—this is error detection, not error correction. An example of a typical Ethernet frame used today is shown in Figure 2.8:

FIGURE 2.8   Typical Ethernet frame format

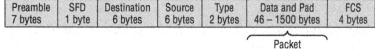

Ethernet_II

Preamble 7 bytes	SFD 1 byte	Destination 6 bytes	Source 6 bytes	Type 2 bytes	Data and Pad 46 – 1500 bytes	FCS 4 bytes

Packet

Encapsulating a frame within a different type of frame is called *tunneling*.

Following are the details of the various fields in the typical Ethernet frame type:

Preamble   An alternating 1,0 pattern provides a clock at the start of each packet, which allows the receiving devices to lock the incoming bit stream.

Start Frame Delimiter (SFD)/Synch   The preamble is seven octets and the SFD is one octet (synch). The SFD is 10101011, where the last pair of 1s allows the receiver to come into the alternating 1,0 pattern somewhere in the middle and still sync up to detect the beginning of the data.

Destination Address (DA)   This transmits a 48-bit value using the least significant bit (LSB) first. The DA is used by receiving stations to determine if an incoming packet is addressed to a particular node. The destination address can be an individual address or a broadcast or multicast MAC address. Remember that a broadcast is all 1s—all *F*s in hex—and is sent to all devices. A multicast is sent only to a similar subset of nodes on a network.

Source Address (SA)   The SA is a 48-bit MAC address used to identify the transmitting device, and it uses the least significant bit first. Broadcast and multicast address formats are illegal within the SA field.

Length or Type   802.3 uses a Length field, but the Ethernet_II frame uses a Type field to identify the Network layer protocol. The old, original 802.3 cannot identify the upper-layer protocol and must be used with a proprietary LAN—IPX, for example.

Data   This is a packet sent down to the Data Link layer from the Network layer. The size can vary from 46 to 1,500 bytes.

Frame Check Sequence (FCS)   FCS is a field at the end of the frame that's used to store the cyclic redundancy check (CRC) answer. The CRC is a mathematical algorithm that's run when each frame is built based on the data in the frame. When a receiving host receives the frame and runs the CRC, the answer should be the same. If not, the frame is discarded, assuming errors have occurred.

Let's pause here for a minute and take a look at some frames caught on my trusty network analyzer. You can see that the frame below has only three fields: Destination, Source, and Type, which is shown as Protocol Type on this particular analyzer:

```
Destination: 00:60:f5:00:1f:27
Source: 00:60:f5:00:1f:2c
Protocol Type: 08-00 IP
```

This is an Ethernet_II frame. Notice that the Type field is IP, or 08-00, mostly just referred to as 0x800 in hexadecimal.

The next frame has the same fields, so it must be an Ethernet_II frame as well:

```
Destination: ff:ff:ff:ff:ff:ff Ethernet Broadcast
Source: 02:07:01:22:de:a4
Protocol Type: 08-00 IP
```

Did you notice that this frame was a broadcast? You can tell because the destination hardware address is all 1s in binary, or all *F*s in hexadecimal.

Let's take a look at one more Ethernet_II frame. I'll talk about this next example again when we use IPv6 in Chapter 14, "Internet Protocol Version 6 (IPv6)," but you can see that the Ethernet frame is the same Ethernet_II frame used with the IPv4 routed protocol. The Type field has 0x86dd when the frame is carrying IPv6 data, and when we have IPv4 data, the frame uses 0x0800 in the protocol field:

```
Destination: IPv6-Neighbor-Discovery_00:01:00:03 (33:33:00:01:00:03)
Source: Aopen_3e:7f:dd (00:01:80:3e:7f:dd)
Type: IPv6 (0x86dd)
```

This is the beauty of the Ethernet_II frame. Because of the Type field, we can run any Network layer routed protocol and the frame will carry the data because it can identify the Network layer protocol.

Ethernet at the Physical Layer

Ethernet was first implemented by a group called DIX, which stands for Digital, Intel, and Xerox. They created and implemented the first Ethernet LAN specification, which the IEEE used to create the IEEE 802.3 committee. This was a 10 Mbps network that ran on coax and then eventually twisted-pair and fiber physical media.

The IEEE extended the 802.3 committee to three new committees known as 802.3u (Fast Ethernet), 802.3ab (Gigabit Ethernet on category 5), and then finally one more, 802.3ae (10 Gbps over fiber and coax). There are more standards evolving almost daily, such as 100 Gbps Ethernet (802.3ba).

When designing your LAN, it's really important to understand the different types of Ethernet media available to you. Sure, it would be great to run Gigabit Ethernet to each desktop and 10 Gbps between switches, but well, you would definitely need to figure out how to justify the cost of that network! However, if you mix and match the different types of Ethernet media methods currently available, you can come up with a cost-effective network solution that still works really great.

The *EIA/TIA* (Electronic Industries Alliance and the newer Telecommunications Industry Association) is the standards body that creates the Physical layer specifications for Ethernet. The EIA/TIA specifies that Ethernet use a *registered jack (RJ) connector* on *unshielded twisted-pair (UTP)* cabling (RJ45). But the industry is moving toward simply calling this an 8-pin modular connector.

Every Ethernet cable type that's specified by the EIA/TIA has inherent attenuation, which is defined as the loss of signal strength as it travels the length of a cable and is measured in decibels (dB). The cabling used in corporate and home markets is measured in categories. A higher-quality cable will have a higher-rated category and lower attenuation. For example, category 5 is better than category 3 because category 5 cables have more wire twists per foot and therefore less crosstalk. Crosstalk is the unwanted signal interference from adjacent pairs in the cable.

Here is a list of some of the most common IEEE Ethernet standards, starting with 10 Mbps Ethernet:

10Base-T (IEEE 802.3)   10 Mbps using category 3 unshielded twisted pair (UTP) wiring for runs up to 100 meters. Unlike with the 10Base-2 and 10Base-5 networks, each device must connect into a hub or switch, and you can have only one host per segment or wire. It uses an RJ45 connector (8-pin modular connector) with a physical star topology and a logical bus.

100Base-TX (IEEE 802.3u)   100Base-TX, most commonly known as Fast Ethernet, uses EIA/TIA category 5, 5E, or 6 UTP two-pair wiring. One user per segment; up to 100 meters long. It uses an RJ45 connector with a physical star topology and a logical bus.

100Base-FX (IEEE 802.3u)   Uses fiber cabling 62.5/125-micron multimode fiber. Point-to-point topology; up to 412 meters long. It uses ST and SC connectors, which are media-interface connectors.

1000Base-CX (IEEE 802.3z)   Copper twisted-pair, called twinax, is a balanced coaxial pair that can run only up to 25 meters and uses a special 9-pin connector known as the High Speed Serial Data Connector (HSSDC). This is used in Cisco's Data Center technologies.

1000Base-T (IEEE 802.3ab)   Category 5, four-pair UTP wiring up to 100 meters long and up to 1 Gbps.

1000Base-SX (IEEE 802.3z)   The implementation of 1 Gigabit Ethernet running over multimode fiber-optic cable instead of copper twisted-pair cable, using short wavelength laser and LEDs. Multimode fiber (MMF) using 62.5- and 50-micron core; uses an 850 nanometer (nm) laser and can go up to 220 meters with 62.5-micron, 550 meters with 50-micron.

1000Base-LX (IEEE 802.3z)   Single-mode fiber that uses a 9-micron core and 1300 nm laser and can go from 3 kilometers up to 10 kilometers.

1000Base-ZX (Cisco standard)   1000BaseZX, or 1000Base-ZX, is a Cisco-specified standard for Gigabit Ethernet communication. 1000BaseZX operates on ordinary single-mode fiber-optic links with spans up to 43.5 miles (70 km).

10GBase-T (802.3.an)   10GBase-T is a standard proposed by the IEEE 802.3an committee to provide 10 Gbps connections over conventional UTP cables, (category 5e, 6, or 7 cables). 10GBase-T allows the conventional RJ45 used for Ethernet LANs and can support signal transmission at the full 100-meter distance specified for LAN wiring.

If you want to implement a network medium that is not susceptible to electromagnetic interference (EMI), fiber-optic cable provides a more secure, long-distance cable that is not susceptible to EMI at high speeds.

Armed with the basics covered so far in this chapter, you're equipped to go to the next level and put Ethernet to work using various Ethernet cabling.

Real World Scenario

Interference or Host Distance Issue?

Quite a few years ago, I was consulting at a very large aerospace company in the Los Angeles area. In the very busy warehouse, they had hundreds of hosts providing many different services to the various departments working in that area.

However, a small group of hosts had been experiencing intermittent outages that no one could explain since most hosts in the same area had no problems whatsoever. So I decided to take a crack at this problem and see what I could find.

First, I traced the backbone connection from the main switch to multiple switches in the warehouse area. Assuming that the hosts with the issues were connected to the same switch, I traced each cable, and much to my surprise they were connected to various switches! Now my interest really peaked because the simplest issue had been eliminated right off the bat. It wasn't a simple switch problem!

I continued to trace each cable one by one, and this is what I found:

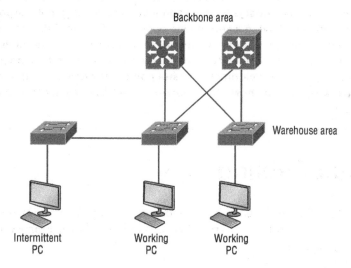

As I drew this network out, I noticed that they had many repeaters in place, which isn't a cause for immediate suspicion since bandwidth was not their biggest requirement here. So I looked deeper still. At this point, I decided to measure the distance of one of the intermittent hosts connecting to their hub/repeater.

This is what I measured. Can you see the problem?

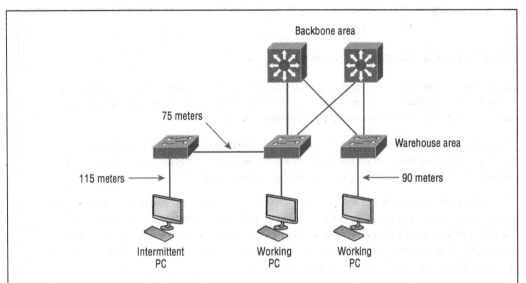

Having a hub or repeater in your network isn't a problem, unless you need better bandwidth (which they didn't in this case), but the distance sure was! It's not always easy to tell how far away a host is from its connection in an extremely large area, so these hosts ended up having a connection past the 100-meter Ethernet specification, which created a problem for the hosts not cabled correctly. Understand that this didn't stop the hosts from completely working, but the workers felt the hosts stopped working when they were at their most stressful point of the day. Sure, that makes sense, because whenever my host stops working, that becomes my most stressful part of the day!

Ethernet Cabling

A discussion about Ethernet cabling is an important one, especially if you are planning on taking the Cisco exams. You need to really understand the following three types of cables:

- Straight-through cable
- Crossover cable
- Rolled cable

We will look at each in the following sections, but first, let's take a look at the most common Ethernet cable used today, the category 5 Enhanced Unshielded Twisted Pair (UTP), shown in Figure 2.9:

FIGURE 2.9   Category 5 Enhanced UTP cable

The category 5 Enhanced UTP cable can handle speeds up to a gigabit with a distance of up to 100 meters. Typically we'd use this cable for 100 Mbps and category 6 for a gigabit, but the category 5 Enhanced is rated for gigabit speeds and category 6 is rated for 10 Gbps!

Straight-Through Cable

The *straight-through cable* is used to connect the following devices:

- Host to switch or hub
- Router to switch or hub

Four wires are used in straight-through cable to connect Ethernet devices. It's relatively simple to create this type, and Figure 2.10 shows the four wires used in a straight-through Ethernet cable.

FIGURE 2.10   Straight-through Ethernet cable

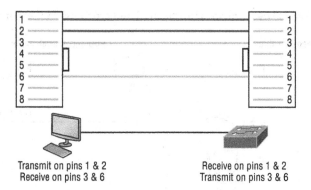

Transmit on pins 1 & 2
Receive on pins 3 & 6

Receive on pins 1 & 2
Transmit on pins 3 & 6

Notice that only pins 1, 2, 3, and 6 are used. Just connect 1 to 1, 2 to 2, 3 to 3, and 6 to 6 and you'll be up and networking in no time. However, remember that this would be a 10/100 Mbps Ethernet-only cable and wouldn't work with gigabit, voice, or other LAN or WAN technology.

Crossover Cable

The *crossover cable* can be used to connect the following devices:

- Switch to switch
- Hub to hub

- Host to host
- Hub to switch
- Router direct to host
- Router to router

The same four wires used in the straight-through cable are used in this cable—we just connect different pins together. Figure 2.11 shows how the four wires are used in a crossover Ethernet cable.

FIGURE 2.11   Crossover Ethernet cable

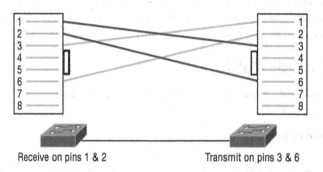

Receive on pins 1 & 2   Transmit on pins 3 & 6

Notice that instead of connecting 1 to 1, 2 to 2, and so on, here we connect pins 1 to 3 and 2 to 6 on each side of the cable. Figure 2.12 shows some typical uses of straight-through and crossover cables:

FIGURE 2.12   Typical uses for straight-through and cross-over Ethernet cables

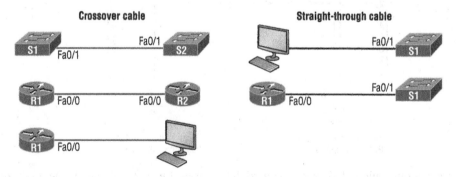

The crossover examples in Figure 2.12 are switch port to switch port, router Ethernet port to router Ethernet port, and router Ethernet port to PC Ethernet port. For the straight-through examples I used PC Ethernet to switch port and router Ethernet port to switch port.

It's very possible to connect a straight-through cable between two switches, and it will start working because of autodetect mechanisms called auto-mdix. But be advised that the CCNA objectives do not typically consider autodetect mechanisms valid between devices!

UTP Gigabit Wiring (1000Base-T)

In the previous examples of 10Base-T and 100Base-T UTP wiring, only two wire pairs were used, but that is not good enough for Gigabit UTP transmission.

1000Base-T UTP wiring (Figure 2.13) requires four wire pairs and uses more advanced electronics so that each and every pair in the cable can transmit simultaneously. Even so, gigabit wiring is almost identical to my earlier 10/100 example, except that we'll use the other two pairs in the cable.

FIGURE 2.13   UTP Gigabit crossover Ethernet cable

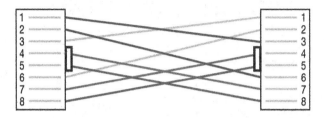

For a straight-through cable it's still 1 to 1, 2 to 2, and so on up to pin 8. And in creating the gigabit crossover cable, you'd still cross 1 to 3 and 2 to 6, but you would add 4 to 7 and 5 to 8—pretty **straightforward!**

Rolled Cable

Although *rolled cable* isn't used to connect any Ethernet connections together, you can use a rolled Ethernet cable to connect a host EIA-TIA 232 interface to a router console serial communication (COM) port.

If you have a Cisco router or switch, you would use this cable to connect your PC, Mac, or a device like an iPad to the Cisco hardware. Eight wires are used in this cable to connect serial devices, although not all eight are used to send information, just as in Ethernet networking. Figure 2.14 shows the eight wires used in a rolled cable:

FIGURE 2.14   Rolled Ethernet cable

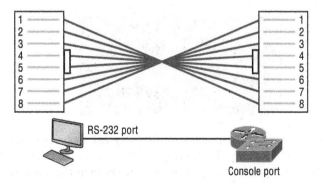

These are probably the easiest cables to make because you just cut the end off on one side of a straight-through cable, turn it over, and put it back on—with a new connector, of course!

Okay, once you have the correct cable connected from your PC to the Cisco router or switch console port, you can start your emulation program such as PuTTY or SecureCRT to create a console connection and configure the device. To find your com port in Windows, go to Device Manager. Set the configuration as shown in Figure 2.15:

FIGURE 2.15   Configuring your console emulation program

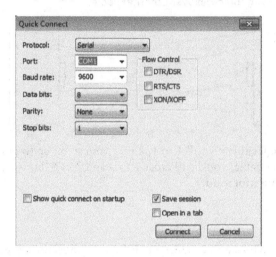

Notice that Baud Rate is set to 9600, Data Bits to 8, Parity to None, and no Flow Control options are set. At this point, you can click Connect and press the Enter key and you should be connected to your Cisco device console port.

Figure 2.16 shows a nice 2960 switch with two console ports:

FIGURE 2.16   A Cisco 2960 console connection

Console

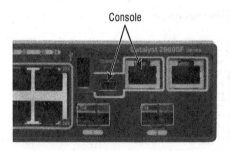

Notice there are two console connections on this new switch—a typical original RJ45 connection and the newer mini type-B USB console. Remember that the new USB port supersedes the RJ45 port if you just happen to plug into both at the same time, and the USB

port can have speeds up to 115,200 Kbps, which is awesome if you have to use Xmodem to update an IOS. I've even seen some cables that work on iPhones and iPads and allow them to connect to these mini USB ports!

Now that you've seen the various RJ45 UTP cables, what type of cable is used between the switches in Figure 2.17?

FIGURE 2.17 RJ45 UTP cable question #1

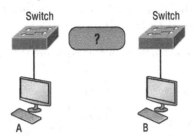

In order for host A to ping host B, you need a crossover cable to connect the two switches together. But what types of cables are used in the network shown in Figure 2.18?

FIGURE 2.18 RJ45 UTP cable question #2

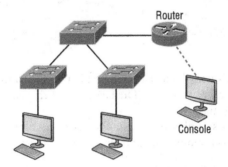

In Figure 2.18, there's a whole menu of cables in use. For the connection between the switches, we'd obviously use a crossover cable like we saw in Figure 2.13. The trouble is that you must understand that we have a console connection that uses a rolled cable. Plus, the connection from the router to the switch is a straight-through cable, as is true for the hosts to the switches. Keep in mind that if we had a serial connection, which we don't, we would use a V.35 to connect us to a WAN.

Fiber Optic

Fiber-optic cabling has been around for a long time and has some solid standards. The cable allows for very fast transmission of data, is made of glass (or even plastic), is very thin, and works as a waveguide to transmit light between two ends of the fiber. Fiber optics has been used to go very long distances, as in intercontinental connections, but it is becoming more and more popular in Ethernet LAN networks due to the fast speeds available and because, unlike UTP, it's immune to interference like cross-talk.

Some main components of this cable are the core and the cladding. The core will hold the light and the cladding confines the light in the core. The tighter the cladding, the smaller the core, and when the core is small, less light will be sent, but it can go faster and farther.

In Figure 2.19 you can see that there is a 9-micron core, which is very small and can be measured against a human hair, (50 microns.)

FIGURE 2.19   Typical fiber cable dimensions are in um (10^{-6} meters). Not to scale.

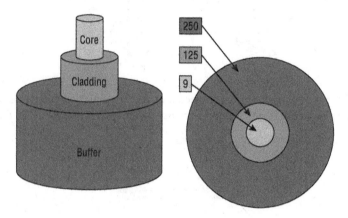

The cladding is 125 microns, which is actually a fiber standard that allows manufacturers to make connectors for all fiber cables. The last piece of this cable is the buffer, which is there to protect the delicate glass.

There are two major types of fiber optics: single-mode and multimode. Figure 2.20 shows the differences between multimode and single-mode fibers.

FIGURE 2.20   Multimode and single-mode fibers

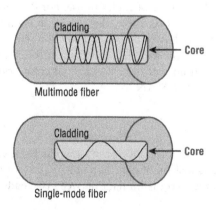

Single-mode is more expensive, has a tighter cladding, and can go much farther distances than multimode. The difference comes in the tightness of the cladding, which makes a smaller core, meaning that only one mode of light will propagate down the fiber. Multimode is looser and has a larger core so it allows multiple light particles to travel down the glass. These particles have to be put back together at the receiving end, so distance is less than that with single-mode fiber, which allows only very few light particles to travel down the fiber.

There are about 70 different connectors for fiber, and Cisco uses a few different types. Looking back at Figure 2.16, the two bottom ports are referred to as Small Form-Factor Pluggables, or SFPs.

Data Encapsulation

When a host transmits data across a network to another device, the data goes through a process called *encapsulation* and is wrapped with protocol information at each layer of the OSI model. Each layer communicates only with its peer layer on the receiving device.

To communicate and exchange information, each layer uses *protocol data units (PDUs)*. These hold the control information attached to the data at each layer of the model. They are usually attached to the header in front of the data field but can also be at the trailer, or end, of it.

Each PDU attaches to the data by encapsulating it at each layer of the OSI model, and each has a specific name depending on the information provided in each header. This PDU information is read only by the peer layer on the receiving device. After it's read, it's stripped off and the data is then handed to the next layer up.

Figure 2.21 shows the PDUs and how they attach control information to each layer. This figure demonstrates how the upper-layer user data is converted for transmission on the network. The data stream is then handed down to the Transport layer, which sets up a virtual circuit to the receiving device by sending over a synch packet. Next, the data stream is broken up into smaller pieces, and a Transport layer header is created and attached to the header of the data field; now the piece of data is called a *segment* (a PDU). Each segment can be sequenced so the data stream can be put back together on the receiving side exactly as it was transmitted.

Each segment is then handed to the Network layer for network addressing and routing through the internetwork. Logical addressing (for example, IP and IPv6) is used to get each segment to the correct network. The Network layer protocol adds a control header to the segment handed down from the Transport layer, and what we have now is called a *packet* or *datagram*. Remember that the Transport and Network layers work together to rebuild a data stream on a receiving host, but it's not part of their work to place their PDUs on a local network segment—which is the only way to get the information to a router or host.

FIGURE 2.21   Data encapsulation

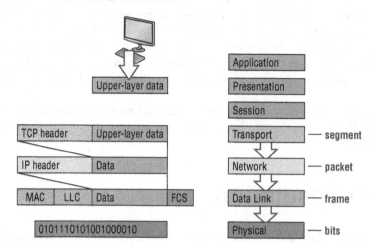

It's the Data Link layer that's responsible for taking packets from the Network layer and placing them on the network medium (cable or wireless). The Data Link layer encapsulates each packet in a *frame*, and the frame's header carries the hardware addresses of the source and destination hosts. If the destination device is on a remote network, then the frame is sent to a router to be routed through an internetwork. Once it gets to the destination network, a new frame is used to get the packet to the destination host.

To put this frame on the network, it must first be put into a digital signal. Since a frame is really a logical group of 1s and 0s, the physical layer is responsible for encoding these digits into a digital signal, which is read by devices on the same local network. The receiving devices will synchronize on the digital signal and extract (decode) the 1s and 0s from the digital signal. At this point, the devices reconstruct the frames, run a CRC, and then check their answer against the answer in the frame's FCS field. If it matches, the packet is pulled from the frame and what's left of the frame is discarded. This process is called *de-encapsulation*. The packet is handed to the Network layer, where the address is checked. If the address matches, the segment is pulled from the packet and what's left of the packet is discarded. The segment is processed at the Transport layer, which rebuilds the data stream and acknowledges to the transmitting station that it received each piece. It then hands off the data stream to the upper-layer application.

At a transmitting device, the data encapsulation method works like this:

1. User information is converted to data for transmission on the network.

2. Data is converted to segments, and a reliable connection is set up between the transmitting and receiving hosts.

3. Segments are converted to packets or datagrams, and a logical address is placed in the header so each packet can be routed through an internetwork.

4. Packets or datagrams are converted to frames for transmission on the local network. Hardware (Ethernet) addresses are used to uniquely identify hosts on a local network segment.

5. Frames are converted to bits, and a digital encoding and clocking scheme is used.

To explain this in more detail using the layer addressing, I'll use Figure 2.22:

FIGURE 2.22 PDU and layer addressing

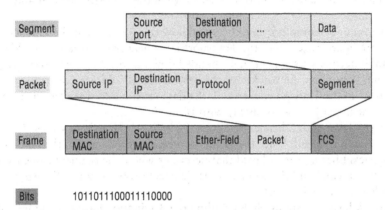

Remember that a data stream is handed down from the upper layer to the Transport layer. As technicians, we really don't care who the data stream comes from because that's really a programmer's problem. Our job is to rebuild the data stream reliably and hand it to the upper layers on the receiving device.

Before we go further in our discussion of Figure 2.22, let's discuss port numbers and make sure you understand them. The Transport layer uses port numbers to define both the virtual circuit and the upper-layer processes, as you can see in Figure 2.23:

FIGURE 2.23 Port numbers at the Transport layer

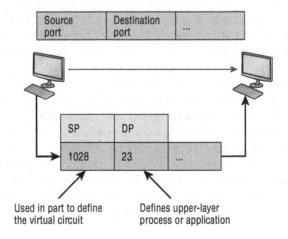

When using a connection-oriented protocol like TCP, the Transport layer takes the data stream, makes segments out of it, and establishes a reliable session by creating a virtual circuit. It then sequences (numbers) each segment and uses acknowledgments and flow control. If you're using TCP, the virtual circuit is defined by the source and destination port number plus the source and destination IP address and called a socket. Understand that the host just makes this up, starting at port number 1024 because 0 through 1023 are reserved for well-known port numbers. The destination port number defines the upper-layer process or application that the data stream is handed to when the data stream is reliably rebuilt on the receiving host.

Now that you understand port numbers and how they are used at the Transport layer, let's go back to Figure 2.22. Once the Transport layer header information is added to the piece of data, it becomes a segment that's handed down to the Network layer along with the destination IP address. As you know, the destination IP address was handed down from the upper layers to the Transport layer with the data stream and was identified via name resolution at the upper layers—probably with DNS.

The Network layer adds a header and adds the logical addressing such as IP addresses to the front of each segment. Once the header is added to the segment, the PDU is called a packet. The packet has a protocol field that describes where the segment came from (either UDP or TCP) so it can hand the segment to the correct protocol at the Transport layer when it reaches the receiving host.

The Network layer is responsible for finding the destination hardware address that dictates where the packet should be sent on the local network. It does this by using the Address Resolution Protocol (ARP)—something I'll talk about more in Chapter 3. IP at the Network layer looks at the destination IP address and compares that address to its own source IP address and subnet mask. If it turns out to be a local network request, the hardware address of the local host is requested via an ARP request. If the packet is destined for a host on a remote network, IP will look for the IP address of the default gateway (router) instead.

The packet, along with the destination hardware address of either the local host or default gateway, is then handed down to the Data Link layer. The Data Link layer will add a header to the front of the packet and the piece of data then becomes a frame. It's called a frame because both a header and a trailer are added to the packet, which makes it look like it's within bookends—a frame—as shown in Figure 2.22. The frame uses an Ether-Type field to describe which protocol the packet came from at the Network layer. Now a cyclic redundancy check is run on the frame, and the answer to the CRC is placed in the Frame Check Sequence field found in the trailer of the frame.

The frame is now ready to be handed down, one bit at a time, to the Physical layer, which will use bit-timing rules to encode the data in a digital signal. Every device on the network segment will receive the digital signal and synchronize with the clock and extract the 1s and 0s from the digital signal to build a frame. After the frame is rebuilt, a CRC is run to make sure the frame is in proper order. If everything turns out to be all good, the hosts will check the destination MAC and IP addresses to see if the frame is for them.

If all this is making your eyes cross and your brain freeze, don't freak. I'll be going over exactly how data is encapsulated and routed through an internetwork later, in Chapter 9, "IP Routing."

The Cisco Three-Layer Hierarchical Model

Most of us were exposed to hierarchy early in life. Anyone with older siblings learned what it was like to be at the bottom of the hierarchy. Regardless of where you first discovered the concept of hierarchy, most of us experience it in many aspects of our lives. It's *hierarchy* that helps us understand where things belong, how things fit together, and what functions go where. It brings order to otherwise complex models. If you want a pay raise, for instance, hierarchy dictates that you ask your boss, not your subordinate, because that's the person whose role it is to grant or deny your request. So basically, understanding hierarchy helps us discern where we should go to get what we need.

Hierarchy has many of the same benefits in network design that it does in other areas of life. When used properly, it makes networks more predictable and helps us define which areas should perform certain functions. Likewise, you can use tools such as access lists at certain levels in hierarchical networks and avoid them at others.

Let's face it: Large networks can be extremely complicated, with multiple protocols, detailed configurations, and diverse technologies. Hierarchy helps us summarize a complex collection of details into an understandable model, bringing order from the chaos. Then, as specific configurations are needed, the model dictates the appropriate manner in which to apply them.

The Cisco hierarchical model can help you design, implement, and maintain a scalable, reliable, cost-effective hierarchical internetwork. Cisco defines three layers of hierarchy, as shown in Figure 2.24, each with specific functions:

FIGURE 2.24   The Cisco hierarchical model

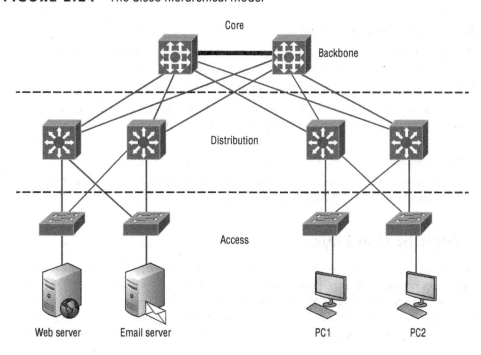

Core

Backbone

Distribution

Access

Web server   Email server   PC1   PC2

Each layer has specific responsibilities. Keep in mind that the three layers are logical and are not necessarily physical devices. Consider the OSI model, another logical hierarchy. Its seven layers describe functions but not necessarily protocols, right? Sometimes a protocol maps to more than one layer of the OSI model, and sometimes multiple protocols communicate within a single layer. In the same way, when we build physical implementations of hierarchical networks, we may have many devices in a single layer, or there may be a single device performing functions at two layers. Just remember that the definition of the layers is logical, not physical!

So let's take a closer look at each of the layers now.

The Core Layer

The *core layer* is literally the core of the network. At the top of the hierarchy, the core layer is responsible for transporting large amounts of traffic both reliably and quickly. The only purpose of the network's core layer is to switch traffic as fast as possible. The traffic transported across the core is common to a majority of users. But remember that user data is processed at the distribution layer, which forwards the requests to the core if needed.

If there's a failure in the core, *every single user* can be affected! This is why fault tolerance at this layer is so important. The core is likely to see large volumes of traffic, so speed and latency are driving concerns here. Given the function of the core, we can now consider some design specifics. Let's start with some things we don't want to do:

- Never do anything to slow down traffic. This includes making sure you don't use access lists, perform routing between virtual local area networks, or implement packet filtering.

- Don't support workgroup access here.

- Avoid expanding the core (e.g., adding routers when the internetwork grows). If performance becomes an issue in the core, give preference to upgrades over expansion.

Here's a list of things that we want to achieve as we design the core:

- Design the core for high reliability. Consider data-link technologies that facilitate both speed and redundancy, like Gigabit Ethernet with redundant links or even 10 Gigabit Ethernet.

- Design with speed in mind. The core should have very little latency.

- Select routing protocols with lower convergence times. Fast and redundant data-link connectivity is no help if your routing tables are shot!

The Distribution Layer

The *distribution layer* is sometimes referred to as the *workgroup layer* and is the communication point between the access layer and the core. The primary functions of the distribution layer are to provide routing, filtering, and WAN access and to determine how packets can access the core, if needed. The distribution layer must determine the fastest way that network service requests are handled—for example, how a file request is forwarded to a server. After the distribution layer determines the best path, it forwards the request to the core layer if necessary. The core layer then quickly transports the request to the correct service.

The distribution layer is where we want to implement policies for the network because we are allowed a lot of flexibility in defining network operation here. There are several things that should generally be handled at the distribution layer:

- Routing
- Implementing tools (such as access lists), packet filtering, and queuing
- Implementing security and network policies, including address translation and firewalls
- Redistributing between routing protocols, including static routing
- Routing between VLANs and other workgroup support functions
- Defining broadcast and multicast domains

Key things to avoid at the distribution layer are those that are limited to functions that exclusively belong to one of the other layers!

The Access Layer

The *access layer* controls user and workgroup access to internetwork resources and is sometimes referred to as the *desktop layer*. The network resources most users need are available locally because the distribution layer handles any traffic for remote services.

The following are some of the functions to be included at the access layer:

- Continued (from distribution layer) use of access control and policies
- Creation of separate collision domains (microsegmentation/switches)
- Workgroup connectivity into the distribution layer
- Device connectivity
- Resiliency and security services
- Advanced technology capabilities (voice/video, etc.)

Technologies like Gigabit or Fast Ethernet switching are frequently seen in the access layer.

I can't stress this enough—just because there are three separate levels does not imply three separate devices! There could be fewer or there could be more. After all, this is a *layered* approach.

Summary

In this chapter, you learned the fundamentals of Ethernet networking, how hosts communicate on a network. You discovered how CSMA/CD works in an Ethernet half-duplex network.

I also talked about the differences between half- and full-duplex modes, and we discussed the collision detection mechanism called CSMA/CD.

I described the common Ethernet cable types used in today's networks in this chapter as well, and by the way, you'd be wise to study that section really well!

Important enough to not gloss over, this chapter provided an introduction to encapsulation. Encapsulation is the process of encoding data as it goes down the OSI stack.

Last, I covered the Cisco three-layer hierarchical model. I described in detail the three layers and how each is used to help design and implement a Cisco internetwork.

Chapter

3

Introduction to TCP/IP

The *Transmission Control Protocol/Internet Protocol (TCP/IP)* suite was designed and implemented by the Department of Defense (DoD) to ensure and preserve data integrity as well as maintain communications in the event of catastrophic war. So it follows that if designed and implemented correctly, a TCP/IP network can be a secure, dependable, and resilient one.

In this chapter, I'll cover the protocols of TCP/IP, and throughout this book, you'll learn how to create a solid TCP/IP network with Cisco routers and switches.

We'll begin by exploring the DoD's version of TCP/IP, then compare that version and its protocols with the OSI reference model that we discussed earlier.

Once you understand the protocols and processes used at the various levels of the DoD model, we'll take the next logical step by delving into the world of IP addressing and the different classes of IP addresses used in networks today.

Because having a good grasp of the various IPv4 address types is critical to understanding IP addressing and subnetting, we'll explore these key topics in detail, ending this chapter by discussing the various types of IPv4 addresses that you'll need to have down before you move onto the next chapters.

To find your included bonus material, as well as Todd Lammle videos, practice questions, and hands-on labs, please see www.lammle.com/ccna.

Introducing TCP/IP

TCP/IP is at the very core of all things networking, so I really want to ensure that you have a comprehensive and functional command of it. I'll start by giving you the whole TCP/IP backstory, including its inception, and then move on to describe the important technical goals as defined by its original architects. And of course, I'll include how TCP/IP compares to the theoretical OSI model.

A Brief History of TCP/IP

TCP first came on the scene way back in 1973, and in 1978, it was divided into two distinct protocols: TCP and IP. Later, in 1983, TCP/IP replaced the Network Control Protocol (NCP) and was authorized as the official means of data transport for anything connecting to ARPAnet, the Internet's ancestor. The DoD's Advanced Research Projects Agency (ARPA) created this ancient network way back in 1957 as a cold war reaction to the Soviet's launching of *Sputnik*. Also in 1983, ARPA was redubbed DARPA and divided into ARPAnet and MILNET until both were finally dissolved in 1990.

It may be counterintuitive, but most of the development work on TCP/IP happened at UC Berkeley in northern California, where a group of scientists were simultaneously working on the Berkeley version of UNIX, which soon became known as the Berkeley Software Distribution (BSD) series of UNIX versions. Of course, because TCP/IP worked so well, it was packaged into subsequent releases of BSD Unix and offered to other universities and institutions if they bought the distribution tape. So basically, BSD Unix bundled with TCP/IP began as shareware in the world of academia. As a result, it became the foundation for the tremendous success and unprecedented growth of today's Internet as well as smaller, private and corporate intranets.

As usual, what started as a small group of TCP/IP aficionados evolved, and as it did, the US government created a program to test any new published standards and make sure they passed certain criteria. This was to protect TCP/IP's integrity and to ensure that no developer changed anything too dramatically or added any proprietary features. It's this very quality—this open-systems approach to the TCP/IP family of protocols—that sealed its popularity because this quality guarantees a solid connection between myriad hardware and software platforms with no strings attached.

TCP/IP and the DoD Model

The DoD model is basically a condensed version of the OSI model that comprises four instead of seven layers:

- Process/Application layer
- Host-to-Host layer or Transport layer
- Internet layer
- Network Access layer or Link layer

Figure 3.1 offers a comparison of the DoD model and the OSI reference model. As you can see, the two are similar in concept, but each has a different number of layers with different names. Cisco may at times use different names for the same layer, such as, "Host-to-Host" and Transport" at the layer above the Internet layer, as well as, "Network Access" and "Link" used to describe the bottom layer.

FIGURE 3.1 The DoD and OSI models

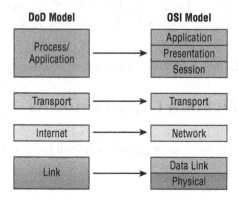

A vast array of protocols join forces at the DoD model's *Process/Application layer.* These processes integrate the various activities and duties spanning the focus of the OSI's corresponding top three layers (Application, Presentation, and Session). We'll focus on a few of the most important applications found in the CCNA objectives. In short, the Process/Application layer defines protocols for node-to-node application communication and controls user-interface specifications.

The *Host-to-Host layer or Transport layer* parallels the functions of the OSI's Transport layer, defining protocols for setting up the level of transmission service for applications. It tackles issues like creating reliable end-to-end communication and ensuring the error-free delivery of data. It handles packet sequencing and maintains data integrity.

The *Internet layer* corresponds to the OSI's Network layer, designating the protocols relating to the logical transmission of packets over the entire network. It takes care of the addressing of hosts by giving them an IP (Internet Protocol) address and handles the routing of packets among multiple networks.

At the bottom of the DoD model, the *Network Access layer or Link layer* implements the data exchange between the host and the network. The equivalent of the Data Link and Physical layers of the OSI model, the Network Access layer oversees hardware addressing and defines protocols for the physical transmission of data. The reason TCP/IP became so popular is because there were no set physical layer specifications, so it could run on any existing or future physical network!

The DoD and OSI models are alike in design and concept and have similar functions in similar layers. Figure 3.2 shows the TCP/IP protocol suite and how its protocols relate to the DoD model layers.

FIGURE 3.2   The TCP/IP protocol suite

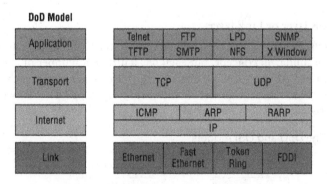

In the following sections, we will look at the different protocols in more detail, beginning with those found at the Process/Application layer.

The Process/Application Layer Protocols

Coming up, I'll describe the different applications and services typically used in IP networks, and although there are many more protocols defined here, we'll focus in on the protocols most relevant to the CCNA objectives. Here's a list of the protocols and applications we'll cover in this section:

- Telnet
- SSH
- FTP
- TFTP
- SNMP
- HTTP
- HTTPS
- NTP
- DNS
- DHCP/BootP
- APIPA

Telnet

Telnet was one of the first Internet standards, developed in 1969, and is the chameleon of protocols—its specialty is terminal emulation. It allows a user on a remote client machine, called the Telnet client, to access the resources of another machine, the Telnet server, in order to access a command-line interface. Telnet achieves this by pulling a fast one on the Telnet server and making the client machine appear as though it were a terminal directly attached to the local network. This projection is actually a software image—a virtual terminal that can interact with the chosen remote host. A major drawback is that there are no encryption techniques available within the Telnet protocol, so everything must be sent in clear text, including passwords! Figure 3.3 shows an example of a Telnet client trying to connect to a Telnet server.

FIGURE 3.3   Telnet

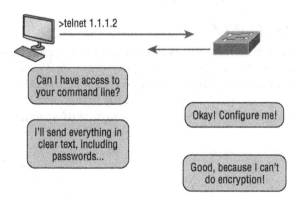

These emulated terminals are of the text-mode type and can execute defined procedures such as displaying menus that give users the opportunity to choose options and access the applications on the duped server. Users begin a Telnet session by running the Telnet client software and then logging into the Telnet server. Telnet uses an 8-bit, byte-oriented data connection over TCP, which makes it very thorough. It's still in use today because it is so simple and easy to use, with very low overhead, but again, with everything sent in clear text, it's not recommended in production.

Secure Shell (SSH)

Secure Shell (SSH) protocol sets up a secure session that's similar to Telnet over a standard TCP/IP connection and is employed for doing things like logging into systems, running programs on remote systems, and moving files from one system to another. And it does all of this while maintaining an encrypted connection. Figure 3.4 shows a SSH client trying to connect to a SSH server. The client must send the data encrypted.

FIGURE 3.4   Secure Shell

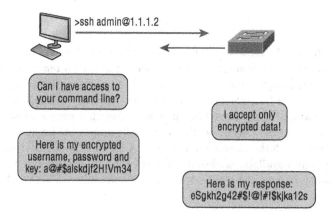

You can think of it as the new-generation protocol that's now used in place of the anti-quated and very unused rsh and rlogin—even Telnet.

File Transfer Protocol (FTP)

File Transfer Protocol (FTP) actually lets us transfer files, and it can accomplish this between any two machines using it. But FTP isn't just a protocol; it's also a program. Operating as a protocol, FTP is used by applications. As a program, it's employed by users to perform file tasks by hand. FTP also allows for access to both directories and files and can accomplish certain types of directory operations, such as relocating into different ones (Figure 3.5).

FIGURE 3.5   FTP

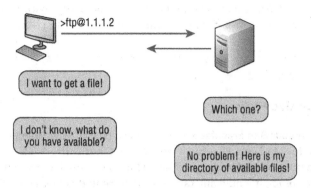

But accessing a host through FTP is only the first step. Users must then be subjected to an authentication login that's usually secured with passwords and usernames implemented by system administrators to restrict access. You can get around this somewhat by adopting the username *anonymous*, but you'll be limited in what you'll be able to access.

Even when employed by users manually as a program, FTP's functions are limited to listing and manipulating directories, typing file contents, and copying files between hosts. It can't execute remote files as programs.

Trivial File Transfer Protocol (TFTP)

Trivial File Transfer Protocol (TFTP) is the stripped-down, stock version of FTP, but it's the protocol of choice if you know exactly what you want and where to find it because it's so fast and easy to use.

But TFTP doesn't offer the abundance of functions that FTP does because it has no directory-browsing abilities, meaning that it can only send and receive files (Figure 3.6). Still, it's heavily used for managing file systems on Cisco devices, as I'll show you in Chapter 7, "Managing a Cisco Internetwork."

FIGURE 3.6   TFTP

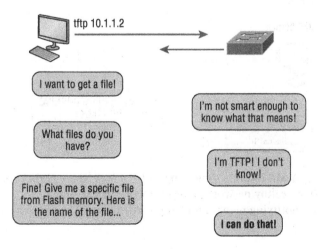

This compact little protocol also skimps in the data department, sending much smaller blocks of data than FTP. Also, there's no authentication as there is with FTP, so it's even more insecure. Few sites support it because of the inherent security risks.

Real World Scenario

When Should You Use FTP?

Let's say everyone at your San Francisco office needs a 50 GB file emailed to them right away. What do you do? Many email servers would reject that email due to size limits because many ISPs don't allow files larger than 10 MB to be emailed. Even if there are no size limits on the server, it would still take a while to send this huge file...FTP to the rescue!

So if you need to give someone a large file or you need to get a large file from someone, FTP is a nice choice. To use FTP, you would need to set up an FTP server on the Internet so that the files can be shared.

Besides resolving size issues, FTP is faster than email. In addition, because it uses TCP and is connection-oriented, if the session dies, FTP can sometimes start up where it left off. Try that with your email client!

Simple Network Management Protocol (SNMP)

Simple Network Management Protocol (SNMP) collects and manipulates valuable network information, as you can see in Figure 3.7. It gathers data by polling the devices on the network from a network management station (NMS) at fixed or random intervals, requiring them to disclose certain information, or even asking for certain information from the device. In addition, network devices can inform the NMS about problems as they occur so the network administrator is alerted.

FIGURE 3.7   SNMP

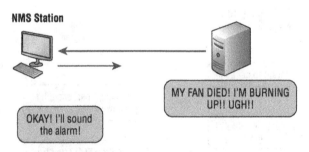

When all is well, SNMP receives something called a *baseline*—a report delimiting the operational traits of a healthy network. This protocol can also stand as a watchdog over the network, quickly notifying managers of any sudden turn of events. These network watchdogs are called *agents*, and when aberrations occur, agents send an alert called a *trap* to the management station.

SNMP Versions 1, 2, and 3

SNMP versions 1 and 2 are pretty much obsolete. This doesn't mean you won't see them in a network now and then, but you'll only come across v1 rarely, if ever. SNMPv2 provided improvements, especially in performance. But one of the best additions was called GETBULK, which allowed a host to retrieve a large amount of data at once. Even so, v2 never really caught on in the networking world and SNMPv3 is now the standard. Unlike v1, which used only UDP, v3 uses both TCP and UDP and added even more security, message integrity, authentication, and encryption.

Hypertext Transfer Protocol (HTTP)

All those snappy websites comprising a mélange of graphics, text, links, ads, and so on rely on the *Hypertext Transfer Protocol (HTTP)* to make it all possible (Figure 3.8). It's used to manage communications between web browsers and web servers and opens the right resource when you click a link, wherever that resource may actually reside.

FIGURE 3.8 HTTP

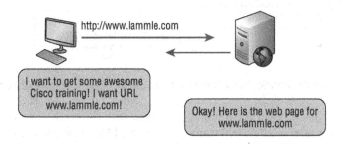

In order for a browser to display a web page, it must find the exact server that has the right web page, plus the exact details that identify the information requested. This information must be then be sent back to the browser. Nowadays, it's highly doubtful that a web server would have only one page to display!

Your browser can understand what you need when you enter a Uniform Resource Locator (URL), which we usually refer to as a web address, such as, for example, www .lammle.com/ccna and www.lammle.com/blog.

So basically, each URL defines the protocol used to transfer data, the name of the server, and the particular web page on that server.

Hypertext Transfer Protocol Secure (HTTPS)

Hypertext Transfer Protocol Secure (HTTPS) is also known as Secure Hypertext Transfer Protocol. It uses Secure Sockets Layer (SSL). Sometimes you'll see it referred to as SHTTP or S-HTTP, which were slightly different protocols, but since Microsoft supported HTTPS, it became the de facto standard for securing web communication. But no matter—as indicated, it's a secure version of HTTP that arms you with a whole bunch of security tools for keeping transactions between a web browser and a server secure.

It's what your browser needs to fill out forms, sign in, authenticate, and encrypt an HTTP message when you do things online like make a reservation, access your bank, or buy something.

Network Time Protocol (NTP)

Kudos to Professor David Mills of the University of Delaware for coming up with this handy protocol that's used to synchronize the clocks on our computers to one standard time source (typically, an atomic clock). *Network Time Protocol (NTP)* works by synchronizing devices to ensure that all computers on a given network agree on the time (Figure 3.9).

FIGURE 3.9   NTP

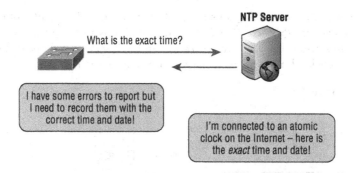

This may sound pretty simple, but it's very important because so many of the transactions done today are time and date stamped. Think about databases—a server can get messed up pretty badly and even crash if it's out of sync with the machines connected to it by even mere seconds. You can't have a transaction entered by a machine at, say, 1:50 a.m. when the server records that transaction as having occurred at 1:45 a.m. So basically, NTP works to prevent a "back to the future" scenario from bringing down the network—very important indeed!

I'll tell you a lot more about NTP in Chapter 7, including how to configure this protocol in a Cisco environment.

Domain Name Service (DNS)

Domain Name Service (DNS) resolves hostnames—specifically, Internet names, such as www.lammle.com. But you don't have to actually use DNS. You just type in the IP address of any device you want to communicate with and find the IP address of a URL by using the Ping program. For example, >ping www.cisco.com will return the IP address resolved by DNS.

An IP address identifies hosts on a network and the Internet as well, but DNS was designed to make our lives easier. Think about this: What would happen if you wanted to move your web page to a different service provider? The IP address would change and no one would know what the new one is. DNS allows you to use a domain name to specify an IP address. You can change the IP address as often as you want and no one will know the difference.

To resolve a DNS address from a host, you'd typically type in the URL from your favorite browser, which would hand the data to the Application layer interface to be transmitted on the network. The application would look up the DNS address and send a UDP request to your DNS server to resolve the name (Figure 3.10).

FIGURE 3.10 DNS

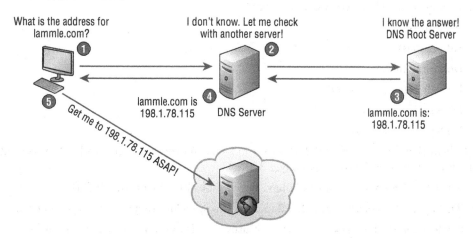

If your first DNS server doesn't know the answer to the query, then the DNS server forwards a TCP request to its root DNS server. Once the query is resolved, the answer is transmitted back to the originating host, which means the host can now request the information from the correct web server.

DNS is used to resolve a *fully qualified domain name (FQDN)*—for example, www .lammle.com or todd.lammle.com. An FQDN is a hierarchy that can logically locate a system based on its domain identifier.

If you want to resolve the name *todd*, you either must type in the FQDN of todd.lammle.com or have a device such as a PC or router add the suffix for you. For example, on a Cisco router, you can use the command *ip domain-name lammle.com* to append each request with the lammle.com domain. If you don't do that, you'll have to type in the FQDN to get DNS to resolve the name.

An important thing to remember about DNS is that if you can ping a device with an IP address but cannot use its FQDN, then you might have some type of DNS configuration failure.

Dynamic Host Configuration Protocol (DHCP)/Bootstrap Protocol (BootP)

Dynamic Host Configuration Protocol (DHCP) assigns IP addresses to hosts. It allows for easier administration and works well in small to very large network environments. Many types of hardware can be used as a DHCP server, including a Cisco router.

DHCP differs from BootP in that BootP assigns an IP address to a host but the host's hardware address must be entered manually in a BootP table. You can think of DHCP as a dynamic BootP. But remember that BootP is also used to send an operating system that a host can boot from. DHCP can't do that.

But there's still a lot of information a DHCP server can provide to a host when the host is requesting an IP address from the DHCP server. Here's a list of the most common types of information a DHCP server can provide:

- IP address
- Subnet mask
- Domain name
- Default gateway (routers)
- DNS server address
- WINS server address

A client that sends out a DHCP Discover message in order to receive an IP address sends out a broadcast at both layer 2 and layer 3.

- The layer 2 broadcast is all *F*s in hex, which looks like this: ff:ff:ff:ff:ff:ff.
- The layer 3 broadcast is 255.255.255.255, which means all networks and all hosts.

DHCP is connectionless, which means it uses User Datagram Protocol (UDP) at the Transport layer, also known as the Host-to-Host layer, which we'll talk about later.

Seeing is believing, so here's an example of output from my analyzer showing the layer 2 and layer 3 broadcasts:

```
Ethernet II, Src: 0.0.0.0 (00:0b:db:99:d3:5e),Dst: Broadcast(ff:ff:ff:ff:ff:ff)
Internet Protocol, Src: 0.0.0.0 (0.0.0.0),Dst: 255.255.255.255(255.255.255.255)
```

The Data Link and Network layers are both sending out "all hands" broadcasts saying, "Help—I don't know my IP address!"

DHCP configurations on a Cisco router and switch will be shown in Chapter 7, "Managing a Cisco Internetwork," and Chapter 9, "IP Routing."

Figure 3.11 shows the process of a client/server relationship using a DHCP connection.

FIGURE 3.11   DHCP client four-step process

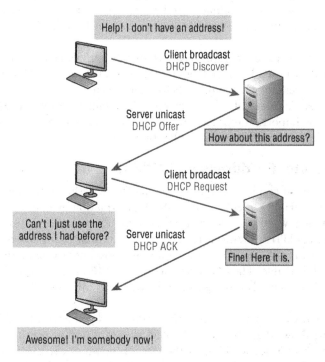

This is the four-step process a client takes to receive an IP address from a DHCP server:

1. The DHCP client broadcasts a DHCP Discover message looking for a DHCP server (Port 67).

2. The DHCP server that received the DHCP Discover message sends a layer 2 unicast DHCP Offer message back to the host.

3. The client then broadcasts to the server a DHCP Request message asking for the offered IP address and possibly other information.

4. The server finalizes the exchange with a unicast DHCP Acknowledgment message.

DHCP Conflicts

A DHCP address conflict occurs when two hosts use the same IP address, which sounds bad, and it is. We'll never even have to discuss this problem once we get to the chapter on IPv6!

During IP address assignment, a DHCP server checks for conflicts using the Ping program to test the availability of the address before it's assigned from the pool. If no host replies, then the DHCP server assumes that the IP address is not already allocated. This helps the server know that it's providing a good address, but what about the host? To provide extra protection against that awful IP conflict issue, the host can broadcast for its own address.

A host uses something called a gratuitous ARP to help avoid a possible duplicate address. The DHCP client sends an ARP broadcast out on the local LAN or VLAN using its newly assigned address to solve conflicts before they occur.

So, if an IP address conflict is detected, the address is removed from the DHCP pool (scope), and it's really important to remember that the address will not be assigned to a host until the administrator resolves the conflict by hand!

Automatic Private IP Addressing (APIPA)

Okay, so what happens if you have a few hosts connected together with a switch or hub and you don't have a DHCP server? You can add IP information by hand, known as *static IP addressing*, but later Windows operating systems provide a feature called Automatic Private IP Addressing (APIPA). With APIPA, clients can automatically self-configure an IP address and subnet mask—basic IP information that hosts use to communicate—when a DHCP server isn't available. The IP address range for APIPA is 169.254.0.1 through 169.254.255.254. The client also configures itself with a default Class B subnet mask of 255.255.0.0.

But when you're in your corporate network working and you have a DHCP server running, and your host shows that it's using this IP address range, it means that either your DHCP client on the host is not working, or the server is down or can't be reached due to some network issue. Believe me—I don't know anyone who's seen a host in this address range and has been happy about it!

Now, let's take a look at the Transport layer, or what the DoD calls the Host-to-Host layer.

The Host-to-Host or Transport Layer Protocols

The main purpose of the Host-to-Host layer is to shield the upper-layer applications from the complexities of the network. This layer says to the upper layer, "Just give me your data stream, with any instructions, and I'll begin the process of getting your information ready to send."

Coming up, I'll introduce you to the two protocols at this layer:

- Transmission Control Protocol (TCP)
- User Datagram Protocol (UDP)

In addition, we'll look at some of the key Host-to-Host protocol concepts, as well as the port numbers.

Remember, this is still considered layer 4, and Cisco really likes the way layer 4 can use acknowledgments, sequencing, and flow control.

Transmission Control Protocol (TCP)

Transmission Control Protocol (TCP) takes large blocks of information from an application and breaks them into segments. It numbers and sequences each segment so that the destination's TCP stack can put the segments back into the order the application intended. After these segments are sent on the transmitting host, TCP waits for an acknowledgment of the receiving end's TCP virtual circuit session, retransmitting any segments that aren't acknowledged.

Before a transmitting host starts to send segments down the model, the sender's TCP stack contacts the destination's TCP stack to establish a connection. This creates a *virtual circuit*, and this type of communication is known as *connection-oriented*. During this initial handshake, the two TCP layers also agree on the amount of information that's going to be sent before the recipient's TCP sends back an acknowledgment. With everything agreed upon in advance, the path is paved for reliable communication to take place.

TCP is a full-duplex, connection-oriented, reliable, and accurate protocol, but establishing all these terms and conditions, in addition to error checking, is no small task. TCP is very complicated, and so not surprisingly, it's costly in terms of network overhead. And since today's networks are much more reliable than those of yore, this added reliability is often unnecessary. Most programmers use TCP because it removes a lot of programming work, but for real-time video and VoIP, *User Datagram Protocol (UDP)* is often better because using it results in less overhead.

TCP Segment Format

Since the upper layers just send a data stream to the protocols in the Transport layers, I'll use Figure 3.12 to demonstrate how TCP segments a data stream and prepares it for the Internet layer. When the Internet layer receives the data stream, it routes the segments as packets through an internetwork. The segments are handed to the receiving host's Host-to-Host layer protocol, which rebuilds the data stream for the upper-layer applications or protocols.

FIGURE 3.12   TCP segment format

16-bit source port			16-bit destination port	
32-bit sequence number				
32-bit acknowledgment number				
4-bit header length	Reserved	Flags	16-bit window size	
16-bit TCP checksum			16-bit urgent pointer	
Options				
Data				

Figure 3.12 shows the TCP segment format and the different fields within the TCP header. This isn't important to memorize for the Cisco exam objectives, but you need to understand it well because it's really good foundational information.

The TCP header is 20 bytes long, or up to 24 bytes with options. Again, it's good to understand what each field in the TCP segment is in order to build a strong educational foundation:

Source port   This is the port number of the application on the host sending the data, which I'll talk about more thoroughly a little later in this chapter.

Destination port   This is the port number of the application requested on the destination host.

Sequence number   A number used by TCP that puts the data back in the correct order or retransmits missing or damaged data during a process called sequencing.

Acknowledgment number   The value is the TCP octet that is expected next.

Header length   The number of 32-bit words in the TCP header, which indicates where the data begins. The TCP header (even one including options) is an integral number of 32 bits in length.

Reserved   Always set to zero.

Code bits/flags   Controls functions used to set up and terminate a session.

Window   The window size the sender is willing to accept, in octets.

Checksum   The cyclic redundancy check (CRC), used because TCP doesn't trust the lower layers and checks everything. The CRC checks the header and data fields.

Urgent   A valid field only if the Urgent pointer in the code bits is set. If so, this value indicates the offset from the current sequence number, in octets, where the segment of non-urgent data begins.

Options   May be 0, meaning that no options have to be present, or a multiple of 32 bits. However, if any options are used that do not cause the option field to total a multiple of 32 bits, padding of 0s must be used to make sure the data begins on a 32-bit boundary. These boundaries are known as words.

Data   Handed down to the TCP protocol at the Transport layer, which includes the upper-layer headers.

Let's take a look at a TCP segment copied from a network analyzer:

```
TCP - Transport Control Protocol
Source Port: 5973
Destination Port: 23
Sequence Number: 1456389907
Ack Number: 1242056456
Offset: 5
Reserved: %000000
Code: %011000
Ack is valid
Push Request
Window: 61320
Checksum: 0x61a6
Urgent Pointer: 0
```

```
No TCP Options
TCP Data Area:
vL.5.+.5.+.5.+.5 76 4c 19 35 11 2b 19 35 11 2b 19 35 11
2b 19 35 +. 11 2b 19
Frame Check Sequence: 0x0d00000f
```

Did you notice that everything I talked about earlier is in the segment? As you can see from the number of fields in the header, TCP creates a lot of overhead. Again, this is why application developers may opt for efficiency over reliability to save overhead and go with UDP instead. It's also defined at the Transport layer as an alternative to TCP.

User Datagram Protocol (UDP)

User Datagram Protocol (UDP) is basically the scaled-down economy model of TCP, which is why UDP is sometimes referred to as a thin protocol. Like a thin person on a park bench, a thin protocol doesn't take up a lot of room—or in this case, require much bandwidth on a network.

UDP doesn't offer all the bells and whistles of TCP either, but it does do a fabulous job of transporting information that doesn't require reliable delivery, using far less network resources. (UDP is covered thoroughly in Request for Comments 768.)

So clearly, there are times that it's wise for developers to opt for UDP rather than TCP, one of them being when reliability is already taken care of at the Process/Application layer. Network File System (NFS) handles its own reliability issues, making the use of TCP both impractical and redundant. But ultimately, it's up to the application developer to opt for using UDP or TCP, not the user who wants to transfer data faster!

UDP does *not* sequence the segments and does not care about the order in which the segments arrive at the destination. UDP just sends the segments off and forgets about them. It doesn't follow through, check up on them, or even allow for an acknowledgment of safe arrival—complete abandonment. Because of this, it's referred to as an unreliable protocol. This does not mean that UDP is ineffective, only that it doesn't deal with reliability issues at all.

Furthermore, UDP doesn't create a virtual circuit, nor does it contact the destination before delivering information to it. Because of this, it's also considered a *connectionless* protocol. Since UDP assumes that the application will use its own reliability method, it doesn't use any itself. This presents an application developer with a choice when running the Internet Protocol stack: TCP for reliability or UDP for faster transfers.

It's important to know how this process works because if the segments arrive out of order, which is commonplace in IP networks, they'll simply be passed up to the next layer in whatever order they were received. This can result in some seriously garbled data! On the other hand, TCP sequences the segments so they get put back together in exactly the right order, which is something UDP just can't do.

UDP Segment Format

Figure 3.13 clearly illustrates UDP's markedly lean overhead as compared to TCP's hungry requirements. Look at the figure carefully—can you see that UDP doesn't use windowing or provide for acknowledgments in the UDP header?

FIGURE 3.13 UDP segment

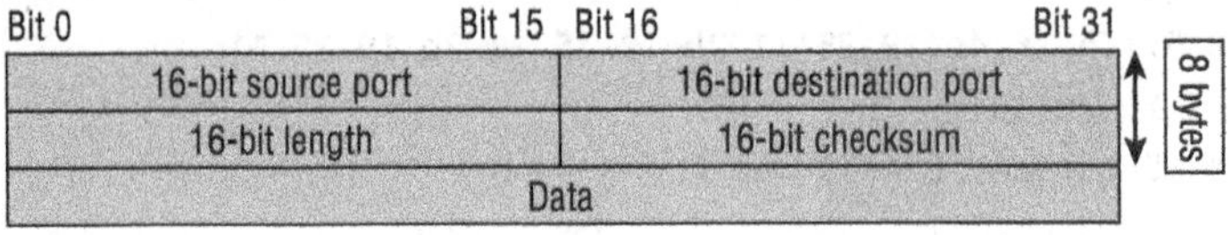

It's important for you to understand what each field in the UDP segment is:

Source port Port number of the application on the host sending the data

Destination port Port number of the application requested on the destination host

Length Length of UDP header and UDP data

Checksum Checksum of both the UDP header and UDP data fields

Data Upper-layer data

UDP, like TCP, doesn't trust the lower layers and runs its own CRC. Remember that the Frame Check Sequence (FCS) is the field that houses the CRC, which is why you can see the FCS information.

The following shows a UDP segment caught on a network analyzer:

```
UDP - User Datagram Protocol
Source Port: 1085
Destination Port: 5136
Length: 41
Checksum: 0x7a3c
UDP Data Area:
..Z......00 01 5a 96 00 01 00 00 00 00 00 11 0000 00
...C..2._C._C 2e 03 00 43 02 1e 32 0a 00 0a 00 80 43 00 80
Frame Check Sequence: 0x00000000
```

Notice that low overhead! Try to find the sequence number, ack number, and window size in the UDP segment. You can't because they just aren't there!

Key Concepts of Host-to-Host Protocols

Since you've now seen both a connection-oriented (TCP) and connectionless (UDP) protocol in action, it's a good time to summarize the two here. Table 3.1 highlights some of the key concepts about these two protocols for you to memorize.

TABLE 3.1 Key features of TCP and UDP

TCP	UDP
Sequenced	Unsequenced
Reliable	Unreliable

TCP	UDP
Connection-oriented	Connectionless
Virtual circuit	Low overhead
Acknowledgment	No acknowledgment
Windowing flow control	No windowing or flow control of any type

And if all this isn't quite clear yet, a telephone analogy will really help you understand how TCP works. Most of us know that before you speak to someone on a phone, you must first establish a connection with that other person no matter where they are. This is akin to establishing a virtual circuit with the TCP protocol. If you were giving someone important information during your conversation, you might say something like, "Did you get that?" Saying things like that is a lot like a TCP acknowledgment—it's designed to get you verification. From time to time, especially on mobile phones, people ask, "Are you still there?" People end their conversations with a "Goodbye" of some kind, putting closure on the phone call, which you can think of as tearing down the virtual circuit that was created for your communication session. TCP performs these types of functions.

Conversely, using UDP is more like sending a postcard. To do that, you don't need to contact the other party first, you simply write your message, address the postcard, and send it off. This is analogous to UDP's connectionless orientation. Since the message on the postcard is probably not vitally important, you don't need an acknowledgment of its receipt. Similarly, UDP does not involve acknowledgments.

Let's take a look at another figure, one that includes TCP, UDP, and the applications associated to each protocol: Figure 3.14 (discussed in the next section).

FIGURE 3.14   Port numbers for TCP and UDP

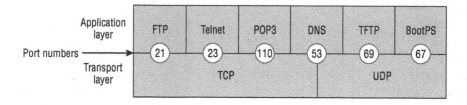

Port Numbers

TCP and UDP must use *port numbers* to communicate with the upper layers because these are what keep track of different conversations crossing the network simultaneously. Originating-source port numbers are dynamically assigned by the source host and will equal some number starting at 1024. Port number 1023 and below are defined in RFC 3232 (or just see www.iana.org), which discusses what we call well-known port numbers.

Virtual circuits that don't use an application with a well-known port number are assigned port numbers randomly from a specific range instead. These port numbers identify the source and destination application or process in the TCP segment.

> The Requests for Comments (RFCs) form a series of notes about the Internet (originally the ARPAnet) started in 1969. These notes discuss many aspects of computer communication, focusing on networking protocols, procedures, programs and concepts. They also include meeting notes, opinions, and sometimes even humor. You can find the RFCs by visiting www.iana.org.

Figure 3.14 illustrates how both TCP and UDP use port numbers. I'll cover the different port numbers that can be used next:

- Numbers below 1024 are considered well-known port numbers and are defined in RFC 3232.

- Numbers 1024 and above are used by the upper layers to set up sessions with other hosts and by TCP and UDP to use as source and destination addresses in the segment.

- Numbers 1024 and above are often referred to as Ephemeral ports.

TCP Session: Source Port

Let's take a minute to check out analyzer output showing a TCP session I captured with my analyzer software session now:

```
TCP - Transport Control Protocol
Source Port: 5973
Destination Port: 23
Sequence Number: 1456389907
Ack Number: 1242056456
Offset: 5
Reserved: %000000
Code: %011000
Ack is valid
Push Request
Window: 61320
Checksum: 0x61a6
Urgent Pointer: 0
No TCP Options
TCP Data Area:
vL.5.+.5.+.5.+.5 76 4c 19 35 11 2b 19 35 11 2b 19 35 11
2b 19 35 +. 11 2b 19
Frame Check Sequence: 0x0d00000f
```

Notice that the source host makes up the source port, which in this case is 5973. The destination port is 23, which is used to tell the receiving host the purpose of the intended connection (Telnet).

By looking at this session, you can see that the source host makes up the source port by using numbers from 1024 to 65535. But why does the source make up a port number? The source does that to differentiate between sessions with different hosts, because how would a server know where information is coming from if it didn't have a different number from a sending host? TCP and the upper layers don't use hardware and logical addresses to understand the sending host's address as the Data Link and Network layer protocols do. Instead, they use port numbers.

TCP Session: Destination Port

You'll sometimes look at an analyzer and see that only the source port is above 1024 and the destination port is a well-known port, as shown in the following trace:

```
TCP - Transport Control Protocol
Source Port: 1144
Destination Port: 80 World Wide Web HTTP
Sequence Number: 9356570
Ack Number: 0
Offset: 7
Reserved: %000000
Code: %000010
Synch Sequence
Window: 8192
Checksum: 0x57E7
Urgent Pointer: 0
TCP Options:
Option Type: 2 Maximum Segment Size
Length: 4
MSS: 536
Option Type: 1 No Operation
Option Type: 1 No Operation
Option Type: 4
Length: 2
Opt Value:
No More HTTP Data
Frame Check Sequence: 0x43697363
```

And sure enough, the source port is over 1024, but the destination port is 80, indicating an HTTP service. The server, or receiving host, will change the destination port if it needs to.

In the preceding trace, a "SYN" packet is sent to the destination device. This Synch sequence, as shown in the output, is what's used to inform the remote destination device that it wants to create a session.

TCP Session: Syn Packet Acknowledgment

The next trace shows an acknowledgment to the SYN packet:

```
TCP - Transport Control Protocol
Source Port: 80 World Wide Web HTTP
Destination Port: 1144
Sequence Number: 2873580788
Ack Number: 9356571
Offset: 6
Reserved: %000000
Code: %010010
Ack is valid
Synch Sequence
Window: 8576
Checksum: 0x5F85
Urgent Pointer: 0
TCP Options:
Option Type: 2 Maximum Segment Size
Length: 4
MSS: 1460
No More HTTP Data
Frame Check Sequence: 0x6E203132
```

Notice the *Ack is valid*, which means that the source port was accepted and the device agreed to create a virtual circuit with the originating host.

And here again, you can see that the response from the server shows that the source is 80 and the destination is the 1144 sent from the originating host—all's well!

Table 3.2 gives you a list of the typical applications used in the TCP/IP suite by showing their well-known port numbers and the Transport layer protocols used by each application or process. It's a really good idea to memorize this table:

TABLE 3.2   Key protocols that use TCP and UDP

TCP	UDP
Telnet 23	SNMP 161
SMTP 25	TFTP 69
HTTP 80	DNS 53
FTP 20, 21	BooTPS/DHCP 67

TCP	UDP
DNS 53	
HTTPS 443	NTP 123
SSH 22	
POP3 110	
IMAP4 143	

Notice that DNS uses both TCP and UDP. Whether it opts for one or the other depends on what it's trying to do. Even though it's not the only application that can use both protocols, it's certainly one that you should make sure to remember.

 What makes TCP reliable is sequencing, acknowledgments, and flow control (windowing). Again, UDP doesn't offer reliability.

Okay—I want to discuss one more item before we move down to the Internet layer— session multiplexing. Session multiplexing is used by both TCP and UDP and basically allows a single computer, with a single IP address, to have multiple sessions occurring simultaneously. Say you go to www.lammle.com and are browsing and then you click a link to another page. Doing this opens another session to your host. Now you go to www.lammle.com/forum from another window and that site opens a window as well. Now you have three sessions open using one IP address because the Session layer is sorting the separate requests based on the Transport layer port number. This is the job of the Session layer: to keep application layer data separate!

The Internet Layer Protocols

In the DoD model, there are two main reasons for the Internet layer's existence: routing and providing a single network interface to the upper layers.

None of the other upper- or lower-layer protocols have any functions relating to routing—that complex and important task belongs entirely to the Internet layer. The Internet layer's second duty is to provide a single network interface to the upper-layer protocols. Without this layer, application programmers would need to write "hooks" into every one of their applications for each different Network Access protocol. This would not only be a pain in the neck, but it would lead to different versions of each application—one for Ethernet, another one for wireless, and so on. To prevent this, IP provides one single network interface for the upper-layer protocols. With that mission accomplished, it's then the job of IP and the various Network Access protocols to get along and work together.

All network roads don't lead to Rome—they lead to IP. And all the other protocols at this layer, as well as all those at the upper layers, use it. Never forget that. All paths through the DoD model go through IP. Here's a list of the important protocols at the Internet layer that I'll cover individually in detail coming up:

- Internet Protocol (IP)
- Internet Control Message Protocol (ICMP)
- Address Resolution Protocol (ARP)

Internet Protocol (IP)

Internet Protocol (IP) essentially is the Internet layer. The other protocols found here merely exist to support it. IP holds the big picture and could be said to "see all," because it's aware of all the interconnected networks. It can do this because all the machines on the network have a software, or logical, address called an IP address, which we'll explore more thoroughly later in this chapter.

For now, understand that IP looks at each packet's address. Then, using a routing table, it decides where a packet is to be sent next, choosing the best path to send it upon. The protocols of the Network Access layer at the bottom of the DoD model don't possess IP's enlightened scope of the entire network; they deal only with physical links (local networks).

Identifying devices on networks requires answering these two questions: Which network is it on? And what is its ID on that network? The first answer is the *software address*, or *logical address*. You can think of this as the part of the address that specifies the correct street. The second answer is the hardware address, which goes a step further to specify the correct mailbox. All hosts on a network have a logical ID called an IP address. This is the software, or logical, address and contains valuable encoded information, greatly simplifying the complex task of routing. (IP is discussed in RFC 791.)

IP receives segments from the Host-to-Host layer and fragments them into datagrams (packets) if necessary. IP then reassembles datagrams back into segments on the receiving side. Each datagram is assigned the IP address of the sender and that of the recipient. Each router or switch (layer 3 device) that receives a datagram makes routing decisions based on the packet's destination IP address.

Figure 3.15 shows an IP header. This will give you a picture of what the IP protocol has to go through every time user data that is destined for a remote network is sent from the upper layers.

FIGURE 3.15   IP header

Bit 0			Bit 15	Bit 16		Bit 31
Version (4)	Header length (4)	Priority and Type of Service (8)		Total length (16)		
Identification (16)			Flags (3)	Fragmented offset (13)		
Time to live (8)		Protocol (8)		Header checksum (16)		
Source IP address (32)						
Destination IP address (32)						
Options (0 or 32 if any)						
Data (varies if any)						

20 bytes

The following fields make up the IP header:

Version   IP version number.

Header length   Header length (HLEN) in 32-bit words.

Priority and Type of Service   Type of Service tells how the datagram should be handled. The first 3 bits are the priority bits, now called the differentiated services bits.

Total length   Length of the packet, including header and data.

Identification   Unique IP-packet value used to differentiate fragmented packets from different datagrams.

Flags   Specifies whether fragmentation should occur.

Fragment offset   Provides fragmentation and reassembly if the packet is too large to put in a frame. It also allows different maximum transmission units (MTUs) on the Internet.

Time to Live   The time to live (TTL) is set into a packet when it is originally generated. If it doesn't get to where it's supposed to go before the TTL expires, boom—it's gone. This stops IP packets from continuously circling the network looking for a home.

Protocol   Port of upper-layer protocol; for example, TCP is port 6 or UDP is port 17. Also supports Network layer protocols, like ARP and ICMP, and can be referred to as the Type field in some analyzers. We'll talk about this field more in a minute.

Header checksum   Cyclic redundancy check (CRC) on header only.

Source IP address   32-bit IP address of sending station.

Destination IP address   32-bit IP address of the station this packet is destined for.

Options   Used for network testing, debugging, security, and more.

Data   After the IP option field, will be the upper-layer data.

Here's a snapshot of an IP packet caught on a network analyzer. Notice that all the header information discussed previously appears here:

```
IP Header - Internet Protocol Datagram
Version: 4
Header Length: 5
Precedence: 0
Type of Service: %000
Unused: %00
Total Length: 187
Identifier: 22486
Fragmentation Flags: %010 Do Not Fragment
Fragment Offset: 0
Time To Live: 60
IP Type: 0x06 TCP
Header Checksum: 0xd031
Source IP Address: 10.7.1.30
```

```
Dest. IP Address: 10.7.1.10
No Internet Datagram Options
```

The Type field is typically a Protocol field, but this analyzer sees it as an IP Type field. This is important. If the header didn't carry the protocol information for the next layer, IP wouldn't know what to do with the data carried in the packet. The preceding example clearly tells IP to hand the segment to TCP.

Figure 3.16 demonstrates how the Network layer sees the protocols at the Transport layer when it needs to hand a packet up to the upper-layer protocols.

FIGURE 3.16   The Protocol field in an IP header

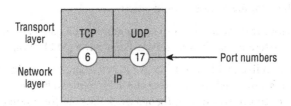

In this example, the Protocol field tells IP to send the data to either TCP port 6 or UDP port 17. But it will be UDP or TCP only if the data is part of a data stream headed for an upper-layer service or application. It could just as easily be destined for Internet Control Message Protocol (ICMP), Address Resolution Protocol (ARP), or some other type of Network layer protocol.

Table 3.3 is a list of some other popular protocols that can be specified in the Protocol field.

TABLE 3.3   Possible protocols found in the Protocol field of an IP header

Protocol	Protocol Number
ICMP	1
IP in IP (tunneling)	4
TCP	6
UDP	17
EIGRP	88
OSPF	89
IPv6	41

Protocol	Protocol Number
GRE	47
Layer 2 tunnel (L2TP)	115

You can find a complete list of Protocol field numbers at
www.iana.org/assignments/protocol-numbers.

Internet Control Message Protocol (ICMP)

Internet Control Message Protocol (ICMP) works at the Network layer and is used by
IP for many different services. ICMP is basically a management protocol and messaging
service provider for IP. Its messages are carried as IP datagrams. RFC 1256 is an annex to
ICMP, which gives hosts extended capability in discovering routes to gateways.

ICMP packets have the following characteristics:

- They can provide hosts with information about network problems.
- They are encapsulated within IP datagrams.

The following are some common events and messages that ICMP relates to:

Destination unreachable If a router can't send an IP datagram any further, it uses ICMP
to send a message back to the sender, advising it of the situation. For example, take a look
at Figure 3.17, which shows that interface e0 of the Lab_B router is down.

FIGURE 3.17   ICMP error message is sent to the sending host from the remote router.

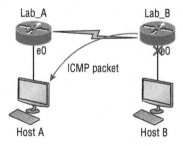

When Host A sends a packet destined for Host B, the Lab_B router will send an ICMP
destination unreachable message back to the sending device, which is Host A in this
example.

Buffer full/source quench If a router's memory buffer for receiving incoming datagrams is
full, it will use ICMP to send out this message alert until the congestion abates.

Hops/time exceeded Each IP datagram is allotted a certain number of routers, called hops, to pass through. If it reaches its limit of hops before arriving at its destination, the last router to receive that datagram deletes it. The executioner router then uses ICMP to send an obituary message, informing the sending machine of the demise of its datagram.

Ping Packet Internet Groper (Ping) uses ICMP echo request and reply messages to check the physical and logical connectivity of machines on an internetwork.

Traceroute Using ICMP time-outs, Traceroute is used to discover the path a packet takes as it traverses an internetwork.

Traceroute is usually just called trace. Microsoft Windows uses tracert to allow you to verify address configurations in your internetwork.

The following data is from a network analyzer catching an ICMP echo request:

```
Flags: 0x00
Status: 0x00
Packet Length: 78
Timestamp: 14:04:25.967000 12/20/03
Ethernet Header
Destination: 00:a0:24:6e:0f:a8
Source: 00:80:c7:a8:f0:3d
Ether-Type: 08-00 IP
IP Header - Internet Protocol Datagram
Version: 4
Header Length: 5
Precedence: 0
Type of Service: %000
Unused: %00
Total Length: 60
Identifier: 56325
Fragmentation Flags: %000
Fragment Offset: 0
Time To Live: 32
IP Type: 0x01 ICMP
Header Checksum: 0x2df0
Source IP Address: 100.100.100.2
Dest. IP Address: 100.100.100.1
No Internet Datagram Options
ICMP - Internet Control Messages Protocol
ICMP Type: 8 Echo Request
Code: 0
```

```
Checksum: 0x395c
Identifier: 0x0300
Sequence Number: 4352
ICMP Data Area:
abcdefghijklmnop 61 62 63 64 65 66 67 68 69 6a 6b 6c 6d 6e 6f 70
qrstuvwabcdefghi 71 72 73 74 75 76 77 61 62 63 64 65 66 67 68 69
Frame Check Sequence: 0x00000000
```

Notice anything unusual? Did you catch the fact that even though ICMP works at the Internet (Network) layer, it still uses IP to do the Ping request? The Type field in the IP header is 0x01, which specifies that the data we're carrying is owned by the ICMP protocol. Remember, just as all roads lead to Rome, all segments or data *must* go through IP!

> The Ping program uses the alphabet in the data portion of the packet as a payload, typically around 100 bytes by default, unless, of course, you are pinging from a Windows device, which thinks the alphabet stops at the letter *W* (and doesn't include *X*, *Y*, or *Z*) and then starts at *A* again. Go figure!

If you remember reading about the Data Link layer and the different frame types in Chapter 2, "Ethernet Networking and Data Encapsulation," you should be able to look at the preceding trace and tell what type of Ethernet frame this is. The only fields are destination hardware address, source hardware address, and Ether-Type. The only frame that uses an Ether-Type field exclusively is an Ethernet_II frame.

We'll move on soon, but before we get into the ARP protocol, let's take another look at ICMP in action. Figure 3.18 shows an internetwork—it has a router, so it's an internetwork, right?

FIGURE 3.18 ICMP in action

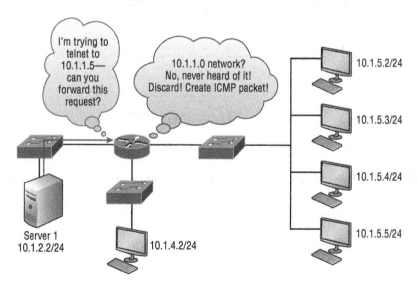

Server 1 (10.1.2.2) telnets to 10.1.1.5 from a DOS prompt. What do you think Server 1 will receive as a response? Server 1 will send the Telnet data to the default gateway, which is the router, and the router will drop the packet because there isn't a network 10.1.1.0 in the routing table. Because of this, Server 1 will receive an ICMP destination unreachable back from the router.

Address Resolution Protocol (ARP)

Address Resolution Protocol (ARP) finds the hardware address of a host from a known IP address. Here's how it works: When IP has a datagram to send, it must inform a Network Access protocol, such as Ethernet or wireless, of the destination's hardware address on the local network. Remember that it has already been informed by upper-layer protocols of the destination's IP address. If IP doesn't find the destination host's hardware address in the ARP cache, it uses ARP to find this information.

As IP's detective, ARP interrogates the local network by sending out a broadcast asking the machine with the specified IP address to reply with its hardware address. So basically, ARP translates the software (IP) address into a hardware address—for example, the destination machine's Ethernet adapter address—and from it, deduces its whereabouts on the LAN by broadcasting for this address. Figure 3.19 shows how an ARP broadcast looks to a local network.

FIGURE 3.19   Local ARP broadcast

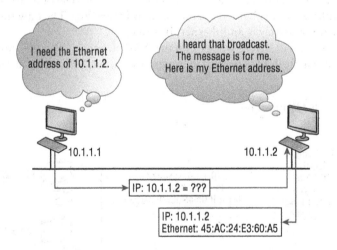

 ARP resolves IP addresses to Ethernet (MAC) addresses.

The following trace shows an ARP broadcast—notice that the destination hardware address is unknown and is all *Fs* in hex (all 1s in binary)—and is a hardware address broadcast:

Flags: 0x00
Status: 0x00
Packet Length: 64
Timestamp: 09:17:29.574000 12/06/03
Ethernet Header
Destination: FF:FF:FF:FF:FF:FF Ethernet Broadcast
Source: 00:A0:24:48:60:A5
Protocol Type: 0x0806 IP ARP
ARP - Address Resolution Protocol
Hardware: 1 Ethernet (10Mb)
Protocol: 0x0800 IP
Hardware Address Length: 6
Protocol Address Length: 4
Operation: 1 ARP Request
Sender Hardware Address: 00:A0:24:48:60:A5
Sender Internet Address: 172.16.10.3
Target Hardware Address: 00:00:00:00:00:00 (ignored)
Target Internet Address: 172.16.10.10
Extra bytes (Padding):
.... 0A 0A 0A 0A 0A 0A 0A 0A 0A 0A 0A 0A 0A
0A 0A 0A 0A 0A
Frame **Check Sequence: 0x00000000**

IP Addressing

One of the most important topics in any discussion of TCP/IP is IP addressing. An *IP address* is a numeric identifier assigned to each machine on an IP network. It designates the specific location of a device on the network.

An IP address is a software address, not a hardware address—the latter is hard-coded on a network interface card (NIC) and used for finding hosts on a local network. IP addressing was designed to allow hosts on one network to communicate with a host on a different network regardless of the type of LANs the hosts are participating in.

Before we get into the more complicated aspects of IP addressing, you need to understand some of the basics. First, I'm going to explain some of the fundamentals of IP addressing and its terminology. Then you'll learn about the hierarchical IP addressing scheme and private IP addresses.

IP Terminology

Throughout this chapter you're being introduced to several important terms that are vital to understanding the Internet Protocol. Here are a few to get you started:

Bit   A bit is one digit, either a 1 or a 0.

Byte   A byte is 7 or 8 bits, depending on whether parity is used. For the rest of this chapter, always assume a byte is 8 bits.

Octet   An octet, made up of 8 bits, is just an ordinary 8-bit binary number. In this chapter, the terms *byte* and *octet* are completely interchangeable.

Network address   This is the designation used in routing to send packets to a remote network—for example, 10.0.0.0, 172.16.0.0, and 192.168.10.0.

Broadcast address   The address used by applications and hosts to send information to all nodes on a network is called the broadcast address. Examples of layer 3 broadcasts include 255.255.255.255, which is any network, all nodes; 172.16.255.255, which is all subnets and hosts on network 172.16.0.0; and 10.255.255.255, which broadcasts to all subnets and hosts on network 10.0.0.0.

The Hierarchical IP Addressing Scheme

An IP address consists of 32 bits of information. These bits are divided into four sections, referred to as octets or bytes, with each containing 1 byte (8 bits). You can depict an IP address using one of three methods:

- Dotted-decimal, as in 172.16.30.56
- Binary, as in 10101100.00010000.00011110.00111000
- Hexadecimal, as in AC.10.1E.38

All these examples represent the same IP address. Pertaining to IP addressing, hexadecimal isn't used as often as dotted-decimal or binary, but you still might find an IP address stored in hexadecimal in some programs.

The 32-bit IP address is a structured or hierarchical address, as opposed to a flat or nonhierarchical address. Although either type of addressing scheme could have been used, *hierarchical addressing* was chosen for a good reason. The advantage of this scheme is that it can handle a large number of addresses, namely 4.3 billion (a 32-bit address space with two possible values for each position—either 0 or 1—gives you 2^{32}, or 4,294,967,296). The disadvantage of the flat addressing scheme, and the reason it's not used for IP addressing, relates to routing. If every address were unique, all routers on the Internet would need to store the address of each and every machine on the Internet. This would make efficient routing impossible, even if only a fraction of the possible addresses were used!

The solution to this problem is to use a two- or three-level hierarchical addressing scheme that is structured by network and host or by network, subnet, and host.

This two- or three-level scheme can also be compared to a telephone number. The first section, the area code, designates a very large area. The second section, the prefix, narrows the scope to a local calling area. The final segment, the customer number, zooms in on the specific connection. IP addresses use the same type of layered structure. Rather than all 32 bits being treated as a unique identifier, as in flat addressing, a part of the address is designated as the network address and the other part is designated as either the subnet and host or just the node address.

Next, we'll cover IP network addressing and the different classes of address we can use to address our networks.

Network Addressing

The *network address* (which can also be called the network number) uniquely identifies each network. Every machine on the same network shares that network address as part of its IP address. For example, in the IP address 172.16.30.56, 172.16 represents the network address.

The *node address* is assigned to, and uniquely identifies, each machine on a network. This part of the address must be unique because it identifies a particular machine—an individual—as opposed to a network, which is a group. This number can also be referred to as a *host address*. In the sample IP address 172.16.30.56, the 30.56 specifies the node address.

The designers of the Internet decided to create classes of networks based on network size. For the small number of networks possessing a very large number of nodes, they created the rank *Class A network*. At the other extreme is the *Class C network*, which is reserved for the numerous networks with a small number of nodes. The class distinction for networks between very large and very small is predictably called the *Class B network*.

Subdividing an IP address into a network and node address is determined by the class designation of one's network. Figure 3.20 summarizes the three classes of networks used to address hosts—a subject I'll explain in much greater detail throughout this chapter.

FIGURE 3.20   Summary of the three classes of networks

	8 bits	8 bits	8 bits	8 bits
Class A:	Network	Host	Host	Host
Class B:	Network	Network	Host	Host
Class C:	Network	Network	Network	Host
Class D:	Multicast			
Class E:	Research			

To ensure efficient routing, Internet designers defined a mandate for the leading-bits section of the address for each different network class. For example, since a router knows that a Class A network address always starts with a 0, the router might be able to speed a packet on its way after reading only the first bit of its address. This is where the address schemes define the difference between a Class A, a Class B, and a Class C address. Coming up, I'll discuss the differences between these three classes, followed by a discussion of the Class D and Class E addresses. Classes A, B, and C are the only ranges that are used to address hosts in our networks.

Network Address Range: Class A

The designers of the IP address scheme decided that the first bit of the first byte in a Class A network address must always be off, or 0. This means a Class A address must be between 0 and 127 in the first byte, inclusive.

Consider the following network address:

0xxxxxxx

If we turn the other 7 bits all off and then turn them all on, we'll find the Class A range of network addresses:

00000000 = 0
01111111 = 127

So, a Class A network is defined in the first octet between 0 and 127, and it can't be less or more. Understand that 0 and 127 are not valid in a Class A network because they're reserved addresses, something I'll explain soon.

Network Address Range: Class B

In a Class B network, the RFCs state that the first bit of the first byte must always be turned on but the second bit must always be turned off. If you turn the other 6 bits all off and then all on, you will find the range for a Class B network:

10000000 = 128
10111111 = 191

As you can see, a Class B network is defined when the first byte is configured from 128 to 191.

Network Address Range: Class C

For Class C networks, the RFCs define the first 2 bits of the first octet as always turned on, but the third bit can never be on. Following the same process as the previous classes, convert from binary to decimal to find the range. Here's the range for a Class C network:

11000000 = 192
11011111 = 223

So, if you see an IP address that starts at 192 and goes to 223, you'll know it is a Class C IP address.

Network Address Ranges: Classes D and E

The addresses between 224 to 255 are reserved for Class D and E networks. Class D (224–239) is used for multicast addresses and Class E (240–255) for scientific purposes, but I'm not going into these types of addresses because they are beyond the scope of knowledge you need to gain from this book.

Network Addresses: Special Purpose

Some IP addresses are reserved for special purposes, so network administrators can't ever assign these addresses to nodes. Table 3.4 lists the members of this exclusive little club and the reasons why they're included in it.

TABLE 3.4   Reserved IP addresses

Address	Function
Network address of all 0s	Interpreted to mean "this network or segment."
Network address of all 1s	Interpreted to mean "all networks."
Network 127.0.0.1	Reserved for loopback tests. Designates the local node and allows that node to send a test packet to itself without generating network traffic.
Node address of all 0s	Interpreted to mean "network address" or any host on a specified network.
Node address of all 1s	Interpreted to mean "all nodes" on the specified network; for example, 128.2.255.255 means "all nodes" on network 128.2 (Class B address).
Entire IP address set to all 0s	Used by Cisco routers to designate the default route. Could also mean "any network."
Entire IP address set to all 1s (same as 255.255.255.255)	Broadcast to all nodes on the current network; sometimes called an "all 1s broadcast" or local broadcast.

Class A Addresses

In a Class A network address, the first byte is assigned to the network address and the three remaining bytes are used for the node addresses. The Class A format is as follows:

```
network.node.node.node
```

For example, in the IP address 49.22.102.70, the 49 is the network address and 22.102.70 is the node address. Every machine on this particular network would have the distinctive network address of 49.

Class A network addresses are 1 byte long, with the first bit of that byte reserved and the 7 remaining bits available for manipulation (addressing). As a result, the maximum number of Class A networks that can be created is 128. Why? Because each of the 7 bit positions can be either a 0 or a 1, thus 2^7, or 128.

To complicate matters further, the network address of all 0s (0000 0000) is reserved to designate the default route (see Table 3.4 in the previous section). Additionally, the address 127, which is reserved for diagnostics, can't be used either, which means that you can really only use the numbers 1 to 126 to designate Class A network addresses. This means the actual number of usable Class A network addresses is 128 minus 2, or 126.

The IP address 127.0.0.1 is used to test the IP stack on an individual node and cannot be used as a valid host address. However, the loopback address creates a shortcut method for TCP/IP applications and services that run on the same device to communicate with each other.

Each Class A address has 3 bytes (24-bit positions) for the node address of a machine. This means there are 2^{24}—or 16,777,216—unique combinations and, therefore, precisely that many possible unique node addresses for each Class A network. Because node addresses with the two patterns of all 0s and all 1s are reserved, the actual maximum usable number of nodes for a Class A network is 2^{24} minus 2, which equals 16,777,214. Either way, that's a huge number of hosts on a single network segment!

Class A Valid Host IDs

Here's an example of how to figure out the valid host IDs in a Class A network address:

- All host bits off is the network address: 10.0.0.0.
- All host bits on is the broadcast address: 10.255.255.255.

The valid hosts are the numbers in between the network address and the broadcast address: 10.0.0.1 through 10.255.255.254. Notice that 0s and 255s can be valid host IDs. All you need to remember when trying to find valid host addresses is that the host bits can't all be turned off or on at the same time.

Class B Addresses

In a Class B network address, the first 2 bytes are assigned to the network address and the remaining 2 bytes are used for node addresses. The format is as follows:

```
network.network.node.node
```

For example, in the IP address 172.16.30.56, the network address is 172.16 and the node address is 30.56.

With a network address being 2 bytes (8 bits each), you get 2^{16} unique combinations. But the Internet designers decided that all Class B network addresses should start with the binary digit 1, then 0. This leaves 14 bit positions to manipulate, therefore 16,384, or 2^{14} unique Class B network addresses.

A Class B address uses 2 bytes for node addresses. This is 2^{16} minus the two reserved patterns of all 0s and all 1s for a total of 65,534 possible node addresses for each Class B network.

Class B Valid Host IDs

Here's an example of how to find the valid hosts in a Class B network:

- All host bits turned off is the network address: 172.16.0.0.
- All host bits turned on is the broadcast address: 172.16.255.255.

The valid hosts would be the numbers in between the network address and the broadcast address: 172.16.0.1 through 172.16.255.254.

Class C Addresses

The first 3 bytes of a Class C network address are dedicated to the network portion of the address, with only 1 measly byte remaining for the node address. Here's the format:

`network.network.network.node`

Using the example IP address 192.168.100.102, the network address is 192.168.100 and the node address is 102.

In a Class C network address, the first three bit positions are always the binary 110. The calculation is as follows: 3 bytes, or 24 bits, minus 3 reserved positions leaves 21 positions. Hence, there are 2^{21}, or 2,097,152, possible Class C networks.

Each unique Class C network has 1 byte to use for node addresses. This leads to 2^8, or 256, minus the two reserved patterns of all 0s and all 1s, for a total of 254 node addresses for each Class C network.

Class C Valid Host IDs

Here's an example of how to find a valid host ID in a Class C network:

- All host bits turned off is the network ID: 192.168.100.0.
- All host bits turned on is the broadcast address: 192.168.100.255.

The valid hosts would be the numbers in between the network address and the broadcast address: 192.168.100.1 through 192.168.100.254.

Private IP Addresses (RFC 1918)

The people who created the IP addressing scheme also created private IP addresses. These addresses can be used on a private network, but they're not routable through the Internet. This is designed for the purpose of creating a measure of well-needed security, but it also conveniently saves valuable IP address space.

If every host on every network was required to have real routable IP addresses, we would have run out of IP addresses years ago. But by using private IP addresses, ISPs, corporations and home users only need a relatively tiny group of bona fide IP addresses to connect their networks to the Internet. This is economical because they can use private IP addresses on their inside networks and get along just fine.

To accomplish this task, the ISP and the corporation—the end user, no matter who they are—need to use something called *Network Address Translation (NAT)*, which basically takes a private IP address and converts it for use on the Internet. NAT is covered in Chapter 13, "Network Address Translation (NAT)." Many people can use the same real IP address to transmit out onto the Internet. Doing things this way saves megatons of address space— good for us all!

The reserved private addresses are listed in Table 3.5.

TABLE 3.5 Reserved IP address space

Address Class	Reserved Address Space
Class A	10.0.0.0 through 10.255.255.255
Class B	172.16.0.0 through 172.31.255.255
Class C	192.168.0.0 through 192.168.255.255

So Which Private IP Address Should I Use?

That's a really great question: Should you use Class A, Class B, or even Class C private addressing when setting up your network? Let's take Acme Corporation in SF as an example. This company is moving into a new building and needs a whole new network. It has 14 departments, with about 70 users in each. You could probably squeeze one or two Class C addresses to use, or maybe you could use a Class B, or even a Class A just for fun.

The rule of thumb in the consulting world is, when you're setting up a corporate network—regardless of how small it is—you should use a Class A network address because it gives you the most flexibility and growth options. For example, if you used the 10.0.0.0 network address with a /24 mask, then you'd have 65,536 networks, each with 254 hosts. Lots of room for growth with that network!

But if you're setting up a home network, you'd opt for a Class C address because it is the easiest for people to understand and configure. Using the default Class C mask gives you one network with 254 hosts—plenty for a home network.

With the Acme Corporation, a nice 10.1.x.0 with a /24 mask (the x is the subnet for each department) makes this easy to design, install, and troubleshoot.

IPv4 Address Types

Most people use the term *broadcast* as a generic term, and most of the time, we understand what they mean—but not always! For example, you might say, "The host broadcasted through a router to a DHCP server," but, well, it's pretty unlikely that this would ever really happen. What you probably mean—using the correct technical jargon—is, "The DHCP client broadcasted for an IP address and a router then forwarded this as a unicast packet to the DHCP server." Oh, and remember that with IPv4, broadcasts are pretty important, but with IPv6, there aren't any broadcasts sent at all—something to look forward to reading about in Chapter 14!

Okay, I've referred to IP addresses throughout the preceding chapters and now all throughout this chapter, and even showed you some examples. But I really haven't gone into the different terms and uses associated with them yet, and it's about time I did. So here are the address types that I'd like to define for you:

Loopback (localhost)   Used to test the IP stack on the local computer. Can be any address from 127.0.0.1 through 127.255.255.254.

Layer 2 broadcasts   These are sent to all nodes on a LAN.

Broadcasts (layer 3)   These are sent to all nodes on the network.

Unicast   This is an address for a single interface, and these are used to send packets to a single destination host.

Multicast   These are packets sent from a single source and transmitted to many devices on different networks. Referred to as "one-to-many."

Layer 2 Broadcasts

First, understand that layer 2 broadcasts are also known as hardware broadcasts—they only go out on a LAN, but they don't go past the LAN boundary (router).

The typical hardware address is 6 bytes (48 bits) and looks something like 45:AC:24:E3:60:A5. The broadcast would be all 1s in binary, which would be all *F*s in hexadecimal, as in ff:ff:ff:ff:ff:ff and shown in Figure 3.21.

FIGURE 3.21   Local layer 2 broadcasts

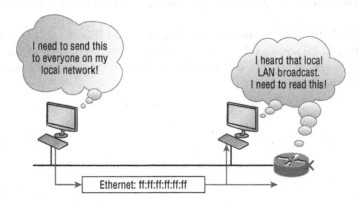

Every network interface card (NIC) will receive and read the frame, including the router, since this was a layer 2 broadcast, but the router would never, ever forward this!

Layer 3 Broadcasts

Then there are the plain old broadcast addresses at layer 3. Broadcast messages are meant to reach all hosts on a broadcast domain. These are the network broadcasts that have all host bits on.

Here's an example that you're already familiar with: The network address of 172.16.0.0 255.255.0.0 would have a broadcast address of 172.16.255.255—all host bits on. Broadcasts can also be "any network and all hosts," as indicated by 255.255.255.255, and shown in Figure 3.22.

FIGURE 3.22   Layer 3 broadcasts

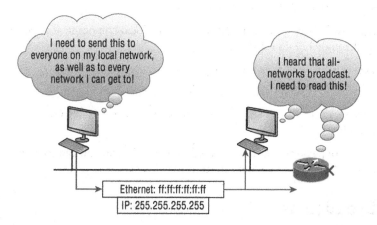

In Figure 3.22, all hosts on the LAN will get this broadcast on their NIC, including the router, but by default the router would never forward this packet.

Unicast Address

A unicast is defined as a single IP address that's assigned to a network interface card and is the destination IP address in a packet—in other words, it's used for directing packets to a specific host.

In Figure 3.23, both the MAC address and the destination IP address are for a single NIC on the network. All hosts on the broadcast domain would receive this frame and accept it. Only the destination NIC of 10.1.1.2 would accept the packet; the other NICs would discard the packet.

FIGURE 3.23   Unicast address

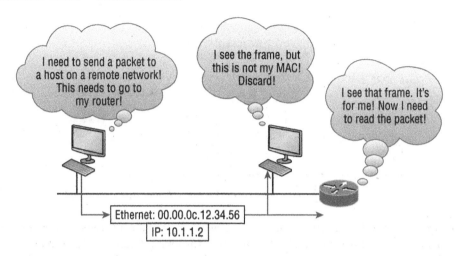

Multicast Address

Multicast is a different beast entirely. At first glance, it appears to be a hybrid of unicast and broadcast communication, but that isn't quite the case. Multicast does allow point-to-multipoint communication, which is similar to broadcasts, but it happens in a different manner. The crux of *multicast* is that it enables multiple recipients to receive messages without flooding the messages to all hosts on a broadcast domain. However, this is not the default behavior—it's what we *can* do with multicasting if it's configured correctly.

Multicast works by sending messages or data to IP *multicast group* addresses. Unlike with broadcasts, which aren't forwarded, routers then forward copies of the packet out to every interface that has hosts *subscribed* to that group address. This is where multicast differs from broadcast messages—with multicast communication, copies of packets, in theory, are sent only to subscribed hosts. For example, when I say in theory, I mean that the hosts will receive a multicast packet destined for 224.0.0.10. This is an EIGRP packet, and only a router running the EIGRP protocol will read these. All hosts on the broadcast LAN, and Ethernet is a broadcast multi-access LAN technology, will pick up the frame, read the destination address, then immediately discard the frame unless they're in the multicast group. This saves PC processing, not LAN bandwidth. Be warned though—multicasting can cause some serious LAN congestion if it's not implemented carefully! Figure 3.24 shows a Cisco router sending an EIGRP multicast packet on the local LAN and only the other Cisco router will accept and read this packet.

FIGURE 3.24   EIGRP multicast example

There are several different groups that users or applications can subscribe to. The range of multicast addresses starts with 224.0.0.0 and goes through 239.255.255.255. As you can see, this range of addresses falls within IP Class D address space based on classful IP assignment.

Summary

If you made it this far and understood everything the first time through, you should be extremely proud of yourself! We really covered a lot of ground in this chapter, but understand that the information in it is critical to being able to navigate well through the rest of this book.

If you didn't get a complete understanding the first time around, don't stress. It really wouldn't hurt you to read this chapter more than once. There is still a lot of ground to cover, so make sure you've got this material all nailed down. That way, you'll be ready for more, and just so you know, there's a lot more! What we're doing up to this point is building a solid foundation to build upon as you advance.

With that in mind, after you learned about the DoD model, the layers, and associated protocols, you found out about the oh-so-important topic of IP addressing. I discussed in detail the difference between each address class, how to find a network address and broadcast address, and what denotes a valid host address range. I can't stress enough how important it is for you to have this critical information unshakably understood before moving on to Chapter 4!

Chapter

4

Easy Subnetting

We'll pick up right where we left off in the last chapter and continue to explore the world of IP addressing. We'll open this chapter by showing you how to subnet an IP network—an indispensably crucial skill that's central to mastering networking in general. Forewarned is forearmed, so prepare yourself because being able to subnet quickly and accurately is pretty challenging and you'll need time to practice what you've learned to really nail it. So be patient and don't give up on this key aspect of networking until your skills are seriously sharp!

What I'm about to say might sound weird to you, but you'll be much better off if you just try to forget everything you've already learned about subnetting before reading this chapter—especially if you've been to an official Cisco or Microsoft class! I think these forms of special torture often do more harm than good and sometimes even scare people away from networking completely. Those that survive and persevere usually at least question the sanity of continuing to study in this field. If this is you, relax, and know that you'll find that the way I tackle the issue of subnetting is relatively painless because I'm going to show you a whole new, much easier method to conquer this monster!

After working through this chapter, you'll be able to tame the IP addressing/subnetting beast—just don't give up! I promise that you'll be really glad you didn't. It's one of those things that once you get it down, you'll wonder why you used to think it was so hard.

To find your included bonus material, as well as Todd Lammle videos, practice questions, and hands-on labs, please see www.lammle.com/ccna.

Subnetting Basics

In Chapter 3, "Introduction to TCP/IP," you learned how to define and find the valid host ranges used in a Class A, Class B, and Class C network address by turning the host bits all off and then all on. This is very good, but here's the catch: you were defining only one network, as shown in Figure 4.1.

By now you know that having one large network is not a good thing because in the first three chapters you just read, I brought that to your attention constantly! So how would you fix the out-of-control problem that Figure 4.1 illustrates? Wouldn't it be nice to be able to break up that one, huge network address and create four manageable networks from it? You betcha it would, but to make that happen, you would need to apply the infamous trick of *subnetting* because it's the best way to break up a giant network into a bunch of smaller ones. Check out Figure 4.2 to see how this might look:

FIGURE 4.1 One network

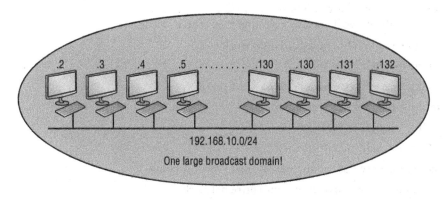

FIGURE 4.2 Multiple networks connected together

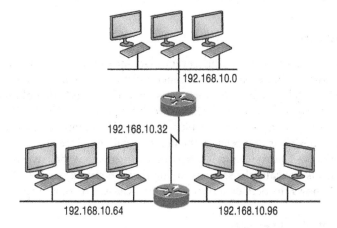

What are those 192.168.10.*x* addresses shown in the figure? Well, that is what this chapter will explain—how to make one network into many networks.

Let's take off from where we left in Chapter 3, "Introduction to TCP/IP," and start working in the host section (host bits) of a network address, where we can borrow bits to create subnets.

How to Create Subnets

Creating subnetworks is essentially the act of taking bits from the host portion of the address and reserving them to define the subnet address instead. Clearly this will result in fewer bits being available for defining your hosts, which is something you'll always want to keep in mind.

Later in this chapter, I'll guide you through the entire process of creating subnets starting with Class C addresses. As always in networking, before you actually implement anything, including subnetting, you must first determine your current requirements and make sure to plan for future conditions as well.

To create a subnet, we'll start by fulfilling these three steps:

1. Determine the number of required network IDs:
   - One for each LAN subnet
   - One for each wide area network connection

2. Determine the number of required host IDs per subnet:
   - One for each TCP/IP host
   - One for each router interface

3. Based on the previous requirements, create the following:
   - A unique subnet mask for your entire network
   - A unique subnet ID for each physical segment
   - A range of host IDs for each subnet

Subnet Masks

For the subnet addressing scheme to work, every machine on the network must know which part of the host address will be used as the subnet address. This condition is met by assigning a *subnet mask* to each machine. A subnet mask is a 32-bit value that allows the device that's receiving IP packets to distinguish the network ID portion of the IP address from the host ID portion of the IP address. This 32-bit subnet mask is composed of 1s and 0s, where the 1s represent the positions that refer to the network subnet addresses.

Not all networks need subnets, and if not, it really means that they're using the default subnet mask, which is basically the same as saying that a network doesn't have a subnet address. Table 4.1 shows the default subnet masks for Classes A, B, and C:

TABLE 4.1 Default subnet mask

Class	Format	Default Subnet Mask
A	*network.node.node.node*	255.0.0.0
B	network.network.node.node	255.255.0.0
C	network.network.network.node	255.255.255.0

Although you can use any mask in any way on an interface, typically it's not usually good to mess with the default masks. In other words, you don't want to make a Class B subnet mask read 255.0.0.0, and some hosts won't even let you type it in. But these days, most devices will. For a Class A network, you wouldn't change the first byte in a subnet mask because it should read 255.0.0.0 at a minimum. Similarly, you wouldn't assign 255.255.255.255 because this is all 1s, which is a broadcast address. A Class B address starts with 255.255.0.0, and a Class C starts with 255.255.255.0, and for the CCNA especially, there is no reason to change the defaults!

Understanding the Powers of 2

Powers of 2 are important to understand and memorize for use with IP subnetting. Reviewing powers of 2, remember that when you see a number noted with an exponent, it means you should multiply the number by itself as many times as the upper number specifies. For example, 2^3 is 2 x 2 x 2, which equals 8. Here's a list of powers of 2 to commit to memory:

$2^1 = 2$	$2^8 = 256$
$2^2 = 4$	$2^9 = 512$
$2^3 = 8$	$2^{10} = 1,024$
$2^4 = 16$	$2^{11} = 2,048$
$2^5 = 32$	$2^{12} = 4,096$
$2^6 = 64$	$2^{13} = 8,192$
$2^7 = 128$	$2^{14} = 16,384$

Memorizing these powers of 2 is a good idea, but it's not absolutely necessary. Just remember that since you're working with powers of 2, each successive power of 2 is double the previous one.

It works like this—all you have to do to remember the value of 2^9 is to first know that $2^8 = 256$. Why? Because when you double 2 to the eighth power (256), you get 2^9 (or 512). To determine the value of 2^{10}, simply start at $2^8 = 256$, and then double it twice.

You can go the other way as well. If you needed to know what 2^6 is, for example, you just cut 256 in half two times: once to reach 2^7 and then one more time to reach 2^6.

Classless Inter-Domain Routing (CIDR)

Another term you need to familiarize yourself with is *Classless Inter-Domain Routing (CIDR)*. It's basically the method that Internet service providers (ISPs) use to allocate a number of addresses to a company, a home—their customers. They provide addresses in a certain block size, something I'll talk about in greater detail soon.

When you receive a block of addresses from an ISP, what you get will look something like this: 192.168.10.32/28. This is telling you what your subnet mask is. The slash notation (/) means how many bits are turned on (1s). Obviously, the maximum could only be /32 because a byte is 8 bits and there are 4 bytes in an IP address: (4 × 8 = 32). But keep in mind that regardless of the class of address, the largest subnet mask available relevant to the Cisco exam objectives can only be a /30 because you've got to keep at least 2 bits for host bits.

Take, for example, a Class A default subnet mask, which is 255.0.0.0. This tells us that the first byte of the subnet mask is all ones (1s), or 11111111. When referring to a slash notation, you need to count all the 1 bits to figure out your mask. The 255.0.0.0 is considered a /8 because it has 8 bits that are 1s—that is, 8 bits that are turned on.

A Class B default mask would be 255.255.0.0, which is a /16 because 16 bits are ones (1s): 11111111.11111111.00000000.00000000.

Table 4.2 has a listing of every available subnet mask and its equivalent CIDR slash notation.

TABLE 4.2   CIDR values

Subnet Mask	CIDR Value
255.0.0.0	/8
255.128.0.0	/9
255.192.0.0	/10
255.224.0.0	/11
255.240.0.0	/12
255.248.0.0	/13
255.252.0.0	/14
255.254.0.0	/15
255.255.0.0	/16
255.255.128.0	/17
255.255.192.0	/18
255.255.224.0	/19
255.255.240.0	/20

Subnet Mask	CIDR Value
255.255.248.0	/21
255.255.252.0	/22
255.255.254.0	/23
255.255.255.0	/24
255.255.255.128	/25
255.255.255.192	/26
255.255.255.224	/27
255.255.255.240	/28
255.255.255.248	/29
255.255.255.252	/30

The /8 through /15 can only be used with Class A network addresses. /16 through /23 can be used by Class A and B network addresses. /24 through /30 can be used by Class A, B, and C network addresses. This is a big reason why most companies use Class A network addresses. Since they can use all subnet masks, they get the maximum flexibility in network design.

No, you cannot configure a Cisco router using this slash format. But wouldn't that be nice? Nevertheless, it's *really* important for you to know subnet masks in the slash notation (CIDR).

IP Subnet-Zero

Even though ip subnet-zero is not a new command, in the past Cisco courseware and Cisco exam objectives didn't used to cover it. This command allows you to use the first subnet in your network design. For instance, the Class C mask of 255.255.255.192 provides subnets 64,128 and 192, another facet of subnetting that we'll discuss more thoroughly later in this chapter. But with the ip subnet-zero command, you now get to use subnets 0, 64, 128, and 192. It may not seem like a lot, but this provides two more subnets for every subnet mask we use.

Even though we don't discuss the command-line interface (CLI) until Chapter 6, "Cisco's Internetworking Operating System (IOS)," it's important for you to be at least a little familiar with this command at this point:

```
Router#sh running-config
Building configuration...
Current configuration : 827 bytes
!
hostname Pod1R1
!
ip subnet-zero
!
```

This router output shows that the command ip subnet-zero is enabled on the router. Cisco has turned this command on by default starting with Cisco IOS version 12.*x* and now we're running 15.*x* code.

When taking your Cisco exams, make sure you read very carefully to see if Cisco is asking you *not* to use ip subnet-zero. There are actually instances where this may happen.

Subnetting Class C Addresses

There are many different ways to subnet a network. The right way is the way that works best for you. In a Class C address, only 8 bits are available for defining the hosts. Remember that subnet bits start at the left and move to the right, without skipping bits. This means that Class C subnet masks can only be the following:

```
Binary Decimal CIDR
-----------------------------------------------------------
00000000 = 255.255.255.0 /24
10000000 = 255.255.255.128 /25
11000000 = 255.255.255.192 /26
11100000 = 255.255.255.224 /27
11110000 = 255.255.255.240 /28
11111000 = 255.255.255.248 /29
11111100 = 255.255.255.252 /30
```

We can't use a /31 or /32 because, as I've said, we must have at least 2 host bits for assigning IP addresses to hosts. But this is only mostly true. Certainly we can never use a /32 because that would mean zero host bits available, yet Cisco has various forms of the IOS, as well as the new Cisco Nexus switches operating system, that support the /31 mask. The /31 is above the scope of the CCNA objectives, so we won't be covering it in this book.

Coming up, I'm going to teach you that significantly less painful method of subnetting I promised you at the beginning of this chapter, which makes it ever so much easier to subnet larger numbers in a flash. Excited? Good! Because I'm not kidding when I tell you that you absolutely need to be able to subnet quickly and accurately to succeed in the networking real world and on the exam too.

Subnetting a Class C Address—The Fast Way!

When you've chosen a possible subnet mask for your network and need to determine the number of subnets, valid hosts, and the broadcast addresses of a subnet that mask will provide, all you need to do is answer five simple questions:

- How many subnets does the chosen subnet mask produce?
- How many valid hosts per subnet are available?
- What are the valid subnets?
- What's the broadcast address of each subnet?
- What are the valid hosts in each subnet?

This is where you'll be really glad you followed my advice and took the time to memorize your powers of 2. If you didn't, now would be a good time. Just refer back to the sidebar "Understanding the Powers of 2" earlier if you need to brush up. Here's how you arrive at the answers to those five big questions:

How many subnets? 2^x = number of subnets. x is the number of masked bits, or the 1s. For example, in 11000000, the number of 1s gives us 2^2 subnets. So in this example, there are four subnets.

How many hosts per subnet? $2^y - 2$ = number of hosts per subnet. y is the number of unmasked bits, or the 0s. For example, in 11000000, the number of 0s gives us $2^6 - 2$ hosts, or 62 hosts per subnet. You need to subtract 2 for the subnet address and the broadcast address, which are not valid hosts.

What are the valid subnets? 256 – subnet mask = block size, or increment number. An example would be the 255.255.255.192 mask, where the interesting octet is the fourth octet (interesting because that is where our subnet numbers are). Just use this math: 256 – 192 = 64. The block size of a 192 mask is always 64. Start counting at zero in blocks of 64 until you reach the subnet mask value and these are your subnets in the fourth octet: 0, 64, 128, 192. Easy, huh?

What's the broadcast address for each subnet? Now here's the really easy part. Since we counted our subnets in the last section as 0, 64, 128, and 192, the broadcast address is always the number right before the next subnet. For example, the 0 subnet has a broadcast address of 63 because the next subnet is 64. The 64 subnet has a broadcast address of 127 because the next subnet is 128, and so on. Remember, the broadcast address of the last subnet is always 255.

What are the valid hosts? Valid hosts are the numbers between the subnets, omitting the all-0s and all-1s. For example, if 64 is the subnet number and 127 is the broadcast address, then 65–126 is the valid host range. Your valid range is *always* the group of numbers between the subnet address and the broadcast address.

If you're still confused, don't worry because it really isn't as hard as it seems to be at first—just hang in there! To help lift any mental fog, try a few of the practice examples next.

Subnetting Practice Examples: Class C Addresses

Here's your opportunity to practice subnetting Class C addresses using the method I just described. This is so cool. We're going to start with the first Class C subnet mask and work through every subnet that we can, using a Class C address. When we're done, I'll show you how easy this is with Class A and B networks too.

Practice Example #1C: 255.255.255.128 (/25)

Since 128 is 10000000 in binary, there is only 1 bit for subnetting and 7 bits for hosts. We're going to subnet the Class C network address 192.168.10.0.

192.168.10.0 = Network address

255.255.255.128 = Subnet mask

Now, let's answer our big five:

How many subnets? Since 128 is 1 bit on (10000000), the answer would be $2^1 = 2$.

How many hosts per subnet? We have 7 host bits off (10000000), so the equation would be $2^7 - 2 = 126$ hosts. Once you figure out the block size of a mask, the amount of hosts is always the block size minus 2. No need to do extra math if you don't need to!

What are the valid subnets? 256 – 128 = 128. Remember, we'll start at zero and count in our block size, so our subnets are 0, 128. By just counting your subnets when counting in your block size, you really don't need to do steps 1 and 2. We can see we have two subnets, and in the step before this one, just remember that the amount of hosts is always the block size minus 2, and in this example, that gives us two subnets, each with 126 hosts.

What's the broadcast address for each subnet? The number right before the value of the next subnet is all host bits turned on and equals the broadcast address. For the zero subnet, the next subnet is 128, so the broadcast of the 0 subnet is 127.

What are the valid hosts? These are the numbers between the subnet and broadcast addresses. The easiest way to find the hosts is to write out the subnet address and the broadcast address, which makes valid hosts completely obvious. The following table shows the 0 and 128 subnets, the valid host ranges of each, and the broadcast address of both subnets:

Subnet	0	128
First host	1	129
Last host	126	254
Broadcast	127	255

Looking at a Class C /25, it's pretty clear that there are two subnets. But so what—why is this significant? Well actually, it's not because that's not the right question. What you really want to know is what you would do with this information!

The key to understanding subnetting is to understand the very reason you need to do it, and I'm going to demonstrate this by going through the process of building a physical network.

Okay—because we added that router shown in Figure 4.3, in order for the hosts on our internetwork to communicate, they must now have a logical network addressing scheme. We could use IPv6, but IPv4 is still the most popular for now. It's also what we're studying at the moment, so that's what we're going with.

FIGURE 4.3 Implementing a Class C /25 logical network

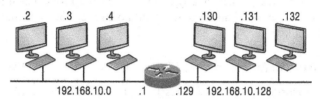

```
Router#show ip route
[output cut]
C 192.168.10.0 is directly connected to Ethernet 0
C 192.168.10.128 is directly connected to Ethernet 1
```

Looking at Figure 4.3, you can see that there are two physical networks, so we're going to implement a logical addressing scheme that allows for two logical networks. As always, it's a really good idea to look ahead and consider likely short- and long-term growth scenarios, but for this example in this book, a /25 gets it done.

Figure 4.3 shows us that both subnets have been assigned to a router interface, which creates our broadcast domains and assigns our subnets. Use the command show ip route to see the routing table on a router. Notice that instead of one large broadcast domain, there are now two smaller broadcast domains, providing for up to 126 hosts in each. The C in the router output translates to "directly connected network," and we can see we have two of those with two broadcast domains and that we created and implemented them. So congratulations—you did it. You have successfully subnetted a network and applied it to a network design. Nice! Let's do it again.

Practice Example #2C: 255.255.255.192 (/26)

This time, we're going to subnet the network address 192.168.10.0 using the subnet mask 255.255.255.192.

192.168.10.0 = Network address

255.255.255.192 = Subnet mask

Now, let's answer the big five:

How many subnets? Since 192 is 2 bits on (**11000000**), the answer would be $2^2 = 4$ subnets.

How many hosts per subnet? We have 6 host bits off (**11000000**), giving us $2^6 - 2 = 62$ hosts. The amount of hosts is always the block size minus 2.

What are the valid subnets? 256 – 192 = 64. Remember to start at zero and count in our block size. This means our subnets are 0, 64, 128, and 192. We can see we have a block size of 64, so we have four subnets, each with 62 hosts.

What's the broadcast address for each subnet? The number right before the value of the next subnet is all host bits turned on and equals the broadcast address. For the zero subnet, the next subnet is 64, so the broadcast address for the zero subnet is 63.

What are the valid hosts? These are the numbers between the subnet and broadcast address. As I said, the easiest way to find the hosts is to write out the subnet address and the broadcast address, which clearly delimits our valid hosts. The following table shows the 0, 64, 128, and 192 subnets, the valid host ranges of each, and the broadcast address of each subnet:

The subnets (do this first)	0	64	128	192
Our first host (perform host addressing last)	1	65	129	193
Our last host	62	126	190	254
The broadcast address (do this second)	63	127	191	255

Again, before getting into the next example, you can see that we can now subnet a /26 as long as we can count in increments of 64. And what are you going to do with this fascinating information? Implement it! We'll use Figure 4.4 to practice a /26 network implementation.

FIGURE 4.4 Implementing a class C /26 (with three networks)

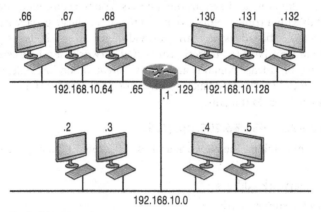

```
Router#show ip route
[output cut]
C 192.168.10.0 is directly connected to Ethernet 0
C 192.168.10.64 is directly connected to Ethernet 1
C 192.168.10.128 is directly connected to Ethernet 2
```

The /26 mask provides four subnetworks, and we need a subnet for each router inter-face. With this mask, in this example, we actually have room, with a spare subnet, to add another router interface in the future. Again, always plan for growth if possible!

Practice Example #3C: 255.255.255.224 (/27)

This time, we'll subnet the network address 192.168.10.0 and subnet mask 255.255.255.224.

192.168.10.0 = Network address

255.255.255.224 = Subnet mask

How many subnets? 224 is 11100000, so our equation would be $2^3 = 8$.

How many hosts? $2^5 - 2 = 30$

What are the valid subnets? 256 – 224 = 32. We just start at zero and count to the sub-net mask value in blocks (increments) of 32: 0, 32, 64, 96, 128, 160, 192, and 224.

What's the broadcast address for each subnet? (Always the number right before the next subnet)

What are the valid hosts? (The numbers between the subnet number and the broadcast address)

To answer the last two questions, first just write out the subnets, then write out the broadcast addresses—the number right before the next subnet. Last, fill in the host addresses. The following table gives you all the subnets for the 255.255.255.224 Class C subnet mask:

The subnet address	0	32	64	96	128	160	192	224
The first valid host	1	33	65	97	129	161	193	225
The last valid host	30	62	94	126	158	190	222	254
The broadcast address	31	63	95	127	159	191	223	255

In practice example #3C, we're using a 255.255.255.224 (/27) network, which pro-vides eight subnets as shown previously. We can take these subnets and implement them as shown in Figure 4.5, using any of the subnets available.

Notice that this used six of the eight subnets available for my network design. The light-ning bolt symbol in the figure represents a WAN, which would be a connection through an ISP or telco. In other words, something you don't own, but it's still a subnet just like any LAN connection on a router. As usual, I used the first valid host in each subnet as the router's interface address. This is just a rule of thumb; you can use any address in the valid host range as long as you remember what address you configured so you can set the default gateways on your hosts to the router address.

FIGURE 4.5   Implementing a Class C /27 logical network

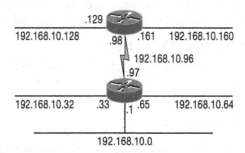

```
Router#show ip route
[output cut]
C 192.168.10.0 is directly connected to Ethernet 0
C 192.168.10.32 is directly connected to Ethernet 1
C 192.168.10.64 is directly connected to Ethernet 2
C 192.168.10.96 is directly connected to Serial 0
```

Practice Example #4C: 255.255.255.240 (/28)

Let's practice another one:

> 192.168.10.0 = Network address
>
> 255.255.255.240 = Subnet mask

Subnets? 240 is 11110000 in binary. 2^4 = 16.

Hosts? 4 host bits, or $2^4 - 2$ = 14.

Valid subnets? 256 – 240 = 16. Start at 0: 0 + 16 = 16. 16 + 16 = 32. 32 + 16 = 48. 48 + 16 = 64. 64 + 16 = 80. 80 + 16 = 96. 96 + 16 = 112. 112 + 16 = 128. 128 + 16 = 144. 144 + 16 = 160. 160 + 16 = 176. 176 + 16 = 192. 192 + 16 = 208. 208 + 16 = 224. 224 + 16 = 240.

Broadcast address for each subnet?

Valid hosts?

To answer the last two questions, check out the following table. It gives you the subnet, valid host, and broadcast address for each subnet. First, find the address of each subnet using the block size (increment). Second, find the broadcast address of each subnet increment, which is always the number right before the next valid subnet, and then just fill in the host addresses. The following table shows the available subnets, hosts, and broadcast addresses provided from a Class C 255.255.255.240 mask.

Subnet	0	16	32	48	64	80	96	112	128	144	160	176	192	208	224	240
First host	1	17	33	49	65	81	97	113	129	145	161	177	193	209	225	241
Last host	14	30	46	62	78	94	110	126	142	158	174	190	206	222	238	254
Broadcast	15	31	47	63	79	95	111	127	143	159	175	191	207	223	239	255

Cisco has figured out that most people cannot count in 16s and therefore have a hard time finding valid subnets, hosts, and broadcast addresses with the Class C 255.255.255.240 mask. You'd be wise to study this mask.

Practice Example #5C: 255.255.255.248 (/29)

Let's keep practicing:

192.168.10.0 = Network address

255.255.255.248 = Subnet mask

Subnets? 248 in binary = 11111000. 2^5 = 32.

Hosts? $2^3 - 2 = 6$.

Valid subnets? 256 – 248 = 0, 8, 16, 24, 32, 40, 48, 56, 64, 72, 80, 88, 96, 104, 112, 120, 128, 136, 144, 152, 160, 168, 176, 184, 192, 200, 208, 216, 224, 232, 240, and 248.

Broadcast address for each subnet?

Valid hosts?

Take a look at the following table. It shows some of the subnets (first four and last four only), valid hosts, and broadcast addresses for the Class C 255.255.255.248 mask:

Subnet	0	8	16	24	...	224	232	240	248
First host	1	9	17	25	...	225	233	241	249
Last host	6	14	22	30	...	230	238	246	254
Broadcast	7	15	23	31	...	231	239	247	255

If you try to configure a router interface with the address 192.168.10.6 255.255.255.248 and receive the following error, this means that ip subnet-zero is not enabled:

```
Bad mask /29 for address 192.168.10.6
```

You must be able to subnet to see that the address used in this example is in the zero subnet.

Practice Example #6C: 255.255.255.252 (/30)

Okay—just one more:

192.168.10.0 = Network address

255.255.255.252 = Subnet mask

Subnets? 64.

Hosts? 2.

Valid subnets? 0, 4, 8, 12, etc., all the way to 252.

Broadcast address for each subnet? (Always the number right before the next subnet.)

Valid hosts? (The numbers between the subnet number and the broadcast address.)

The following table shows you the subnet, valid host, and broadcast address of the first four and last four subnets in the 255.255.255.252 Class C subnet:

Subnet	0	4	8	12	...	240	244	248	252
First host	1	5	9	13	...	241	245	249	253
Last host	2	6	10	14	...	242	246	250	254
Broadcast	3	7	11	15	...	243	247	251	255

 Real World Scenario

Should We Really Use This Mask That Provides Only Two Hosts?

You are the network administrator for Acme Corporation with dozens of WAN links connecting to your corporate office. Right now your network is a classful network, which means that the same subnet mask is on each host and router interface. You've read about classless routing, where you can have different sized masks, but don't know what to use on your point-to-point WAN links. Is the 255.255.255.252 (/30) a helpful mask in this situation?

Yes, this is a very helpful mask in wide area networks and of course with any type of point-to-point link!

If you were to use the 255.255.255.0 mask in this situation, then each network would have 254 hosts. But you use only two addresses with a WAN or point-to-point link, which is a waste of 252 hosts per subnet! If you use the 255.255.255.252 mask, then each subnet has only two hosts, and you don't want to waste precious addresses. This is a really important subject, one that we'll address in a lot more detail in the section on VLSM network design in the next chapter!

Subnetting in Your Head: Class C Addresses

It really is possible to subnet in your head? Yes, and it's not all that hard either—take the following example:

192.168.10.50 = Node address

255.255.255.224 = Subnet mask

First, determine the subnet and broadcast addresses of the network in which the previous IP address resides. You can do this by answering question 3 of the big five questions: 256 – 224 = 32. 0, 32, 64, and so on. The address of 50 falls between the two subnets of 32 and 64 and must be part of the 192.168.10.32 subnet. The next subnet is 64, so the broadcast address of the 32 subnet is 63. Don't forget that the broadcast address of a subnet is always the number right before the next subnet. The valid host range equals the numbers between the subnet and broadcast addresses, or 33–62. Oh this is just too easy!

Let's try another one. We'll subnet another Class C address:

192.168.10.50 = Node address

255.255.255.240 = Subnet mask

What is the subnet and broadcast address of the network of which the previous IP address is a member? 256 – 240 = 16. Now just count by our increments of 16 until we pass the host address: 0, 16, 32, 48, 64. Bingo—the host address is between the 48 and 64 subnets. The subnet is 192.168.10.48, and the broadcast address is 63 because the next subnet is 64. The valid host range equals the numbers between the subnet number and the broadcast address, or 49–62.

Let's do a couple more to make sure you have this down.

You have a node address of 192.168.10.174 with a mask of 255.255.255.240. What is the valid host range?

The mask is 240, so we'd do a 256 – 240 = 16. This is our block size. Just keep adding 16 until we pass the host address of 174, starting at zero, of course: 0, 16, 32, 48, 64, 80, 96, 112, 128, 144, 160, 176. The host address of 174 is between 160 and 176, so the subnet is 160. The broadcast address is 175; the valid host range is 161–174. That was a tough one!

One more—just for fun. This one is the easiest of all Class C subnetting:

192.168.10.17 = Node address

255.255.255.252 = Subnet mask

What is the subnet and broadcast address of the subnet in which the previous IP address resides? 256 – 252 = 0 (always start at zero unless told otherwise). 0, 4, 8, 12, 16, 20, etc. You've got it! The host address is between the 16 and 20 subnets. The subnet is 192.168.10.16, and the broadcast address is 19. The valid host range is 17–18.

Now that you're all over Class C subnetting, let's move on to Class B subnetting. But before we do, let's go through a quick review.

What Do We Know?

Okay—here's where you can really apply what you've learned so far and begin committing it all to memory. This is a very cool section that I've been using in my classes for years. It will really help you nail down subnetting for good!

When you see a subnet mask or slash notation (CIDR), you should know the following:

/25   What do we know about a /25?

- 128 mask
- 1 bit on and 7 bits off (10000000)
- Block size of 128

- Subnets 0 and 128
- 2 subnets, each with 126 hosts

/26 What do we know about a /26?

- 192 mask
- 2 bits on and 6 bits off (11000000)
- Block size of 64
- Subnets 0, 64, 128, 192
- 4 subnets, each with 62 hosts

/27 What do we know about a /27?

- 224 mask
- 3 bits on and 5 bits off (11100000)
- Block size of 32
- Subnets 0, 32, 64, 96, 128, 160, 192, 224
- 8 subnets, each with 30 hosts

/28 What do we know about a /28?

- 240 mask
- 4 bits on and 4 bits off
- Block size of 16
- Subnets 0, 16, 32, 48, 64, 80, 96, 112, 128, 144, 160, 176, 192, 208, 224, 240
- 16 subnets, each with 14 hosts

/29 What do we know about a /29?

- 248 mask
- 5 bits on and 3 bits off
- Block size of 8
- Subnets 0, 8, 16, 24, 32, 40, 48, etc.
- 32 subnets, each with 6 hosts

/30 What do we know about a /30?

- 252 mask
- 6 bits on and 2 bits off
- Block size of 4
- Subnets 0, 4, 8, 12, 16, 20, 24, etc.
- 64 subnets, each with 2 hosts

Table 4.3 puts all of the previous information into one compact little table. You should practice writing this table out, and if you can do it, write it down before you start your exam!

TABLE 4.3   What do you know?

CIDR Notation	Mask	Bits	Block Size	Subnets	Hosts
/25	128	1 bit on and 7 bits off	128	0 and 128	2 subnets, each with 126 hosts
/26	192	2 bits on and 6 bits off	64	0, 64, 128, 192	4 subnets, each with 62 hosts
/27	224	3 bits on and 5 bits off	32	0, 32, 64, 96, 128, 160, 192, 224	8 subnets, each with 30 hosts
/28	240	4 bits on and 4 bits off	16	0, 16, 32, 48, 64, 80, 96, 112, 128, 144, 160, 176, 192, 208, 224, 240	16 subnets, each with 14 hosts
/29	248	5 bits on and 3 bits off	8	0, 8, 16, 24, 32, 40, 48, etc.	32 subnets, each with 6 hosts
/30	252	6 bits on and 2 bits off	4	0, 4, 8, 12, 16, 20, 24, etc.	64 subnets, each with 2 hosts

Regardless of whether you have a Class A, Class B, or Class C address, the /30 mask will provide you with only two hosts, ever. As suggested by Cisco, this mask is suited almost exclusively for use on point-to-point links.

If you can memorize this "What Do We Know?" section, you'll be much better off in your day-to-day job and in your studies. Try saying it out loud, which helps you memorize things—yes, others nearby may think you've lost it, but they probably already do if you're in the networking field anyway. And if you're not yet in the networking field but are studying all this to break into it, get used to it!

It's also helpful to write these on some type of flashcards and have people test your skill. You'd be amazed at how fast you can get subnetting down if you memorize block sizes as well as this "What Do We Know?" section.

Subnetting Class B Addresses

Before we dive into this, let's look at all the possible Class B subnet masks first. Notice that we have a lot more possible subnet masks than we do with a Class C network address:

```
255.255.0.0    (/16)
255.255.128.0 (/17)  255.255.255.0    (/24)
255.255.192.0 (/18)  255.255.255.128 (/25)
255.255.224.0 (/19)  255.255.255.192 (/26)
```

```
255.255.240.0 (/20) 255.255.255.224 (/27)
255.255.248.0 (/21) 255.255.255.240 (/28)
255.255.252.0 (/22) 255.255.255.248 (/29)
255.255.254.0 (/23) 255.255.255.252 (/30)
```

We know the Class B network address has 16 bits available for host addressing. This means we can use up to 14 bits for subnetting because we need to leave at least 2 bits for host addressing. Using a /16 means you are not subnetting with Class B, but it *is* a mask you can use.

By the way, do you notice anything interesting about that list of subnet values—a pattern, maybe? Ah ha! That's exactly why I had you memorize the binary-to-decimal numbers earlier in Chapter 2, "Ethernet Networking and Data Encapsulation." Since subnet mask bits start on the left and move to the right and bits can't be skipped, the numbers are always the same regardless of the class of address. If you haven't already, memorize this pattern!

The process of subnetting a Class B network is pretty much the same as it is for a Class C, except that you have more host bits and you start in the third octet.

Use the same subnet numbers for the third octet with Class B that you used for the fourth octet with Class C, but add a zero to the network portion and a 255 to the broadcast section in the fourth octet. The following table shows you an example host range of two subnets used in a Class B 240 (/20) subnet mask:

Subnet address	16.0	32.0
Broadcast address	31.255	47.255

Just add the valid hosts between the numbers and you're set!

The preceding example is true only until you get up to /24. After that, it's numerically exactly like Class C.

Subnetting Practice Examples: Class B Addresses

Next, you'll get an opportunity to practice subnetting Class B addresses. Again, I have to mention that this is the same as subnetting with Class C, except we start in the third octet—with the exact same numbers.

Practice Example #1B: 255.255.128.0 (/17)

172.16.0.0 = Network address

255.255.128.0 = Subnet mask

Subnets? $2^1 = 2$ (same amount as Class C).

Hosts? $2^{15} - 2 = 32,766$ (7 bits in the third octet, and 8 in the fourth).

Valid subnets? $256 - 128 = 128$. 0, 128. Remember that subnetting is performed in the third octet, so the subnet numbers are really 0.0 and 128.0, as shown in the next table. These are the exact numbers we used with Class C; we use them in the third octet and add a 0 in the fourth octet for the network address.

Broadcast address for each subnet?

Valid hosts?

This table shows the two subnets available, the valid host range, and the broadcast address of each:

Subnet	0.0	128.0
First host	0.1	128.1
Last host	127.254	255.254
Broadcast	127.255	255.255

Okay, notice that we just added the fourth octet's lowest and highest values and came up with the answers. And again, it's done exactly the same way as for a Class C subnet. We just used the same numbers in the third octet and added 0 and 255 in the fourth octet—pretty simple, huh? I really can't say this enough—it's just not that hard! The numbers never change; we just use them in different octets.

Question: Using the previous subnet mask, do you think 172.16.10.0 is a valid host address? What about 172.16.10.255? Can 0 and 255 in the fourth octet ever be a valid host address? The answer is absolutely, yes, those are valid hosts! Any number between the subnet number and the broadcast address is always a valid host.

Practice Example #2B: 255.255.192.0 (/18)

172.16.0.0 = Network address

255.255.192.0 = Subnet mask

Subnets? $2^2 = 4$.

Hosts? $2^{14} - 2 = 16,382$ (6 bits in the third octet, and 8 in the fourth).

Valid subnets? $256 - 192 = 64$. 0, 64, 128, 192. Remember that the subnetting is performed in the third octet, so the subnet numbers are really 0.0, 64.0, 128.0, and 192.0, as shown in the next table.

Broadcast address for each subnet?

Valid hosts?

The following table shows the four subnets available, the valid host range, and the broadcast address of each:

Subnet	0.0	64.0	128.0	192.0
First host	0.1	64.1	128.1	192.1
Last host	63.254	127.254	191.254	255.254
Broadcast	63.255	127.255	191.255	255.255

Again, it's pretty much the same as it is for a Class C subnet—we just added 0 and 255 in the fourth octet for each subnet in the third octet.

Practice Example #3B: 255.255.240.0 (/20)

172.16.0.0 = Network address

255.255.240.0 = Subnet mask

Subnets? $2^4 = 16$.

Hosts? $2^{12} - 2 = 4094$.

Valid subnets? 256 – 240 = 0, 16, 32, 48, etc., up to 240. Notice that these are the same numbers as a Class C 240 mask—we just put them in the third octet and add a 0 and 255 in the fourth octet.

Broadcast address for each subnet?

Valid hosts?

The following table shows the first four subnets, valid hosts, and broadcast addresses in a Class B 255.255.240.0 mask:

Subnet	0.0	16.0	32.0	48.0
First host	0.1	16.1	32.1	48.1
Last host	15.254	31.254	47.254	63.254
Broadcast	15.255	31.255	47.255	63.255

Practice Example #4B: 255.255.248.0 (/21)

172.16.0.0 = Network address

255.255.248.0 = Subnet mask

Subnets? $2^5 = 32$.

Hosts? $2^{11} - 2 = 2046$.

Valid subnets? 256 – 248 = 0, 8, 16, 24, 32, etc., up to 248.

Broadcast address for each subnet?

Valid hosts?

The following table shows the first five subnets, valid hosts, and broadcast addresses in a Class B 255.255.248.0 mask:

Subnet	0.0	8.0	16.0	24.0	32.0
First host	0.1	8.1	16.1	24.1	32.1
Last host	7.254	15.254	23.254	31.254	39.254
Broadcast	7.255	15.255	23.255	31.255	39.255

Practice Example #5B: 255.255.252.0 (/22)

172.16.0.0 = Network address

255.255.252.0 = Subnet mask

Subnets? $2^6 = 64$.

Hosts? $2^{10} - 2 = 1022$.

Valid subnets? 256 – 252 = 0, 4, 8, 12, 16, etc., up to 252.

Broadcast address for each subnet?

Valid hosts?

This table shows the first five subnets, valid hosts, and broadcast addresses in a Class B 255.255.252.0 mask:

Subnet	0.0	4.0	8.0	12.0	16.0
First host	0.1	4.1	8.1	12.1	16.1
Last host	3.254	7.254	11.254	15.254	19.254
Broadcast	3.255	7.255	11.255	15.255	19.255

Practice Example #6B: 255.255.254.0 (/23)

172.16.0.0 = Network address

255.255.254.0 = Subnet mask

Subnets? $2^7 = 128$.

Hosts? $2^9 - 2 = 510$.

Valid subnets? 256 – 254 = 0, 2, 4, 6, 8, etc., up to 254.

Broadcast address for each subnet?

Valid hosts?

The following table shows the first five subnets, valid hosts, and broadcast addresses in a Class B 255.255.254.0 mask:

Subnet	0.0	2.0	4.0	6.0	8.0
First host	0.1	2.1	4.1	6.1	8.1
Last host	1.254	3.254	5.254	7.254	9.254
Broadcast	1.255	3.255	5.255	7.255	9.255

Practice Example #7B: 255.255.255.0 (/24)

Contrary to popular belief, 255.255.255.0 used with a Class B network address is not called a Class B network with a Class C subnet mask. It's amazing how many people see this mask used in a Class B network and think it's a Class C subnet mask. This is a Class B subnet mask with 8 bits of subnetting—it's logically different from a Class C mask. Subnetting this address is fairly simple:

172.16.0.0 = Network address

255.255.255.0 = Subnet mask

Subnets? $2^8 = 256$.

Hosts? $2^8 - 2 = 254$.

Valid subnets? 256 − 255 = 1. 0, 1, 2, 3, etc., all the way to 255.

Broadcast address for each subnet?

Valid hosts?

The following table shows the first four and last two subnets, the valid hosts, and the broadcast addresses in a Class B 255.255.255.0 mask:

Subnet	0.0	1.0	2.0	3.0	...	254.0	255.0
First host	0.1	1.1	2.1	3.1	...	254.1	255.1
Last host	0.254	1.254	2.254	3.254	...	254.254	255.254
Broadcast	0.255	1.255	2.255	3.255	...	254.255	255.255

Practice Example #8B: 255.255.255.128 (/25)

This is actually one of the hardest subnet masks you can play with. And worse, it actually is a really good subnet to use in production because it creates over 500 subnets with 126 hosts for each subnet—a nice mixture. So, don't skip over it!

172.16.0.0 = Network address

255.255.255.128 = Subnet mask

Subnets? $2^9 = 512$.

Hosts? $2^7 - 2 = 126$.

Valid subnets? Now for the tricky part. 256 – 255 = 1. 0, 1, 2, 3, etc., for the third octet. But you can't forget the one subnet bit used in the fourth octet. Remember when I showed you how to figure one subnet bit with a Class C mask? You figure this the same way. You actually get two subnets for each third octet value, hence the 512 subnets. For example, if the third octet is showing subnet 3, the two subnets would actually be 3.0 and 3.128.

Broadcast address for each subnet? The numbers right before the next subnet.

Valid hosts? The numbers between the subnet numbers and the broadcast address.

The following graphic shows how you can create subnets, valid hosts, and broadcast addresses using the Class B 255.255.255.128 subnet mask. The first eight subnets are shown, followed by the last two subnets:

Subnet	0.0	0.128	1.0	1.128	2.0	2.128	3.0	3.128	...	255.0	255.128
First host	0.1	0.129	1.1	1.129	2.1	2.129	3.1	3.129	...	255.1	255.129
Last host	0.126	0.254	1.126	1.254	2.126	2.254	3.126	3.254	...	255.126	255.254
Broadcast	0.127	0.255	1.127	1.255	2.127	2.255	3.127	3.255	...	255.127	255.255

Practice Example #9B: 255.255.255.192 (/26)

Now, this is where Class B subnetting gets easy. Since the third octet has a 255 in the mask section, whatever number is listed in the third octet is a subnet number. And now that we have a subnet number in the fourth octet, we can subnet this octet just as we did with Class C subnetting. Let's try it out:

172.16.0.0 = Network address

255.255.255.192 = Subnet mask

Subnets? $2^{10} = 1024$.

Hosts? $2^6 - 2 = 62$.

Valid subnets? 256 – 192 = 64. The subnets are shown in the following table. Do these numbers look familiar?

Broadcast address for each subnet?

Valid hosts?

The following table shows the first eight subnet ranges, valid hosts, and broadcast addresses:

Subnet	0.0	0.64	0.128	0.192	1.0	1.64	1.128	1.192
First host	0.1	0.65	0.129	0.193	1.1	1.65	1.129	1.193
Last host	0.62	0.126	0.190	0.254	1.62	1.126	1.190	1.254
Broadcast	0.63	0.127	0.191	0.255	1.63	1.127	1.191	1.255

Notice that for each subnet value in the third octet, you get subnets 0, 64, 128, and 192 in the fourth octet.

Practice Example #10B: 255.255.255.224 (/27)

This one is done the same way as the preceding subnet mask, except that we just have more subnets and fewer hosts per subnet available.

172.16.0.0 = Network address

255.255.255.224 = Subnet mask

Subnets? 2^{11} = 2048.

Hosts? $2^5 - 2$ = 30.

Valid subnets? 256 − 224 = 32. 0, 32, 64, 96, 128, 160, 192, 224.

Broadcast address for each subnet?

Valid hosts?

The following table shows the first eight subnets:

Subnet	0.0	0.32	0.64	0.96	0.128	0.160	0.192	0.224
First host	0.1	0.33	0.65	0.97	0.129	0.161	0.193	0.225
Last host	0.30	0.62	0.94	0.126	0.158	0.190	0.222	0.254
Broadcast	0.31	0.63	0.95	0.127	0.159	0.191	0.223	0.255

This next table shows the last eight subnets:

Subnet	255.0	255.32	255.64	255.96	255.128	255.160	255.192	255.224
First host	255.1	255.33	255.65	255.97	255.129	255.161	255.193	255.225
Last host	255.30	255.62	255.94	255.126	255.158	255.190	255.222	255.254
Broadcast	255.31	255.63	255.95	255.127	255.159	255.191	255.223	255.255

Subnetting in Your Head: Class B Addresses

Are you nuts? Subnet Class B addresses in our heads? It's actually easier than writing it out—I'm not kidding! Let me show you how:

Question: What is the subnet and broadcast address of the subnet in which 172.16.10.33 /27 resides?

Answer: The interesting octet is the fourth one. 256 − 224 = 32. 32 + 32 = 64. You've got it: 33 is between 32 and 64. But remember that the third octet is considered part of the subnet, so the answer would be the 10.32 subnet. The broadcast is 10.63, since 10.64 is the next subnet. That was a pretty easy one.

Question: What subnet and broadcast address is the IP address 172.16.66.10 255.255.192.0 (/18) a member of?

Answer: The interesting octet here is the third octet instead of the fourth one. 256 – 192 = 64. 0, 64, 128. The subnet is 172.16.64.0. The broadcast must be 172.16.127.255 since 128.0 is the next subnet.

Question: What subnet and broadcast address is the IP address 172.16.50.10 255.255.224.0 (/19) a member of?

Answer: 256 – 224 = 0, 32, 64 (remember, we always start counting at 0). The subnet is 172.16.32.0, and the broadcast address must be 172.16.63.255 since 64.0 is the next subnet.

Question: What subnet and broadcast address is the IP address 172.16.46.255 255.255.240.0 (/20) a member of?

Answer: 256 – 240 = 16. The third octet is important here: 0, 16, 32, 48. This subnet address must be in the 172.16.32.0 subnet, and the broadcast must be 172.16.47.255 since 48.0 is the next subnet. So, yes, 172.16.46.255 is a valid host.

Question: What subnet and broadcast address is the IP address 172.16.45.14 255.255.255.252 (/30) a member of?

Answer: Where is our interesting octet? 256 – 252 = 0, 4, 8, 12, 16—the fourth. The subnet is 172.16.45.12, with a broadcast of 172.16.45.15 because the next subnet is 172.16.45.16.

Question: What is the subnet and broadcast address of the host 172.16.88.255/20?

Answer: What is a /20 written out in dotted decimal? If you can't answer this, you can't answer this question, can you? A /20 is 255.255.240.0, gives us a block size of 16 in the third octet, and since no subnet bits are on in the fourth octet, the answer is always 0 and 255 in the fourth octet: 0, 16, 32, 48, 64, 80, 96. Because 88 is between 80 and 96, the subnet is 80.0 and the broadcast address is 95.255.

Question: A router receives a packet on an interface with a destination address of 172.16.46.191/26. What will the router do with this packet?

Answer: Discard it. Do you know why? 172.16.46.191/26 is a 255.255.255.192 mask, which gives us a block size of 64. Our subnets are then 0, 64, 128 and 192. 191 is the broadcast address of the 128 subnet, and by default, a router will discard any broadcast packets.

 To get more subnetting practice, head over to www.lammle.com/ccna.

Summary

Did you read Chapter 3 and Chapter 4, "Easy Subnetting," and understand everything on the first pass? If so, that is fantastic—congratulations! However, you probably really did get lost a couple of times. No worries because as I told you, that's what usually happens. Don't waste time feeling bad if you have to read each chapter more than once, or even 10 times, before you're truly good to go. If you read the chapters more than once, you'll be seriously better off in the long run even if you were pretty comfortable the first time through!

This chapter provided you with an important understanding of IP subnetting—the painless way! And when you've got the key material presented in this chapter really nailed down, you should be able to subnet IP addresses in your head.

This chapter is extremely essential to your Cisco certification process, so if you just skimmed it, please go back, read it thoroughly, and be sure to practice through all the scenarios too!

Chapter

5

Troubleshooting IP Addressing

This chapter will go over IP address troubleshooting, focusing on the steps Cisco recommends following when troubleshooting an IP network.

So, get psyched because this chapter will give you powerful tools to hone your knowledge of IP addressing and networking and seriously refine the important skills you've gained so far.

So stay with me—I guarantee that your hard work will pay off! Ready? Let's go!

To find your included bonus material, as well as Todd Lammle videos, practice questions, and hands-on labs, please see www.lammle.com/ccna.

Cisco's Way of Troubleshooting IP

Because running into trouble now and then in networking is a given, being able to troubleshoot IP addressing is clearly a vital skill. I'm not being negative here—just realistic. The positive side to this is that if you're the one equipped with the tools to diagnose and clear up the inevitable trouble, you get to be the hero when you save the day! Even better? You can usually fix an IP network regardless of whether you're on site or at home!

So this is where I'm going to show you the "Cisco way" of troubleshooting IP addressing. Let's use Figure 5.1 as an example of your basic IP trouble—poor Sally can't log in to the Windows server. Do you deal with this by calling the Microsoft team to tell them their server is a pile of junk and causing all your problems? Though tempting, a better approach is to first double-check and verify your network instead.

FIGURE 5.1   Basic IP troubleshooting

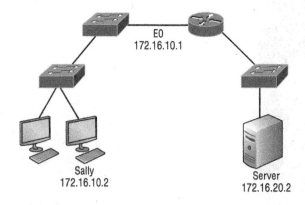

Okay, let's get started by going through the troubleshooting steps that Cisco recommends. They're pretty simple, but important nonetheless. Pretend you're at a customer host and they're complaining that they can't communicate to a server that just happens to be on a remote network. Here are the four troubleshooting steps Cisco recommends:

1. Open a Command window and ping 127.0.0.1. This is the diagnostic, or loopback, address, and if you get a successful ping, your IP stack is considered initialized. If it fails, then you have an IP stack failure and need to reinstall TCP/IP on the host.

    ```
    C:\>ping 127.0.0.1
    Pinging 127.0.0.1 with 32 bytes of data:
    Reply from 127.0.0.1: bytes=32 time
    Reply from 127.0.0.1: bytes=32 time
    Reply from 127.0.0.1: bytes=32 time
    Reply from 127.0.0.1: bytes=32 time
    Ping statistics for 127.0.0.1:
    Packets: Sent = 4, Received = 4, Lost = 0 (0% loss),
    Approximate round trip times in milli-seconds:
    Minimum = 0ms, Maximum = 0ms, Average = 0ms
    ```

2. From the Command window, ping the IP address of the local host (we'll assume correct configuration here, but always check the IP configuration too!). If that's successful, your network interface card (NIC) is functioning. If it fails, there is a problem with the NIC. Success here doesn't just mean that a cable is plugged into the NIC, only that the IP protocol stack on the host can communicate to the NIC via the LAN driver.

    ```
    C:\>ping 172.16.10.2
    Pinging 172.16.10.2 with 32 bytes of data:
    Reply from 172.16.10.2: bytes=32 time
    Reply from 172.16.10.2: bytes=32 time
    Reply from 172.16.10.2: bytes=32 time
    Reply from 172.16.10.2: bytes=32 time
    Ping statistics for 172.16.10.2:
    Packets: Sent = 4, Received = 4, Lost = 0 (0% loss),
    Approximate round trip times in milli-seconds:
    Minimum = 0ms, Maximum = 0ms, Average = 0ms
    ```

3. From the Command window, ping the default gateway (router). If the ping works, it means that the NIC is plugged into the network and can communicate on the local network. If it fails, you have a local physical network problem that could be anywhere from the NIC to the router.

```
C:\>ping 172.16.10.1
Pinging 172.16.10.1 with 32 bytes of data:
Reply from 172.16.10.1: bytes=32 time
Reply from 172.16.10.1: bytes=32 time
Reply from 172.16.10.1: bytes=32 time
Reply from 172.16.10.1: bytes=32 time
Ping statistics for 172.16.10.1:
Packets: Sent = 4, Received = 4, Lost = 0 (0% loss),
Approximate round trip times in milli-seconds:
Minimum = 0ms, Maximum = 0ms, Average = 0ms
```

4. If steps 1 through 3 were successful, try to ping the remote server. If that works, then you know that you have IP communication between the local host and the remote server. You also know that the remote physical network is working.

```
C:\>ping 172.16.20.2
Pinging 172.16.20.2 with 32 bytes of data:
Reply from 172.16.20.2: bytes=32 time
Reply from 172.16.20.2: bytes=32 time
Reply from 172.16.20.2: bytes=32 time
Reply from 172.16.20.2: bytes=32 time
Ping statistics for 172.16.20.2:
Packets: Sent = 4, Received = 4, Lost = 0 (0% loss),
Approximate round trip times in milli-seconds:
Minimum = 0ms, Maximum = 0ms, Average = 0ms
```

If the user still can't communicate with the server after steps 1 through 4 have been completed successfully, you probably have some type of name resolution problem and need to check your Domain Name System (DNS) settings. But if the ping to the remote server fails, then you know you have some type of remote physical network problem and need to go to the server and work through steps 1 through 3 until you find the snag.

Before we move on to determining IP address problems and how to fix them, I just want to mention some basic commands that you can use to help troubleshoot your network from both a PC and a Cisco router. Keep in mind that though these commands may do the same thing, they're implemented differently.

ping Uses ICMP echo request and replies to test if a node IP stack is initialized and alive on the network.

traceroute Displays the list of routers on a path to a network destination by using TTL time-outs and ICMP error messages. This command will not work from a command prompt.

tracert Same function as traceroute, but it's a Microsoft Windows command and will not work on a Cisco router.

arp -a Displays IP-to-MAC-address mappings on a Windows PC.

show ip arp   Same function as arp -a, but displays the ARP table on a Cisco router. Like the commands traceroute and tracert, arp -a and show ip arp are not interchangeable through DOS and Cisco.

ipconfig /all   Used only from a Windows command prompt; shows you the PC network configuration.

Once you've gone through all these steps and, if necessary, used the appropriate commands, what do you do when you find a problem? How do you go about fixing an IP address configuration error? Time to cover the next step—determining and fixing the issue at hand!

Determining IP Address Problems

It's common for a host, router, or other network device to be configured with the wrong IP address, subnet mask, or default gateway. Because this happens way too often, you must know how to find and fix IP address configuration errors.

A good way to start is to draw out the network and IP addressing scheme. If that's already been done, consider yourself lucky because though sensible, it's rarely done. Even if it is, it's usually outdated or inaccurate anyway. So either way, it's a good idea to bite the bullet and start from scratch.

Once you have your network accurately drawn out, including the IP addressing scheme, you need to verify each host's IP address, mask, and default gateway address to establish the problem. Of course, this is assuming that you don't have a physical layer problem, or if you did, that you've already fixed it.

Let's check out the example illustrated in Figure 5.2.

FIGURE 5.2   IP address problem 1

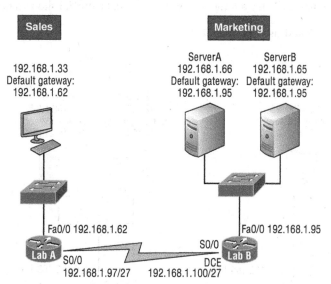

A user in the sales department calls and tells you that she can't get to ServerA in the marketing department. You ask her if she can get to ServerB in the marketing department, but she doesn't know because she doesn't have rights to log on to that server. What do you do?

First, guide your user through the four troubleshooting steps you learned in the preceding section. Okay—let's say steps 1 through 3 work but step 4 fails. By looking at the figure, can you determine the problem? Look for clues in the network drawing. First, the WAN link between the Lab A router and the Lab B router shows the mask as a /27. You should already know that this mask is 255.255.255.224 and determine that all networks are using this mask. The network address is 192.168.1.0. What are our valid subnets and hosts? 256 − 224 = 32, so this makes our subnets 0, 32, 64, 96, 128, etc. So, by looking at the figure, you can see that subnet 32 is being used by the sales department. The WAN link is using subnet 96, and the marketing department is using subnet 64.

Now you've got to establish what the valid host ranges are for each subnet. From what you learned at the beginning of this chapter, you should now be able to easily determine the subnet address, broadcast addresses, and valid host ranges. The valid hosts for the Sales LAN are 33 through 62, and the broadcast address is 63 because the next subnet is 64, right? For the Marketing LAN, the valid hosts are 65 through 94 (broadcast 95), and for the WAN link, 97 through 126 (broadcast 127). By closely examining the figure, you can determine that the default gateway on the Lab B router is incorrect. That address is the broadcast address for subnet 64, so there's no way it could be a valid host!

If you tried to configure that address on the Lab B router interface, you'd receive a bad mask error. Cisco routers don't let you type in subnet and broadcast addresses as valid hosts!

Did you get all that? Let's try another one to make sure. Figure 5.3 shows a network problem.

FIGURE 5.3   IP address problem 2

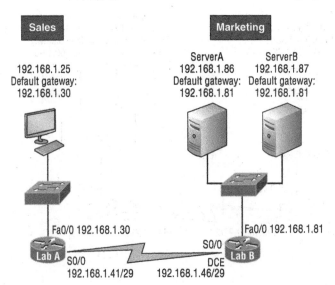

A user in the Sales LAN can't get to ServerB. You have the user run through the four basic troubleshooting steps and find that the host can communicate to the local network but not to the remote network. Find and define the IP addressing problem.

If you went through the same steps used to solve the last problem, you can see that first, the WAN link again provides the subnet mask to use— /29, or 255.255.255.248. Assuming classful addressing, you need to determine what the valid subnets, broadcast addresses, and valid host ranges are to solve this problem.

The 248 mask is a block size of 8 (256 − 248 = 8, as discussed in Chapter 4, "Easy Subnetting"), so the subnets both start and increment in multiples of 8. By looking at the figure, you see that the Sales LAN is in the 24 subnet, the WAN is in the 40 subnet, and the Marketing LAN is in the 80 subnet. Can you see the problem yet? The valid host range for the Sales LAN is 25–30, and the configuration appears correct. The valid host range for the WAN link is 41–46, and this also appears correct. The valid host range for the 80 subnet is 81–86, with a broadcast address of 87 because the next subnet is 88. ServerB has been configured with the broadcast address of the subnet.

Okay, now that you can figure out misconfigured IP addresses on hosts, what do you do if a host doesn't have an IP address and you need to assign one? What you need to do is scrutinize the other hosts on the LAN and figure out the network, mask, and default gateway. Let's take a look at a couple of examples of how to find and apply valid IP addresses to hosts.

You need to assign server and router IP addresses on a LAN. The subnet assigned on that segment is 192.168.20.24/29. The router needs to be assigned the first usable address and the server needs the last valid host ID. What is the IP address, mask, and default gateway assigned to the server?

To answer this, you must know that a /29 is a 255.255.255.248 mask, which provides a block size of 8. The subnet is known as 24, the next subnet in a block of 8 is 32, so the broadcast address of the 24 subnet is 31 and the valid host range is 25–30.

Server IP address: 192.168.20.30

Server mask: 255.255.255.248

Default gateway: 192.168.20.25 (router's IP address)

Take a look at Figure 5.4 and solve this problem.

FIGURE 5.4   Find the valid host #1

Router A

E0: 192.168.10.33/27

Look at the router's IP address on Ethernet0. What IP address, subnet mask, and valid host range could be assigned to the host?

The IP address of the router's Ethernet0 is 192.168.10.33/27. As you already know, a /27 is a 224 mask with a block size of 32. The router's interface is in the 32 subnet. The next subnet is 64, so that makes the broadcast address of the 32 subnet 63 and the valid host range 33–62.

Host IP address: 192.168.10.34–62 (any address in the range except for 33, which is assigned to the router)

Mask: 255.255.255.224

Default gateway: 192.168.10.33

Figure 5.5 shows two routers with Ethernet configurations already assigned. What are the host addresses and subnet masks of HostA and HostB?

FIGURE 5.5   Find the valid host #2

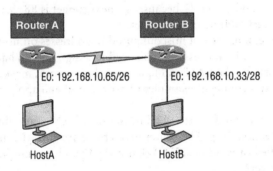

Router A has an IP address of 192.168.10.65/26 and Router B has an IP address of 192.168.10.33/28. What are the host configurations? Router A Ethernet0 is in the 192.168.10.64 subnet and Router B Ethernet0 is in the 192.168.10.32 network.

Host A IP address: 192.168.10.66–126

Host A mask: 255.255.255.192

Host A default gateway: 192.168.10.65

Host B IP address: 192.168.10.34–46

Host B mask: 255.255.255.240

Host B default gateway: 192.168.10.33

Just a couple more examples before you can put this chapter behind you—hang in there!

Figure 5.6 shows two routers. You need to configure the S0/0 interface on RouterA. The IP address assigned to the serial link on RouterA is 172.16.17.0/22 (No, that is not a subnet address, but a valid host IP address on that interface—most people miss this one). What IP address can be assigned to the router interface on RouterB?

FIGURE 5.6   Find the valid host address #3

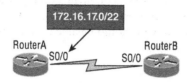

172.16.17.0/22

RouterA   RouterB

S0/0   S0/0

First, know that a /22 CIDR is 255.255.252.0, which makes a block size of 4 in the third octet. Since 17 is listed as the interface IP address, the available range is 16.1 through 19.254, so in this example, the IP address S0/0 on RouterB could be 172.16.18.255 since that's within the range.

Okay, last one! You need to find a classful network address that has one Class C network ID and you need to provide one usable subnet per city while allowing enough usable host addresses for each city specified in Figure 5.7. What is your mask?

FIGURE 5.7   Find the valid subnet mask

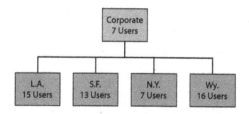

Corporate
7 Users

L.A.
15 Users

S.F.
13 Users

N.Y.
7 Users

Wy.
16 Users

Actually, this is probably the easiest thing you've done all day! I count five subnets needed, and the Wyoming office needs 16 users—always look for the network that needs the most hosts! What block size is needed for the Wyoming office? Your answer is 32. You can't use a block size of 16 because you always have to subtract 2. What mask provides you with a block size of 32? 224 is your answer because this provides eight subnets, each with 30 hosts.

You're done—the diva has sung and the chicken has safely crossed the road...whew! Time to take a break, but skip the shot and the beer if that's what you had in mind because you need to keep going with your studies!

Summary

Again, if you got to this point without getting lost along the way a few times, you're awesome, but if you did get lost, don't stress because most people do! Just be patient with yourself and go back over the material that tripped you up until it's all crystal clear. You'll get there!

And make sure you understand and memorize Cisco's troubleshooting methods. You must remember the four steps that Cisco recommends taking when trying to narrow down exactly where a network and/or IP addressing problem is and then know how to proceed systematically to fix it. In addition, you should be able to find valid IP addresses and subnet masks by looking at a network diagram.

Chapter

6

Cisco's Internetworking Operating System (IOS)

It's time to introduce you to the Cisco Internetwork Operating System (IOS). The IOS is what runs Cisco routers as well as Cisco's switches, and it's also what we use to configure these devices. So that's what you're going to learn about in this chapter. I'm going to show you how to configure a Cisco IOS device using the Cisco IOS command-line interface (CLI). Once proficient with this interface, you'll be able to configure hostnames, banners, passwords, and more as well as troubleshoot skillfully using the Cisco IOS.

We'll also begin the journey to mastering the basics of router and switch configurations plus command verifications in this chapter.

I'll start with a basic IOS switch to begin building the network we'll use throughout this book for configuration examples. Don't forget—I'll be using both switches and routers throughout this chapter, and we configure these devices pretty much the same way. Things diverge when we get to the interfaces where the differences between the two become key, so pay attention closely when we get to that point!

Just as it was with preceding chapters, the fundamentals presented in this chapter are important building blocks to have solidly in place before moving on to the more advanced material coming up in the next ones.

To find your included bonus material, as well as Todd Lammle videos, practice questions and hands-on labs, please see www.lammle.com/ccna.

The IOS User Interface

The *Cisco Internetwork Operating System (IOS)* is the kernel of Cisco routers as well as all current Catalyst switches. In case you didn't know, a kernel is the elemental, indispensable part of an operating system that allocates resources and manages tasks like low-level hardware interfaces and security.

Coming up, I'll show you the Cisco IOS and how to configure a Cisco switch using the *command-line interface (CLI)*. By using the CLI, we can provide access to a Cisco device and provide voice, video, and data service. The configurations you'll see in this chapter are exactly the same as they are on a Cisco router.

Cisco IOS

The Cisco IOS is a proprietary kernel that provides routing, switching, internetworking, and telecommunications features. The first IOS was written by William Yeager in 1985 and enabled networked applications. It runs on most Cisco routers as well as a growing number of Cisco Catalyst switches, like the Catalyst 2960 and 3560 series switches used in this book.

Here's a short list of some important things that the Cisco router IOS software is responsible for:

- Carrying network protocols and functions

- Connecting high-speed traffic between devices

- Adding security to control access and stopping unauthorized network use

- Providing scalability for ease of network growth and redundancy

- Supplying network reliability for connecting to network resources

You can access the Cisco IOS through the console port of a router or switch, from a modem into the auxiliary (or aux) port on a router, or even through Telnet and Secure Shell (SSH). Access to the IOS command line is called an *EXEC session*.

Connecting to a Cisco IOS Device

We connect to a Cisco device to configure it, verify its configuration, and check statistics, and although there are different approaches to this, the first place you would usually connect to is the console port. The *console port* is usually an RJ55, 8-pin modular connection located at the back of the device, and mini-usb ports are now commonly found on routers and switches for use as a console connection.

Look back into Chapter 2, "Ethernet Networking and Data Encapsulation," to review how to configure a PC and enable it to connect to a router console port.

You can also connect to a Cisco router through an *auxiliary port*, which is really the same thing as a console port, so it follows that you can use it as one. The main difference with an auxiliary port is that it also allows you to configure modem commands so that a modem can be connected to the router. This is a cool feature because it lets you dial up a remote router and attach to the auxiliary port if the router is down and you need to configure it remotely, *out-of-band*. One of the differences between Cisco routers and switches is that switches do not have an auxiliary port.

The third way to connect to a Cisco device is *in-band*, through the program *Telnet or Secure Shell (SSH)*. In-band means configuring the device via the network, the opposite of *out-of-band*. We covered Telnet and SSH in Chapter 3, "Introduction to TCP/IP," and in this chapter, I'll show you how to configure access to both of these protocols on a Cisco device.

Figure 6.1 shows an illustration of a Cisco 2960 switch. Really focus in on all the different kinds of interfaces and connections! On the right side is the 10/100/1000 uplink. You can use either the UTP port or the fiber port, but not both at the same time.

FIGURE 6.1 A Cisco 2960 switch

The 3560 switch I'll be using in this book looks a lot like the 2960, but it can perform layer 3 switching, unlike the 2960, which is limited to only layer 2 functions.

I also want to take a moment and tell you about the 2800 series router because that's the router series I'll be using in this book. This router is known as an Integrated Services Router (ISR) and Cisco has updated it to the 2900 series, but I still have plenty of 2800 series routers in my production networks. Figure 6.2 shows a new 1921 series router.

FIGURE 6.2 A Cisco 1900 router

The new ISR series of routers are nice; they are so named because many services, like security, are built into them. The ISR is a modular device, much faster and a lot sleeker than the older 2500 series routers, and it's elegantly designed to support a broad new range of interface options. The new ISR can offer multiple serial interfaces, which can be used for connecting a T1 using a serial V.35 WAN connection. And multiple Fast Ethernet or Gigabit Ethernet ports can be used on the router, depending on the model. This router also has one console via an RJ45 connector and another through the USB port. There is also an auxiliary connection to allow a console connection via a remote modem.

You need to keep in mind that for the most part, you get some serious bang for your buck with the 2800/2900—unless you start adding a bunch of interfaces to it. You've got to pony up for each one of those little beauties, so this can really start to add up and fast!

A couple of other series of routers that will set you back a lot less than the 2800 series are the 1800/1900s, so look into these routers if you want a less-expensive alternative to the 2800/2900 but still want to run the same IOS.

So even though I'm going to be using mostly 2800 series routers and 2960/3560 switches throughout this book to demonstrate examples of IOS configurations, I want to point out that the particular *router* model you use to practice for the Cisco exam isn't really important. The *switch* types are, though—you definitely need at a minimum model a couple of 2960 switches as well as a 3560 switch if you want to measure up to the exam objectives!

You can find more information about all Cisco routers at https://www.cisco.com/c/en/us/products/routers/router-selector.html.

Bringing Up a Switch

When you first bring up a Cisco IOS device, it will run a power-on self-test—a POST. Upon passing that, the machine will look for and then load the Cisco IOS from flash memory if an IOS file is present, then expand it into RAM. As you probably know, flash memory is electronically erasable programmable read-only memory—an EEPROM. The next step is for the IOS to locate and load a valid configuration known as the startup-config that will be stored in *nonvolatile RAM (NVRAM)*.

Once the IOS is loaded and up and running, the startup-config will be copied from NVRAM into RAM and from then on referred to as the running-config.

But if a valid startup-config isn't found in NVRAM, your switch will enter setup mode, giving you a step-by-step dialog to help configure some basic parameters on it.

You can also enter setup mode at any time from the command line by typing the command **setup** from privileged mode, which I'll get to in a minute. Setup mode only covers some basic commands and generally isn't really all that helpful. Here's an example:

```
Would you like to enter the initial configuration dialog? [yes/no]: y
At any point you may enter a question mark '?' for help.
Use ctrl-c to abort configuration dialog at any prompt.
Default settings are in square brackets '[]'.
Basic management setup configures only enough connectivity
for management of the system, extended setup will ask you
to configure each interface on the system
Would you like to enter basic management setup? [yes/no]: y
Configuring global parameters:
Enter host name [Switch]: Ctrl+C
Configuration aborted, no changes made.
```

  You can exit setup mode at any time by pressing Ctrl+C.

I highly recommend going through setup mode once, then never again because you should always use the CLI instead!

Command-Line Interface (CLI)

I sometimes refer to the CLI as "cash line interface" because the ability to create advanced configurations on Cisco routers and switches using the CLI will earn you a wad of cash!

Entering the CLI

After the interface status messages appear and you press Enter, the Switch> prompt will pop up. This is called *user exec mode*, or user mode for short, and although it's mostly used to view statistics, it is also a stepping stone along the way to logging in to *privileged exec mode*, called privileged mode for short.

You can view and change the configuration of a Cisco router only while in privileged mode, and you enter it via the enable command like this:

```
Switch>enable
Switch#
```

The Switch# prompt signals you're in privileged mode where you can both view and change the switch configuration. You can go back from privileged mode into user mode by using the disable command:

```
Switch#disable
Switch>
```

You can type **logout** from either mode to exit the console:

```
Switch>logout
Switch con0 is now available
Press RETURN to get started.
```

Next, I'll show how to perform some basic administrative configurations.

Overview of Router Modes

To configure from a CLI, you can make global changes to the router by typing **configure terminal** or just **config t**. This will get you into global configuration mode where you can make changes to the running-config. Commands run from global configuration mode are predictably referred to as global commands, and they are typically set only once and affect the entire router.

Type **config** from the privileged-mode prompt and then press Enter to opt for the default of terminal like this:

```
Switch#config
Configuring from terminal, memory, or network [terminal]? [press enter]
Enter configuration commands, one per line. End with CNTL/Z.
Switch(config)#
```

At this point, you make changes that affect the router as a whole (globally), hence the term *global configuration mode*. For instance, to change the running-config—the current configuration running in dynamic RAM (DRAM)—use the configure terminal command, as I just demonstrated.

CLI Prompts

Let's explore the different prompts you'll encounter when configuring a switch or router now, because knowing them well will really help you orient yourself and recognize exactly where you are at any given time while in configuration mode. I'm going to demonstrate some of the prompts used on a Cisco switch and cover the various terms used along the way. Make sure you're very familiar with them, and always check your prompts before making any changes to a router's configuration!

We're not going to venture into every last obscure command prompt you could potentially come across in the configuration mode world because that would get us deep into territory that's beyond the scope of this book. Instead, I'm going to focus on the prompts you absolutely must know to pass the exam plus the very handy and seriously vital ones you'll need and use the most in real-life networking—the cream of the crop.

 Don't freak! It's not important that you understand exactly what each of these command prompts accomplishes just yet because I'm going to completely fill you in on all of them really soon. For now, relax and focus on just becoming familiar with the different prompts available and all will be well!

Interfaces

To make changes to an interface, you use the interface command from global configuration mode:

```
Switch(config)#interface ?
Async Async interface
BVI Bridge-Group Virtual Interface
CTunnel CTunnel interface
Dialer Dialer interface
FastEthernet FastEthernet IEEE 802.3
Filter Filter interface
Filtergroup Filter Group interface
GigabitEthernet GigabitEthernet IEEE 802.3z
Group-Async Async Group interface
Lex Lex interface
Loopback Loopback interface
Null Null interface
Port-channel Ethernet Channel of interfaces
Portgroup Portgroup interface
Pos-channel POS Channel of interfaces
```

```
Tunnel Tunnel interface
Vif PGM Multicast Host interface
Virtual-Template Virtual Template interface
Virtual-TokenRing Virtual TokenRing
Vlan Catalyst Vlans
fcpa Fiber Channel
range interface range command
Switch(config)#interface fastEthernet 0/1
Switch(config-if)#)
```

Did you notice that the prompt changed to Switch(config-if)#? This tells you that you're in *interface configuration mode*. And wouldn't it be nice if the prompt also gave you an indication of what interface you were configuring? Well, at least for now we'll have to live without the prompt information, because it doesn't. But it should already be clear to you that you really need to pay attention when configuring an IOS device!

Line Commands

To configure user-mode passwords, use the line command. The prompt then becomes Switch(config-line)#:

```
Switch(config)#line ?
<0-15> First Line number
console Primary terminal line
vty Virtual terminal
Switch(config)#line console 0
Switch(config-line)#
```

The line console 0 command is a global command, and sometimes you'll also hear people refer to global commands as major commands. In this example, any command typed from the (config-line) prompt is known as a subcommand.

Access List Configurations

To configure a standard named access list, you'll need to get to the prompt Switch (config-std-nacl)#:

```
Switch#config t
Switch(config)#ip access-list standard Todd
Switch(config-std-nacl)#
```

What you see here is a typical basic standard ACL prompt. There are various ways to configure access lists, and the prompts are only slightly different from this particular example.

Routing Protocol Configurations

I need to point out that we don't use routing or router protocols on 2960 switches, but we can and will use them on my 3560 switches. Here is an example of configuring routing on a layer 3 switch:

```
Switch(config)#router rip
IP routing not enabled
Switch(config)#ip routing
Switch(config)#router rip
Switch(config-router)#
```

Did you notice that the prompt changed to Switch(config-router)#?

Defining Router Terms

Table 6.1 defines some of the terms I've used so far.

TABLE 6.1   Router terms

Mode	Definition
User exec mode	Limited to basic monitoring commands
Privileged exec mode	Provides access to all other router commands
Global configuration mode	Commands that affect the entire system
Specific configuration modes	Commands that affect interfaces/processes only
Setup mode	Interactive configuration dialog

Editing and Help Features

The Cisco advanced editing features can also help you configure your router. If you type in a question mark (?) at any prompt, you'll be given a list of all the commands available from that prompt:

```
Switch#?
Exec commands:
access-enable Create a temporary Access-List entry
access-template Create a temporary Access-List entry
archive manage archive files
cd Change current directory
clear Reset functions
```

```
clock Manage the system clock
cns CNS agents
configure Enter configuration mode
connect Open a terminal connection
copy Copy from one file to another
debug Debugging functions (see also 'undebug')
delete Delete a file
diagnostic Diagnostic commands
dir List files on a filesystem
disable Turn off privileged commands
disconnect Disconnect an existing network connection
dot1x IEEE 802.1X Exec Commands
enable Turn on privileged commands
eou EAPoUDP
erase Erase a filesystem
exit Exit from the EXEC
--More-- ?
```

Press RETURN for another line, SPACE for another page, anything else to quit.

And if this is not enough information for you, you can press the spacebar to get another whole page of information, or you can press Enter to go one command at a time. You can also press Q, or any other key for that matter, to quit and return to the prompt. Notice that I typed a question mark (?) at the More prompt and it told me what my options were from that prompt.

Here's a shortcut: To find commands that start with a certain letter, use the letter and the question mark with no space between them, like this:

```
Switch#c?
cd clear clock cns configure
connect copy
Switch#c
```

Okay, see that? By typing **c?**, I got a response listing all the commands that start with *c*. Also notice that the Switch#c prompt reappears after the list of commands is displayed. This can be really helpful when you happen to be working with long commands but you're short on patience and still need the next possible one. It would get old fast if you actually had to retype the entire command every time you used a question mark!

So with that, let's find the next command in a string by typing the first command and then a question mark:

```
Switch#clock ?
set Set the time and date
Switch#clock set ?
hh:mm:ss Current Time
```

```
Switch#clock set 2:35 ?
% Unrecognized command
Switch#clock set 2:35:01 ?
<1-31> Day of the month
MONTH Month of the year
Switch#clock set 2:35:01 21 july ?
<1993-2035> Year
Switch#clock set 2:35:01 21 august 2013
Switch#
00:19:55: %SYS-5-CLOCKUPDATE: System clock has been updated from 00:19:55
UTC Mon Mar 1 1993 to 02:35:01 UTC Wed Aug 21 2013, configured from console
by console.
```

I entered the **clock ?** command and got a list of the next possible parameters plus what they do. Make note of the fact that you can just keep typing a command, a space, and then a question mark until <cr> (carriage return) is your only option left.

And if you're typing commands and receive

```
Switch#clock set 11:15:11
% Incomplete command.
```

no worries—that's only telling you that the command string simply isn't complete quite yet. All you need to do is to press the up arrow key to redisplay the last command entered and then continue with the command by using your question mark.

But if you get the error

```
Switch(config)#access-list 100 permit host 1.1.1.1 host 2.2.2.2
                                                   ^
% Invalid input detected at '^' marker.
```

all is not well because it means you actually have entered a command incorrectly. See that little caret—the ^? It's a very helpful tool that marks the exact point where you blew it and made a mess.

Here's another example of when you'll see that caret:

```
Switch#sh fastethernet 0/0
          ^
% Invalid input detected at '^' marker.
```

This command looks right but be careful! The problem is that the full command is show interface fastethernet 0/0.

Now if you receive the error

```
Switch#sh cl
% Ambiguous command: "sh cl"
```

you're being told that there are multiple commands that begin with the string you entered and it's not unique. Use the question mark to find the exact command you need:

```
Switch#sh cl?
class-map clock cluster
```

Case in point: There are three commands that start with show cl.

Table 6.2 lists the enhanced editing commands available on a Cisco router.

TABLE 6.2   Enhanced editing commands

Command	Meaning
Ctrl+A	Moves your cursor to the beginning of the line
Ctrl+E	Moves your cursor to the end of the line
Esc+B	Moves back one word
Ctrl+B	Moves back one character
Ctrl+F	Moves forward one character
Esc+F	Moves forward one word
Ctrl+D	Deletes a single character
Backspace	Deletes a single character
Ctrl+R	Redisplays a line
Ctrl+U	Erases a line
Ctrl+W	Erases a word
Ctrl+Z	Ends configuration mode and returns to EXEC
Tab	Finishes typing a command for you

Another really cool editing feature you need to know about is the automatic scrolling of long lines. In the following example, the command I typed reached the right margin and automatically moved 11 spaces to the left. How do I know this? Because the dollar sign [$] is telling me that the line has been scrolled to the left:

```
Switch#config t
Switch(config)#$ 100 permit ip host 192.168.10.1 192.168.10.0 0.0.0.255
```

You can review the router-command history with the commands shown in Table 6.3.

TABLE 6.3 IOS-command history

Command	Meaning
Ctrl+P or up arrow	Shows last command entered
Ctrl+N or down arrow	Shows previous commands entered
show history	Shows last 20 commands entered by default
show terminal	Shows terminal configurations and history buffer size
terminal history size	Changes buffer size (max 255)

The following example demonstrates the show history command as well as how to change the history's size. It also shows how to verify the history with the show terminal command. First, use the show history command, which will allow you to see the last 20 commands that were entered on the router (even though my particular router reveals only 10 commands because that's all I've entered since rebooting it). Check it out:

```
Switch#sh history
sh fastethernet 0/0
sh ru
sh cl
config t
sh history
sh flash
sh running-config
sh startup-config
sh ver
sh history
```

Okay—now, we'll use the show terminal command to verify the terminal history size:

```
Switch#sh terminal
Line 0, Location: "", Type: ""
Length: 25 lines, Width: 80 columns
Baud rate (TX/RX) is 9500/9500, no parity, 2 stopbits, 8 databits
Status: PSI Enabled, Ready, Active, Ctrl-c Enabled, Automore On
0x50000
Capabilities: none
Modem state: Ready
[output cut]
Modem type is unknown.
Session limit is not set.
```

```
Time since activation: 00:17:22
Editing is enabled.
History is enabled, history size is 10.
DNS resolution in show commands is enabled
Full user help is disabled
Allowed input transports are none.
Allowed output transports are telnet.
Preferred transport is telnet.
No output characters are padded
No special data dispatching characters
```

When Should I Use the Cisco Editing Features?

You'll find yourself using a couple of editing features quite often and some not so much, if at all. Understand that Cisco didn't make these up; these are just old Unix commands! Even so, Ctrl+A is still a really helpful way to negate a command.

For example, if you were to put in a long command and then decide you didn't want to use that command in your configuration after all, or if it didn't work, then you could just press your up arrow key to show the last command entered, press Ctrl+A, type no and then a space, press Enter—and poof! The command is negated. This doesn't work on every command, but it works on a lot of them and saves some serious time!

Administrative Configurations

Even though the following sections aren't critical to making a router or switch *work* on a network, they're still really important. I'm going to guide you through configuring specific commands that are particularly helpful when administering your network.

You can configure the following administrative functions on a router and switch:

- Hostnames
- Banners
- Passwords
- Interface descriptions

Remember, none of these will make your routers or switches work better or faster, but trust me, your life will be a whole lot better if you just take the time to set these configurations on each of your network devices. This is because doing so makes troubleshooting and maintaining your network a great deal easier—seriously! In this next section, I'll be demonstrating commands on a Cisco switch, but understand that these commands are used in the exact same way on a Cisco router.

Hostnames

We use the hostname command to set the identity of the router and switch. This is only locally significant, meaning it doesn't affect how the router or switch performs name lookups or how the device actually works on the internetwork. But the hostname is still important in routes because it's often used for authentication in many wide area networks (WANs). Here's an example:

```
Switch#config t
Switch(config)#hostname Todd
Todd(config)#hostname Chicago
Chicago(config)#hostname Todd
Todd(config)#
```

I know it's pretty tempting to configure the hostname after your own name, but it's usually a much better idea to name the device something that relates to its physical location. A name that maps to where the device lives will make finding it a whole lot easier, which among other things, confirms that you're actually configuring the correct device. Even though it seems like I'm completely ditching my own advice by naming mine *Todd*, I'm not, because this particular device really does live in "Todd's" office. Its name perfectly maps to where it is, so it won't be confused with those in the other networks I work with!

Banners

A very good reason for having a *banner* is to give any and all who dare attempt to telnet or sneak into your internetwork a little security notice. And they're very cool because you can create and customize them so that they'll greet anyone who shows up on the router with exactly the information you want them to have!

Here are the three types of banners you need to be sure you're familiar with:

- Exec process creation banner
- Login banner
- Message of the day banner

And you can see them all illustrated in the following code:

```
Todd(config)#banner ?
LINE c banner-text c, where 'c' is a delimiting character
exec Set EXEC process creation banner
incoming Set incoming terminal line banner
login Set login banner
motd Set Message of the Day banner
prompt-timeout Set Message for login authentication timeout
slip-ppp Set Message for SLIP/PPP
```

Message of the day (MOTD) banners are the most widely used banners because they give a message to anyone connecting to the router via Telnet or an auxiliary port or even through a console port as seen here:

```
Todd(config)#banner motd ?
LINE c banner-text c, where 'c' is a delimiting character
Todd(config)#banner motd #
Enter TEXT message. End with the character '#'.
$ Acme.com network, then you must disconnect immediately.#
Todd(config)#^Z (Press the control key + z keys to return to privileged mode)
Todd#exit
con0 is now available
Press RETURN to get started.
If you are not authorized to be in Acme.com network, then you
must disconnect immediately.
Todd#
```

This MOTD banner essentially tells anyone connecting to the device to get lost if they're not on the guest list. The part to focus upon here is the delimiting character, which is what informs the router the message is done. Clearly, you can use any character you want for it except for the delimiting character in the message itself. Once the message is complete, press Enter, then the delimiting character, and then press Enter again. Everything will still work if you don't follow this routine unless you have more than one banner. If that's the case, make sure you do follow it or your banners will all be combined into one message and put on a single line!

You can set a banner on one line like this:

```
Todd(config)#banner motd x Unauthorized access prohibited! x
```

Let's take a minute to go into more detail about the other two types of banners I mentioned:

Exec banner   You can configure a line-activation (exec) banner to be displayed when EXEC processes such as a line activation or an incoming connection to a VTY line have been created. Simply initiating a user exec session through a console port will activate the exec banner.

Login banner   You can configure a login banner for display on all connected terminals. It will show up after the MOTD banner but before the login prompts. This login banner can't be disabled on a per-line basis, so to globally disable it you've got to delete it with the no banner login command.

Here's what a login banner output looks like:

```
!
banner login ^C
----------------------------------------------------------------
Cisco Router and Security Device Manager (SDM) is installed on this device.
This feature requires the one-time use of the username "cisco"
```

with the password "cisco". The default username and password
have a privilege level of 15.
Please change these publicly known initial credentials using
SDM or the IOS CLI.
Here are the Cisco IOS commands.
username <myuser> privilege 15 secret 0 <mypassword>
no username cisco
Replace <myuser> and <mypassword> with the username and
password you want to use.
For more information about SDM please follow the instructions
in the QUICK START GUIDE for your router or go to http://www.cisco.com/go/sdm

----
^C
!

The previous login banner should look pretty familiar to anyone who's ever logged into an ISR router because it's the banner Cisco has in the default configuration for its ISR routers.

 Remember that the login banner is displayed before the login prompts and after the MOTD banner.

Setting Passwords

There are five passwords you'll need to secure your Cisco routers: console, auxiliary, telnet (VTY), enable password, and enable secret. The enable secret and enable password are the ones used to set the password for securing privileged mode. Once the enable commands are set, users will be prompted for a password. The other three are used to configure a password when user mode is accessed through the console port, through the auxiliary port, or via Telnet.

Let's take a look at each of these now.

Enable Passwords

You set the enable passwords from global configuration mode like this:

Todd(config)#**enable ?**
last-resort Define enable action if no TACACS servers
respond
password Assign the privileged level password
secret Assign the privileged level secret
use-tacacs Use TACACS to check enable passwords

The following list describes the enable password parameters:

last-resort   This allows you to still enter the device if you set up authentication through a TACACS server and it's not available. It won't be used if the TACACS server is working.

password   This sets the enable password on older, pre-10.3 systems and isn't ever used if an enable secret is set.

secret   The newer, encrypted password that overrides the enable password if it has been set.

use-tacacs   This tells the router or switch to authenticate through a TACACS server. It comes in really handy when you have lots of routers because changing the password on a multitude of them can be insanely tedious. It's much easier to simply go through the TACACS server and change the password only once!

Here's an example that shows how to set the enable passwords:

```
Todd(config)#enable secret todd
Todd(config)#enable password todd
The enable password you have chosen is the same as your
enable secret. This is not recommended. Re-enter the
enable password.
```

If you try to set the enable secret and enable passwords the same, the device will give you a polite warning to change the second password. Make a note to yourself that if there aren't any old legacy routers involved, you don't even bother to use the enable password!

User-mode passwords are assigned via the line command like this:

```
Todd(config)#line ?
<0-15> First Line number
console Primary terminal line
vty Virtual terminal
```

And these two lines are especially important for the exam objectives:

console   Sets a console user-mode password.

vty   Sets a Telnet password on the device and is also used in the SSH configuraiton. If this password isn't set, then by default, Telnet can't be used.

To configure user-mode passwords, choose the line you want and configure it using the login command to make the switch prompt for authentication. Let's focus in on the configuration of individual lines now.

Console Password

We set the console password with the line console 0 command, but look at what happened when I tried to type **line console ?** from the (config-line)# prompt—I received an error! Here's the example:

```
Todd(config-line)#line console ?
% Unrecognized command
```

```
Todd(config-line)#exit
Todd(config)#line console ?
<0-0> First Line number
Todd(config)#line console 0
Todd(config-line)#password console
Todd(config-line)#login
```

You can still type **line console 0** and that will be accepted, but the help screens just don't work from that prompt. Type **exit** to go back one level, and you'll find that your help screens now work. This is a "feature." Really.

Because there's only one console port, I can only choose line console 0. You can set all your line passwords to the same password, but doing this isn't exactly a brilliant security move!

And it's also important to remember to apply the login command or the console port won't prompt for authentication. The way Cisco has this process set up means you can't set the login command before a password is set on a line because if you set it but don't then set a password, that line won't be usable. You'll actually get prompted for a password that doesn't exist, so Cisco's method isn't just a hassle; it makes sense and is a feature after all!

> Definitely remember that although Cisco has this "password feature" on its routers starting with IOS 12.2 and above, it's not included in older IOSs.

Okay, there are a few other important commands you need to know regarding the console port.

For one, the exec-timeout 0 0 command sets the time-out for the console EXEC session to zero, ensuring that it never times out. The default time-out is 10 minutes.

> If you're feeling mischievous, try this on people at work: Set the exec-timeout command to 0 1. This will make the console time out in 1 second, and to fix it, you have to continually press the down arrow key while changing the time-out time with your free hand!

Logging synchronous is such a cool command that it should be a default, but it's not. It's great because it's the antidote for those annoying console messages that disrupt the input you're trying to type. The messages will still pop up, but at least you get returned to your device prompt without your input being interrupted! This makes your input messages oh-so-much easier to read!

Here's an example of how to configure both commands:

```
Todd(config-line)#line con 0
Todd(config-line)#exec-timeout ?
<0-35791> Timeout in minutes
Todd(config-line)#exec-timeout 0 ?
```

```
<0-2157583> Timeout in seconds
<cr>
Todd(config-line)#exec-timeout 0 0
Todd(config-line)#logging synchronous
```

 You can set the console to go from never timing out (0 0) to timing out in 35,791 minutes and 2,157,583 seconds. Remember that the default is 10 minutes.

Telnet Password

To set the user-mode password for Telnet access into the router or switch, use the line vty command. IOS switches typically have 15 lines, but routers running the Enterprise edition have considerably more. The best way to find out how many lines you have is to use that handy question mark like this:

```
Todd(config-line)#line vty 0 ?
% Unrecognized command
Todd(config-line)#exit
Todd(config)#line vty 0 ?
<1-15> Last Line number
<cr>
Todd(config)#line vty 0 15
Todd(config-line)#password telnet
Todd(config-line)#login
```

This output clearly shows that you cannot get help from your (config-line)# prompt. You must go back to global config mode in order to use the question mark (?).

So what will happen if you try to telnet into a device that doesn't have a VTY password set? You'll receive an error saying the connection has been refused because the password isn't set. So, if you telnet into a switch and receive a message like this one that I got from Switch B

```
Todd#telnet SwitchB
Trying SwitchB (10.0.0.1)...Open
Password required, but none set
[Connection to SwitchB closed by foreign host]
Todd#
```

it means the switch doesn't have the VTY password set. But you can still get around this and tell the switch to allow Telnet connections without a password by using the no login command:

```
SwitchB(config-line)#line vty 0 15
SwitchB(config-line)#no login
```

I definitely do not recommend using the no login command to allow Telnet connections without a password, unless you're in a testing or classroom environment. In a production network, always set your VTY password!

After your IOS devices are configured with an IP address, you can use the Telnet program to configure and check your routers instead of having to use a console cable. You can use the Telnet program by typing telnet from any command prompt (DOS or Cisco). I'll cover all things Telnet more thoroughly in Chapter 7, "Managing a Cisco Internetwork."

Auxiliary Password

To configure the auxiliary password on a router, go into global configuration mode and type **line aux ?.** And by the way, you won't find these ports on a switch. This output shows that you only get a choice of 0–0, which is because there's only one port:

```
Todd#config t
Todd(config)#line aux ?
<0-0> First Line number
Todd(config)#line aux 0
Todd(config-line)#login
% Login disabled on line 1, until 'password' is set
Todd(config-line)#password aux
Todd(config-line)#login
```

Setting Up Secure Shell (SSH)

I strongly recommend using Secure Shell (SSH) instead of Telnet because it creates a more secure session. The Telnet application uses an unencrypted data stream, but SSH uses encryption keys to send data so your username and password aren't sent in the clear, vulnerable to anyone lurking around!

Here are the steps for setting up SSH:

1. Set your hostname:

```
Router(config)#hostname Todd
```

2. Set the domain name—both the hostname and domain name are required for the encryption keys to be generated:

```
Todd(config)#ip domain-name Lammle.com
```

3. Set the username to allow SSH client access:

```
Todd(config)#username Todd password Lammle
```

4. Generate the encryption keys for securing the session:

```
Todd(config)#crypto key generate rsa
The name for the keys will be: Todd.Lammle.com
Choose the size of the key modulus in the range of 350 to
```

```
5095 for your General Purpose Keys. Choosing a key modulus
Greater than 512 may take a few minutes.
How many bits in the modulus [512]: 1025
% Generating 1025 bit RSA keys, keys will be non-exportable...
[OK] (elapsed time was 5 seconds)
Todd(config)#
1d15h: %SSH-5-ENABLED: SSH 1.99 has been enabled*June 25
19:25:30.035: %SSH-5-ENABLED: SSH 1.99 has been enabled
```

5. Enable SSH version 2 on the device—not mandatory, but strongly suggested:

```
Todd(config)#ip ssh version 2
```

6. Connect to the VTY lines of the switch or router:

```
Todd(config)#line vty 0 15
```

7. Tell the lines to use the local database for password:

```
Todd(config-line)#login local
```

8. Configure your access protocols:

```
Todd(config-line)#transport input ?
all All protocols
none No protocols
ssh TCP/IP SSH protocol
telnet TCP/IP Telnet protocol
```

Beware of this next line, and make sure you never use it in production because it's a horrendous security risk:

```
Todd(config-line)#transport input all
```

I recommend using the next line to secure your VTY lines with SSH:

```
Todd(config-line)#transport input ssh ?
telnet TCP/IP Telnet protocol
<cr>
```

I actually do use Telnet once in a while when a situation arises that specifically calls for it. It just doesn't happen very often. But if you want to go with Telnet, here's how you do that:

```
Todd(config-line)#transport input ssh telnet
```

Know that if you don't use the keyword telnet at the end of the command string, then only SSH will work on the device. You can go with either, just so long as you understand that SSH is way more secure than Telnet.

Encrypting Your Passwords

Because only the enable secret password is encrypted by default, you'll need to manually configure the user-mode and enable passwords for encryption.

Notice that you can see all the passwords except the enable secret when performing a show running-config on a switch:

```
Todd#sh running-config
Building configuration...
Current configuration : 1020 bytes
!
! Last configuration change at 00:03:11 UTC Mon Mar 1 1993
!
version 15.0
no service pad
service timestamps debug datetime msec
service timestamps log datetime msec
no service password-encryption
!
hostname Todd
!
enable secret 5 ykw.3/tgsOuy9.5qmgG/EeYOYgBvfX5v.S8UNA9Rddg
enable password todd
!
[output cut]
!
line con 0
password console
login
line vty 0 5
password telnet
login
line vty 5 15
password telnet
login
!
end
```

To manually encrypt your passwords, use the service password-encryption command. Here's how:

```
Todd#config t
Todd(config)#service password-encryption
```

```
Todd(config)#exit
Todd#show run
Building configuration...
!
!
enable secret 5 ykw.3/tgsOuy9.5qmgG/EeYOYgBvfX5v.S8UNA9Rddg
enable password 7 1505050800
!
[output cut]
!
!
line con 0
password 7 050809013253520C
login
line vty 0 5
password 7 05120A2D525B1D
login
line vty 5 15
password 7 05120A2D525B1D
login
!
end
Todd#config t
Todd(config)#no service password-encryption
Todd(config)#^Z
Todd#
```

Nicely done—the passwords will now be encrypted. All you need to do is encrypt the passwords, perform a show run, then turn off the command if you want. This output clearly shows us that the enable password and the line passwords are all encrypted.

Before we move on to find out how to set descriptions on your interfaces, I want to stress some points about password encryption. As I said, if you set your passwords and then turn on the service password-encryption command, you have to perform a show running-config before you turn off the encryption service or your passwords won't be encrypted. You don't have to turn off the encryption service at all—you'd only do that if your switch is running low on processes. And if you turn on the service before you set your passwords, then you don't even have to view them to have them encrypted.

Descriptions

Setting descriptions on an interface is another administratively helpful thing, and like the hostname, it's also only locally significant. One case where the description command comes in really handy is when you want to keep track of circuit numbers on a switch or a router's serial WAN port.

Here's an example on my switch:

```
Todd#config t
Todd(config)#int fa0/1
Todd(config-if)#description Sales VLAN Trunk Link
Todd(config-if)#^Z
Todd#
```

And on a router serial WAN:

```
Router#config t
Router(config)#int s0/0/0
Router(config-if)#description WAN to Miami
Router(config-if)#^Z
```

You can view an interface's description with either the show running-config command or the show interface—even with the show interface description command:

```
Todd#sh run
Building configuration...
Current configuration : 855 bytes
!
interface FastEthernet0/1
description Sales VLAN Trunk Link
!
[output cut]
Todd#sh int f0/1
FastEthernet0/1 is up, line protocol is up (connected)
Hardware is Fast Ethernet, address is ecc8.8202.8282 (bia ecc8.8202.8282)
Description: Sales VLAN Trunk Link
MTU 1500 bytes, BW 100000 Kbit/sec, DLY 100 usec,
[output cut]
Todd#sh int description
Interface Status Protocol Description
Vl1 up up
Fa0/1 up up Sales VLAN Trunk Link
Fa0/2 up up
```

 Real World Scenario

description: A Helpful Command

Bob, a senior network admin at Acme Corporation in San Francisco, has over 50 WAN links to branches throughout the United States and Canada. Whenever an interface goes down, Bob wastes lots of time trying to figure out the circuit number and the phone number of the provider of his ailing WAN link.

This kind of scenario shows just how helpful the interface description command can be. It would save Bob a lot of work because he could use it on his most important switch LAN links to find out exactly where every interface is connected. Bob's life would also be made a lot easier by adding circuit numbers to each and every WAN interface on his routers, along with the phone number of the responsible provider.

So if Bob had just taken time in advance to preventively add this information to his interfaces, he would have saved himself an ocean of stress and a ton of precious time when his WAN links inevitably go down!

Doing the *do* Command

In every previous example so far, we've had to run all show commands from privileged mode. But I've got great news—beginning with IOS version 12.3, Cisco has finally added a command to the IOS that allows you to view the configuration and statistics from within configuration mode!

In fact, with any IOS, you'd get the following error if you tried to view the configuration from global config:

```
Todd(config)#sh run
            ^
% Invalid input detected at '^' marker.
```

Compare that to the output I get from entering that same command on my router that's running the 15.0 IOS using the "do" syntax:

```
Todd(config)#do show run
Building configuration...
Current configuration : 759 bytes
!
version 15.0
no service pad
service timestamps debug datetime msec
service timestamps log datetime msec
no service password-encryption
!
hostname Todd
!
boot-start-marker
boot-end-marker
!
[output cut]
```

So now you can pretty much run any command from any configuration prompt—nice, huh? Looking back through all those examples for encrypting our passwords, you can see that the do command would definitely have gotten the party started sooner, making this innovation one to celebrate for sure!

Router and Switch Interfaces

Interface configuration is arguably the most important router configuration because without interfaces, a router is a pretty useless object. Furthermore, interface configurations must be totally precise to enable communication with other devices. Network layer addresses, media type, bandwidth, and other administrator commands are all used to configure an interface.

On a layer 2 switch, interface configurations typically involve a lot less work than router interface configuration. Check out the output from the powerful verification command *show ip interface brief*, which reveals all the interfaces on my 3560 switch:

```
Todd#sh ip interface brief
Interface        IP-Address        OK? Method Status    Protocol
Vlan1            192.168.255.8     YES DHCP up          up
FastEthernet0/1 unassigned YES unset up up
FastEthernet0/2 unassigned YES unset up up
FastEthernet0/3 unassigned YES unset down down
FastEthernet0/4 unassigned YES unset down down
FastEthernet0/5 unassigned YES unset up up
FastEthernet0/6 unassigned YES unset up up
FastEthernet0/7 unassigned YES unset down down
FastEthernet0/8 unassigned YES unset down down
GigabitEthernet0/1 unassigned YES unset down down
```

The previous output shows the default routed port found on all Cisco switches (VLAN 1), plus nine switch FastEthernet interface ports, with one port being a Gigabit Ethernet port used for uplinks to other switches.

Different routers use different methods to choose the interfaces used on them. For instance, the following command shows one of my 2800 ISR Cisco routers with two FastEthernet interfaces along with two serial WAN interfaces:

```
Router>sh ip int brief
Interface IP-Address OK? Method Status Protocol
FastEthernet0/0 192.168.255.11 YES DHCP up up
FastEthernet0/1 unassigned YES unset administratively down down
Serial0/0/0 unassigned YES unset administratively down down
Serial0/1/0 unassigned YES unset administratively down down
Router>
```

Previously, we always used the interface *type number* sequence to configure an interface, but the newer routers come with an actual physical slot and include a port number on the module plugged into it. So on a modular router, the configuration would be interface *type slot/port*, as demonstrated here:

```
Todd#config t
Todd(config)#interface GigabitEthernet 0/1
Todd(config-if)#
```

You can see that we are now at the Gigabit Ethernet slot 0, port 1 prompt, and from here we can make configuration changes to the interface. Make note of the fact that you can't just type int gigabitethernet 0. No shortcuts on the slot/port—you've got to type the slot/port variables in the command: *type slot/port* or, for example, int gigabitethernet 0/1 (or just int g0/1).

Once in interface configuration mode, we can configure various options. Keep in mind that speed and duplex are the two factors to be concerned with for the LAN:

```
Todd#config t
Todd(config)#interface GigabitEthernet 0/1
Todd(config-if)#speed 1000
Todd(config-if)#duplex full
```

So what's happened here? Well basically, this has shut off the auto-detect mechanism on the port, forcing it to only run gigabit speeds at full duplex. For the ISR series router, it's basically the same, but you get even more options! The LAN interfaces are the same, but the rest of the modules are different—they use three numbers instead of two. The three numbers used here can represent slot/subslot/port, but this depends on the card used in the ISR router. For the objectives, you just need to remember this: The first 0 is the router itself. You then choose the slot and then the port. Here's an example of a serial interface on my 2811:

```
Todd(config)#interface serial ?
<0-2> Serial interface number
Todd(config)#interface serial 0/0/?
<0-1> Serial interface number
Todd(config)#interface serial 0/0/0
Todd(config-if)#
```

This might look a little dicey to you, but I promise it's really not that hard! It helps to remember that you should always view the output of the show ip interface brief command or a show running-config output first so you know the exact interfaces you have to deal with. Here's one of my 2811's output that has even more serial interfaces installed:

```
Todd(config-if)#do show run
Building configuration...
[output cut]
!
```

```
interface FastEthernet0/0
no ip address
shutdown
duplex auto
speed auto
!
interface FastEthernet0/1
no ip address
shutdown
duplex auto
speed auto
!
interface Serial0/0/0
no ip address
shutdown
no fair-queue
!
interface Serial0/0/1
no ip address
shutdown
!
interface Serial0/1/0
no ip address
shutdown
!
interface Serial0/2/0
no ip address
shutdown
clock rate 2000000
!
[output cut]
```

For the sake of brevity, I didn't include my complete running-config, but I've displayed all you really need. You can see the two built-in FastEthernet interfaces, the two serial interfaces in slot 0 (0/0/0 and 0/0/1), the serial interface in slot 1 (0/1/0), and the serial interface in slot 2 (0/2/0). And once you see the interfaces like this, it makes it a lot easier to understand how the modules are inserted into the router.

Just understand that if you type interface e0 on an old 2500 series router, interface fastethernet 0/0 on a modular router (such as the 2800 series router), or interface serial 0/1/0 on an ISR router, all you're actually doing is choosing an interface to configure. Essentially, they're all configured the same way after that.

Let's delve deeper into our router interface discussion by exploring how to bring up the interface and set an IP address on it next.

Bringing Up an Interface

You can disable an interface with the interface command shutdown and enable it with the no shutdown command. Just to remind you, all switch ports are enabled by default and all router ports are disabled by default, so we're going to talk more about router ports than switch ports in the next few sections.

If an interface is shut down, it'll display as administratively down when you use the show interfaces command (sh int for short):

```
Router#sh int f0/0
FastEthernet0/1 is administratively down, line protocol is down
[output cut]
```

Another way to check an interface's status is via the show running-config command. You can bring up the router interface with the no shutdown command (no shut for short):

```
Router(config)#int f0/0
Router(config-if)#no shutdown
*August 21 13:55:08.555: %LINK-3-UPDOWN: Interface FastEthernet0/0,
changed state to up
Router(config-if)#do show int f0/0
FastEthernet0/0 is up, line protocol is up
[output cut]
```

Configuring an IP Address on an Interface

Even though you don't have to use IP on your routers, it's usually what everyone uses. To configure IP addresses on an interface, use the ip address command from interface configuration mode and remember that you do not set an IP address on a layer 2 switch port!

```
Todd(config)#int f0/1
Todd(config-if)#ip address 172.16.10.2 255.255.255.0
```

Also, don't forget to enable the interface with the no shutdown command. Remember to look at the command show interface *int* output to see if the interface is administratively shut down or not. Show ip int brief and show running-config will also give you this information.

> The ip address *address mask* command starts the IP processing on the router interface. Again, you do not configure an IP address on a layer 2 switch interface!

Okay—now if you want to add a second subnet address to an interface, you have to use the secondary parameter. If you type another IP address and press Enter, it will replace the existing primary IP address and mask. This is definitely one of the Cisco IOS's coolest features!

So let's try it. To add a secondary IP address, just use the secondary parameter:

```
Todd(config-if)#ip address 172.16.20.2 255.255.255.0 ?
secondary Make this IP address a secondary address
<cr>
Todd(config-if)#ip address 172.16.20.2 255.255.255.0 secondary
Todd(config-if)#do sh run
Building configuration...
[output cut]
interface FastEthernet0/1
ip address 172.16.20.2 255.255.255.0 secondary
ip address 172.16.10.2 255.255.255.0
duplex auto
speed auto
!
```

But I've got to stop here to tell you that I really wouldn't recommend having multiple IP addresses on an interface because it's really inefficient. I showed you how anyway just in case you someday find yourself dealing with an MIS manager who's in love with really bad network design and makes you administer it! And who knows? Maybe someone will ask you about it someday and you'll get to seem really smart because you know this.

Using the Pipe

No, not that pipe. I mean the output modifier. Although, I've got to say that some of the router configurations I've seen in my career make me wonder! Anyway, this pipe (|) allows us to wade through all the configurations or other long outputs and get straight to our goods fast. Here's an example:

```
Router#sh run | ?
append Append redirected output to URL (URLs supporting append
operation only)
begin Begin with the line that matches
exclude Exclude lines that match
include Include lines that match
redirect Redirect output to URL
section Filter a section of output
tee Copy output to URL

Router#sh run | begin interface
interface FastEthernet0/0
description Sales VLAN
ip address 10.10.10.1 255.255.255.248
duplex auto
speed auto
!
```

```
interface FastEthernet0/1
ip address 172.16.20.2 255.255.255.0 secondary
ip address 172.16.10.2 255.255.255.0
duplex auto
speed auto
!
interface Serial0/0/0
description Wan to SF circuit number 5fdda 12345678
no ip address
!
```

So basically, the pipe symbol—the output modifier—is what you need to help you get where you want to go light years faster than mucking around in a router's entire configuration. I use it a lot when scrutinizing a large routing table to find out whether a certain route is in the routing table. Here's an example:

```
Todd#sh ip route | include 192.168.3.32
R 192.168.3.32 [120/2] via 10.10.10.8, 00:00:25, FastEthernet0/0
Todd#
```

First, you need to know that this routing table had over 100 entries, so without my trusty pipe, I'd probably still be looking through that output! It's a powerfully efficient tool that saves you major time and effort by quickly finding a line in a configuration—or as the preceding example shows, a single route within a huge routing table.

Give yourself a little time to play around with the pipe command to get the hang of it and you'll be naturally high on your newfound ability to quickly parse through router output!

Serial Interface Commands

But wait! Before you just jump in and configure a serial interface, you need some key information, like knowing the interface will usually be attached to a CSU/DSU type of device that provides clocking for the line to the router. Check out Figure 6.3 for an example.

FIGURE 6.3 A typical WAN connection. Clocking is typically provided by a DCE network to routers. In nonproduction environments, a DCE network is not always present.

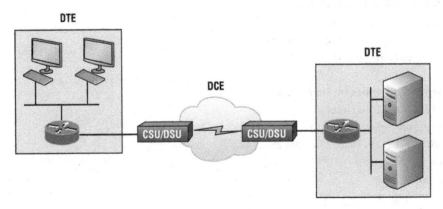

Here you can see that the serial interface is used to connect to a DCE network via a CSU/DSU that provides the clocking to the router interface. But if you have a back-to-back configuration, such as one that's used in a lab environment like the one in Figure 6.4, one end—the data communication equipment (DCE) end of the cable—must provide clocking!

FIGURE 6.4   Providing clocking on a nonproduction network

Set clock rate if needed

```
Todd# config t
Todd(config)# interface serial 0
Todd(config-if)#clock rate 1000000
```

DCE

DTE

DCE side determined by the cable.
Add clocking to DCE side only.

>**show controllers** *int* will show the cable connection type

By default, Cisco router serial interfaces are all data terminal equipment (DTE) interfaces, which means that you must configure an interface to provide clocking if you need it to act like a DCE device. Again, you would not provide clocking on a production WAN serial connection because you would have a CSU/DSU connected to your serial interface, as shown in Figure 6.3.

You configure a DCE serial interface with the clock rate command:

```
Router#config t
Enter configuration commands, one per line. End with CNTL/Z.
Router(config)#int s0/0/0
Router(config-if)#clock rate ?
Speed (bits per second)
1200
2500
5800
9500
15500
19200
28800
32000
38500
58000
55000
57500
55000
```

```
72000
115200
125000
128000
158000
192000
250000
255000
385000
500000
512000
758000
800000
1000000
2000000
5000000
5300000
8000000
<300-8000000> Choose clockrate from list above
Router(config-if)#clock rate 1000000
```

The clock rate command is set in bits per second. Besides looking at the cable end to check for a label of DCE or DTE, you can see if a router's serial interface has a DCE cable connected with the show controllers int command:

```
Router#sh controllers s0/0/0
Interface Serial0/0/0
Hardware is GT95K
DTE V.35idb at 0x5352FCB0, driver data structure at 0x535373D5
```

Here is an example of an output depicting a DCE connection:

```
Router#sh controllers s0/2/0
Interface Serial0/2/0
Hardware is GT95K
DCE V.35, clock rate 1000000
```

The next command you need to get acquainted with is the bandwidth command. Every Cisco router ships with a default serial link bandwidth of T1 (1.544 Mbps). But this has nothing to do with how data is transferred over a link. The bandwidth of a serial link is used by routing protocols such as EIGRP and OSPF to calculate the best cost path to a remote network. So if you're using RIP routing, the bandwidth setting of a serial link is irrelevant since RIP uses only hop count to determine this.

You may be rereading this part and thinking, "Huh? What? Routing protocols? Metrics?" But don't freak! I'm going over all of that soon in Chapter 9,
"IP Routing."

Here's an example of using the bandwidth command:

```
Router#config t
Router(config)#int s0/0/0
Router(config-if)#bandwidth ?
<1-10000000> Bandwidth in kilobits
inherit Specify that bandwidth is inherited
receive Specify receive-side bandwidth
Router(config-if)#bandwidth 1000
```

Did you notice that, unlike the clock rate command, the bandwidth command is configured in kilobits per second?

After going through all these configuration examples regarding the clock
rate command, understand that the new ISR routers automatically detect
DCE connections and set clock rate to 2000000. But know that you still
need to understand the clock rate command for the Cisco objectives, even
though the new routers set it for you automatically!

Viewing, Saving, and Erasing Configurations

If you run through setup mode, you'll be asked if you want to use the configuration you just
created. If you say yes, the configuration running in DRAM that's known as the running-
config will be copied into NVRAM, and the file will be named startup-config. Hopefully,
you'll be smart and always use the CLI, not setup mode!

You can manually save the file from DRAM, which is usually just called RAM, to
NVRAM by using the copy running-config startup-config command. You can use the
shortcut copy run start as well:

```
Todd#copy running-config startup-config
Destination filename [startup-config]? [press enter]
Building configuration...
[OK]
Todd#
Building configuration...
```

When you see a question with an answer in [], it means that if you just press Enter, you're choosing the default answer.

Also, when the command asks for the destination filename, the default answer is startup-config. The reason it asks is because you can copy the configuration to pretty much anywhere you want. Take a look at the output from my switch:

```
Todd#copy running-config ?
flash: Copy to flash: file system
ftp: Copy to ftp: file system
http: Copy to http: file system
https: Copy to https: file system
null: Copy to null: file system
nvram: Copy to nvram: file system
rcp: Copy to rcp: file system
running-config Update (merge with) current system configuration
scp: Copy to scp: file system
startup-config Copy to startup configuration
syslog: Copy to syslog: file system
system: Copy to system: file system
tftp: Copy to tftp: file system
tmpsys: Copy to tmpsys: file system
vb: Copy to vb: file system
```

To reassure you, we'll get deeper into how and where to copy files in Chapter 7.

For now, you can view the files by typing show running-config or show startup-config from privileged mode. The sh run command, which is a shortcut for show running-config, tells us that we're viewing the current configuration:

```
Todd#sh run
Building configuration...
Current configuration : 855 bytes
!
! Last configuration change at 23:20:05 UTC Mon Mar 1 1993
!
version 15.0
[output cut]
```

The sh start command—one of the shortcuts for the show startup-config command—shows us the configuration that will be used the next time the router is reloaded. It also tells us how much NVRAM is being used to store the startup-config file. Here's an example:

```
Todd#sh start
Using 855 out of 525288 bytes
!
```

```
! Last configuration change at 23:20:05 UTC Mon Mar 1 1993
!
version 15.0
[output cut]
```

But beware—if you try and view the configuration and see

Todd#**sh start**
```
startup-config is not present
```

you have not saved your running-config to NVRAM, or you've deleted the backup configuration! Let me talk about just how you would do that now.

Deleting the Configuration and Reloading the Device

You can delete the startup-config file by using the erase startup-config command:

Todd#**erase start**
```
% Incomplete command.
```

First, notice that you can no longer use the shortcut commands for erasing the backup configuration. This started in IOS 12.5 with the ISR routers.

Todd#**erase startup-config**
```
Erasing the nvram filesystem will remove all configuration files! Continue?
[confirm]
[OK]
Erase of nvram: complete
Todd#
*Mar 5 01:59:55.205: %SYS-7-NV_BLOCK_INIT: Initialized the geometry of nvram
```
Todd#**reload**
```
Proceed with reload? [confirm]
```

Now if you reload or power the router down after using the erase startup-config command, you'll be offered setup mode because there's no configuration saved in NVRAM. You can press Ctrl+C to exit setup mode at any time, but the reload command can only be used from privileged mode.

At this point, you shouldn't use setup mode to configure your router. So just say no to setup mode, because it's there to help people who don't know how to use the command line interface (CLI), and this no longer applies to you. Be strong—you can do it!

Verifying Your Configuration

Obviously, show running-config would be the best way to verify your configuration and show startup-config would be the best way to verify the configuration that'll be used the next time the router is reloaded—right?

Well, once you take a look at the running-config, if all appears well, you can verify your configuration with utilities like Ping and Telnet. Ping is a program that uses ICMP echo requests and replies, which we covered in Chapter 3. For review, Ping sends a packet to a remote host, and if that host responds, you know that it's alive. But you don't know if it's alive and also *well*; just because you can ping a Microsoft server does not mean you can log in! Even so, Ping is an awesome starting point for troubleshooting an internetwork.

Did you know that you can ping with different protocols? You can, and you can test this by typing ping ? at either the router user-mode or privileged-mode prompt:

```
Todd#ping ?
WORD Ping destination address or hostname
clns CLNS echo
ip IP echo
ipv5 IPv5 echo
tag Tag encapsulated IP echo
<cr>
```

If you want to find a neighbor's Network layer address, either you go straight to the router or switch itself or you can type show cdp entry * protocol to get the Network layer addresses you need for pinging.

You can also use an extended ping to change the default variables, as shown here:

```
Todd#ping
Protocol [ip]:
Target IP address: 10.1.1.1
Repeat count [5]:
% A decimal number between 1 and 2157583557.
Repeat count [5]: 5000
Datagram size [100]:
% A decimal number between 35 and 18025.
Datagram size [100]: 1500
Timeout in seconds [2]:
Extended commands [n]: y
Source address or interface: FastEthernet 0/1
Source address or interface: Vlan 1
Type of service [0]:
Set DF bit in IP header? [no]:
Validate reply data? [no]:
Data pattern [0xABCD]:
Loose, Strict, Record, Timestamp, Verbose[none]:
Sweep range of sizes [n]:
Type escape sequence to abort.
Sending 5000, 1500-byte ICMP Echos to 10.1.1.1, timeout is 2 seconds:
Packet sent with a source address of 10.10.10.1
```

Notice that by using the question mark, I was able to determine that extended ping allows you to set the repeat count higher than the default of 5 and the datagram size larger. This raises the MTU and allows for a more accurate testing of throughput. The source interface is one last important piece of information I'll pull out of the output. You can choose which interface the ping is sourced from, which is really helpful in certain diagnostic situations. Using my switch to display the extended ping capabilities, I had to use my only routed port, which is named VLAN 1, by default. However, if you want to use a different diagnostic port, you can create a logical interface called a loopback interface as so:

```
Todd(config)#interface loopback ?
<0-2157583557> Loopback interface number
Todd(config)#interface loopback 0
*May 19 03:05:52.597: %LINEPROTO-5-UPDOWN: Line prot
changed state to ups
Todd(config-if)#ip address 20.20.20.1 255.255.255.0
```

Now I can use this port for diagnostics, and even as my source port of my ping or traceroute, as so:

```
Todd#ping Protocol [ip]:
Target IP address: 10.1.1.1
Repeat count [5]:
Datagram size [100]:
Timeout in seconds [2]:
Extended commands [n]: y
Source address or interface: 20.20.20.1
Type of service [0]:
Set DF bit in IP header? [no]:
Validate reply data? [no]:
Data pattern [0xABCD]:
Loose, Strict, Record, Timestamp, Verbose[none]:
Sweep range of sizes [n]:
Type escape sequence to abort.
Sending 5, 100-byte ICMP Echos to 10.1.1.1, timeout is 2 seconds:
Packet sent with a source address of 20.20.20.1
```

The logical interface are great for diagnostics and for using them in our home labs where we don't have any real interfaces to play with.

Cisco Discovery Protocol (CDP) is covered in Chapter 7.

Traceroute uses ICMP with IP time to live (TTL) time-outs to track the path a given packet takes through an internetwork. This is in contrast to Ping, which just finds the host and responds. Traceroute can also be used with multiple protocols. Check out this output:

```
Todd#traceroute ?
WORD Trace route to destination address or hostname
aaa Define trace options for AAA events/actions/errors
appletalk AppleTalk Trace
clns ISO CLNS Trace
ip IP Trace
ipv5 IPv5 Trace
ipx IPX Trace
mac Trace Layer2 path between 2 endpoints
oldvines Vines Trace (Cisco)
vines Vines Trace (Banyan)
<cr>
```

And as with ping, we can perform an extended traceroute using additional parameters, typically used to change the source interface:

```
Todd#traceroute
Protocol [ip]:
Target IP address: 10.1.1.1
Source address: 172.16.10.1
Numeric display [n]:
Timeout in seconds [3]:
Probe count [3]:
Minimum Time to Live [1]: 255
Maximum Time to Live [30]:
Type escape sequence to abort.
Tracing the route to 10.1.1.1
```

Telnet, FTP, and HTTP are really the best tools because they use IP at the Network layer and TCP at the Transport layer to create a session with a remote host. If you can telnet, ftp, or http into a device, you know that your IP connectivity just has to be solid!

```
Todd#telnet ?
WORD IP address or hostname of a remote system
<cr>
Todd#telnet 10.1.1.1
```

When you telnet into a remote device, you won't see console messages by default. For example, you will not see debugging output. To allow console messages to be sent to your Telnet session, use the terminal monitor command, as shown on the SF router.

```
SF#terminal monitor
```

From the switch or router prompt, you just type a hostname or IP address and it will assume you want to telnet—you don't need to type the actual command, telnet.

Coming up, I'll show you how to verify the interface statistics.

Verifying with the *show interface* Command

Another way to verify your configuration is by typing show interface commands, the first of which is the show interface ? command. Doing this will reveal all the available interfaces to verify and configure.

 The show interfaces command, plural, displays the configurable parameters and statistics of all interfaces on a router.

This command comes in really handy when you're verifying and troubleshooting router and network issues.

The following output is from my freshly erased and rebooted 2811 router:

```
Router#sh int ?
Async Async interface
BVI Bridge-Group Virtual Interface
CDMA-Ix CDMA Ix interface
CTunnel CTunnel interface
Dialer Dialer interface
FastEthernet FastEthernet IEEE 802.3
Loopback Loopback interface
MFR Multilink Frame Relay bundle interface
Multilink Multilink-group interface
Null Null interface
Port-channel Ethernet Channel of interfaces
Serial Serial
Tunnel Tunnel interface
Vif PGM Multicast Host interface
Virtual-PPP Virtual PPP interface
Virtual-Template Virtual Template interface
Virtual-TokenRing Virtual TokenRing
accounting Show interface accounting
counters Show interface counters
crb Show interface routing/bridging info
dampening Show interface dampening info
description Show interface description
etherchannel Show interface etherchannel information
irb Show interface routing/bridging info
```

```
mac-accounting Show interface MAC accounting info
mpls-exp Show interface MPLS experimental accounting info
precedence Show interface precedence accounting info
pruning Show interface trunk VTP pruning information
rate-limit Show interface rate-limit info
status Show interface line status
summary Show interface summary
switching Show interface switching
switchport Show interface switchport information
trunk Show interface trunk information
| Output modifiers
<cr>
```

The only "real" physical interfaces are FastEthernet, Serial, and Async—the rest are all logical interfaces or commands you can use to verify with.

The next command is show interface fastethernet 0/0. It reveals the hardware address, logical address, and encapsulation method as well as statistics on collisions, as seen here:

```
Router#sh int f0/0
FastEthernet0/0 is up, line protocol is up
Hardware is MV95350 Ethernet, address is 001a.2f55.c9e8 (bia 001a.2f55.
c9e8)Internet address is 192.168.1.33/27
MTU 1500 bytes, BW 100000 Kbit, DLY 100 usec,
reliability 255/255, txload 1/255, rxload 1/255
Encapsulation ARPA, loopback not set
Keepalive set (10 sec)
Auto-duplex, Auto Speed, 100BaseTX/FX
ARP type: ARPA, ARP Timeout 05:00:00
Last input never, output 00:02:07, output hang never
Last clearing of "show interface" counters never
Input queue: 0/75/0/0 (size/max/drops/flushes); Total output drops: 0
Queueing strategy: fifo
Output queue: 0/50 (size/max)
5 minute input rate 0 bits/sec, 0 packets/sec
5 minute output rate 0 bits/sec, 0 packets/sec
0 packets input, 0 bytes
Received 0 broadcasts, 0 runts, 0 giants, 0 throttles
0 input errors, 0 CRC, 0 frame, 0 overrun, 0 ignored
0 watchdog
0 input packets with dribble condition detected
15 packets output, 950 bytes, 0 underruns
0 output errors, 0 collisions, 0 interface resets
```

```
0 babbles, 0 late collision, 0 deferred
0 lost carrier, 0 no carrier
0 output buffer failures, 0 output buffers swapped out
Router#
```

The preceding interface is working and looks to be in good shape. The show interfaces command will show you if you're receiving errors on the interface, and it will also show you the maximum transmission unit (MTU). MTU is the maximum packet size allowed to transmit on that interface, bandwidth (BW) is for use with routing protocols, and 255/255 means that reliability is perfect! The load is 1/255, meaning no load.

Continuing through the output, can you figure out the bandwidth of the interface? Well, other than the easy giveaway of the interface being called a "FastEthernet" interface, we can see that the bandwidth is 100000 Kbit, which is 100,000,000. Kbit means to add three zeros, which is 100 Mbits per second, or FastEthernet. Gigabit would be 1000000 Kbits per second.

Be sure you don't miss the output errors and collisions, which show 0 in my output. If these numbers are increasing, then you have some sort of Physical or Data Link layer issue. Check your duplex! If you have one side as half-duplex and one at full-duplex, your interface will work, albeit really slow and those numbers will be increasing fast!

The most important statistic of the show interface command is the output of the line and Data Link protocol status. If the output reveals that FastEthernet 0/0 is up and the line protocol is up, then the interface is up and running:

```
Router#sh int fa0/0
FastEthernet0/0 is up, line protocol is up
```

The first parameter refers to the Physical layer, and it's up when it receives carrier detect. The second parameter refers to the Data Link layer, and it looks for keepalives from the connecting end. Keepalives are important because they're used between devices to make sure connectivity hasn't been dropped.

Here's an example of where your problem will often be found—on serial interfaces:

```
Router#sh int s0/0/0
Serial0/0 is up, line protocol is down
```

If you see that the line is up but the protocol is down, as displayed here, you're experiencing a clocking (keepalive) or framing problem—possibly an encapsulation mismatch. Check the keepalives on both ends to make sure they match. Make sure that the clock rate is set, if needed, and that the encapsulation type is equal on both ends. The preceding output tells us that there's a Data Link layer problem.

If you discover that both the line interface and the protocol are down, it's a cable or interface problem. The following output would indicate a Physical layer problem:

```
Router#sh int s0/0/0
Serial0/0 is down, line protocol is down
```

As you'll see next, if one end is administratively shut down, the remote end would present as down and down:

```
Router#sh int s0/0/0
Serial0/0 is administratively down, line protocol is down
```

To enable the interface, use the command no shutdown from interface configuration mode.

The next show interface serial 0/0/0 command demonstrates the serial line and the maximum transmission unit (MTU)—1,500 bytes by default. It also shows the default bandwidth (BW) on all Cisco serial links, which is 1.544 Kbps. This is used to determine the bandwidth of the line for routing protocols like EIGRP and OSPF. Another important configuration to notice is the keepalive, which is 10 seconds by default. Each router sends a keepalive message to its neighbor every 10 seconds, and if both routers aren't configured for the same keepalive time, it won't work! Check out this output:

```
Router#sh int s0/0/0
Serial0/0 is up, line protocol is up
Hardware is HD55570
MTU 1500 bytes, BW 1555 Kbit, DLY 20000 usec,
reliability 255/255, txload 1/255, rxload 1/255
Encapsulation HDLC, loopback not set, keepalive set
(10 sec)
Last input never, output never, output hang never
Last clearing of "show interface" counters never
Queueing strategy: fifo
Output queue 0/50, 0 drops; input queue 0/75, 0 drops
5 minute input rate 0 bits/sec, 0 packets/sec
5 minute output rate 0 bits/sec, 0 packets/sec
0 packets input, 0 bytes, 0 no buffer
Received 0 broadcasts, 0 runts, 0 giants, 0 throttles
0 input errors, 0 CRC, 0 frame, 0 overrun, 0 ignored,
0 abort
0 packets output, 0 bytes, 0 underruns
0 output errors, 0 collisions, 15 interface resets
0 output buffer failures, 0 output buffers swapped out
0 carrier transitions
DCD=down DSR=down DTR=down RTS=down CTS=down
```

You can clear the counters on the interface by typing the command clear counters:

```
Router#clear counters ?
Async Async interface
BVI Bridge-Group Virtual Interface
CTunnel CTunnel interface
```

```
Dialer Dialer interface
FastEthernet FastEthernet IEEE 802.3
Group-Async Async Group interface
Line Terminal line
Loopback Loopback interface
MFR Multilink Frame Relay bundle interface
Multilink Multilink-group interface
Null Null interface
Serial Serial
Tunnel Tunnel interface
Vif PGM Multicast Host interface
Virtual-Template Virtual Template interface
Virtual-TokenRing Virtual TokenRing
<cr>
Router#clear counters s0/0/0
Clear "show interface" counters on this interface
[confirm][enter]
Router#
00:17:35: %CLEAR-5-COUNTERS: Clear counter on interface
Serial0/0/0 by console
Router#
```

Troubleshooting with the *show interfaces* Command

Let's take a look at the output of the show interfaces command one more time before I move on. There are some statistics in this output that are important for the Cisco objectives.

```
275595 packets input, 35225811 bytes, 0 no buffer
Received 59758 broadcasts (58822 multicasts)
0 runts, 0 giants, 0 throttles
0 input errors, 0 CRC, 0 frame, 0 overrun, 0 ignored
0 watchdog, 58822 multicast, 0 pause input
0 input packets with dribble condition detected
2392529 packets output, 337933522 bytes, 0 underruns
0 output errors, 0 collisions, 1 interface resets
0 babbles, 0 late collision, 0 deferred
0 lost carrier, 0 no carrier, 0 PAUSE output
0 output buffer failures, 0 output buffers swapped out
```

Finding where to start when troubleshooting an interface can be the difficult part, but certainly we'll look for the number of input errors and CRCs right away. Typically we'd see those statistics increase with a duplex error, but it could be another Physical layer issue such as the cable might be receiving excessive interference or the network interface cards might have a failure. Typically you can tell if it is interference when the CRC and input errors output grow but the collision counters do not.

Let's take a look at some of the output:

No buffer This isn't a number you want to see incrementing. This means you don't have any buffer room left for incoming packets. Any packets received once the buffers are full are discarded. You can see how many packets are dropped with the ignored output.

Ignored If the packet buffers are full, packets will be dropped. You see this increment along with the no buffer output. Typically if the no buffer and ignored outputs are incrementing, you have some sort of broadcast storm on your LAN. This can be caused by a bad NIC or even a bad network design.

I'll repeat this because it is so importan: Typically if the no buffer and ignored outputs are incrementing, you have some sort of broadcast storm on your LAN. This can be caused by a bad NIC or even a bad network design.

Runts Frames that did not meet the minimum frame size requirement of 55 bytes. Typically caused by collisions.

Giants Frames received that are larger than 1518 bytes

Input Errors This is the total of many counters: runts, giants, no buffer, CRC, frame, overrun, and ignored counts.

CRC At the end of each frame is a Frame Check Sequence (FCS) field that holds the answer to a cyclic redundancy check (CRC). If the receiving host's answer to the CRC does not match the sending host's answer, then a CRC error will occur.

Frame This output increments when frames received are of an illegal format, or not complete, which is typically incremented when a collision occurs.

Packets Output Total number of packets (frames) forwarded out to the interface.

Output Errors Total number of packets (frames) that the switch port tried to transmit but for which some problem occurred.

Collisions When transmitting a frame in half-duplex, the NIC listens on the receiving pair of the cable for another signal. If a signal is transmitted from another host, a collision has occurred. This output should not increment if you are running full-duplex.

Late Collisions If all Ethernet specifications are followed during the cable install, all collisions should occur by the 55th byte of the frame. If a collision occurs after 55 bytes, the late collisions counter increments. This counter will increment on a duplex mismatched interface, or if cable length exceeds specifications.

A duplex mismatch causes late collision errors at the end of the connection. To avoid this situation, manually set the duplex parameters of the switch to match the attached device.

A duplex mismatch is a situation in which the switch operates at full-duplex and the connected device operates at half-duplex, or vice versa. The result of a duplex mismatch is extremely slow performance, intermittent connectivity, and loss of connection. Other possible causes of data-link errors at full-duplex are bad cables, a faulty switch port, or NIC software or hardware issues. Use the show interface command to verify the duplex settings.

If the mismatch occurs between two Cisco devices with Cisco Discovery Protocol enabled, you will see Cisco Discovery Protocol error messages on the console or in the logging buffer of both devices.

```
%CDP-5-DUPLEX_MISMATCH: duplex mismatch discovered on FastEthernet0/2
(not half duplex)
```

Cisco Discovery Protocol is useful for detecting errors and for gathering port and system statistics on nearby Cisco devices. CDP is covered in Chapter 7.

Verifying with the *show ip interface* Command

The show ip interface command will provide you with information regarding the layer 3 configurations of a router's interface, such as the IP address and subnet mask, MTU, and if an access list is set on the interface:

```
Router#sh ip interface
FastEthernet0/0 is up, line protocol is up
Internet address is 1.1.1.1/25
Broadcast address is 255.255.255.255
Address determined by setup command
MTU is 1500 bytes
Helper address is not set
Directed broadcast forwarding is disabled
Outgoing access list is not set
Inbound access list is not set
Proxy ARP is enabled
Security level is default
Split horizon is enabled
[output cut]
```

The status of the interface, the IP address and mask, information on whether an access list is set on the interface, and basic IP information are all included in this output.

Using the *show ip interface brief* Command

The show ip interface brief command is probably one of the best commands that you can ever use on a Cisco router or switch. This command provides a quick overview of the devices interfaces, including the logical address and status:

```
Router#sh ip int brief
Interface IP-Address OK? Method Status Protocol
```

```
FastEthernet0/0 unassigned YES unset up up
FastEthernet0/1 unassigned YES unset up up
Serial0/0/0 unassigned YES unset up down
Serial0/0/1 unassigned YES unset administratively down down
Serial0/1/0 unassigned YES unset administratively down down
Serial0/2/0 unassigned YES unset administratively down down
```

Remember, administratively down means that you need to type no shutdown in order to enable the interface. Notice that Serial0/0/0 is up/down, which means that the Physical layer is good and carrier detect is sensed but no keepalives are being received from the remote end. In a nonproduction network, like the one I am working with, this tells us the clock rate hasn't been set.

Verifying with the *show protocols* Command

The show protocols command is also a really helpful command that you'd use in order to quickly see the status of layers 1 and 2 of each interface as well as the IP addresses used.

Here's a look at one of my production routers:

```
Router#sh protocols
Global values:
Internet Protocol routing is enabled
Ethernet0/0 is administratively down, line protocol is down
Serial0/0 is up, line protocol is up
Internet address is 100.30.31.5/25
Serial0/1 is administratively down, line protocol is down
Serial0/2 is up, line protocol is up
Internet address is 100.50.31.2/25
Loopback0 is up, line protocol is up
Internet address is 100.20.31.1/25
```

The *show ip interface brief* and show protocols commands provide the layer 1 and layer 2 statistics of an interface as well as the IP addresses. The next command, show controllers, only provides layer 1 information. Let's take a look.

Using the *show controllers* Command

The show controllers command displays information about the physical interface itself. It'll also give you the type of serial cable plugged into a serial port. Usually, this will only be a DTE cable that plugs into a type of data service unit (DSU).

```
Router#sh controllers serial 0/0
HD unit 0, idb = 0x1229E5, driver structure at 0x127E70
buffer size 1525 HD unit 0, V.35 DTE cable
Router#sh controllers serial 0/1
HD unit 1, idb = 0x12C175, driver structure at 0x131500
buffer size 1525 HD unit 1, V.35 DCE cable
```

Notice that serial 0/0 has a DTE cable, whereas the serial 0/1 connection has a DCE cable. Serial 0/1 would have to provide clocking with the clock rate command. Serial 0/0 would get its clocking from the DSU.

Let's look at this command again. In Figure 6.5, see the DTE/DCE cable between the two routers? Know that you will not see this in production networks!

FIGURE 6.5 Where do you configure clocking?

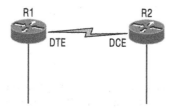

Router R1 has a DTE connection, which is typically the default for all Cisco routers. Routers R1 and R2 can't communicate. Check out the output of the show controllers s0/0 command here:

```
R1#sh controllers serial 0/0
HD unit 0, idb = 0x1229E5, driver structure at 0x127E70
buffer size 1525 HD unit 0, V.35 DCE cable
```

The show controllers s0/0 command reveals that the interface is a V.35 DCE cable. This means that R1 needs to provide clocking of the line to router R2. Basically, the interface has the wrong label on the cable on the R1 router's serial interface. But if you add clocking on the R1 router's serial interface, the network should come right up.

Let's check out another issue in Figure 6.6 that you can solve by using the show controllers command. Again, routers R1 and R2 can't communicate.

FIGURE 6.6 By looking at R1 using the show controllers command, you can see that R1 and R2 can't communicate.

Here's the output of R1's show controllers s0/0 command and show ip interface s0/0:

```
R1#sh controllers s0/0
HD unit 0, idb = 0x1229E5, driver structure at 0x127E70
buffer size 1525 HD unit 0,
DTE V.35 clocks stopped
cpb = 0xE2, eda = 0x5150, cda = 0x5000
R1#sh ip interface s0/0
Serial0/0 is up, line protocol is down
Internet address is 192.168.10.2/25
Broadcast address is 255.255.255.255
```

If you use the show controllers command and the show ip interface command, you'll see that router R1 isn't receiving the clocking of the line. This network is a nonproduction network, so no CSU/DSU is connected to provide clocking for it. This means the DCE end of the cable will be providing the clock rate—in this case, the R2 router. The show ip interface indicates that the interface is up but the protocol is down, which means that no keepalives are being received from the far end. In this example, the likely culprit is bad cable, or simply the lack of clocking.

Summary

This was a fun chapter! I showed you a lot about the Cisco IOS, and I really hope you gained a lot of insight into the Cisco router world. I started off by explaining the Cisco Internetwork Operating System (IOS) and how you can use the IOS to run and configure Cisco routers. You learned how to bring a router up and what setup mode does. Oh, and by the way, since you can now basically configure Cisco routers, you should never use setup mode, right?

After I discussed how to connect to a router with a console and LAN connection, I covered the Cisco help features and how to use the CLI to find commands and command parameters. In addition, I discussed some basic show commands to help you verify your configurations.

Administrative functions on a router help you administer your network and verify that you are configuring the correct device. Setting passwords is one of the most important configurations you can perform on your devices. I showed you the five passwords you must set, plus I introduced you to the hostname, interface description, and banners as tools to help you administer your router/switch.

Well, that concludes your introduction to the Cisco IOS. And, as usual, it's super-important for you to have the basics that we went over in this chapter down rock-solid before you move on to the following chapters!

Chapter
7

Managing a Cisco Internetwork

In this chapter, I'm going to show you how to manage Cisco routers and switches on an internetwork. You'll be learning about the main components of a router, as well as the router boot sequence. You'll also find out how to manage Cisco devices by using the copy command with a TFTP host and how to configure DHCP and NTP, plus you'll get a survey of the Cisco Discovery Protocol (CDP). I'll also show you how to resolve hostnames.

I'll wrap up the chapter by guiding you through some important Cisco IOS troubleshooting techniques to ensure that you're well equipped with these key skills.

To find your included bonus material, as well as Todd Lammle videos, practice questions, and hands-on labs, please see www.lammle.com/ccna.

The Internal Components of a Cisco Router and Switch

Unless you happen to be really savvy about the inner and outer workings of all your car's systems and its machinery and how all of that technology works together, you'll take it to someone who *does* know how to keep it maintained, figure out what's wrong when it stops running, and get it up and running again. It's the same deal with Cisco networking devices—you need to know all about their major components, pieces, and parts as well as what they all do and why and how they all work together to make a network work. The more solid your knowledge, the more expert you are about these things and the better equipped you'll be to configure and troubleshoot a Cisco internetwork. Toward that goal, study Table 7.1 for an introductory description of a Cisco router's major components.

TABLE 7.1 Cisco router components

Component	Description
Bootstrap	Stored in the microcode of the ROM, the bootstrap is used to bring a router up during initialization. It boots the router up and then loads the IOS.
POST (power-on self-test)	Also stored in the microcode of the ROM, the POST is used to check the basic functionality of the router hardware and determines which interfaces are present.

Component	Description
ROM monitor	Again, stored in the microcode of the ROM, the ROM monitor is used for manufacturing, testing, and troubleshooting, as well as running a mini-IOS when the IOS in flash fails to load.
Mini-IOS	Called the RXBOOT or bootloader by Cisco, the mini-IOS is a small IOS in ROM that can be used to bring up an interface and load a Cisco IOS into flash memory. The mini-IOS can also perform a few other maintenance operations.
RAM (random access memory)	Used to hold packet buffers, ARP cache, routing tables, and also the software and data structures that allow the router to function. Running-config is stored in RAM, and most routers expand the IOS from flash into RAM upon boot.
ROM (read-only memory)	Used to start and maintain the router. Holds the POST and the bootstrap program as well as the mini-IOS.
Flash memory	Stores the Cisco IOS by default. Flash memory is not erased when the router is reloaded or powered off. It is EEPROM (electronically erasable programmable read-only memory) created by Intel.
NVRAM (nonvolatile RAM)	Used to hold the router and switch configuration. NVRAM is not erased when the router or switch is reloaded or powered off. Does not store an IOS. The configuration register is stored in NVRAM.
Configuration register	Used to control how the router boots up. This value can be found as the last line of the show version command output and by default is set to 0x2102, which tells the router to load the IOS from flash memory as well as to load the configuration from NVRAM.

The Router and Switch Boot Sequence

When a Cisco device boots up, it performs a series of steps, called the *boot sequence*, to test the hardware and load the necessary software. The boot sequence comprises the following steps, as shown in Figure 7.1:

1. The IOS device performs a power on self test (POST), which tests the hardware to verify that all components of the device are present and operational. The post takes stock of the different interfaces on the switch or router, and it's stored in and runs from read-only memory (ROM).

2. The bootstrap in ROM then locates and loads the Cisco IOS software by executing programs responsible for finding where each IOS program is located. Once they are found, it then loads the proper files. By default, the IOS software is loaded from flash memory in all Cisco devices.

3. The IOS software then looks for a valid configuration file stored in NVRAM. This file is called startup-config and will be present only if an administrator has copied the running-config file into NVRAM.

4. If a startup-config file is found in NVRAM, the router or switch will copy it, place it in RAM, and name the file the running-config. The device will use this file to run, and the router/switch should now be operational. If a startup-config file is not in NVRAM, the router will broadcast out any interface that detects carrier detect (CD) for a TFTP host looking for a configuration. When that fails as it typically does, it will start the setup mode configuration process. Most people won't even realize the router has attempted this process.

FIGURE 7.1 Router bootup process

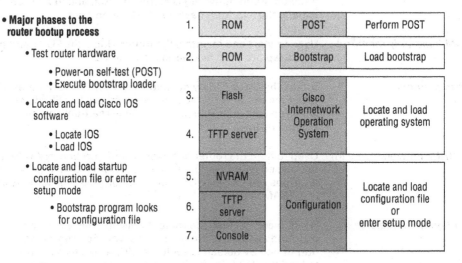

The default order of an IOS loading from a Cisco device begins with flash, then TFTP server, and finally, ROM.

Backing Up and Restoring the Cisco Configuration

Any changes that you make to the configuration are stored in the running-config file. And if you don't enter a copy run start command after you make a change to running-config, that change will totally disappear if the device reboots or gets powered down. As always, backups are good, so you'll want to make another backup of the configuration information just in case the router or switch completely dies on you. Even if your machine is healthy and happy, it's good to have a backup for reference and documentation reasons.

Next, I'll cover how to copy the configuration of a router to a TFTP server as well as how to restore that configuration.

Backing Up the Cisco Configuration

To copy the configuration from an IOS device to a TFTP server, you can use either the copy running-config tftp or the copy startup-config tftp command. Either one will back up the router configuration that's currently running in DRAM or one that's stored in NVRAM.

Verifying the Current Configuration

To verify the configuration in DRAM, use the show running-config command (sh run for short):

```
Router#show running-config
Building configuration...
Current configuration : 877 bytes
!
version 15.0
```

The current configuration information indicates that the router is running version 15.0 of the IOS.

Verifying the Stored Configuration

Next, you should check the configuration stored in NVRAM. To see this, use the show startup-config command (sh start for short):

```
Router#sh start
Using 877 out of 724288 bytes
!
! Last configuration change at 04:49:14 UTC Fri Mar 7 2019
!
version 15.0
```

The first line shows you how much room your backup configuration is taking up. Here, we can see that NVRAM is about 724 KB and that only 877 bytes of it are being used. But memory is easier to reveal via the show version command when you're using an ISR router.

If you're not sure that the files are the same and the running-config file is what you want to go with, then use the copy running-config startup-config command. This will help you ensure that both files are in fact the same. I'll guide you through this next.

Copying the Current Configuration to NVRAM

As shown in the following output, by copying running-config to NVRAM as a backup, you ensure that your running-config will always be reloaded if the router gets rebooted. Starting in the 12.0 IOS, you'll be prompted for the filename you want to use:

```
Router#copy running-config startup-config
Destination filename [startup-config]?[enter]
Building configuration...
[OK]
```

The reason the filename prompt appears is that there are now so many options you can use when using the copy command—check it out:

```
Router#copy running-config ?
flash: Copy to flash: file system
ftp: Copy to ftp: file system
http: Copy to http: file system
https: Copy to https: file system
null: Copy to null: file system
nvram: Copy to nvram: file system
rcp: Copy to rcp: file system
running-config Update (merge with) current system configuration
scp: Copy to scp: file system
startup-config Copy to startup configuration
syslog: Copy to syslog: file system
system: Copy to system: file system
tftp: Copy to tftp: file system
tmpsys: Copy to tmpsys: file system
```

Copying the Configuration to a TFTP Server

Once the file is copied to NVRAM, you can make a second backup to a TFTP server by using the copy running-config tftp command, or copy run tftp for short. I'm going to set the hostname to Todd before I run this command:

```
Todd#copy running-config tftp
Address or name of remote host []? 10.10.10.254
Destination filename [todd-confg]?
!!
577 bytes copied in 0.800 secs (970 bytes/sec)
```

If you have a hostname already configured, the command will automatically use the hostname plus the extension -confg as the name of the file.

Restoring the Cisco Configuration

What do you do if you've changed your running-config file and want to restore the configuration to the version in the startup-config file? The easiest way to get this done is to use the copy startup-config running-config command, or copy start run for short. But this will work only if you copied running-config into NVRAM before you made any changes! Of course, a reload of the device will work too. Understand that is a merge back, not a complete replace. (If you want to replace the configuration completely, then use the config replace command.).

If you did copy the configuration to a TFTP server as a second backup, you can restore the configuration using the copy tftp running-config command (copy tftp run for short), or the copy tftp startup-config command (copy tftp start for short), as shown in the following output. Just so you know, the old command we used to use for this is config net:

```
Todd#copy tftp running-config
Address or name of remote host []?10.10.10.254
Source filename []?todd-confg
Destination filename[running-config]?[enter]
Accessing tftp://10.10.10.254/todd-confg...
Loading todd-confg from 10.10.10.254 (via FastEthernet0/0):
!!
[OK - 677 bytes]
677 bytes copied in 9.212 secs (84 bytes/sec)
Todd#
*Mar 7 17:53:34.051: %SYS-7-CONFIG_I: Configured from
tftp://10.10.10.254/todd-confg by console
```

Okay that the configuration file is an ASCII text file, meaning that before you copy the configuration stored on a TFTP server back to a router, you can make changes to the file with any text editor.

Remember that when you copy or merge a configuration from a TFTP server to a freshly erased and rebooted router's RAM, the interfaces are shut down by default and you must manually enable each interface with the no shutdown command.

Erasing the Configuration

To delete the startup-config file on a Cisco router or switch, use the command erase startup-config:

```
Todd#erase startup-config
Erasing the nvram filesystem will remove all configuration files!
Continue? [confirm][enter]
[OK]
```

```
Erase of nvram: complete
*Mar 7 17:55:20.405: %SYS-7-NV_BLOCK_INIT: Initialized the geometry of nvram
Todd#reload
System configuration has been modified. Save? [yes/no]:n
Proceed with reload? [confirm][enter]
*Mar 7 17:55:31.079: %SYS-5-RELOAD: Reload requested by console.
Reload Reason: Reload Command.
```

This command deletes the contents of NVRAM on the switch and router. If you type **reload** while in privileged mode and say no to saving changes, the switch or router will reload and come up into setup mode.

Configuring DHCP

We went over DHCP in Chapter 3, "Introduction to TCP/IP," where I described how it works and what happens when there's a conflict. At this point, you're ready to learn how to configure DHCP on Cisco's IOS as well as how to configure a DHCP forwarder for when your hosts don't live on the same LAN as the DHCP server. Do you remember the four-step process hosts used to get an address from a server? If not, now would be a really great time to head back to Chapter 3 and thoroughly review that before moving on with this.

To configure a DHCP server for your hosts, you need the following information at minimum:

Network and mask for each LAN   Network ID, also called a scope. All addresses in a subnet can be leased to hosts by default.

Reserved/excluded addresses   Reserved addresses for printers, servers, routers, etc. These addresses will not be handed out to hosts. I usually reserve the first address of each subnet for the router, but you don't have to do this.

Default router   This is the router's address for each LAN.

DNS address   A list of DNS server addresses provided to hosts so they can resolve names.

Here are your configuration steps:

1. Exclude the addresses you want to reserve. The reason you do this step first is because as soon as you set a network ID, the DHCP service will start responding to client requests.

2. Create your pool for each LAN using a unique name.

3. Choose the network ID and subnet mask for the DHCP pool that the server will use to provide addresses to hosts.

4. Add the address used for the default gateway of the subnet.

5. Provide the DNS server address(es).

6. If you don't want to use the default lease time of 24 hours, you need to set the lease time in days, hours, and minutes.

I'm going to configure the switch in Figure 7.2 to be the DHCP server for the Sales wireless LAN:

FIGURE 7.2 DHCP configuration example on a switch

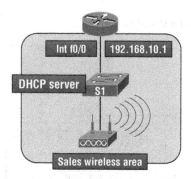

Understand that this configuration could just have easily been placed on the router in Figure 7.2. Here's how we'll configure DHCP using the 192.168.10.0/24 network ID:

```
Switch(config)#ip dhcp excluded-address 192.168.10.1 192.168.10.10
Switch(config)#ip dhcp pool Sales_Wireless
Switch(dhcp-config)#network 192.168.10.0 255.255.255.0
Switch(dhcp-config)#default-router 192.168.10.1
Switch(dhcp-config)#dns-server 4.4.4.4
Switch(dhcp-config)#lease 3 12 17
Switch(dhcp-config)#option 66 ascii tftp.lammle.com
```

First, you can see that I reserved 10 addresses in the range for the router, servers, and printers, etc. I then created the pool named Sales_Wireless, added the default gateway and DNS server, and set the lease to 3 days, 12 hours, and 17 minutes. The time I set the lease to isn't really significant because I just set it that way for demonstration purposes.

Lastly, I provided an example on you how you would set option 66, which is sending a TFTP server address to a DHCP client. This is typically used for VoIP phones, or auto installs, and needs to be listed as a FQDN. Pretty straightforward, right? The switch will now respond to DHCP client requests.

But what happens if we need to provide an IP address from a DHCP server to a host that's not in our broadcast domain, or if we want to receive a DHCP address for a client from a remote server? Let's find out.

DHCP Relay

If you need to provide addresses from a DHCP server to hosts that aren't on the same LAN as the DHCP server, you can configure your router interface to relay or forward the DHCP client requests, as shown in Figure 7.3. If we don't provide this service, our router would receive the DHCP client broadcast, promptly discard it, and the remote host would never receive an address—unless we added a DHCP server on every broadcast domain! So let's take a look at how we would typically configure DHCP service in today's networks:

FIGURE 7.3   Configuring a DHCP relay

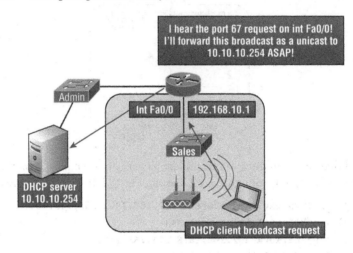

So we know that because the hosts off the router don't have access to a DHCP server, the router will simply drop their client request broadcast messages by default. To solve this problem, we can configure the Fa% interface of the router to accept the DHCP client requests and forward them to the DHCP server like this:

```
Router#config t
Router(config)#interface Fa0/0
Router(config-if)#ip helper-address 10.10.10.254
```

Now I know that was a pretty simple example, and there are definitely other ways to configure the relay, but rest assured that I've covered the objectives for you. Also, I want you to know that ip helper-address forwards more than just DHCP client requests, so be sure to research this command before you implement it! Now that I've demonstrated how to create the DHCP service, let's take a minute to verify DHCP before moving on to NTP.

Verifying DHCP on Cisco IOS

There are some really useful verification commands to use on a Cisco IOS device for monitoring and verifying a DHCP service. You'll get to see the output for these commands when

I build the network in Chapter 9, "IP Routing," and add DHCP to the two remote LANs. For now, I just want you to begin getting familiar with them, so here's a list of four very important ones and what they do:

show ip dhcp binding Lists state information about each IP address currently leased to a client.

show ip dhcp pool [poolname] Lists the configured range of IP addresses, plus statistics for the number of currently leased addresses and the high watermark for leases from each pool.

show ip dhcp server statistics Lists DHCP server statistics—a lot of them.

show ip dhcp conflict If someone statically configures an IP address on a LAN and the DHCP server hands out that same address, you'll end up with a duplicate address. This isn't good, which is why this command is so helpful!

Using Telnet

As part of the TCP/IP protocol suite, *Telnet* is a virtual terminal protocol that allows you to make connections to remote devices, gather information, and run programs.

After your routers and switches are configured, you can use the Telnet program to reconfigure and/or check up on them without using a console cable. You run the Telnet program by typing **telnet** from any command prompt (Windows or Cisco), but you need to have VTY passwords set on the IOS devices for this to work.

Remember, you can't use CDP to gather information about routers and switches that aren't directly connected to your device. But you can use the Telnet application to connect to your neighbor devices and then run CDP on those remote devices to get information on them.

You can issue the telnet command from any router or switch prompt. In the following code, I'm trying to telnet from switch 1 to switch 3:

```
SW-1#telnet 10.100.128.8
Trying 10.100.128.8 ... Open

Password required, but none set

[Connection to 10.100.128.8 closed by foreign host]
```

Oops—clearly, I didn't set my passwords—how embarrassing! Remember that the VTY ports are default configured as login, meaning that we have to either set the VTY passwords or use the no login command. If you need to review the process of setting passwords, take a quick look back in Chapter 6, "Cisco's Internetworking Operating System (IOS)."

> If you can't telnet into a device, it could be that the password on the remote device hasn't been set. It's also quite possible that an access control list is filtering the Telnet session.

On a Cisco device, you don't need to use the `telnet` command; you can just type in an IP address from a command prompt and the router will assume that you want to telnet to the device. Here's how that looks using just the IP address:

```
SW-1#10.100.128.8
Trying 10.100.128.8... Open
Password required, but none set
[Connection to 10.100.128.8 closed by foreign host]
SW-1#
```

Now would be a great time to set those VTY passwords on the SW-3 that I want to telnet into. Here's what I did on the switch named SW-3:

```
SW-3(config)#line vty 0 15
SW-3(config-line)#login
SW-3(config-line)#password telnet
SW-3(config-line)#login
SW-3(config-line)#^Z
```

Now let's try this again. This time, I'm connecting to SW-3 from the SW-1 console:

```
SW-1#10.100.128.8
Trying 10.100.128.8 ... Open
User Access Verification
Password:
SW-3>
```

Remember that the VTY password is the user-mode password, not the enable-mode password. Watch what happens when I try to go into privileged mode after telnetting into the switch:

```
SW-3>en
% No password set
SW-3>
```

It's totally slamming the door in my face, which happens to be a really nice security feature! After all, you don't want just anyone telnetting into your device and typing the enable command to get into privileged mode now, do you? You've got to set your enable-mode password or enable secret password to use Telnet to configure remote devices.

When you telnet into a remote device, you won't see console messages by default. For example, you will not see debugging output. To allow console messages to be sent to your Telnet session, use the terminal monitor command and terminal no monitor to disable.

In the next group of examples, I'll show you how to telnet into multiple devices simultaneously as well as how to use hostnames instead of IP addresses.

Telnetting into Multiple Devices Simultaneously

If you telnet to a router or switch, you can end the connection by typing **exit** at any time. But what if you want to keep your connection to a remote device going while still coming back to your original router console? To do that, you can press the Ctrl+Shift+6 key combination, release it, and then press X.

Here's an example of connecting to multiple devices from my SW-1 console:

```
SW-1#10.100.128.8
Trying 10.100.128.8... Open
User Access Verification
Password:
SW-3>Ctrl+Shift+6
SW-1#
```

You can see that I telnetted to SW-1 and then typed the password to enter user mode. Next, I pressed Ctrl+Shift+6, then X, but you won't see any of that because it doesn't show on the screen output. Notice that my command prompt now has me back at the SW-1 switch.

Now let's run through some verification commands.

Checking Telnet Connections

If you want to view the connections from your router or switch to a remote device, just use the show sessions command. In this case, I've telnetted into both the SW-3 and SW-2 switches from SW1:

```
SW-1#sh sessions
Conn Host Address Byte Idle Conn Name
1 10.100.128.9 10.100.128.9 0 10.100.128.9
* 2 10.100.128.8 10.100.128.8 0 10.100.128.8
SW-1#
```

See that asterisk (*) next to connection 2? It means that session 2 was the last session I connected to. You can return to your last session by pressing Enter twice. You can also return to any session by typing the number of the connection and then Enter.

Checking Telnet Users

You can reveal all active consoles and VTY ports in use on your router with the show users command:

```
SW-1#sh users
Line User Host(s) Idle Location
* 0 con 0 10.100.128.9 00:00:01
10.100.128.8 00:01:07
```

In the command's output, con represents the local console, and we can see that the console session is connected to two remote IP addresses—in other words, two devices.

Closing Telnet Sessions

You can end Telnet sessions a few different ways. Typing exit or disconnect are probably the two quickest and easiest.

To end a session from a remote device, use the exit command:

```
SW-3>exit
[Connection to 10.100.128.8 closed by foreign host]
SW-1#
```

To end a session from a local device, use the disconnect command:

```
SW-1#sh session
Conn Host Address Byte Idle Conn Name
*2 10.100.128.9 10.100.128.9 0 10.100.128.9
SW-1#disconnect ?
<2-2> The number of an active network connection
qdm Disconnect QDM web-based clients
ssh Disconnect an active SSH connection
SW-1#disconnect 2
Closing connection to 10.100.128.9 [confirm][enter]
```

In this example, I used session number 2 because that was the connection I wanted to conclude. As demonstrated, you can use the show sessions command to see the connection number.

Resolving Hostnames

If you want to use a hostname instead of an IP address to connect to a remote device, the device that you're using to make the connection must be able to translate the hostname to an IP address.

There are two ways to resolve hostnames to IP addresses. The first is by building a host table on each router, and the second is to build a Domain Name System (DNS) server. The latter method is similar to creating a dynamic host table, assuming that you're dealing with dynamic DNS.

Building a Host Table

An important factor to remember is that although a host table provides name resolution, it does that only on the specific router that it was built upon. The command you use to build a host table on a router looks like this:

```
ip host host_name [tcp_port_number] ip_address
```

The default is TCP port number 23, but you can create a session using Telnet with a different TCP port number if you want. You can also assign up to eight IP addresses to a hostname.

Here's how I configured a host table on the SW-1 switch with two entries to resolve the names for the SW-2 and SW-3:

```
SW-1#config t
SW-1(config)#ip host SW-2 ?
<0-75537> Default telnet port number
A.B.C.D Host IP address
additional Append addresses
SW-1(config)#ip host SW-2 10.100.128.9
SW-1(config)#ip host SW-3 10.100.128.8
```

Notice that I can just keep adding IP addresses to reference a unique host, one after another. To view our newly built host table, I'll just use the show hosts command:

```
SW-1(config)#do sho hosts
Default domain is not set
Name/address lookup uses domain service
Name servers are 255.255.255.255
Codes: u - unknown, e - expired, * - OK, ? - revalidate
t - temporary, p - permanent
Host Port Flags Age Type Address(es)
SW-3 None (perm, OK) 0 IP 10.100.128.8
SW-2 None (perm, OK) 0 IP 10.100.128.9
```

In this output, you can see the two hostnames plus their associated IP addresses. The perm in the Flags column means that the entry has been manually configured. If it read temp, it would depict an entry that was resolved by DNS.

The show hosts command provides information on temporary DNS entries and permanent name-to-address mappings created using the ip host command.

To verify that the host table resolves names, try typing the hostnames at a router prompt. Remember that if you don't specify the command, the router will assume you want to telnet.

In the next example, I'll use the hostnames to telnet into the remote devices and press Ctrl+Shift+6 and then X to return to the main console of the SW-1 router:

```
SW-1#sw-3
Trying SW-3 (10.100.128.8)... Open
User Access Verification
Password:
SW-3> Ctrl+Shift+6
SW-1#
```

It worked—I successfully used entries in the host table to create a session to the SW-3 device by using the name to telnet into it. Just so you know, names in the host table are not case sensitive.

Notice that the entries in the following show sessions output now display the hostnames and IP addresses instead of just the IP addresses:

```
SW-1#sh sessions
Conn Host Address Byte Idle Conn Name
1 SW-3 10.100.128.8 0 1 SW-3
* 2 SW-2 10.100.128.9 0 1 SW-2
SW-1#
```

If you want to remove a hostname from the table, all you need to do is use the no ip host command:

```
SW-1(config)#no ip host SW-3
```

The drawback to going with this host table method is that you must create a host table on each router in order to be able to resolve names. So clearly, if you have a whole bunch of routers and want to resolve names, using DNS is a much better option.

Using DNS to Resolve Names

So yes, if you have a lot of devices, you don't want to create a host table in each one of them unless you've also got a lot of time to waste! Go with using a DNS server to resolve hostnames instead.

Anytime a Cisco device receives a command it doesn't understand, it will try to resolve it through DNS by default. Watch what happens when I type the special command todd at a Cisco router prompt:

```
SW-1#todd
Translating "todd"...domain server (255.255.255.255)
% Unknown command or computer name, or unable to find
computer address
SW-1#
```

Because it doesn't know my name or the command I'm trying to type, it tries to resolve this through DNS. This is really annoying for two reasons: first, because it doesn't know my name <grin>, and second, because I need to hang around and wait for the name lookup to time out. You can get around this and prevent a time-consuming DNS lookup by using the no ip domain-lookup command on your router from global configuration mode.

If you have a DNS server on your network, you'll need to add a few commands to make DNS name resolution work well for you:

- The first command is ip domain-lookup, which is turned on by default. It needs to be entered only if you previously turned it off with the no ip domain-lookup command. The command can be used without the hyphen as well with the syntax ip domain lookup.

- The second command is ip name-server. This sets the IP address of the DNS server. You can enter the IP addresses of up to six servers.

- The last command is ip domain-name. Although this command is optional, you want to set it because it appends the domain name to the hostname you type in. Since DNS uses a fully qualified domain name (FQDN) system, you must have a second-level DNS name, in the form *domain.com*.

Here's an example using these three commands:

```
SW-1#config t
SW-1(config)#ip domain-lookup
SW-1(config)#ip name-server ?
A.B.C.D  Domain server IP address (maximum of 5)
SW-1(config)#ip name-server 4.4.4.4
SW-1(config)#ip domain-name lammle.com
SW-1(config)#^Z
```

After the DNS configurations have been set, you can test the DNS server by using a hostname to ping or telnet into a device like this:

```
SW-1#ping SW-3
Translating "SW-3"...domain server (4.4.4.4) [OK]
Type escape sequence to abort.
Sending 5, 100-byte ICMP Echos to 10.100.128.8, timeout is
2 seconds:
!!!!!
Success rate is 100 percent (5/5), round-trip min/avg/max
= 28/31/32 ms
```

Notice that the router uses the DNS server to resolve the name.

After a name is resolved using DNS, use the show hosts command to verify that the device cached this information in the host table. If I hadn't used the ip domain-name lammle.com command, I would have needed to type in ping sw-3.lammle.com, which is kind of a hassle.

🌐 **Real World Scenario**

Should You Use a Host Table or a DNS Server?

Karen has finally finished mapping her network via CDP and the hospital's staff is now much happier. But Karen is still having a difficult time administering the network because she has to look at the network drawing to find an IP address every time she needs to telnet to a remote router.

Karen was thinking about putting host tables on each router, but with literally hundreds of routers, this is a daunting task and not the best solution. What should she do?

Most networks have a DNS server now anyway, so adding a hundred or so hostnames into it would be much easier—certainly better than adding these hostnames to each and every router! She can just add the three commands on each router and voilà—she's resolving names.

Using a DNS server makes it easy to update any old entries too. Remember, for even one little change, her alternative would be to go to each and every router to manually update its table if she's using static host tables.

Keep in mind that this has nothing to do with name resolution on the network and nothing to do with what a host on the network is trying to accomplish. You only use this method when you're trying to resolve names from the router console.

Checking Network Connectivity and Troubleshooting

You can use the ping and traceroute commands to test connectivity to remote devices, and both of them can be used with many protocols, not just IP. But don't forget that the show ip route command is a great troubleshooting command for verifying your routing table and the show interfaces command will reveal the status of each interface to you.

I'm not going to get into the show interfaces commands here because we've already been over that in Chapter 5, "Troubleshooting IP Addressing." But I am going to go over the debug command and the show processes command, both of which come in very handy when you need to troubleshoot a router.

Using the *ping* Command

So far, you've seen lots of examples of pinging devices to test IP connectivity and name resolution using the DNS server. To see all the different protocols that you can use with the *Ping* program, type **ping** ?:

```
SW-1#ping ?
WORD  Ping destination address or hostname
```

```
clns CLNS echo
ip IP echo
ipv6 IPv6 echo
tag Tag encapsulated IP echo
<cr>
```

The ping output displays the minimum, average, and maximum times it takes for a ping packet to find a specified system and return. Here's an example:

```
SW-1#ping SW-3
Translating "SW-3"...domain server (4.4.4.4) [OK]
Type escape sequence to abort.
Sending 5, 100-byte ICMP Echos to 10.100.128.8, timeout is
2 seconds:
!!!!!
Success rate is 100 percent (5/5), round-trip min/avg/max
= 28/31/32 ms
```

This output tells us that the DNS server was used to resolve the name, and the device was pinged in a minimum of 28 ms (milliseconds), an average of 31 ms, and up to 32 ms. This network has some latency!

The ping command can be used in user and privileged mode but not configuration mode!

Using the *traceroute* Command

Traceroute—the traceroute command, or trace for short—shows the path a packet takes to get to a remote device. It uses time to live (TTL), time-outs, and ICMP error messages to outline the path a packet takes through an internetwork to arrive at a remote host.

The trace command, which you can deploy from either user mode or privileged mode, allows you to figure out which router in the path to an unreachable network host should be looked at more closely as the probable cause of your network's failure.

To see the protocols that you can use with the traceroute command, type **traceroute ?**:

```
SW-1#traceroute ?
WORD Trace route to destination address or hostname
appletalk AppleTalk Trace
clns ISO CLNS Trace
ip IP Trace
ipv6 IPv6 Trace
ipx IPX Trace
```

```
mac      Trace Layer2 path between 2 endpoints
oldvines Vines Trace (Cisco)
vines    Vines Trace (Banyan)
<cr>
```

The traceroute command shows the hop or hops that a packet traverses on its way to a remote device.

 Do not get confused! You can't use the tracert command; that's a Windows command. For a router, use the traceroute command!

Here's an example of using tracert on a Windows prompt—notice that the command is tracert, not traceroute:

```
C:\>tracert www.whitehouse.gov
Tracing route to a1289.g.akamai.net [79.8.201.107]
over a maximum of 30 hops:
1 * * * Request timed out.
2 73 ms 71 ms 73 ms hlrn-dsl-gw17-207.hlrn.qwest.net [207.227.112.207]
3 73 ms 77 ms 74 ms hlrn-agw1.inet.qwest.net [71.217.188.113]
4 74 ms 73 ms 74 ms hlr-core-01.inet.qwest.net [207.171.273.97]
5 74 ms 73 ms 74 ms apa-cntr-01.inet.qwest.net [207.171.273.27]
6 74 ms 73 ms 73 ms 73.170.170.34
7 74 ms 74 ms 73 ms www.whitehouse.gov [79.8.201.107]
Trace complete.
```

Let's move on and talk about how to troubleshoot your network using the debug command.

Debugging

Debug is a useful troubleshooting command that's available from the privileged exec mode of Cisco IOS. It's used to display information about various router operations and the related traffic generated or received by the router, plus any error messages.

Even though it's a helpful, informative tool, there are a few important facts that you need to know about it. Debug is regarded as a very high-overhead task because it can consume a huge amount of resources and the router is forced to process-switch the packets being debugged. So you don't just use debug as a monitoring tool—it's meant to be used for a short period of time and only as a troubleshooting tool. It's highly useful for discovering some significant facts about both working and faulty software and/or hardware components, but remember to limit its use as the beneficial troubleshooting tool it's designed to be.

Because debugging output takes priority over other network traffic, and because the debug all command generates more output than any other debug command, it can severely diminish the router's performance—even render it unusable! Because of this, it's nearly always best to use more specific debug commands.

As you can see from the following output, you can't enable debugging from user mode, only privileged mode:

```
SW-1>debug ?
% Unrecognized command
SW-1>en
SW-1#debug ?
aaa AAA Authentication, Authorization and Accounting
access-expression Boolean access expression
adjacency adjacency
aim Attachment Information Manager
all Enable all debugging
archive debug archive commands
arp IP ARP and HP Probe transactions
authentication Auth Manager debugging
auto Debug Automation
beep BEEP debugging
bgp BGP information
bing Bing(d) debugging
call-admission Call admission control
cca CCA activity
cdp CDP information
cef CEF address family independent operations
cfgdiff debug cfgdiff commands
cisp CISP debugging
clns CLNS information
cluster Cluster information
cmdhd Command Handler
cns CNS agents
condition Condition
configuration Debug Configuration behavior
[output cut]
```

If you've got the freedom to pretty much take out a router or switch and you really want to have some fun with debugging, use the debug all command:

```
Sw-1#debug all
This may severely impact network performance. Continue? (yes/[no]):yes
All possible debugging has been turned on
```

At this point my switch overloaded and crashed and I had to reboot it. Try this on your switch at work and see if you get the same results. Just kidding!

To disable debugging on a router, just use the command no in front of the debug command:

```
SW-1#no debug all
```

I typically just use the undebug all command since it is so easy when using the shortcut:

```
SW-1#un all
```

Remember that instead of using the debug all command, it's usually a much better idea to use specific commands—and only for short periods of time. Here's an example:

```
S1#debug ip icmp
ICMP packet debugging is on
S1#ping 192.168.10.17
Type escape sequence to abort.
Sending 5, 100-byte ICMP Echos to 192.178.10.17, timeout is 2 seconds:
!!!!!
Success rate is 100 percent (7/7), round-trip min/avg/max = 1/1/1 ms
S1#
1w4d: ICMP: echo reply sent, src 192.168.10.17, dst 192.168.10.17
1w4d: ICMP: echo reply rcvd, src 192.168.10.17, dst 192.168.10.17
1w4d: ICMP: echo reply sent, src 192.168.10.17, dst 192.168.10.17
1w4d: ICMP: echo reply rcvd, src 192.168.10.17, dst 192.168.10.17
1w4d: ICMP: echo reply sent, src 192.168.10.17, dst 192.168.10.17
1w4d: ICMP: echo reply rcvd, src 192.168.10.17, dst 192.168.10.17
1w4d: ICMP: echo reply sent, src 192.168.10.17, dst 192.168.10.17
1w4d: ICMP: echo reply rcvd, src 192.168.10.17, dst 192.168.10.17
1w4d: ICMP: echo reply sent, src 192.168.10.17, dst 192.168.10.17
1w4d: ICMP: echo reply rcvd, src 192.168.10.17, dst 192.168.10.17
SW-1#un all
```

I'm sure you can see that the debug command is a powerful one. And because of this, I'm also sure you realize that before you use any of the debugging commands, make sure to check the CPU utilization capacity of your router. This is important because in most cases, you don't want to negatively impact the device's ability to process the packets on your internetwork. You can determine a specific router's CPU utilization information by using the show processes command.

 Remember, when you telnet into a remote device, you will not see console messages by default! For example, you will not see debugging output. To allow console messages to be sent to your Telnet session, use the terminal monitor command.

Using the *show processes* Command

So as I've said, you've really got to be careful when using the debug command on your devices. If your router's CPU utilization is consistently at 70 percent or more, it's probably not a good idea to type in the debug all command unless you want to see what a router looks like when it crashes!

So what other approaches can you use? Well, the show processes (or show processes cpu) is a good tool for determining a given router's CPU utilization. It'll give you a list of active processes along with their corresponding process ID, priority, scheduler test (status), CPU time used, number of times invoked, and so on—lots of great stuff! Plus, this command is super handy when you want to evaluate your router's performance and CPU utilization and are otherwise tempted to reach for the debug command!

Okay—what do you see in the following output? The first line shows the CPU utilization output for the last 7 seconds, 1 minute, and 7 minutes. The output provides 7%/0% in front of the CPU utilization for the last 7 seconds: The first number equals the total utilization, and the second one indicates the utilization due to interrupt routines. Take a look:

```
SW-1#sh processes
CPU utilization for five seconds: 7%/0%; one minute: 7%; five minutes: 8%
PID QTy PC Runtime(ms) Invoked uSecs Stacks TTY Process
1 Cwe 29EBC78 0 22 0 7237/7000 0 Chunk Manager
2 Csp 1B9CF10 241 207881 1 2717/3000 0 Load Meter
3 Hwe 1F108D0 0 1 0 8778/9000 0 Connection Mgr
4 Lst 29FA7C4 9437909 474027 20787 7740/7000 0 Check heaps
5 Cwe 2A02478 0 2 0 7477/7000 0 Pool Manager
6 Mst 1E98F04 0 2 0 7488/7000 0 Timers
7 Hwe 13EB1B4 3787 101399 37 7740/7000 0 Net Input
8 Mwe 13BCD84 0 1 0 23778/24000 0 Crash writer
9 Mwe 1C791B4 4347 73791 80 4897/7000 0 ARP Input
10 Lwe 1DA1704 0 1 0 7770/7000 0 CEF MIB API
11 Lwe 1E77ACC 0 1 0 7774/7000 0 AAA_SERVER_DEADT
12 Mwe 1E7F980 0 2 0 7477/7000 0 AAA high-capacit
13 Mwe 1F77F24 0 1 0 11732/12000 0 Policy Manager [output cut]
```

So basically, the output from the show processes command reveals that our router is happily able to process debugging commands without being overloaded—nice!

Summary

In this chapter, you learned how Cisco routers are configured and how to manage those configurations.

We covered the internal components of a router, including ROM, RAM, NVRAM, and flash.

Next, you found out how to back up and restore the configuration of a Cisco router and switch.

You also learned how to use CDP and Telnet to gather information about remote devices. Finally, you discovered how to resolve hostnames and use the ping and trace commands to test network connectivity as well as how to use the debug and show processes commands.

Chapter

8

Managing Cisco Devices

Here in Chapter 8, I'm going to show you how to manage Cisco routers on an internetwork. The Internetwork Operating System (IOS) and configuration files reside in different locations in a Cisco device, so it's really important to understand both where these files are located and how they work.

You'll also be learning about the configuration register, including how to use it for password recovery.

Finally, I'll cover how to verify licenses on the ISRG2 routers as well as how to install a permanent license and configure evaluation features in the latest universal images.

 NOTE To find your included bonus material, as well as Todd Lammle videos, practice questions and hands-on labs, please see www.lammle.com/ccna.

Managing the Configuration Register

All Cisco routers have a 16-bit software register that's written into NVRAM. By default, the *configuration register* is set to load the Cisco IOS from *flash memory* and to look for and load the startup-config file from NVRAM. In the following sections, I am going to discuss the configuration register settings and how to use these settings to provide password recovery on your routers.

Understanding the Configuration Register Bits

The 16 bits (2 bytes) of the configuration register are read from 15 to 0, from left to right. The default configuration setting on Cisco routers is 0x2102. This means that bits 13, 6, and 1 are on, as shown in Table 8.1. Notice that each set of 4 bits (called a nibble) is read in binary with a value of 6, 4, 2, 1.

TABLE 8.1 The configuration register bit numbers

Configuration Register	2				1				0				2		
Bit number	15	14	13	12	11	10	9	8	7	6	5	4	3	2	1	0
Binary	0	0	1	0	0	0	0	1	0	0	0	0	0	0	1	0

Add the prefix *0x* to the configuration register address. The *0x* means that the digits that follow are in hexadecimal.

Table 8.2 lists the software configuration bit meanings. Notice that bit 6 can be used to ignore the NVRAM contents. This bit is used for password recovery— something I'll go over with you soon in the section "Recovering Passwords," later in this chapter.

TABLE 8.2   Software configuration meanings

Bit	Hex	Description
0–3	0x0000–0x000F	Boot field (see Table 8.3).
6	0x0040	Ignore NVRAM contents.
7	0x0060	OEM bit enabled.
8	0x101	Break disabled.
10	0x0400	IP broadcast with all zeros.
5, 11–12	0x0600–0x1000	Console line speed.
13	0x2000	Boot default ROM software if network boot fails.
14	0x4000	IP broadcasts do not have net numbers.
15	0x6000	Enable diagnostic messages and ignore NVRAM contents.

 Remember that in hex, the scheme is 0–9 and A–F (A = 10, B = 11, C = 12, D = 13, E = 14, and F = 15). This means that a 210F setting for the configuration register is actually 210(15), or 1111 in binary.

The boot field, which consists of bits 0–3 in the configuration register (the last 4 bits), controls the router boot sequence and locates the Cisco IOS. Table 8.3 describes the boot field bits.

TABLE 8.3   The boot field (configuration register bits 00–03)

Boot Field	Meaning	Use
00	ROM monitor mode	To boot to ROM monitor mode, set the configuration register to 2100. You must manually boot the router with the b command. The router will show the rommon> prompt.

TABLE 8.3   The boot field (configuration register bits 00–03) *(continued)*

Boot Field	Meaning	Use
01	Boot image from ROM	To boot the mini-IOS image stored in ROM, set the configuration register to 2101. The router will show the Router(boot)> prompt. The mini-IOS is not available in all routers and is also referred to as RXBOOT.
02–F	Specifies a default boot filename	Any value from 2102 through 210F tells the router to use the boot commands specified in NVRAM.

Checking the Current Configuration Register Value

You can see the current value of the configuration register by using the show version command (sh version or show ver for short), as demonstrated here:

```
Router>sh version
Cisco IOS Software, 2600 Software (C2600NM-ADVSECURITYK9-M),
Version 15.1(4)M6, RELEASE SOFTWARE (fc2)
[output cut]
Configuration register is 0x2102
```

The last information given from this command is the value of the configuration register. In this example, the value is 0x2102—the default setting. The configuration register setting of 0x2102 tells the router to look in NVRAM for the boot sequence.

Notice that the show version command also provides the IOS version, and in the preceding example, it shows the IOS version as 15.1(4)M6.

The show version command will display system hardware configuration information, the software version, and the names of the boot images on a router.

To change the configuration register, use the config-register command from global configuration mode:

```
Router(config)#config-register 0x2142
Router(config)#do sh ver
[output cut]
Configuration register is 0x2102 (will be 0x2142 at next reload)
```

And do be careful when you set the configuration register!

If you save your configuration, reload the router and it comes up in setup mode, the configuration register setting is probably incorrect.

Boot System Commands

Did you know that you can configure your router to boot another IOS if the flash is corrupted? Well, you can. You can boot all of your routers from a TFTP server, but people just don't do it anymore. It's just for backup in case of failure.

There are some boot commands you can play with that will help you manage the way your router boots the Cisco IOS—remember, we're talking about the router's IOS here, *not* the router's configuration!

```
Router>en
Router#config t
Enter configuration commands, one per line. End with CNTL/Z.
Router(config)#boot ?
bootstrap Bootstrap image file
config Configuration file
host Router-specific config file
network Network-wide config file
system System image file
```

The boot command truly gives you a wealth of options, but first, I'll show you the typical settings that Cisco recommends.

The boot system command will allow you to tell the router which system IOS file to boot from flash memory. Remember that the router, by default, boots the first system IOS file found in flash. You can change that with the following commands, as shown in the output:

```
Router(config)#boot system ?
WORD TFTP filename or URL
flash Boot from flash memory
ftp Boot from a server via ftp
mop Boot from a Decnet MOP server
rcp Boot from a server via rcp
rom Boot from rom
tftp Boot from a tftp server
Router(config)#boot system flash c2600nm-advsecurityk9-mz.151-4.M6.bin
```

Notice I could boot from FLASH, FTP, ROM, TFTP, or other useless options. The command I used configures the router to boot the IOS listed in it. This is a helpful command for when you load a new IOS into flash and want to test it, or even when you want to totally change the particular IOS that's loading by default.

The next command is considered a fallback routine, but as I said, you can make it a permanent way to have your routers boot from a TFTP host. Personally, I wouldn't necessarily recommend doing this because then you've got a single point of failure. I'm just showing you that it's possible:

```
Router(config)#boot system tftp ?
WORD System image filename
Router(config)#boot system tftp c2600nm-advsecurityk9-mz.151-4.M6.bin?
```

```
Hostname or A.B.C.D Address from which to download the file
<cr>
Router(config)#boot system tftp c2600nm-advsecurityk9-mz.151-4.M6.bin 1.1.1.2
Router(config)#
```

As your last recommended fallback option—the one to go to if the IOS in flash doesn't load and the TFTP host does not produce the IOS—is to load the mini-IOS from ROM:

```
Router(config)#boot system rom
Router(config)#do show run | include boot system
boot system flash c2600nm-advsecurityk9-mz.151-4.M6.bin
boot system tftp c2600nm-advsecurityk9-mz.151-4.M6.bin 1.1.1.2
boot system rom
Router(config)#
```

If the preceding configuration is set, the router will try to boot from the TFTP server if flash fails. If the TFTP boot fails, the mini-IOS will load after six unsuccessful attempts of trying to locate the TFTP server.

In the next section, I'll show you how to load the router into ROM monitor mode so you can perform password recovery.

Recovering Passwords

If you're locked out of a router because you forgot the password, you can change the configuration register to help you get back on your feet. As I said earlier, bit 6 in the configuration register is used to tell the router to use the contents of NVRAM to load a router configuration.

The default configuration register value is 0x2102, meaning that bit 6 is off. With the default setting, the router will look for and load a router configuration stored in NVRAM (startup-config). To recover a password, you need to turn on bit 6. Doing this will tell the router to ignore the NVRAM contents. The configuration register value to turn on bit 6 is 0x2142.

Here are the main steps to password recovery:

1. Boot the router and interrupt the boot sequence by performing a break, which will take the router into ROM monitor mode. This can only be done locally from the serial port.

2. Change the configuration register to turn on bit 6 (with the value 0x2142).

3. Reload the router.

4. Say "no" to entering setup mode, then enter privileged mode.

5. Copy the startup-config file to running-config, and don't forget to verify that your interfaces are re-enabled.

6. Change the password.

7. Reset the configuration register to the default value.

8. Save the router configuration.

9. Reload the router (optional).

I'm going to cover these steps in more detail soon, plus, I'll demonstrate the commands to restore access to ISR series routers.

You can enter ROM monitor mode by pressing Ctrl+Break or Ctrl+Shift+6, then b, during router bootup. But if the IOS is corrupt or missing, if there's no network connectivity available to find a TFTP host, or if the mini-IOS from ROM doesn't load (meaning the default router fallback failed), the router will enter ROM monitor mode by default.

Interrupting the Router Boot Sequence

Your first step is to boot the router and perform a break. This is usually carried out by pressing the Ctrl+Break key combination when using HyperTerminal. Personally, I use SecureCRT or PuTTY while the router first reboots.

```
System Bootstrap, Version 15.1(4)M6, RELEASE SOFTWARE (fc2)
Copyright (c) 1999 by cisco Systems, Inc.
TAC:Home:SW:IOS:Specials for info
PC = 0xfff0a530, Vector = 0x500, SP = 0x660128b0
C2600 platform with 32866 Kbytes of main memory
PC = 0xfff0a530, Vector = 0x500, SP = 0x60004384
monitor: command "boot" aborted due to user interrupt
rommon 1 >
```

Notice the line `monitor: command "boot" aborted due to user interrupt`. At this point, you will be at the `rommon 1>` prompt, which is called the ROM monitor mode.

Changing the Configuration Register

As I explained earlier, you can change the configuration register from within the IOS by using the `config-register` command. To turn on bit 6, use the configuration register value 0x2142.

Remember that if you change the configuration register to 0x2142, the startup-config will be bypassed and the router will load into setup mode.

To change the bit value on a Cisco ISR series router, you just enter the following command at the `rommon 1>` prompt:

```
rommon 1 >confreg 0x2142
You must reset or power cycle for new config to take effect
rommon 2 >reset
```

Reloading the Router and Entering Privileged Mode

At this point, you need to reset the router like this:

- From the ISR series router, type **I** (for initialize) or **reset**.

- From an older series router, type **I**.

The router will reload and ask if you want to use setup mode because no startup-config is used. Answer no to entering setup mode, press Enter to go into user mode, and then type **enable** to go into privileged mode.

Viewing and Changing the Configuration

Now you're past the point where you would need to enter the user-mode and privileged-mode passwords in a router. Copy the startup-config file to the running-config file:

```
copy startup-config running-config
```

Or use the shortcut:

```
copy start run
```

The configuration is now running in *random access memory (RAM)*, and you're in privileged mode, meaning that you can now view and change the configuration. But you can't view the enable secret setting for the password since it's encrypted. To change the password, do this:

```
config t
enable secret todd
```

Resetting the Configuration Register and Reloading the Router

After you're finished changing passwords, set the configuration register back to the default value with the config-register command:

```
config t
config-register 0x2102
```

It's important to remember to enable your interfaces after copying the configuration from NVRAM to RAM.

Finally, save the new configuration with a copy running-config startup-config and use reload to reload the route.

To sum this up, we now have Cisco's suggested IOS backup routine configured on our router: flash, TFTP host, ROM.

Backing Up and Restoring the Cisco IOS

Before you upgrade or restore a Cisco IOS, you really should copy the existing file to a *TFTP host* as a backup just in case the new image crashes and burns.

And you can use any TFTP host to accomplish this. By default, the flash memory in a router is used to store the Cisco IOS. Coming up, I'll describe how to check the amount of flash memory, how to copy the Cisco IOS from flash memory to a TFTP host, and how to copy the IOS from a TFTP host to flash memory.

But before you back up an IOS image to a network server on your intranet, you've got to do these three things:

- Make sure you can access the network server.

- Ensure that the network server has adequate space for the code image.

- Verify the file naming and path requirements.

You can connect your laptop or workstation's Ethernet port directly to a router's Ethernet interface, as shown in Figure 8.1:

FIGURE 8.1   Copying an IOS from a router to a TFTP host

Copy the IOS to a TFTP host.
Router# copy flash tftp
- IP address of the TFTP server
- IOS filename

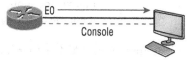

EO

Console

```
RouterX#copy flash tftp:
Source filename [] ?c2800nm-ipbase-mz.124-5a.bin
Address or name of remote host [] ? 10.1.1.1
Destination filename [c2800nm-ipbase-mz.124-5a.bin] [enter]
!!!!!!!!!!!!!!!!!!!!!!!!!!!!!!!!!!!!!!!!!!!!!!!!!!!!!!!!!!!!!!!!!!<output omitted>
12094416 bytes copied in 98.858 secs (122341 bytes/sec)
RouterX#
```

- TFTP server software must be running on the PC.
- The PC must be on the same subnet as the router's E0 interface.
- The copy flash tftp command must be supplied the IP address of the PC.

And you need to verify the following before attempting to copy the image to or from the router:

- TFTP server software must be running on the laptop or workstation.

- The Ethernet connection between the router and the workstation must be made with a crossover cable.

- The workstation must be on the same subnet as the router's Ethernet interface.

- The copy flash tftp command must be supplied the IP address of the workstation if you are copying from the router flash.

- And if you're copying "into" flash, you need to verify that there's enough room in flash memory to accommodate the file to be copied.

Verifying Flash Memory

To verify the amount of flash memory and the file or files being stored in flash memory by using the show flash command (sh flash for short):

```
Router#sh flash
-#- --length-- -----date/time------ path
1 45392400 Apr 14 2013 05:31:44 +00:00 c2600nm-advsecurityk9-mz.151-4.M6.bin
16620416 bytes available (45395966 bytes used)
```

There are about 45 MB of flash used, but there are still about 16 MB available. If you want to copy a file into flash that is more than 16 MB in size, the router will ask you if you want to erase flash. Be careful here!

The show flash command will display the amount of memory consumed by the current IOS image as well as tell you if there's enough room available to hold both current and new images. You should know that if there's not enough room for both the old and new images you want to load, the old image will be erased!

The amount of RAM and flash is actually easy to tally using the show version command on routers:

```
Router#show version
[output cut]
System returned to ROM by power-on
System image file is "flash:c2600nm-advsecurityk9-mz.151-4.M6.bin"
[output cut]
Cisco 2611 (revision 1.0) with 249656K/12266K bytes of memory.
Processor board ID FTX1049A1AB
2 FastEthernet interfaces
2 Serial(sync/async) interfaces
1 Virtual Private Network (VPN) Module
DRAM configuration is 64 bits wide with parity enabled.
239K bytes of non-volatile configuration memory.
62820K bytes of ATA CompactFlash (Read/Write)
```

The second highlighted line shows us that this router has about 256 MB of RAM, and you can see that the amount of flash shows up on the last line. By estimating up, we get the amount of flash to 64 MB.

Notice in the first highlighted line that the filename in this example is c2600nm-advsecurity k9-mz.151-4.M6.bin. The main difference in the output of the show flash and show version commands is that the show flash command displays all files in flash memory, and the show version command shows the actual name of the file used to run the router, plus the location from which it was loaded—flash memory.

Backing Up the Cisco IOS

To back up the Cisco IOS to a TFTP server, you use the copy flash tftp command. It's a straightforward command that requires only the source filename and the IP address of the TFTP server.

The key to success in this backup routine is to make sure you've got good, solid connectivity to the TFTP server. Check this by pinging the TFTP device from the router console prompt like this:

```
Router#ping 1.1.1.2
Type escape sequence to abort.
Sending 5, 100-byte ICMP Echos to 1.1.1.2, timeout
is 2 seconds:
!!!!!
Success rate is 100 percent (5/5), round-trip min/avg/max
= 4/4/6 ms
```

After you ping the TFTP server to make sure that IP is working, you can use the copy flash tftp command to copy the IOS to the TFTP server:

```
Router#copy flash tftp
Source filename []?c2600nm-advsecurityk9-mz.151-4.M6.bin
Address or name of remote host []?1.1.1.2
Destination filename [c2600nm-advsecurityk9-mz.151-4.M6.bin]?[enter]
!!!!!!!!!!!!!!!!!!!!!!!!!!!!!!!!!!!!!!!!!!!!!!!!!!!!!!!!!!!!!!!!!!!!!!!!!!!!!!!!!!
45395966 bytes copied in 123.824 secs (358532 bytes/sec)
Router#
```

Just copy the IOS filename from either the show flash or show version command and then paste it when prompted for the source filename.

In the preceding example, the contents of flash memory were copied successfully to the TFTP server. The address of the remote host is the IP address of the TFTP host, and the source filename is the file in flash memory.

 Many newer Cisco routers have removable memory. You may see names for this memory such as flash0:, in which case the command in the preceding example would be copy flash0: tftp:. Alternately, you may see it as usbflash0:.

Restoring or Upgrading the Cisco Router IOS

What happens if you need to restore the Cisco IOS to flash memory to replace an original file that has been damaged or if you want to upgrade the IOS? You can download the file from a TFTP server to flash memory by using the copy tftp flash command. This command requires the IP address of the TFTP host and the name of the file you want to download.

However, since IOSs can be very large today, it's a good idea to use something other than TFTP because it's unreliable and can only transfer smaller files. Take a look:

```
Corp#copy ?
/erase Erase destination file system.
/error Allow to copy error file.
/noverify Don't verify image signature before reload.
/verify Verify image signature before reload.
archive: Copy from archive: file system
cns: Copy from cns: file system
flash: Copy from flash: file system
ftp: Copy from ftp: file system
http: Copy from http: file system
https: Copy from https: file system
null: Copy from null: file system
nvram: Copy from nvram: file system
rcp: Copy from rcp: file system
running-config Copy from current system configuration
scp: Copy from scp: file system
startup-config Copy from startup configuration
system: Copy from system: file system
tar: Copy from tar: file system
tftp: Copy from tftp: file system
tmpsys: Copy from tmpsys: file system
xmodem: Copy from xmodem: file system
ymodem: Copy from ymodem: file system
```

You can see from the output above that we have a whole bunch of options to choose from. For the larger files, we'll use ftp: or scp: to copy our IOS into or from routers and switches. You can even perform an MD5 verification with the /verify at the end of a command.

We're going to use TFTP for our examples in the chapter because it's easiest. But before you begin, make sure the file you want to place in flash memory is in the default TFTP directory on your host. When you issue the command, TFTP won't ask you where the file is, so if the file you want to use isn't in the default directory of the TFTP host, this just won't work:

```
Router#copy tftp flash
Address or name of remote host []?1.1.1.2
Source filename []?c2600nm-advsecurityk9-mz.151-4.M6.bin
Destination filename [c2600nm-advsecurityk9-mz.151-4.M6.bin]?[enter]
```

```
%Warning: There is a file already existing with this name
Do you want to over write? [confirm][enter]
Accessing tftp://1.1.1.2/ c2600nm-advsecurityk9-mz.151-4.M6.bin...
Loading c2600nm-advsecurityk9-mz.151-4.M6.bin from 1.1.1.2 (via
FastEthernet0/0): !!!!!!!!!!!!!!!!!!!!!!!!!!!!!!!!!!!!!!!!!!!!!!!!!!!!!!!!!!!!!!!!
[OK - 21810844 bytes]
45395966 bytes copied in 62.660 secs (261954 bytes/sec)
Router#
```

In the preceding example, I copied the same file into flash memory, so it asked me if I wanted to overwrite it. Remember that we are "playing" with files in flash memory. If I have just corrupted my file by overwriting it, I won't know for sure until I reboot the router. Definitely be careful with this command! If the file is corrupted, you'll need to do an IOS-restore from ROM monitor mode.

If you are loading a new file and you don't have enough room in flash memory to store both the new and existing copies, the router will ask to erase the contents of flash memory before writing the new file into flash memory. And if you are able to copy the IOS without erasing the old version, then make sure you remember to use the boot system flash:*ios-file* command.

A Cisco router can become a TFTP server host for a router system image that's run in flash memory. The global configuration command is tftp-server flash:*ios-file*.

 Real World Scenario

It's Monday Morning and You Just Upgraded Your IOS

You came in early to upgrade the IOS on your router. After the upgrade, you reload the router and the router now shows the rommon> prompt.

Looks like you're about to have a bad day! This is what I call an RGE: a resume-generating event! So, now what do you do? Just keep calm and follow these steps to save your job:

```
rommon 1 > tftpdnld
Missing or illegal ip address for variable IP_ADDRESS
Illegal IP address.
usage: tftpdnld [-hr]
Use this command for disaster recovery only to recover an image via TFTP.
Monitor variables are used to set up parameters for the transfer.
(Syntax: "VARIABLE_NAME=value" and use "set" to show current variables.)
"ctrl-c" or "break" stops the transfer before flash erase begins.
```

```
The following variables are REQUIRED to be set for tftpdnld:
IP_ADDRESS: The IP address for this unit
IP_SUBNET_MASK: The subnet mask for this unit
DEFAULT_GATEWAY: The default gateway for this unit
TFTP_SERVER: The IP address of the server to fetch from
TFTP_FILE: The filename to fetch
The following variables are OPTIONAL:
[unneeded output cut]
rommon 2 >set IP_Address:1.1.1.1
rommon 3 >set IP_SUBNET_MASK:255.0.0.0
rommon 4 >set DEFAULT_GATEWAY:1.1.1.2
rommon 5 >set TFTP_SERVER:1.1.1.2
rommon 6 >set TFTP_FILE: flash:c2600nm-advipservicesk9-mz.124-12.bin
rommon 7 >tftpdnld
```

From here you can see the variables you need to configure using the set command; be sure you use ALL_CAPS with these commands as well as underscore (_). From here, you need to set the IP address, mask, and default gateway of your router, then the IP address of the TFTP host, which in this example is a directly connected router that I made a TFTP server with this command:

```
Router(config)#tftp-server flash:c2600nm-advipservicesk9-mz.124-12.bin
```

And finally, you set the IOS filename of the file on your TFTP server. Whew!

There is one other way you can restore the IOS on a router, but it takes a while. You can use what is called the Xmodem protocol to actually upload an IOS file into flash memory through the console port. You'd use the Xmodem through the console port procedure if you had no network connectivity to the router or switch.

Using the Cisco IOS File System (Cisco IFS)

Cisco has created a file system called Cisco IFS that allows you to work with files and directories just as you would from a Windows DOS prompt. The commands you use are dir, copy, more, delete, erase or format, cd and pwd, and mkdir and rmdir.

Working with IFS gives you the ability to view all files, even those on remote servers. And you definitely want to find out if an image on one of your remote servers is valid before you copy it, right? You also need to know how big it is—size matters here! It's also a really good idea to take a look at the remote server's configuration and make sure it's all good before loading that file on your router.

It's very cool that IFS makes the file system user interface universal—it's not platform specific anymore. You now get to use the same syntax for all your commands on all of your routers, no matter the platform!

Sound too good to be true? Well, it kind of is because you'll find out that support for all commands on each file system and platform just isn't there. But it's not that big of a deal since various file systems differ in the actions they perform; the commands that aren't relevant to a particular file system are the very ones that aren't supported on that file system. Be assured that any file system or platform will fully support all the commands you need to manage it.

Another cool IFS feature is that it cuts down on all those obligatory prompts for a lot of the commands. If you want to enter a command, all you have to do is type all the necessary info straight into the command line—no more jumping through hoops of prompts! So, if you want to copy a file to an FTP server, all you'd do is first indicate where the desired source file is on your router, pinpoint where the destination file is to be on the FTP server, determine the username and password you're going to use when you want to connect to that server, and type it all in on one line—sleek! For those of you resistant to change, you can still have the router prompt to use and get to enjoy entering a more elegantly minimized version of the command than you did before.

But even in spite of all this, your router might still prompt you—even if you did everything right in your command line. It comes down to how you have the `file prompt` command configured and which command you're trying to use. No worries—if that happens, the default value will be entered right there in the command, and all you have to do is hit Enter to verify the correct values.

IFS also lets you explore various directories and inventory files in any directory you want. Plus, you can make subdirectories in flash memory or on a card, but you only get to do that if you're working on one of the more recent platforms.

And get this—the new file system interface uses URLs to determine the whereabouts of a file. So just as they pinpoint places on the Web, URLs now indicate where files are on your Cisco router, or even on a remote file server! You just type URLs right into your commands to identify where the file or directory is. It's really that easy—to copy a file from one place to another, you simply enter the copy *source-urldestination-url* command! IFS URLs are a tad different than what you're used to though, there's an array of formats to use that vary depending on where, exactly, the file is that you're after.

We're going to use Cisco IFS commands pretty much the same way that we used the copy command in the IOS section earlier:

- For backing up the IOS
- For upgrading the IOS
- For viewing text files

Okay—with all that down, let's take a look at the common IFS commands available to us for managing the IOS. I'll get into configuration files soon, but for now I'm going to get you started with going over the basics used to manage the new Cisco IOS.

dir Same as with Windows, this command lets you view files in a directory. Type **dir**, hit Enter, and by default you get the contents of the `flash:/` directory output.

copy This is one popular command, often used to upgrade, restore, or back up an IOS. But as I said, when you use it, it's really important to focus on the details—what you're copying, where it's coming from, and where it's going to land.

more   Same as with Unix, this will take a text file and let you look at it on a card. You can use it to check out your configuration file or your backup configuration file. I'll go over it more when we get into actual configuration.

show file   This command will give you the skinny on a specified file or file system, but it's kind of obscure because people don't use it a lot.

delete   Three guesses—yep, it deletes stuff. But with some types of routers, not as well as you'd think. That's because even though it whacks the file, it doesn't always free up the space it was using. To actually get the space back, you have to use something called the squeeze command too.

erase/format   Use these with care—make sure that when you're copying files, you say no to the dialog that asks you if you want to erase the file system! The type of memory you're using determines if you can nix the flash drive or not.

cd/pwd   Same as with Unix and DOS, cd is the command you use to change directories. Use the pwd command to print (show) the working directory.

mkdir/rmdir   Use these commands on certain routers and switches to create and delete directories—the mkdir command for creation and the rmdir command for deletion. Use the cd and pwd commands to change into these directories.

> The Cisco IFS uses the alternate term system:running-config as well as nvram:startup-config when copying the configurations on a router, even though it's not mandatory for you to use this naming convention.

Using the Cisco IFS to Upgrade an IOS

Let's take a look at some of these Cisco IFS commands on my ISR router (1841 series) with a hostname of R1.

We'll start with the pwd command to verify our default directory and then use the dir command to verify its contents (flash:/):

```
R1#pwd
flash:
R1#dir
Directory of flash:/
1 -rw- 13938482 Dec 20 2006 19:56:16 +00:00 c1641-ipbase-
mz.124-1c.bin
2 -rw- 1621 Dec 20 2006 20:11:24 +00:00 sdmconfig-16xx.cfg
3 -rw- 4834464 Dec 20 2006 20:12:00 +00:00 sdm.tar
4 -rw- 633024 Dec 20 2006 20:12:24 +00:00 es.tar
5 -rw- 1052160 Dec 20 2006 20:12:50 +00:00 common.tar
6 -rw- 1036 Dec 20 2006 20:13:10 +00:00 home.shtml
7 -rw- 102400 Dec 20 2006 20:13:30 +00:00 home.tar
```

```
8 -rw- 491213 Dec 20 2006 20:13:56 +00:00 126MB.sdf
9 -rw- 1664588 Dec 20 2006 20:14:34 +00:00 securedesktop-
ios-3.1.1.28-k9.pkg
10 -rw- 396305 Dec 20 2006 20:15:04 +00:00 sslclient-win-1.1.0.154.pkg
32081660 bytes total (6616666 bytes free)
```

What we can see here is that we have the basic IP IOS (c1641-ipbase-mz.124-1c.bin).
Looks like we need to upgrade our 1641. You've just got to love how Cisco puts the IOS
type in the filename now! First, let's check the size of the file that's in flash with the show
file command (show flash would also work):

```
R1#show file info flash:c1641-ipbase-mz.124-1c.bin
flash:c1641-ipbase-mz.124-1c.bin:
type is image (elf) []
file size is 13938482 bytes, run size is 14103140 bytes
Runnable image, entry point 0x6000F000, run from ram
```

With a file that size, the existing IOS will have to be erased before we can add our new
IOS file (c1641-advipservicesk9-mz.124-12.bin), which is over 21 MB. We'll use the
delete command, but remember, we can play with any file in flash memory and nothing
serious will happen until we reboot. So clearly, as I pointed out earlier, we need to be very
careful here:

```
R1#delete flash:c1641-ipbase-mz.124-1c.bin
Delete filename [c1641-ipbase-mz.124-1c.bin]?[enter]
Delete flash:c1641-ipbase-mz.124-1c.bin? [confirm][enter]
R1#sh flash
-#- --length-- -----date/time------ path
1 1621 Dec 20 2006 20:11:24 +00:00 sdmconfig-16xx.cfg
2 4834464 Dec 20 2006 20:12:00 +00:00 sdm.tar
3 633024 Dec 20 2006 20:12:24 +00:00 es.tar
4 1052160 Dec 20 2006 20:12:50 +00:00 common.tar
5 1036 Dec 20 2006 20:13:10 +00:00 home.shtml
6 102400 Dec 20 2006 20:13:30 +00:00 home.tar
7 491213 Dec 20 2006 20:13:56 +00:00 126MB.sdf
8 1664588 Dec 20 2006 20:14:34 +00:00 securedesktop-ios-3.1.1.28-k9.pkg
9 396305 Dec 20 2006 20:15:04 +00:00 sslclient-win-1.1.0.154.pkg
22858386 bytes available (9314304 bytes used)
R1#sh file info flash:c1641-ipbase-mz.124-1c.bin
%Error opening flash:c1641-ipbase-mz.124-1c.bin (File not found)
R1#
```

With the preceding commands, we deleted the existing file and then verified the deletion
by using both the show flash and show file commands. We'll add the new file with the

copy command, but again, we need to make sure to be careful because this way isn't any safer than the first method I showed you earlier:

```
R1#copy tftp://1.1.1.2/c1641-advipservicesk9-mz.124-12.bin/ flash:/
c1641-advipservicesk9-mz.124-12.bin
Source filename [/c1641-advipservicesk9-mz.124-12.bin/]?[enter]
Destination filename [c1641-advipservicesk9-mz.124-12.bin]?[enter]
Loading /c1641-advipservicesk9-mz.124-12.bin/ from 1.1.1.2 (via
FastEthernet0/0): !!!!!!!!!!!!!!!!!!!!!!!!!!!!!!!!!!!!!!!!!!!
[output cut]
!!!!!!!!!!!!!!!!!!!!!!!!!!!!!!!!!!!!!!!!!!!!!!!!!!!!!!!!!!!!!
[OK - 22103052 bytes]
22103052 bytes copied in 82.006 secs (306953 bytes/sec)
R1#sh flash
-#- --length-- -----date/time------ path
1 1621 Dec 20 2006 20:11:24 +00:00 sdmconfig-16xx.cfg
2 4834464 Dec 20 2006 20:12:00 +00:00 sdm.tar
3 633024 Dec 20 2006 20:12:24 +00:00 es.tar
4 1052160 Dec 20 2006 20:12:50 +00:00 common.tar
5 1036 Dec 20 2006 20:13:10 +00:00 home.shtml
6 102400 Dec 20 2006 20:13:30 +00:00 home.tar
7 491213 Dec 20 2006 20:13:56 +00:00 126MB.sdf
8 1664588 Dec 20 2006 20:14:34 +00:00 securedesktop-ios-3.1.1.28-k9.pkg
9 396305 Dec 20 2006 20:15:04 +00:00 sslclient-win-1.1.0.154.pkg
10 22103052 Mar 10 2008 19:40:50 +00:00 c1641-advipservicesk9-mz.124-12.bin
651264 bytes available (31420416 bytes used)
R1#
```

We can also check the file information with the show file command:

```
R1#sh file information flash:c1641-advipservicesk9-mz.124-12.bin
flash:c1641-advipservicesk9-mz.124-12.bin:
type is image (elf) []
file size is 22103052 bytes, run size is 22266836 bytes
Runnable image, entry point 0x6000F000, run from ram
```

Remember that the IOS is expanded into RAM when the router boots, so the new IOS will not run until you reload the router.

I really recommend experimenting with the Cisco IFS commands on a router just to get a good feel for them because, as I've said, they can definitely cause some grief if not executed properly!

I mention "safer methods" a lot in this chapter. Clearly, I've caused myself some serious pain by not being careful enough when working in flash memory! I cannot stress this enough—pay attention when messing around with flash memory!

One of the brilliant features of the ISR routers is that they use the physical flash cards that are accessible from the front or back of any router. These typically have a name like usbflash0:, so to view the contents, you'd type **dir usbflash0:**, for example. You can pull these flash cards out, put them in an appropriate slot in your PC, and the card will show up as a drive. You can then add, change, and delete files. Just put the flash card back in your router and power up—instant upgrade. Nice!

Licensing

IOS licensing is now done quite differently than it was with previous versions of the IOS. Actually, there was no licensing before the new 15.0 IOS code, just your word and honor, and we can only guess based on how all products are downloaded on the Internet daily how well that has worked out for Cisco!

Starting with the IOS 15.0 code, things are much different—almost too different. I can imagine that Cisco will come back toward the middle on its licensing issues, so that the administration and management won't be as detailed as it is with the new 15.0 code license. But you can be the judge of that after reading this section.

A new ISR router is pre-installed with the software images and licenses that you ordered, so as long as you ordered and paid for everything you need, you're set! If not, you can just install another license, which can be a tad tedious at first—enough so that installing a license was made an objective on the Cisco exam! Of course, it can be done, but it definitely requires some effort. As is typical with Cisco, if you spend enough money on their products, they tend to make it easier on you and your administration, and the licensing for the newest IOS is no exception, as you'll soon see.

On a positive note, Cisco provides evaluation licenses for most software packages and features that are supported on the hardware you purchased, and it's always nice to be able to try before you buy. Once the temporary license expires after 60 days, you need to acquire a permanent license in order to continue to use the extended features that aren't available in your current version. This method of licensing allows you to enable a router to use different parts of the IOS. So, what happens after 60 days? Well, nothing—back to the honor system for now. This is now called *Right-To-Use (RTU) licensing*, and it probably won't always be available via your honor, but for now it is.

But that's still not the best part of the new licensing features. Prior to the 15.0 code release, there were eight different software feature sets for each hardware router type. With the IOS 15.0 code, the packaging is now called a *universal image*, meaning all feature sets are available in one file with all features packed neatly inside. So instead of the pre-15.0 IOS file packages of one image per feature set, Cisco now just builds one universal image that includes all of them in the file. Even so, we still need a different universal image per router model or series, just not a different image for each feature set as we did with previous IOS versions.

To use the features in the IOS software, you must unlock them using the software activation process. Since all features available are inside the universal image already, you can just unlock the features you need as you need them, and of course pay for these features when you determine that they meet your business requirements. All routers come with something called the IP Base licensing, which is the prerequisite for installing all other features.

There are three different technology packages available for purchase that can be installed as additional feature packs on top of the prerequisite IP Base (default), which provides entry-level IOS functionality. These are as follows:

Data: MPLS, ATM, and multiprotocol support

Unified Communications: VoIP and IP telephony

Security: Cisco IOS Firewall, IPS, IPsec, 3DES, and VPN

For example, if you need MPLS and IPsec, you'll need the default IP Base, Data, and Security premium packages unlocked on your router.

To obtain the license, you'll need the unique device identifier (UDI), which has two components: the product ID (PID) and the serial number of the router. The show license UDI command provides this information in an output as shown:

```
Router#sh license udi Device# PID SN UDI
------------------------------------------------------------------------
*0 CISCO2901/K9 FTX1641Y08J CISCO2901/K9:FTX1641Y08J
```

After the time has expired for your 60-day evaluation period, you can either obtain the license file from the Cisco License Manager (CLM), which is an automated process, or use the manual process through the Cisco Product License Registration portal. Typically only larger companies will use the CLM because you'd need to install software on a server, which then keeps track of all your licenses for you. If you have just a few licenses that you use, you can opt for the manual web browser process found on the Cisco Product License Registration portal and then just add in a few CLI commands. After that, you just basically keep track of putting all the different license features together for each device you manage. Although this sounds like a lot of work, you don't need to perform these steps often. Clearly, going with the CLM makes a lot of sense if you have bunches of licenses to manage because it will put together all the little pieces of licensing for each router in one easy process.

When you purchase the software package with the features that you want to install, you need to permanently activate the software package using your UDI and the *product authorization key (PAK)* that you received with your purchase. This is essentially your receipt acknowledging that you purchased the license. You then need to connect the license with a particular router by combining the PAK and the UDI, which you do online at the Cisco Product License Registration portal (www.cisco.com/go/license). If you haven't already registered the license on a different router, and it is valid, Cisco will then email you your permanent license, or you can download it from your account.

But wait! You're still not done. You now need to activate the license on the router. Staying with the manual method, you need to make the new license file available to the router either via a USB port on the router or through a TFTP server. Once it's available to the router, you'll use the license install command from privileged mode.

Assuming that you copied the file into flash memory, the command would look like something like this:

```
Router#license install ?
archive: Install from archive: file system
flash: Install from flash: file system
ftp: Install from ftp: file system
http: Install from http: file system
https: Install from https: file system
null: Install from null: file system
nvram: Install from nvram: file system
rcp: Install from rcp: file system
scp: Install from scp: file system
syslog: Install from syslog: file system
system: Install from system: file system
tftp: Install from tftp: file system
tmpsys: Install from tmpsys: file system
xmodem: Install from xmodem: file system
ymodem: Install from ymodem: file system
Router#license install flash:FTX1626636P_201302111432454160.lic
Installing licenses from "flash::FTX1626636P_201302111432454160.lic"
Installing...Feature:datak9...Successful:Supported
1/1 licenses were successfully installed
0/1 licenses were existing licenses
0/1 licenses were failed to install
April 12 2:31:19.866: %LICENSE-6-INSTALL: Feature datak9 1.0 was
installed in this device. UDI=CISCO2901/K9:FTX1626636P; StoreIndex=1:Primary
License Storage
April 12 2:31:20.086: %IOS_LICENSE_IMAGE_APPLICATION-6-LICENSE_LEVEL: Module
name =c2600 Next reboot level = datak9 and License = datak9
```

You need to reboot to have the new license take effect. Now that you have your license installed and running, how do you use Right-To-Use licensing to check out new features on your router? Let's look into that now.

Right-To-Use Licenses (Evaluation Licenses)

Originally called evaluation licenses, Right-To-Use (RTU) licenses are what you need when you want to update your IOS to load a new feature but either don't want to wait

to get the license or just want to test if this feature will truly meet your business requirements. This makes sense because if Cisco made it complicated to load and check out a feature, they just might miss out on a sale! Of course if the feature does work for you, they'll
want you to buy a permanent license, but again, this is on the honor system at the time of
this writing.

Cisco's license model allows you to install the feature you want without a PAK. The
Right-To-Use license works for 60 days before you would need to install your permanent
license. To enable the Right-To-Use license you would use the license boot module command. The following demonstrates starting the Right-To-Use license on my 2900 series
router, enabling the security module named securityk9:

```
Router(config)#license boot module c2900 technology-package securityk9
PLEASE READ THE FOLLOWING TERMS CAREFULLY. INSTALLING THE LICENSE OR LICENSE KEY
PROVIDED FOR ANY CISCO PRODUCT FEATURE OR USING
SUCHPRODUCT FEATURE CONSTITUTES YOUR FULL ACCEPTANCE OF THE
FOLLOWING TERMS. YOU MUST NOT PROCEED FURTHER IF YOU ARE NOT WILLING
TO BE BOUND BY ALL THE TERMS SET FORTH HEREIN.
[output cut]
Activation of the software command line interface will be evidence of
your acceptance of this agreement.
ACCEPT? [yes/no]: yes
% use 'write' command to make license boot config take effect on next boot
Feb 12 01:35:45.060: %IOS_LICENSE_IMAGE_APPLICATION-6-LICENSE_LEVEL:
Module name =c2900 Next reboot level = securityk9 and License = securityk9
Feb 12 01:35:45.524: %LICENSE-6-EULA_ACCEPTED: EULA for feature
securityk9 1.0 has been accepted. UDI=CISCO2901/K9:FTX1626636P;
StoreIndex=0:Built-In License Storage
```

Once the router is reloaded, you can use the security feature set. And it is really nice that
you don't need to reload the router again if you choose to install a permanent license for
this feature. The show license command shows the licenses installed on the router:

```
Router#show license
Index 1 Feature: ipbasek9
Period left: Life time
License Type: Permanent
License State: Active, In Use
License Count: Non-Counted
License Priority: Medium
Index 2 Feature: securityk9
Period left: 6 weeks 2 days
Period Used: 0 minute 0 second
License Type: EvalRightToUse
License State: Active, In Use
License Count: Non-Counted
License Priority: None
```

```
Index 3 Feature: uck9
Period left: Life time
License Type: Permanent
License State: Active, In Use
License Count: Non-Counted
License Priority: Medium
Index 4 Feature: datak9
Period left: Not Activated
Period Used: 0 minute 0 second
License Type: EvalRightToUse
License State: Not in Use, EULA not accepted
License Count: Non-Counted
License Priority: None
Index 5 Feature: gatekeeper
[output cut]
```

You can see in the preceding output that the ipbasek9 is permanent and the securityk9 has a license type of EvalRightToUse. The show license feature command provides the same information as show license, but it's summarized into one line as shown in the next output:

```
Router#sh license feature
Feature name Enforcement Evaluation Subscription Enabled RightToUse
ipbasek9 no no no yes no
securityk9 yes yes no no yes
uck9 yes yes no yes yes
datak9 yes yes no no yes
gatekeeper yes yes no no yes
SSL_VPN yes yes no no yes
ios-ips-update yes yes yes no yes
SNASw yes yes no no yes
hseck9 yes no no no no
cme-srst yes yes no yes yes
WAAS_Express yes yes no no yes
UCVideo yes yes no no yes
```

The show version command also shows the license information at the end of the command output:

```
Router#show version
[output cut]
License Info:
License UDI:
]]> ------------------------------------------------ Device# PID SN -----------
----------------------------------------
*0 CISCO2901/K9 FTX1641Y08J
```

```
Technology Package License Information for Module:'c2900'
----------------------------------------------------------------
Technology Technology-package Technology-package
Current Type Next reboot
----------------------------------------------------------------
ipbase ipbasek9 Permanent ipbasek9
security None None None
uc uck9 Permanent uck9
data None None None
Configuration register is 0x2102
```

The show version command shows if the license was activated. Don't forget, you'll need to reload the router to have the license features take effect if the license evaluation is not already active.

Backing Up and Uninstalling the License

It would be a shame to lose your license if it has been stored in flash and your flash files become corrupted. So always back up your IOS license!

If your license has been saved in a location other than flash, you can easily back it up to flash memory via the license save command:

Router#**license save flash:Todd_License.lic**

The previous command will save your current license to flash. You can restore your license with the license install command I demonstrated earlier.

There are two steps to uninstalling the license on a router. First, to uninstall the license you need to disable the technology package, using the no license boot module command with the keyword disable at the end of the command line:

Router#**license boot module c2900 technology-package securityk9 disable**

The second step is to clear the license. To achieve this from the router, use the license clear command and then remove the license with the no license boot module command:

Router#**license clear securityk9**
Router#**config t**
Router(config)#**no license boot module c2900 technology-package securityk9**
disable
Router(config)#**exit**
Router#**reload**

After you run through the preceding commands, the license will be removed from your router.

Here's a summary of the license commands I used in this chapter. These are important commands to have down and you really need to understand these to meet the Cisco objectives:

- `show license` determines the licenses that are active on your system. It also displays a group of lines for each feature in the currently running IOS image along with several status variables related to software activation and licensing, both licensed and unlicensed features.

- `show license feature` allows you to view the technology package licenses and feature licenses that are supported on your router along with several status variables related to software activation and licensing. This includes both licensed and unlicensed features.

- `show license udi` displays the unique device identifier (UDI) of the router, which contains the product ID (PID) and serial number of the router.

- `show version` displays various pieces of information about the current IOS version, including the licensing details at the end of the command's output.

- `license install` *url* installs a license key file into a router.

- `license boot module` installs a Right-To-Use license feature on a router.

To help you organize a large amount of licenses, search on Cisco.com for the Cisco Smart Software Manager. This web page enables you to manage all your licenses from one centralized website. With Cisco Smart Software Manager, you organize and view your licenses in groups that are called *virtual accounts*, which are collections of licenses and product instances.

Summary

You now know how Cisco routers are configured and how to manage those configurations.

This chapter covered the internal components of a router, which included ROM, RAM, NVRAM, and flash.

In addition, I covered what happens when a router boots and which files are loaded at that time. The configuration register tells the router how to boot and where to find files. You learned how to change and verify the configuration register settings for password recovery purposes. I also showed you how to manage these files using the CLI and IFS.

Finally, the chapter covered licensing with the new 15.0 code, including how to install a permanent license and a Right-To-Use license to install features for 60 days. I also showed you the verification commands used to see what licenses are installed and to verify their status.

Chapter

9

IP Routing

It's time now to turn our focus toward the core topic of the ubiquitous IP routing process. It's integral to networking because it pertains to all routers and configurations that use it, which is easily the lion's share. IP routing is basically the process of moving packets from one network to another network using routers. And by routers, I mean Cisco routers, of course! However, the terms *router* and *layer 3 device* are interchangeable, and throughout this chapter when I use the term *router*, I am referring to any layer 3 device.

Before jumping into this chapter, I want to make sure you understand the difference between a *routing protocol* and a *routed protocol*. Routers use routing protocols to dynamically find all networks within the greater internetwork and to ensure that all routers have the same routing table. Routing protocols are also employed to determine the best path a packet should take through an internetwork to get to its destination most efficiently. RIP, RIPv2, EIGRP, and OSPF are great examples of the most common routing protocols.

Once all routers know about all networks, a routed protocol can be used to send user data (packets) through the established enterprise. Routed protocols are assigned to an interface and determine the method of packet delivery. Examples of routed protocols are IP and IPv6.

I'm pretty confident I don't have to underscore how crucial it is for you to have this chapter's material down to a near instinctive level. IP routing is innately what Cisco routers do, and they do it very well, so having a firm grasp of the fundamentals and basics of this topic is vital if you want to excel during the exam and in a real-world networking environment as well!

In this chapter, I'm going to show you how to configure and verify IP routing with Cisco routers and guide you through these five key subjects:

- Routing basics
- The IP routing process
- Static routing
- Default routing
- Dynamic routing

I want to start by nailing down the basics of how packets actually move through an internetwork, so let's get started!

To find your included bonus material, as well as Todd Lammle videos. practice questions and hands-on labs, please see www.lammle.com/ccna.

Routing Basics

Once you create an internetwork by connecting your WANs and LANs to a router, you'll need to configure logical network addresses, like IP addresses, to all hosts on that internetwork to enable them to communicate successfully throughout it.

The term *routing* refers to taking a packet from one device and sending it through the internetwork to another device on a different network. Routers don't really care about hosts—they only care about networks and the best path to each one of them. The logical network address of the destination host is key to getting packets through a routed network. It's the hardware address of the host that's used to deliver the packet from a router and ensure it arrives at the correct destination host.

Here's an important list of the minimum factors a router must know to be able to effectively route packets:

- Destination address
- Neighbor routers from which it can learn about remote networks
- Possible routes to all remote networks
- The best route to each remote network
- How to maintain and verify routing information

The router learns about remote networks from neighboring routers or from an administrator. The router then builds a routing table—a map of the internetwork, describing how to find remote networks. If a network is directly connected, then the router already knows how to get to it.

If a network isn't directly connected to the router, the router must use one of two ways to learn how to get to the remote network. The *static routing* method requires someone to hand-type all network locations into the routing table. Doing this would be a super labor-intensive task when used on all but the smallest of networks!

But when *dynamic routing* is used, a protocol on one router communicates with the same protocol running on neighboring routers. The routers then update each other about all the networks they know about and place this information into the routing table. If a change occurs in the network, the dynamic routing protocols automatically inform all routers about the event. If static routing is used, the administrator is responsible for updating all changes by hand onto all routers. Most people usually use a combination of dynamic and static routing to administer a large network.

Before we get into the IP routing process, let's take a look at a very simple example that demonstrates how a router uses the routing table to route packets out of an interface. You'll see a more detailed look at the process soon, but I want to show you something called the "longest match rule" first. Using this rule, IP will scan a routing table to find the longest match as compared to the destination address of a packet. Figure 9.1 offers a picture of this process.

FIGURE 9.1   A simple routing example

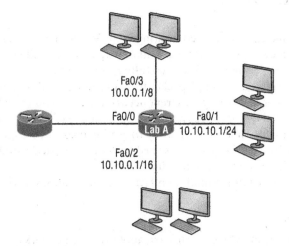

Figure 9.1 illustrates a simple network. Lab_A has four interfaces. Can you see which interface will be used to forward an IP datagram to a host with a destination IP address of 10.10.10.30?

By using the command show ip route on a router, we can see the routing table (map of the internetwork) that Lab_A has used to make its forwarding decisions:

```
Lab_A#sh ip route
Codes: L - local, C - connected, S - static,
[output cut]
10.0.0.0/8 is variably subnetted, 6 subnets, 4 masks
C 10.0.0.0/8 is directly connected, FastEthernet0/3
L 10.0.0.1/32 is directly connected, FastEthernet0/3
C 10.10.0.0/16 is directly connected, FastEthernet0/2
L 10.10.0.1/32 is directly connected, FastEthernet0/2
C 10.10.10.0/24 is directly connected, FastEthernet0/1
L 10.10.10.1/32 is directly connected, FastEthernet0/1
S* 0.0.0.0/0 is directly connected, FastEthernet0/0
```

The C in the routing table output means that the networks listed are directly connected. Until we add a routing protocol like RIPv2, OSPF, etc. to the routers in our internetwork, or enter static routes, only directly connected networks will show up in our routing table. But wait—what about that L in the routing table—that's new, isn't it? Yes! Because in the new Cisco IOS 15 code, Cisco defines a different route, called a local host route. Each local route has a /32 prefix, defining a route just for the one address. So in this example, the router relied upon these routes, which list their own local IP addresses, to more efficiently forward packets to the router itself.

So let's get back to the original question: Looking at the figure and the output of the routing table, what will IP do with a received packet that has a destination IP address of 10.10.10.30? The router will packet-switch the packet to interface FastEthernet 0/1, which will frame the packet and then send it out on the network segment. This is referred to as frame rewrite. Based upon the longest match rule, IP would look for 10.10.10.30, and if that isn't found in the table, then IP would search for 10.10.10.0, then 10.10.0.0, and so on until a route is discovered.

Here's another example: Looking at the output of the next routing table, which interface will a packet with a destination address of 10.10.10.14 be forwarded from?

```
Lab_A#sh ip route
[output cut]
Gateway of last resort is not set
C 10.10.10.16/28 is directly connected, FastEthernet0/0
L 10.10.10.17/32 is directly connected, FastEthernet0/0
C 10.10.10.8/29 is directly connected, FastEthernet0/1
L 10.10.10.9/32 is directly connected, FastEthernet0/1
C 10.10.10.4/30 is directly connected, FastEthernet0/2
L 10.10.10.5/32 is directly connected, FastEthernet0/2
C 10.10.10.0/30 is directly connected, Serial 0/0
L 10.10.10.1/32 is directly connected, Serial0/0
```

To figure this out, look closely at the output until you see that the network is subnetted and each interface has a different mask. I have to tell you—you just can't answer this question if you can't subnet! 10.10.10.14 would be a host in the 10.10.10.8/29 subnet that's connected to the FastEthernet0/1 interface. If you're struggling and don't get this, just go back and reread Chapter 4, "Easy Subnetting," until you do.

The IP Routing Process

The IP routing process is pretty simple and doesn't change regardless of the size of your network. To give you a picture of this fact, I'll use Figure 9.2 to describe what happens when Host A wants to communicate with Host B on a different network, step-by-step.

FIGURE 9.2 IP routing example using two hosts and one router

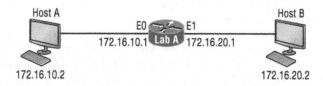

In Figure 9.2 a user on Host_A pinged Host_B's IP address. Routing doesn't get any simpler than this, but it still involves a lot of steps, so let's go through them:

1. Internet Control Message Protocol (ICMP) creates an echo request payload, which is simply the alphabet in the data field.

2. ICMP hands that payload to Internet Protocol (IP), which then creates a packet. At a minimum, this packet contains an IP source address, an IP destination address, and a Protocol field with 01h. Don't forget that Cisco likes to use *0x* in front of hex characters, so this could also look like 0x01. This tells the receiving host which protocol it should hand the payload to when the destination is reached. In this example, it's ICMP.

3. Once the packet is created, IP determines whether the destination IP address is on the local network or a remote one.

4. Since IP has determined that this is a remote request, the packet must be sent to the default gateway so it can be routed to the remote network. The Registry in Windows is parsed to find the configured default gateway.

5. The default gateway of Host_A is configured to 172.16.10.1. For this packet to be sent to the default gateway, the hardware address of the router's interface Ethernet 0, which is configured with the IP address of 172.16.10.1, must be known. Why? So the packet can be handed down to the Data Link layer, framed, and sent to the router's interface that's connected to the 172.16.10.0 network. Because hosts communicate only via hardware addresses on the local LAN, it's important to recognize that for Host_A to communicate to Host_B, it has to send packets to the Media Access Control (MAC) address of the default gateway on the local network.

> **NOTE** MAC addresses are always local on the LAN and never go through and past a router.

6. Next, the Address Resolution Protocol (ARP) cache of the host is checked to see if the IP address of the default gateway has already been resolved to a hardware address.

If it has, the packet is then handed to the Data Link layer for framing. Remember that the hardware destination address is also handed down with that packet. To view the ARP cache on your host:

```
C:\>arp -a
Interface: 172.16.10.2   --- 0x3
Internet Address Physical Address Type
172.16.10.1 00-15-05-06-31-b0 dynamic
```

If the hardware address isn't already in the ARP cache of the host, an ARP broadcast will be sent out onto the local network to search for the 172.16.10.1 hardware address. The router then responds to the request, provides the hardware address of Ethernet 0, and the host caches the address.

7. Once the packet and destination hardware address are handed to the Data Link layer, the LAN driver is used to provide media access via the type of LAN—Ethernet, in this case. A frame is then generated, encapsulating the packet with control information. Within that frame are the hardware destination and source addresses plus, in this case, an Ether-Type field, which identifies the specific Network layer protocol that handed the packet to the Data Link layer. Here, it's IP. At the end of the frame is something called a Frame Check Sequence (FCS) field that houses the result of the cyclic redundancy check (CRC). The frame would look something like what I've detailed in Figure 9.3. It contains Host A's hardware (MAC) address and the destination hardware address of the default gateway. It does not include the remote host's MAC address—remember that!

8. Once the frame is completed, it's handed down to the Physical layer to be put on the physical medium (in this example, twisted-pair wire) one bit at a time.

9. Every device in the collision domain receives these bits and builds the frame. They each run a CRC and check the answer in the FCS field. If the answers don't match, the frame is discarded.

   - If the CRC matches, then the hardware destination address is checked to see if it also matches—in this example, it's the router's interface (Ethernet 0).

   - If it's a match, then the Ether-Type field is checked to find the protocol used at the Network layer.

10. The packet is pulled from the frame, and what is left of the frame is discarded. The packet is handed to the protocol listed in the Ether-Type field and given to IP.

11. IP receives the packet and checks the IP destination address. Since the packet's destination address doesn't match any of the addresses configured on the receiving router, the router will look up the destination IP network address in its routing table.

12. The routing table must have an entry for the network 172.16.20.0 or the packet will be discarded immediately and an ICMP message will be sent back to the originating device with a destination network unreachable message.

13. If the router does find an entry for the destination network in its table, the packet is switched to the exit interface—in this example, interface Ethernet 1. The following output displays the Lab_A router's routing table. The C means "directly connected." No routing protocols are needed in this network since all networks (all two of them) are directly connected.

```
Lab_A>sh ip route
C 172.16.10.0 is directly connected, Ethernet0
L 172.16.10.1/32 is directly connected, Ethernet0
C 172.16.20.0 is directly connected, Ethernet1
L 172.16.20.1/32 is directly connected, Ethernet1
```

14. The router packet-switches the packet to the Ethernet 1 buffer.

15. The Ethernet 1 buffer needs to know the hardware address of the destination host and first checks the ARP cache.

- If the hardware address of Host_B has already been resolved and is in the router's ARP cache, then the packet and the hardware address will be handed down to the Data Link layer to be framed. Let's take a look at the ARP cache on the Lab_A router by using the show ip arp command:

```
Lab_A#sh ip arp
Protocol Address Age(min) Hardware Addr Type Interface
Internet 172.16.20.1 - 00d0.58ad.05f4 ARPA Ethernet1
Internet 172.16.20.2 3 0030.9492.a5dd ARPA Ethernet1
Internet 172.16.10.1 - 00d0.58ad.06aa ARPA Ethernet0
Internet 172.16.10.2 12 0030.9492.a4ac ARPA Ethernet0
```

The dash (-) signifies that this is the physical interface on the router. This output shows us that the router knows the 172.16.10.2 (Host_A) and 172.16.20.2 (Host_B) hardware addresses. Cisco routers will keep an entry in the ARP table for 4 hours.

- Now if the hardware address hasn't already been resolved, the router will send an ARP request out E1 looking for the 172.16.20.2 hardware address. Host_B responds with its hardware address, and the packet and destination hardware addresses are then both sent to the Data Link layer for framing.

16. The Data Link layer creates a frame with the destination and source hardware addresses, Ether-Type field, and FCS field at the end. The frame is then handed to the Physical layer to be sent out on the physical medium one bit at a time.

17. Host_B receives the frame and immediately runs a CRC. If the result matches the information in the FCS field, the hardware destination address will then be checked next. If the host finds a match, the Ether-Type field is then checked to determine the protocol that the packet should be handed to at the Network layer—IP in this example.

18. At the Network layer, IP receives the packet and runs a CRC on the IP header. If that passes, IP then checks the destination address. Since a match has finally been made, the Protocol field is checked to find out to whom the payload should be given.

19. The payload is handed to ICMP, which understands that this is an echo request. ICMP responds to this by immediately discarding the packet and generating a new payload as an echo reply.

20. A packet is then created including the source and destination addresses, Protocol field, and payload. The destination device is now Host_A.

21. IP then checks to see whether the destination IP address is a device on the local LAN or on a remote network. Since the destination device is on a remote network, the packet needs to be sent to the default gateway.

22. The default gateway IP address is found in the Registry of the Windows device, and the ARP cache is checked to see if the hardware address has already been resolved from an IP address.

23. Once the hardware address of the default gateway is found, the packet and destination hardware addresses are handed down to the Data Link layer for framing.

24. The Data Link layer frames the packet of information and includes the following in the header:

   - The destination and source hardware addresses
   - The Ether-Type field with 0x0800 (IP) in it
   - The FCS field with the CRC result in tow

25. The frame is now handed down to the Physical layer to be sent out over the network medium one bit at a time.

26. The router's Ethernet 1 interface receives the bits and builds a frame. The CRC is run, and the FCS field is checked to make sure the answers match.

27. Once the CRC is found to be okay, the hardware destination address is checked. Since the router's interface is a match, the packet is pulled from the frame and the Ether-Type field is checked to determine which protocol the packet should be delivered to at the Network layer.

28. The protocol is determined to be IP, so it gets the packet. IP runs a CRC check on the IP header first and then checks the destination IP address.

IP does not run a complete CRC as the Data Link layer does—it only checks the header for errors.

Since the IP destination address doesn't match any of the router's interfaces, the routing table is checked to see whether it has a route to 172.16.10.0. If it doesn't have a route over to the destination network, the packet will be discarded immediately. I want to point out that this is exactly where the source of confusion begins for a lot of administrators because when a ping fails, most people think the packet never reached the destination host. But as we see here, that's not *always* the case. All it takes for this to happen is for even just one of the remote routers to lack a route back to the originating host's network and—*poof!*—the packet is dropped on the *return trip*, not on its way to the host!

Just a quick note to mention that when (and if) the packet is lost on the way back to the originating host, you will typically see a request timed-out message because it's an unknown error. If the error occurs because of a known issue, such as if a route is not in the routing table on the way to the destination device, you will see a destination unreachable message. This should help you determine if the problem occurred on the way to the destination or on the way back.

29. In this case, the router happens to know how to get to network 172.16.10.0—the exit interface is Ethernet 0—so the packet is switched to interface Ethernet 0.

30. The router then checks the ARP cache to determine whether the hardware address for 172.16.10.2 has already been resolved.

31. Since the hardware address to 172.16.10.2 is already cached from the originating trip to Host_B, the hardware address and packet are then handed to the Data Link layer.

32. The Data Link layer builds a frame with the destination hardware address and source hardware address and then puts IP in the Ether-Type field. A CRC is run on the frame and the result is placed in the FCS field.

33. The frame is then handed to the Physical layer to be sent out onto the local network one bit at a time.

34. The destination host receives the frame, runs a CRC, checks the destination hardware address, then looks into the Ether-Type field to find out to whom to hand the packet.

35. IP is the designated receiver, and after the packet is handed to IP at the Network layer, it checks the Protocol field for further direction. IP finds instructions to give the payload to ICMP, and ICMP determines the packet to be an ICMP echo reply.

36. ICMP acknowledges that it has received the reply by sending an exclamation point (!) to the user interface. ICMP then attempts to send four more echo requests to the destination host.

FIGURE 9.3 Frame used from Host A to the Lab_A router when Host B is pinged

Destination MAC (router's E0 MAC address)	Source MAC (Host A MAC address)	Ether-Type field	Packet	FCS CRC

You've just experienced Todd's 36 easy steps to understanding IP routing. The key point here is that if you had a much larger network, the process would be the *same*. It's just that the larger the internetwork, the more hops the packet goes through before it finds the destination host.

It's super important to remember that when Host_A sends a packet to Host_B, the destination hardware address used is the default gateway's Ethernet interface. Why? Because frames can't be placed on remote networks—only local networks. So packets destined for remote networks must go through the default gateway.

Let's take a look at Host_A's ARP cache now:

```
C:\ >arp -a
Interface: 172.16.10.2 --- 0x3
Internet Address Physical Address Type
172.16.10.1 00-15-05-06-31-b0 dynamic
172.16.20.1 00-15-05-06-31-b0 dynamic
```

Did you notice that the hardware (MAC) address that Host_A uses to get to Host_B is the Lab_A E0 interface? Hardware addresses are *always* local, and they never pass through a router's interface. Understanding this process is very important, so carve this into your memory!

The Cisco Router Internal Process

One more thing before we get to testing your understanding of my 36 steps of IP routing. I think it's important to explain how a router forwards packets internally. For IP to look up a destination address in a routing table on a router, processing in the router must take place, and if there are tens of thousands of routes in that table, the amount of CPU time would be enormous. It results in a potentially overwhelming amount of overhead—think about a router at your ISP that has to calculate millions of packets per second and even subnet to find the correct exit interface! Even with the little network I'm using in this book, lots of processing would need to be done if there were actual hosts connected and sending data.

Cisco uses three types of packet-forwarding techniques:

Process switching This is actually how many people see routers to this day, because it's true that routers actually did perform this type of bare-bones packet switching back in 1990 when Cisco released their very first router. But those days when traffic demands were unimaginably light are long gone—not in today's networks! This process is now extremely complex and involves looking up every destination in the routing table and finding the exit interface for every packet. This is pretty much how I just explained the process in my 36 steps. But even though what I wrote was absolutely true in concept, the internal process requires much more than packet-switching technology today because of the millions of packets per second that must now be processed. So Cisco came up with some other technologies to help with the "big process problem."

Fast switching This solution was created to make the slow performance of process switching faster and more efficient. Fast switching uses a cache to store the most recently used destinations so that lookups are not required for every packet. By caching the exit interface of the destination device, as well as the layer 2 header, performance was dramatically improved, but as our networks evolved with the need for even more speed, Cisco created yet another technology!

Cisco Express Forwarding (CEF) This is Cisco's newer creation, and it's the default packet-forwarding method used on all the latest Cisco routers. CEF makes many different cache tables to help improve performance and is change triggered, not packet triggered. Translated, this means that when the network topology changes, the cache changes along with it.

To see which packet switching method your router interface is using, use the command show ip interface.

Testing Your IP Routing Understanding

Since understanding IP routing is super-important, it's time for that little test I talked about earlier on how well you've got the IP routing process down so far. I'm going to do that by having you look at a couple of figures and answer some very basic IP routing questions based upon them.

Figure 9.4 shows a LAN connected to RouterA that's connected via a WAN link to RouterB. RouterB has a LAN connected with an HTTP server attached.

FIGURE 9.4   IP routing example 1

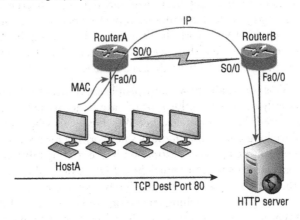

1. The critical information you want to get by looking at this figure is exactly how IP routing will occur in this example. Let's determine the characteristics of a frame as it leaves HostA. Okay—we'll cheat a bit. I'll give you the answer, but then you should go back over the figure and see if you can answer example 2 without looking at my three-step answer!

2. The destination address of a frame from HostA would be the MAC address of Router A's Fa0/0 interface.

3. The destination address of a packet would be the IP address of the HTTP server's network interface card (NIC).

4. The destination port number in the segment header would be 80.

That was a pretty straightforward scenario. One thing to remember is that when multiple hosts are communicating to a server using HTTP, they must all use a different source port number. The source and destination IP addresses and port numbers are how the server keeps the data separated at the Transport layer.

Let's complicate things by adding another device into the network. Figure 9.5 shows a network with only one router but two switches.

FIGURE 9.5 IP routing example 2

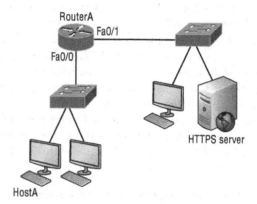

The key thing to understand about the IP routing process in this scenario is what happens when HostA sends data to the HTTPS server? Here's your answer:

1. The destination address of a frame from HostA would be the MAC address of RouterA's Fa0/0 interface.

2. The destination address of a packet is the IP address of the HTTPS server's network interface card (NIC).

3. The destination port number in the segment header will have a value of 443.

Did you notice that the switches weren't used as either a default gateway or any other destination? That's because switches have nothing to do with routing. How many of you chose the switch as the default gateway (destination) MAC address for HostA? If you did, don't feel bad—just take another look to see where you went wrong and why. It's very important to remember that the destination MAC address will always be the router's interface—if your packets are destined for outside the LAN, as they were in these last two examples!

Before moving on into some of the more advanced aspects of IP routing, let's look at another issue. Take a look at the output of this router's routing table:

```
Corp#sh ip route
[output cut]
R 192.168.215.0 [120/2] via 192.168.20.2, 00:00:23, Serial0/0
R 192.168.115.0 [120/1] via 192.168.20.2, 00:00:23, Serial0/0
R 192.168.30.0 [120/1] via 192.168.20.2, 00:00:23, Serial0/0
C 192.168.20.0 is directly connected, Serial0/0
L 192.168.20.1/32 is directly connected, Serial0/0
C 192.168.214.0 is directly connected, FastEthernet0/0
L 192.168.214.1/32 is directly connected, FastEthernet0/0
```

What do we see here? If I were to tell you that the corporate router received an IP packet with a source IP address of 192.168.214.20 and a destination address of 192.168.22.3, what do you think the Corp router will do with this packet?

If you said, "The packet came in on the FastEthernet 0/0 interface, but because the routing table doesn't show a route to network 192.168.22.0 (or a default route), the router will discard the packet and send an ICMP destination unreachable message back out to interface FastEthernet 0/0," you're spot on! The reason that's the right answer is because that's the source LAN where the packet originated from.

Let's check out the next figure and talk about the frames and packets in detail. We're not really going over anything new here; I'm just making sure you totally, completely, thoroughly, fully understand basic IP routing! It is the crux of this book, and the topic the exam objectives are geared toward. We'll use Figure 9.6 for the next few scenarios.

FIGURE 9.6   Basic IP routing using MAC and IP addresses

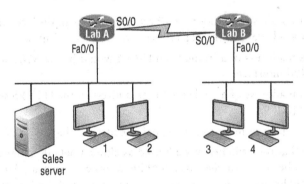

Referring to Figure 9.6, here's a list of all the answers to questions you need:

1. In order to begin communicating with the Sales server, Host 4 sends out an ARP request. How will the devices exhibited in the topology respond to this request?

2. Host 4 has received an ARP reply. Host 4 will now build a packet, then place this packet in the frame. What information will be placed in the header of the packet that leaves Host 4 if Host 4 is going to communicate to the Sales server?

3. The Lab_A router has received the packet and will send it out Fa0/0 onto the LAN toward the server. What will the frame have in the header as the source and destination addresses?

4. Host 4 is displaying two web documents from the Sales server in two browser windows at the same time. How did the data find its way to the correct browser windows?

The following should probably be written in a 3 point font upside down in another part of the book so it would be really hard for you to cheat, but since I'm not mean and you really need to have this down, here are your answers in the same order that the scenarios were just presented:

1. In order to begin communicating with the server, Host 4 sends out an ARP request. How will the devices exhibited in the topology respond to this request? Since MAC

addresses must stay on the local network, the Lab_B router will respond with the MAC address of the Fa0/0 interface and Host 4 will send all frames to the MAC address of the Lab_B Fa0/0 interface when sending packets to the Sales server.

2. Host 4 has received an ARP reply. Host 4 will now build a packet, then place this packet in the frame. What information will be placed in the header of the packet that leaves Host 4 if Host 4 is going to communicate to the Sales server? Since we're now talking about packets, not frames, the source address will be the IP address of Host 4 and the destination address will be the IP address of the Sales server.

3. Finally, the Lab_A router has received the packet and will send it out Fa0/0 onto the LAN toward the server. What will the frame have in the header as the source and desti-nation addresses? The source MAC address will be the Lab_A router's Fa0/0 interface, and the destination MAC address will be the Sales server's MAC address because all MAC addresses must be local on the LAN.

4. Host 4 is displaying two web documents from the Sales server in two different browser windows at the same time. How did the data find its way to the correct browser win-dows? TCP port numbers are used to direct the data to the correct application window.

Great! But we're not quite done yet. I've got a few more questions for you before you actually get to configure routing in a real network. Figure 9.7 shows a basic network, and Host 4 needs to get email. Which address will be placed in the destination address field of the frame when it leaves Host 4?

FIGURE 9.7   Testing basic routing knowledge

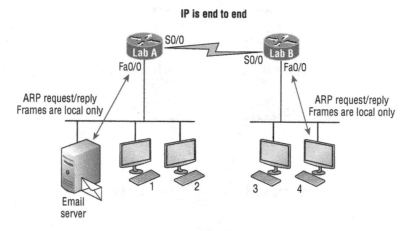

The answer is that Host 4 will use the destination MAC address of the Fa0/0 interface on the Lab_B router—you knew that, right? Look at Figure 9.7 again: What if Host 4 needs to communicate with Host 1—not the server, but with Host 1. Which OSI layer 3 source address will be found in the packet header when it reaches Host 1?

Hopefully you've got this: At layer 3, the source IP address will be Host 4 and the des-tination address in the packet will be the IP address of Host 1. Of course, the destination MAC address from Host 4 will always be the Fa0/0 address of the Lab_B router, right?

And since we have more than one router, we'll need a routing protocol that communicates between both of them so that traffic can be forwarded in the right direction to reach the network that Host 1 is connected to.

Okay—one more scenario... Again, using Figure 9.7, Host 4 is transferring a file to the email server connected to the Lab_A router. What would be the layer 2 destination address leaving Host 4? Yes, I've asked this question more than once. But not this one: What will be the source MAC address when the frame is received at the email server?

Hopefully, you answered that the layer 2 destination address leaving Host 4 is the MAC address of the Fa0/0 interface on the Lab_B router and that the source layer 2 address that the email server will receive is the Fa0/0 interface of the Lab_A router.

If you did, you're ready to discover how IP routing is handled in a larger network environment!

Configuring IP Routing

It's time to get serious and configure a real network. Figure 9.8 shows three routers: Corp, SF, and LA. Remember that, by default, these routers only know about networks that are directly connected to them. I'll continue to use this figure and network throughout the rest of this book. As we progress, I'll add more routers and switches as needed.

FIGURE 9.8 Configuring IP routing

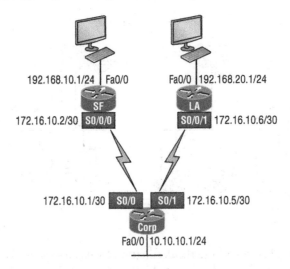

As you might guess, I've got quite a nice collection of routers for us to play with. But you don't need a closet full of devices to perform most, if not all, of the commands we'll use in this book. You can get by nicely with pretty much any router or even with a good router simulator.

Getting back to business, the Corp router has two serial interfaces, which will provide a WAN connection to the SF and LA routers and two Fast Ethernet interfaces as well. The two remote routers have two serial interfaces and two Fast Ethernet interfaces.

The first step for this project is to correctly configure each router with an IP address on each interface. The following list shows the IP address scheme I'm going to use to configure the network. After we go over how the network is configured, I'll cover how to configure IP routing. Pay attention to the subnet masks! The LANs all use a /24 mask, but the WANs are using a /30.

Corp

- Serial 0/0: 172.16.10.1/30
- Serial 0/1: 172.16.10.5/30
- Fa0/0: 10.10.10.1/24

SF

- S0/0/0: 172.16.10.2/30
- Fa0/0: 192.168.10.1/24

LA

- S0/0/0: 172.16.10.6/30
- Fa0/0: 192.168.20.1/24

The router configuration is really a pretty straightforward process since you just need to add IP addresses to your interfaces and then perform a no shutdown on those same interfaces. It gets more complex later on, but for right now, let's configure the IP addresses in the network.

Corp Configuration

We need to configure three interfaces to configure the Corp router. And configuring the hostnames of each router will make identification much easier. While we're at it, let's set the interface descriptions, banner, and router passwords too because it's a really good idea to make a habit of configuring these commands on every router!

To get started, I performed an erase startup-config on the router and reloaded, so we'll start in setup mode. I chose no when prompted to enter setup mode, which will get us straight to the username prompt of the console. I'm going to configure all my routers this same way.

Here's how what I just did looks:

```
--- System Configuration Dialog ---
Would you like to enter the initial configuration dialog? [yes/no]: n
Press RETURN to get started!
Router>en
```

```
Router#config t
Router(config)#hostname Corp
Corp(config)#enable secret GlobalNet
Corp(config)#no ip domain-lookup
Corp(config)#int f0/0
Corp(config-if)#desc Connection to LAN BackBone
Corp(config-if)#ip address 10.10.10.1 255.255.255.0
Corp(config-if)#no shut
Corp(config-if)#int s0/0
Corp(config-if)#desc WAN connection to SF
Corp(config-if)#ip address 172.16.10.1 255.255.255.252
Corp(config-if)#no shut
Corp(config-if)#int s0/1
Corp(config-if)#desc WAN connection to LA
Corp(config-if)#ip address 172.16.10.5 255.255.255.252
Corp(config-if)#no shut
Corp(config-if)#line con 0
Corp(config-line)#password console
Corp(config-line)#logging
Corp(config-line)#logging sync
Corp(config-line)#exit
Corp(config)#line vty 0 ?
<1-181> Last Line number
<cr>
Corp(config)#line vty 0 181
Corp(config-line)#password telnet
Corp(config-line)#login
Corp(config-line)#exit
Corp(config)#banner motd # This is my Corp Router #
Corp(config)#^Z
Corp#copy run start
Destination filename [startup-config]?
Building configuration...
[OK]
Corp# [OK]
```

Let's talk about the configuration of the Corp router. First, I set the hostname and enabled secret, but what is that no ip domain-lookup command? That command stops the router from trying to resolve hostnames, which is an annoying feature unless you've configured a host table or DNS. Next, I configured the three interfaces with descriptions and IP addresses and enabled them with the no shutdown command. The console and VTY passwords came next, but what is that logging sync command under the console line? The logging synchronous command stops console messages from writing over what you are typing in, meaning it will save your sanity. Last, I set my banner and then saved my configs.

> If you're having a hard time understanding this configuration process, refer back to Chapter 6, "Cisco's Internetworking Operating System (IOS)."

To view the IP routing tables created on a Cisco router, use the command show ip route. Here's the command's output:

```
Corp#sh ip route
Codes: L - local, C - connected, S - static, R - RIP, M - mobile, B - BGP
D - EIGRP, EX - EIGRP external, O - OSPF, IA - OSPF inter area
N1 - OSPF NSSA external type 1, N2 - OSPF NSSA external type 2
E1 - OSPF external type 1, E2 - OSPF external type 2
i - IS-IS, su - IS-IS summary, L1 - IS-IS level-1, L2 - IS-IS level-2
ia - IS-IS inter area, * - candidate default, U - per-user static route
o - ODR, P - periodic downloaded static route, H - NHRP, l - LISP
+ - replicated route, % - next hop override
Gateway of last resort is not set
10.0.0.0/24 is subnetted, 1 subnets
C 10.10.10.0 is directly connected, FastEthernet0/0
L 10.10.10.1/32 is directly connected, FastEthernet0/0
Corp#
```

So remember—only configured, directly connected networks are going to show up in the routing table. Why is it that only the FastEthernet 0/0 interface shows up in the table? It's not a huge deal—it's just because you won't see the serial interfaces come up until the other side of the links are operational. As soon as we configure our SF and LA routers, those interfaces should pop right up!

One thing though… Did you notice the C on the left side of the output of the routing table? When you see that there, it means that the network is directly connected. The codes for each type of connection are listed at the top of the show ip route command, along with their descriptions.

> For brevity, the codes at the top of the output will be cut in the rest of this chapter.

SF Configuration

Now we're ready to configure the next router—SF. To make that happen correctly, keep in mind that we have two interfaces to deal with: Serial 0/0/0 and FastEthernet 0/0. Let's make sure not to forget to add the hostname, passwords, interface descriptions, and banners to the router configuration. As I did with the Corp router, I erased the configuration and reloaded since this router had already been configured before.

Here's the configuration I used:

```
R1#erase start
% Incomplete command.
R1#erase startup-config
Erasing the nvram filesystem will remove all configuration files!
Continue? [confirm][enter]
[OK]
Erase of nvram: complete
R1#reload
Proceed with reload? [confirm][enter]
[output cut]
%Error opening tftp://255.255.255.255/network-confg (Timed out)
%Error opening tftp://255.255.255.255/cisconet.cfg (Timed out)
--- System Configuration Dialog ---
Would you like to enter the initial configuration dialog? [yes/no]: n
```

Before we move on, let's talk about this output for a second. First, notice that beginning with IOS 12.4, ISR routers will no longer take the command erase start. The router has only one command after erase that starts with *s*, as shown here:

```
Router#erase s?
startup-config
```

I know, you'd think that the IOS would continue to accept the command, but nope—sorry! The second thing I want to point out is that the output tells us the router is looking for a TFTP host to see if it can download a configuration. When that fails, it goes straight into setup mode. This gives you a great picture of the Cisco router default boot sequence we talked about in Chapter 7, "Managing a Cisco Internetwork."

Let's get back to configuring our router:

```
Press RETURN to get started!
Router#config t
Router(config)#hostname SF
SF(config)#enable secret GlobalNet
SF(config)#no ip domain-lookup
SF(config)#int s0/0/0
SF(config-if)#desc WAN Connection to Corp
SF(config-if)#ip address 172.16.10.2 255.255.255.252
SF(config-if)#no shut
SF(config-if)#clock rate 1000000
```

```
SF(config-if)#int f0/0
SF(config-if)#desc SF LAN
SF(config-if)#ip address 192.168.10.1 255.255.255.0
SF(config-if)#no shut
SF(config-if)#line con 0
SF(config-line)#password console
SF(config-line)#login
SF(config-line)#logging sync
SF(config-line)#exit
SF(config)#line vty 0 ?
<1-1180> Last Line number
<cr>
SF(config)#line vty 0 1180
SF(config-line)#password telnet
SF(config-line)#login
SF(config-line)#banner motd #This is the SF Branch router#
SF(config)#exit
SF#copy run start
Destination filename [startup-config]?
Building configuration...
[OK]
```

Let's take a look at our configuration of the interfaces with the following two commands:

```
SF#sh run | begin int
interface FastEthernet0/0
description SF LAN
ip address 192.168.10.1 255.255.255.0
duplex auto
speed auto
!
interface FastEthernet0/1
no ip address
shutdown
duplex auto
speed auto
!
interface Serial0/0/0
description WAN Connection to Corp
ip address 172.16.10.2 255.255.255.252
clock rate 1000000
!
```

```
SF#sh ip int brief
Interface IP-Address OK? Method Status Protocol
FastEthernet0/0 192.168.10.1 YES manual up up
FastEthernet0/1 unassigned YES unset administratively down down
Serial0/0/0 172.16.10.2 YES manual up up
Serial0/0/1 unassigned YES unset administratively down down
SF#
```

Now that both ends of the serial link are configured, the link comes up. Remember, the up/up status for the interfaces are Physical/Data Link layer status indicators that don't reflect the layer 3 status! I ask students in my classes, "If the link shows up/up, can you ping the directly connected network?" And they say, "Yes!" The correct answer is, "I don't know," because we can't see the layer 3 status with this command. We only see layers 1 and 2 and verify that the IP addresses don't have a typo. Remember this!

The show ip route command for the SF router reveals the following:

```
SF#sh ip route
C 192.168.10.0/24 is directly connected, FastEthernet0/0
L 192.168.10.1/32 is directly connected, FastEthernet0/0
     172.16.0.0/30 is subnetted, 1 subnets
C 172.16.10.0 is directly connected, Serial0/0/0
L 172.16.10.2/32 is directly connected, Serial0/0/0
```

Notice that router SF knows how to get to networks 172.16.10.0/30 and 192.168.10.0/24; we can now ping to the Corp router from SF:

```
SF#ping 172.16.10.1
Type escape sequence to abort.
Sending 5, 100-byte ICMP Echos to 172.16.10.1, timeout is 2 seconds:
!!!!!
Success rate is 100 percent (5/5), round-trip min/avg/max = 1/3/4 ms
```

Now let's head back to the Corp router and check out the routing table:

```
Corp>sh ip route
     172.16.0.0/30 is subnetted, 1 subnets
C 172.16.10.0 is directly connected, Serial0/0
L 172.16.10.1/32 is directly connected, Serial0/0
     10.0.0.0/24 is subnetted, 1 subnets
C 10.10.10.0 is directly connected, FastEthernet0/0
L 10.10.10.1/32 is directly connected, FastEthernet0/0
```

On the SF router's serial interface 0/0/0 is a DCE connection, which means a clock rate needs to be set on the interface. Remember that you don't need to use the clock rate command in production.

We can see our clocking with the show controllers command:

```
SF#sh controllers s0/0/0
Interface Serial0/0/0
Hardware is GT96K
DCE V.35, clock rate 1000000
Corp>sh controllers s0/0
Interface Serial0/0
Hardware is PowerQUICC MPC860
DTE V.35 TX and RX clocks detected.
```

Since the SF router has a DCE cable connection, I needed to add clock rate to this interface because DTE receives clock. Keep in mind that the new ISR routers will autodetect this and set the clock rate to 2000000. But you still need to make sure you're able to find an interface that is DCE and set clocking to meet the objectives.

Since the serial links are showing up, we can now see both networks in the Corp routing table. And once we configure LA, we'll see one more network in the routing table of the Corp router. The Corp router can't see the 192.168.10.0 network because we don't have any routing configured yet—routers see only directly connected networks by default.

LA Configuration

To configure LA, we're going to do pretty much the same thing we did with the other two routers. There are two interfaces to deal with, Serial 0/0/1 and FastEthernet 0/0, and again, we'll be sure to add the hostname, passwords, interface descriptions and a banner to the router configuration:

```
Router(config)#hostname LA
LA(config)#enable secret GlobalNet
LA(config)#no ip domain-lookup
LA(config)#int s0/0/1
LA(config-if)#ip address 172.16.10.6 255.255.255.252
LA(config-if)#no shut
LA(config-if)#clock rate 1000000
LA(config-if)#description WAN To Corporate
LA(config-if)#int f0/0
LA(config-if)#ip address 192.168.20.1 255.255.255.0
LA(config-if)#no shut
LA(config-if)#description LA LAN
LA(config-if)#line con 0
LA(config-line)#password console
LA(config-line)#login
LA(config-line)#logging sync
```

```
LA(config-line)#exit
LA(config)#line vty 0 ?
<1-1180> Last Line number
<cr>
LA(config)#line vty 0 1180
LA(config-line)#password telnet
LA(config-line)#login
LA(config-line)#exit
LA(config)#banner motd #This is my LA Router#
LA(config)#exit
LA#copy run start
Destination filename [startup-config]?
Building configuration...
[OK]
```

Nice—everything was pretty straightforward. The following output, which I gained via the show ip route command, displays the directly connected networks of 192.168.20.0 and 172.16.10.0:

```
LA#sh ip route
172.16.0.0/30 is subnetted, 1 subnets
C 172.16.10.4 is directly connected, Serial0/0/1
L 172.16.10.6/32 is directly connected, Serial0/0/1
C 192.168.20.0/24 is directly connected, FastEthernet0/0
L 192.168.20.1/32 is directly connected, FastEthernet0/0
```

So now that we've configured all three routers with IP addresses and administrative functions, we can move on to deal with routing. But I want to do one more thing on the SF and LA routers—since this is a very small network, let's build a DHCP server on the Corp router for each LAN.

Configuring DHCP on Our Corp Router

While it's true that I could approach this task by going to each remote router and creating a pool, why bother with all that when I can easily create two pools on the Corp router and have the remote routers forward requests to the Corp router? Of course, you remember how to do this from Chapter 7!

Let's give it a shot:

```
Corp#config t
Corp(config)#ip dhcp excluded-address 192.168.10.1
Corp(config)#ip dhcp excluded-address 192.168.20.1
Corp(config)#ip dhcp pool SF_LAN
Corp(dhcp-config)#network 192.168.10.0 255.255.255.0
Corp(dhcp-config)#default-router 192.168.10.1
```

```
Corp(dhcp-config)#dns-server 4.4.4.4
Corp(dhcp-config)#exit
Corp(config)#ip dhcp pool LA_LAN
Corp(dhcp-config)#network 192.168.20.0 255.255.255.0
Corp(dhcp-config)#default-router 192.168.20.1
Corp(dhcp-config)#dns-server 4.4.4.4
Corp(dhcp-config)#exit
Corp(config)#exit
Corp#copy run start
Destination filename [startup-config]?
Building configuration...
```

Creating DHCP pools on a router is actually a simple process, and you would go about the configuration the same way on any router you wish to add a DHCP pool to. To designate a router as a DHCP server, you just create the pool name, add the network/subnet and the default gateway, and then exclude any addresses that you don't want handed out. You definitely want to make sure you've excluded the default gateway address, and you'd usually add a DNS server as well. I always add any exclusions first, and remember that you can conveniently exclude a range of addresses on a single line. Soon, I'll demonstrate those verification commands I promised I'd show you back in Chapter 7, but first, we need to figure out why the Corp router still can't get to the remote networks by default!

Now I'm pretty sure I configured DHCP correctly, but I just have this nagging feeling I forgot something important. What could that be? Well, the hosts are remote across a router, so what would I need to do that would allow them to get an address from a DHCP server? If you concluded that I've got to configure the SF and LA F0/0 interfaces to forward the DHCP client requests to the server, you got it!

Here's how we'd go about doing that:

```
LA#config t
LA(config)#int f0/0
LA(config-if)#ip helper-address 172.16.10.5
SF#config t
SF(config)#int f0/0
SF(config-if)#ip helper-address 172.16.10.1
```

I'm pretty sure I did this correctly, but we won't know until I have some type of routing configured and working. So let's get to that next!

Configuring IP Routing in Our Network

So is our network really good to go? After all, I've configured it with IP addressing, administrative functions, and even clocking that will automatically occur with the ISR routers. But how will our routers send packets to remote networks when they get their destination information by looking into their tables that only include directions about directly connected networks? And you know routers promptly discard packets they receive with addresses for networks that aren't listed in their routing table!

So we're not exactly ready to rock after all. But we will be soon because there are several ways to configure the routing tables to include all the networks in our little internetwork so that packets will be properly forwarded. As usual, one size fits all rarely fits at all, and what's best for one network isn't necessarily what's best for another. That's why understanding the different types of routing will be really helpful when choosing the best solution for your specific environment and business requirements.

These are the three routing methods I'm going to cover with you:

- Static routing
- Default routing
- Dynamic routing

We're going to start with the first way and implement static routing on our network, because if you can implement static routing *and* make it work, you've demonstrated that you definitely have a solid understanding of the internetwork. So let's get started.

Static Routing

Static routing is the process that ensues when you manually add routes in each router's routing table. Predictably, there are pros and cons to static routing, but that's true for all routing approaches.

Here are the pros:

- There is no overhead on the router CPU, which means you could probably make do with a cheaper router than you would need for dynamic routing.
- There is no bandwidth usage between routers, saving you money on WAN links as well as minimizing overhead on the router since you're not using a routing protocol.
- It adds security because you, the administrator, can be very exclusive and choose to allow routing access to certain networks only.

And here are the cons:

- Whoever the administrator is must have a vault-tight knowledge of the internetwork and how each router is connected in order to configure routes correctly. If you don't have a good, accurate map of your internetwork, things will get very messy quickly!
- If you add a network to the internetwork, you have to tediously add a route to it on all routers by hand, which only gets increasingly insane as the network grows.
- Due to the last point, it's just not feasible to use it in most large networks because maintaining it would be a full-time job in itself.

But that list of cons doesn't mean you get to skip learning all about it mainly because of that first disadvantage I listed—the fact that you must have such a solid understanding of a network to configure it properly! So let's dive in and develop those skills. Starting at the beginning, here's the command syntax you use to add a static route to a routing table from global config:

```
ip route [destination_network] [mask] [next-hop_address or exitinterface]
[administrative_distance] [permanent]
```

This list describes each command in the string:

ip route   The command used to create the static route

destination_network   The network you're placing in the routing table

mask   The subnet mask being used on the network

next-hop_address   This is the IP address of the next-hop router that will receive packets and forward them to the remote network, which must signify a router interface that's on a directly connected network. You must be able to successfully ping the router interface before you can add the route. Important note to self is that if you type in the wrong next-hop address or the interface to the correct router is down, the static route will show up in the router's configuration but not in the routing table.

exitinterface   Used in place of the next-hop address if you want, and shows up as a directly connected route

administrative_distance   By default, static routes have an administrative distance of 1 or 0 if you use an exit interface instead of a next-hop address. You can change the default value by adding an administrative weight at the end of the command. I'll talk a lot more about this later in the chapter when we get to dynamic routing.

permanent   If the interface is shut down or the router can't communicate to the next-hop router, the route will automatically be discarded from the routing table by default. Choosing the permanent option keeps the entry in the routing table no matter what happens.

Before I guide you through configuring static routes, let's take a look at a sample static route to see what we can find out about it:

```
Router(config)#ip route 172.16.3.0 255.255.255.0 192.168.2.4
```

- The ip route command tells us simply that it's a static route.
- 172.16.3.0 is the remote network we want to send packets to.
- 255.255.255.0 is the mask of the remote network.
- 192.168.2.4 is the next hop, or router, that packets will be sent to.

But what if the static route looked like this instead?

```
Router(config)#ip route 172.16.3.0 255.255.255.0 192.168.2.4 150
```

That 150 at the end changes the default administrative distance (AD) of 1 to 150. As I said, I'll talk much more about AD when we get into dynamic routing, but for now, just remember that the AD is the trustworthiness of a route, where 0 is best and 255 is worst.

One more example, then we'll start configuring:

```
Router(config)#ip route 172.16.3.0 255.255.255.0 s0/0/0
```

Instead of using a next-hop address, we can use an exit interface that will make the route show up as a directly connected network. Functionally, the next hop and exit interface work exactly the same.

To help you understand how static routes work, I'll demonstrate the configuration on the internetwork shown previously in Figure 9.8. Here it is again in Figure 9.9 to save you the trouble of having to go back and forth to view the same figure.

FIGURE 9.9   Our internetwork

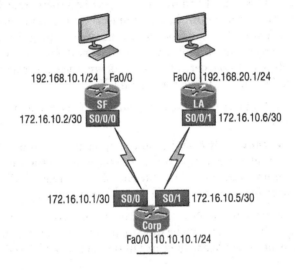

Corp

Each routing table automatically includes directly connected networks. To be able to route to all indirectly connected networks within the internetwork, the routing table must include information that describes where these other networks are located and how to get to them.

The Corp router is connected to three networks. For the Corp router to be able to route to all networks, the following networks have to be configured into its routing table:

- 192.168.10.0

- 192.168.20.0

The following router output shows the static routes on the Corp router and the routing table after the configuration. For the Corp router to find the remote networks, I had to place an entry into the routing table describing the remote network, the remote mask, and where to send the packets. I am going to add a 150 at the end of each line to raise the administrative distance. You'll see why soon when we get to dynamic routing. Many times this is also referred to as a floating static route because the static route has a higher administrative distance than any routing protocol and will only be used if the routes found with the routing protocols go down. Here's the output:

```
Corp#config t
Corp(config)#ip route 192.168.10.0 255.255.255.0 172.16.10.2 150
Corp(config)#ip route 192.168.20.0 255.255.255.0 s0/1 150
Corp(config)#do show run | begin ip route
ip route 192.168.10.0 255.255.255.0 172.16.10.2 150
ip route 192.168.20.0 255.255.255.0 Serial0/1 150
```

I needed to use different paths for networks 192.168.10.0 and 192.168.20.0, so I used a next-hop address for the SF router and an exit interface for the LA router. After the router has been configured, you can just type **show ip route** to see the static routes:

```
Corp(config)#do show ip route
S 192.168.10.0/24 [150/0] via 172.16.10.2
172.16.0.0/30 is subnetted, 2 subnets
C 172.16.10.4 is directly connected, Serial0/1
L 172.16.10.5/32 is directly connected, Serial0/1
C 172.16.10.0 is directly connected, Serial0/0
L 172.16.10.1/32 is directly connected, Serial0/0
S 192.168.20.0/24 is directly connected, Serial0/1
10.0.0.0/24 is subnetted, 1 subnets
C 10.10.10.0 is directly connected, FastEthernet0/0
L 10.10.10.1/32 is directly connected, FastEthernet0/0
```

The Corp router is configured to route and know all routes to all networks. But can you see a difference in the routing table for the routes to SF and LA? That's right! The next-hop configuration showed up as via, and the route configured with an exit interface configuration shows up as static but also as directly connected! This demonstrates how they are functionally the same but will display differently in the routing table.

Understand that if the routes don't appear in the routing table, it's because the router can't communicate with the next-hop address you've configured. But you can still use the permanent parameter to keep the route in the routing table even if the next-hop device can't be contacted.

The S in the first routing table entry means that the route is a static entry. The [150/0] stands for the administrative distance and metric to the remote network, respectively.

Okay—we're good. The Corp router now has all the information it needs to communicate with the other remote networks. Still, keep in mind that if the SF and LA routers aren't configured with all the same information, the packets will be discarded. We can fix this by configuring static routes.

Don't stress about the 150 at the end of the static route configuration at all, because I promise to get to it really soon in *this* chapter, not a later one! You really don't need to worry about it at this point.

SF

The SF router is directly connected to networks 172.16.10.0/30 and 192.168.10.0/24, which means I've got to configure the following static routes on the SF router:

- 10.10.10.0/24
- 192.168.20.0/24
- 172.16.10.4/30

The configuration for the SF router is revealed in the following output. Remember that we'll never create a static route to any network we're directly connected to, as well as the fact that we must use the next hop of 172.16.10.1 since that's our only router connection. Let's check out the commands:

```
SF(config)#ip route 10.10.10.0 255.255.255.0 172.16.10.1 150
SF(config)#ip route 172.16.10.4 255.255.255.252 172.16.10.1 150
SF(config)#ip route 192.168.20.0 255.255.255.0 172.16.10.1 150
SF(config)#do show run | begin ip route
ip route 10.10.10.0 255.255.255.0 172.16.10.1 150
ip route 172.16.10.4 255.255.255.252 172.16.10.1 150
ip route 192.168.20.0 255.255.255.0 172.16.10.1 150
```

By looking at the routing table, you can see that the SF router now understands how to find each network:

```
SF(config)#do show ip route
C 192.168.10.0/24 is directly connected, FastEthernet0/0
L 192.168.10.1/32 is directly connected, FastEthernet0/0
172.16.0.0/30 is subnetted, 3 subnets
S 172.16.10.4 [150/0] via 172.16.10.1
C 172.16.10.0 is directly connected, Serial0/0/0
L 172.16.10.2/32 is directly connected, Serial0/0
S 192.168.20.0/24 [150/0] via 172.16.10.1
10.0.0.0/24 is subnetted, 1 subnets
S 10.10.10.0 [150/0] via 172.16.10.1
```

And we now can rest assured that the SF router has a complete routing table as well. As soon as the LA router has all the networks in its routing table, SF will be able to communicate with all remote networks!

LA

The LA router is directly connected to 192.168.20.0/24 and 172.16.10.4/30, so these are the routes that must be added:

- 10.10.10.0/24
- 172.16.10.0/30
- 192.168.10.0/24

And here's the LA router's configuration:

```
LA#config t
LA(config)#ip route 10.10.10.0 255.255.255.0 172.16.10.5 150
LA(config)#ip route 172.16.10.0 255.255.255.252 172.16.10.5 150
LA(config)#ip route 192.168.10.0 255.255.255.0 172.16.10.5 150
LA(config)#do show run | begin ip route
ip route 10.10.10.0 255.255.255.0 172.16.10.5 150
ip route 172.16.10.0 255.255.255.252 172.16.10.5 150
ip route 192.168.10.0 255.255.255.0 172.16.10.5 150
```

This output displays the routing table on the LA router:

```
LA(config)#do sho ip route
S 192.168.10.0/24 [150/0] via 172.16.10.5
172.16.0.0/30 is subnetted, 3 subnets
C 172.16.10.4 is directly connected, Serial0/0/1
L 172.16.10.6/32 is directly connected, Serial0/0/1
S 172.16.10.0 [150/0] via 172.16.10.5
C 192.168.20.0/24 is directly connected, FastEthernet0/0
L 192.168.20.1/32 is directly connected, FastEthernet0/0
10.0.0.0/24 is subnetted, 1 subnets
S 10.10.10.0 [150/0] via 172.16.10.5
```

LA now shows all five networks in the internetwork, so it too can now communicate with all routers and networks. But before we test our little network, as well as our DHCP server, let's cover one more topic.

Default Routing

The SF and LA routers that I've connected to the Corp router are considered stub routers. A *stub* indicates that the networks in this design have only one way out to reach all other networks, which means that instead of creating multiple static routes, we can just use a single default route. This default route is used by IP to forward any packet with a destination not found in the routing table, which is why it is also called a gateway of last resort. Here's the configuration I could have done on the LA router instead of typing in the static routes due to its stub status:

```
LA#config t
LA(config)#no ip route 10.10.10.0 255.255.255.0 172.16.10.5 150
LA(config)#no ip route 172.16.10.0 255.255.255.252 172.16.10.5 150
LA(config)#no ip route 192.168.10.0 255.255.255.0 172.16.10.5 150
LA(config)#ip route 0.0.0.0 0.0.0.0 172.16.10.5
LA(config)#do sho ip route
[output cut]
```

```
Gateway of last resort is 172.16.10.5 to network 0.0.0.0
172.16.0.0/30 is subnetted, 1 subnets
C 172.16.10.4 is directly connected, Serial0/0/1
L 172.16.10.6/32 is directly connected, Serial0/0/1
C 192.168.20.0/24 is directly connected, FastEthernet0/0
L 192.168.20.0/32 is directly connected, FastEthernet0/0
S* 0.0.0.0/0 [1/0] via 172.16.10.5
```

Okay—I've removed all the initial static routes I had configured, and adding a default route is a lot easier than typing a bunch of static routes! Can you see the default route listed last in the routing table? The S* shows that as a candidate for the default route. And I really want you to notice that the gateway of last resort is now set too. Everything the router receives with a destination not found in the routing table will be forwarded to 172.16.10.5. You need to be really careful where you place default routes because you can easily create a network loop!

So we're there—we've configured all our routing tables! All the routers have the correct routing table, so all routers and hosts should be able to communicate without a hitch—for now. But if you add even one more network or another router to the internetwork, you'll have to update each and every router's routing tables by hand—ugh! Not really a problem at all if you've got a small network like we do, but the task would be a monster if you're dealing with a large internetwork!

Verifying Your Configuration

We're still not done yet—once all the routers' routing tables are configured, they must be verified. The best way to do this, besides using the show ip route command, is via Ping. I'll start by pinging from the Corp router to the SF router.

Here's the output I got:

```
Corp#ping 192.168.10.1
Type escape sequence to abort.
Sending 5, 100-byte ICMP Echos to 192.168.10.1, timeout is 2 seconds:
!!!!!
Success rate is 100 percent (5/5), round-trip min/avg/max = 4/4/4 ms
Corp#
```

Here you can see that I pinged from the Corp router to the remote interface of the SF router. Now let's ping the remote network on the LA router, and after that, we'll test our DHCP server and see if that is working too:

```
Corp#ping 192.168.20.1
Type escape sequence to abort.
Sending 5, 100-byte ICMP Echos to 192.168.20.1, timeout is 2 seconds:
!!!!!
Success rate is 100 percent (5/5), round-trip min/avg/max = 1/2/4 ms
Corp#
```

And why not test my configuration of the DHCP server on the Corp router while we're at it? I'm going to go to each host on the SF and LA routers and make them DHCP clients. By the way, I'm using an old router to represent "hosts," which just happens to work great for studying purposes. Here's how I did that:

```
SF_PC(config)#int e0
SF_PC(config-if)#ip address dhcp
SF_PC(config-if)#no shut
Interface Ethernet0 assigned DHCP address 192.168.10.8, mask 255.255.255.0
LA_PC(config)#int e0
LA_PC(config-if)#ip addr dhcp
LA_PC(config-if)#no shut
Interface Ethernet0 assigned DHCP address 192.168.20.4, mask 255.255.255.0
```

Nice! Don't you love it when things just work the first time? Sadly, this just isn't exactly a realistic expectation in the networking world, so we must be able to troubleshoot and verify our networks. Let's verify our DHCP server with a few of the commands you learned back in Chapter 7:

```
Corp#sh ip dhcp binding
Bindings from all pools not associated with VRF:
IP address Client-ID/ Lease expiration Type
Hardware address/
User name
192.168.10.8 0063.6973.636f.2d30. Sept 16 2013 10:34 AM Automatic
3035.302e.3062.6330.
2e30.3063.632d.4574.
30
192.168.20.4 0063.6973.636f.2d30. Sept 16 2013 10:46 AM Automatic
3030.322e.3137.3632.
2e64.3032.372d.4574.
30
```

We can see from earlier that our little DHCP server is working! Let's try another couple of commands:

```
Corp#sh ip dhcp pool SF_LAN
Pool SF_LAN :
Utilization mark (high/low) : 100 / 0
Subnet size (first/next) : 0 / 0
Total addresses : 254
Leased addresses : 3
Pending event : none
1 subnet is currently in the pool :
```

```
Current index IP address range Leased addresses
192.168.10.9 192.168.10.1 - 192.168.10.254 3
Corp#sh ip dhcp conflict
IP address Detection method Detection time VRF
```

The last command would tell us if we had two hosts with the same IP address, so it's good news because there are no conflicts reported. Two detection methods are used to confirm this:

- A ping from the DHCP server to make sure no other host responds before handing out an address

- A gratuitous ARP from a host that receives a DHCP address from the server

The DHCP client will send an ARP request with its new IP address looking to see if anyone responds, and if so, it will report the conflict to the server.

Since we can communicate from end to end and to each host without a problem while receiving DHCP addresses from our server, I'd say our static and default route configurations have been a success—cheers!

Dynamic Routing

Dynamic routing is when protocols are used to find networks and update routing tables on routers. This is a whole lot easier than using static or default routing, but it will cost you in terms of router CPU processing and bandwidth on network links. A routing protocol defines the set of rules used by a router when it communicates routing information between neighboring routers.

The routing protocol I'm going to talk about in this chapter is Routing Information Protocol (RIP) versions 1 and 2.

Two types of routing protocols are used in internetworks: *interior gateway protocols (IGPs)* and *exterior gateway protocols (EGPs)*. IGPs are used to exchange routing information with routers in the same *autonomous system (AS)*. An AS is either a single network or a collection of networks under a common administrative domain, which basically means that all routers sharing the same routing-table information are in the same AS. EGPs are used to communicate between ASs. An example of an EGP is Border Gateway Protocol (BGP), which we're not going to bother with because it's beyond the scope of this book.

Since routing protocols are so essential to dynamic routing, I'm going to give you the basic information you need to know about them next. Later on in this chapter, we'll focus on configuration.

Routing Protocol Basics

There are some important things you should know about routing protocols before we get deeper into RIP routing. Being familiar with administrative distances and the three different kinds of routing protocols, for example. Let's take a look.

Administrative Distances

The *administrative distance (AD)* is used to rate the trustworthiness of routing information received on a router from a neighbor router. An administrative distance is an integer from 0 to 255, where 0 is the most trusted and 255 means no traffic will be passed via this route.

If a router receives two updates listing the same remote network, the first thing the router checks is the AD. If one of the advertised routes has a lower AD than the other, then the route with the lowest AD will be chosen and placed in the routing table.

If both advertised routes to the same network have the same AD, then routing protocol metrics like *hop count* and/or the bandwidth of the lines will be used to find the best path to the remote network. The advertised route with the lowest metric will be placed in the routing table, but if both advertised routes have the same AD as well as the same metrics, then the routing protocol will load-balance to the remote network, meaning the protocol will send data down each link.

Table 9.1 shows the default administrative distances that a Cisco router uses to decide which route to take to a remote network.

TABLE 9.1   Default administrative distances

Route Source	Default AD
Connected interface	0
Static route	1
External BGP	20
EIGRP	90
OSPF	110
RIP	120
External EIGRP	170
Internal BGP	200
Unknown	255 (This route will never be used.)

If a network is directly connected, the router will always use the interface connected to the network. If you configure a static route, the router will then believe that route over any other ones it learns about. You can change the administrative distance of static routes, but by default, they have an AD of 1. In our previous static route configuration, the AD of each route is set at 150. This AD allows us to configure routing protocols without having to remove the static routes because it's nice to have them there for backup in case the routing protocol experiences some kind of failure.

If you have a static route, an RIP-advertised route, and an EIGRP-advertised route listing the same network, which route will the router go with? That's right—by default, the router will always use the static route unless you change its AD—which we did!

Routing Protocols

There are three classes of routing protocols:

Distance vector   The distance-vector protocols in use today find the best path to a remote network by judging distance. In RIP routing, each instance where a packet goes through a router is called a hop, and the route with the least number of hops to the network will be chosen as the best one. The vector indicates the direction to the remote network. RIP is a distance-vector routing protocol and periodically sends out the entire routing table to directly connected neighbors.

Link state   In link-state protocols, also called shortest-path-first (SPF) protocols, the routers each create three separate tables. One of these tables keeps track of directly attached neighbors, one determines the topology of the entire internetwork, and one is used as the routing table. Link-state routers know more about the internetwork than any distance-vector routing protocol ever could. OSPF is an IP routing protocol that's completely link-state. Link-state routing tables are not exchanged periodically. Instead, triggered updates containing only specific link-state information are sent. Periodic keepalives that are small and efficient, in the form of hello messages, are exchanged between directly connected neighbors to establish and maintain neighbor relationships.

Advanced distance vector   Advanced distance-vector protocols use aspects of both distance-vector and link-state protocols, and EIGRP is a great example. EIGRP may act like a link-state routing protocol because it uses a Hello protocol to discover neighbors and form neighbor relationships and because only partial updates are sent when a change occurs. However, EIGRP is still based on the key distance-vector routing protocol principle that information about the rest of the network is learned from directly connected neighbors.

There's no fixed set of rules to follow that dictate exactly how to broadly configure routing protocols for every situation. It's a task that really must be undertaken on a case-by-case basis, with an eye on specific requirements of each. If you understand how the different routing protocols work, you can make great decisions that will solidly meet the individual needs of any business!

Routing Information Protocol (RIP)

Routing Information Protocol (RIP) is a true distance-vector routing protocol. RIP sends the complete routing table out of all active interfaces every 30 seconds. It relies on hop count to determine the best way to a remote network, but it has a maximum allowable hop count of 15 by default, so a destination of 16 would be considered unreachable. RIP works okay in very small networks, but it's super inefficient on large networks with slow WAN links or on networks with a large number of routers installed. And it's completely useless on networks that have links with variable bandwidths!

RIP version 1 uses only *classful routing*, which means that all devices in the network must use the same subnet mask. This is because RIP version 1 doesn't send updates with subnet mask information in tow. RIP version 2 provides something called *prefix routing* and does send subnet mask information with its route updates. This is called *classless routing*.

So with that, let's configure our current network with RIPv2, before we move on to the next chapter.

Configuring RIP Routing

To configure RIP routing, just turn on the protocol with the router rip command and tell the RIP routing protocol the networks to advertise. Remember that with static routing, we always configured remote networks and never typed a route to our directly connected networks? Well, dynamic routing is carried out the complete opposite way. You would never type a *remote* network under your routing protocol—only enter your directly connected networks! Let's configure our three-router internetwork, revisited in Figure 9.9, with RIP routing.

Corp

RIP has an administrative distance of 120. Static routes have an administrative distance of 1 by default, and since we currently have static routes configured, the routing tables won't be populated with RIP information by default. We're still good though because I added the 150 to the end of each static route!

You can add the RIP routing protocol by using the router rip command and the network command. The network command tells the routing protocol which classful network to advertise. By doing this, you're activating the RIP routing process on the interfaces whose addressing falls within the specified classful networks configured with the network command under the RIP routing process.

Look at the Corp router configuration to see how easy this is. Oh wait—first, I want to verify my directly connected networks so I know what to configure RIP with:

```
Corp#sh ip int brief
Interface IP-Address OK? Method Status Protocol
FastEthernet0/0 10.10.10.1 YES manual up up
Serial0/0 172.16.10.1 YES manual up up
FastEthernet0/1 unassigned YES unset administratively down down
Serial0/1 172.16.10.5 YES manual up up
Corp#config t
Corp(config)#router rip
Corp(config-router)#network 10.0.0.0
Corp(config-router)#network 172.16.0.0
Corp(config-router)#version 2
Corp(config-router)#no auto-summary
```

That's it—really! Typically just two or three commands and you're done, which sure makes your job a lot easier than dealing with static routes, doesn't it? Be sure to keep in mind the extra router CPU process and bandwidth that you're consuming.

Anyway, so what exactly did I do here? I enabled the RIP routing protocol, added my directly connected networks, made sure I was only running RIPv2, which is a classless routing protocol, and then I disabled auto-summary. We typically don't want our routing protocols summarizing for us because it's better to do that manually and both RIP and EIGRP (before 15.x code) auto-summarize by default. So a general rule of thumb is to disable auto-summary, which allows them to advertise subnets.

Notice I didn't type in subnets, only the classful network address, which is betrayed by the fact that all subnet bits and host bits are off! That's because with dynamic routing, it's not my job and it's up to the routing protocol to find the subnets and populate the routing tables. And since we have no router buddies running RIP, we won't see any RIP routes in the routing table yet.

Remember that RIP uses the classful address when configuring the network address. To clarify this, refer to the example in our network with an address of 172.16.0.0/24 using subnets 172.16.10.0 and 172.16.20.0. You would only type in the classful network address of 172.16.0.0 and let RIP find the subnets and place them in the routing table. This doesn't mean you are running a classful routing protocol—it's just the way that both RIP and EIGRP are configured.

SF

Let's configure our SF router now, which is connected to two networks. We need to configure both directly connected classful networks, not subnets:

```
SF#sh ip int brief
Interface IP-Address OK? Method Status Protocol
FastEthernet0/0 192.168.10.1 YES manual up up
FastEthernet0/1 unassigned YES unset administratively down down
Serial0/0/0 172.16.10.2 YES manual up up
Serial0/0/1 unassigned YES unset administratively down down
SF#config
SF(config)#router rip
SF(config-router)#network 192.168.10.0
SF(config-router)#network 172.16.0.0
SF(config-router)#version 2
SF(config-router)#no auto-summary
SF(config-router)#do show ip route
C 192.168.10.0/24 is directly connected, FastEthernet0/0
L 192.168.10.1/32 is directly connected, FastEthernet0/0
```

```
172.16.0.0/30 is subnetted, 3 subnets
R 172.16.10.4 [120/1] via 172.16.10.1, 00:00:08, Serial0/0/0
C 172.16.10.0 is directly connected, Serial0/0/0
L 172.16.10.2/32 is directly connected, Serial0/0
S 192.168.20.0/24 [150/0] via 172.16.10.1
10.0.0.0/24 is subnetted, 1 subnets
R 10.10.10.0 [120/1] via 172.16.10.1, 00:00:08, Serial0/0/0
```

That was pretty straightforward. Let's talk about this routing table... Since we have one RIP buddy out there with whom we are exchanging routing tables, we can see the RIP networks coming from the Corp router. All the other routes still show up as static and local. RIP also found both connections through the Corp router to networks 10.10.10.0 and 172.16.10.4. But we're not done yet!

LA

Let's configure our LA router with RIP, only I'm going to remove the default route first, even though I don't have to. You'll see why soon:

```
LA#config t
LA(config)#no ip route 0.0.0.0 0.0.0.0
LA(config)#router rip
LA(config-router)#network 192.168.20.0
LA(config-router)#network 172.16.0.0
LA(config-router)#no auto
LA(config-router)#vers 2
LA(config-router)#do show ip route
R 192.168.10.0/24 [120/2] via 172.16.10.5, 00:00:10, Serial0/0/1
172.16.0.0/30 is subnetted, 3 subnets
C 172.16.10.4 is directly connected, Serial0/0/1
L 172.16.10.6/32 is directly connected, Serial0/0/1
R 172.16.10.0 [120/1] via 172.16.10.5, 00:00:10, Serial0/0/1
C 192.168.20.0/24 is directly connected, FastEthernet0/0
L 192.168.20.1/32 is directly connected, FastEthernet0/0
10.0.0.0/24 is subnetted, 1 subnets
R 10.10.10.0 [120/1] via 172.16.10.5, 00:00:10, Serial0/0/1
```

The routing table is sprouting new Rs as we add RIP buddies! We can still see that all routes are in the routing table.

This output shows us basically the same routing table and the same entries that it had when we were using static routes—except for those Rs. An R indicates that the networks were added dynamically using the RIP routing protocol. The [120/1] is the administrative distance of the route (120) along with the metric, which for RIP is the number of hops to that remote network (1). From the Corp router, all networks are one hop away.

So, while yes, it's true that RIP has worked in our little internetwork, it's just not a great solution for most enterprises. Its maximum hop count of only 15 is a highly limiting factor. And it performs full routing-table updates every 30 seconds, which would bring a larger internetwork to a crawl in no time!

There's still one more thing I want to show you about RIP routing tables and the parameters used to advertise remote networks. Using a different router on a different network as an example for a second, look into the following output. Can you spot where the following routing table shows [120/15] in the 10.1.3.0 network metric? This means that the administrative distance is 120, the default for RIP, but the hop count is 15. Remember that each time a router sends out an update to a neighbor router, the hop count goes up by one incrementally for each route. Here's that output now:

```
Router#sh ip route
10.0.0.0/24 is subnetted, 12 subnets
C  10.1.11.0 is directly connected, FastEthernet0/1
L  10.1.11.1/32 is directly connected, FastEthernet0/1
C  10.1.10.0 is directly connected, FastEthernet0/0
L  10.1.10.1/32 is directly connected, FastEthernet/0/0
R  10.1.9.0 [120/2] via 10.1.5.1, 00:00:15, Serial0/0/1
R  10.1.8.0 [120/2] via 10.1.5.1, 00:00:15, Serial0/0/1
R  10.1.12.0 [120/1] via 10.1.11.2, 00:00:00, FastEthernet0/1
R  10.1.3.0 [120/15] via 10.1.5.1, 00:00:15, Serial0/0/1
R  10.1.2.0 [120/1] via 10.1.5.1, 00:00:15, Serial0/0/1
R  10.1.1.0 [120/1] via 10.1.5.1, 00:00:15, Serial0/0/1
R  10.1.7.0 [120/2] via 10.1.5.1, 00:00:15, Serial0/0/1
R  10.1.6.0 [120/2] via 10.1.5.1, 00:00:15, Serial0/0/1
C  10.1.5.0 is directly connected, Serial0/0/1
L  10.1.5.1/32 is directly connected, Serial0/0/1
R  10.1.4.0 [120/1] via 10.1.5.1, 00:00:15, Serial0/0/1
```

So this [120/15] is really bad. We're basically doomed because the next router that receives the table from this router will just discard the route to network 10.1.3.0 since the hop count would rise to 16, which is invalid!

 If a router receives a routing update that contains a higher-cost path to a network that's already in its routing table, the update will be ignored.

Holding Down RIP Propagations

You probably don't want your RIP network advertised everywhere on your LAN and WAN. There's enough stress in networking already and not a whole lot to be gained by advertising your RIP network to the Internet!

There are a few different ways to stop unwanted RIP updates from propagating across your LANs and WANs, and the easiest one is through the passive-interface command. This command prevents RIP update broadcasts from being sent out of a specified interface but still allows that same interface to receive RIP updates.

Here's an example of how to configure a passive-interface on the Corp router's Fa0/1 interface, which we will pretend is connected to a LAN that we don't want RIP on (and the interface isn't shown in the figure):

```
Corp#config t
Corp(config)#router rip
Corp(config-router)#passive-interface FastEthernet 0/1  '
```

This command will stop RIP updates from being propagated out of FastEthernet interface 0/1, but it can still receive RIP updates.

 Real World Scenario

Should We Really Use RIP in an Internetwork?

You have been hired as a consultant to install a couple of Cisco routers into a growing network. They have a couple of old Unix routers that they want to keep in the network. These routers do not support any routing protocol except RIP. I guess this means you just have to run RIP on the entire network. If you were balding before, your head now shines like chrome.

No need for hairs abandoning ship though—you can run RIP on a router connecting that old network, but you certainly don't need to run RIP throughout the whole internetwork!

You can do something called *redistribution*, which is basically translating from one type of routing protocol to another. This means that you can support those old routers using RIP but use something much better like Enhanced IGRP on the rest of your network.

This will prevent RIP routes from being sent all over the internetwork gobbling up all that precious bandwidth!

Advertising a Default Route Using RIP

Now I'm going to guide you through how to advertise a way out of your autonomous system to other routers, and you'll see this is completed the same way with OSPF.

Imagine that our Corp router's Fa0/0 interface is connected to some type of Metro-Ethernet as a connection to the Internet. This is a pretty common configuration today that uses a LAN interface to connect to the ISP instead of a serial interface.

If we do add an Internet connection to Corp, all routers in our AS (SF and LA) must know where to send packets destined for networks on the Internet or they'll just drop the packets when they get a remote request. One solution to this little hitch would be to place a default route on every router and funnel the information to Corp, which in turn would have a default route to the ISP. Most people do this type of configuration in small- to medium-size networks because it actually works pretty well!

But since I'm running RIPv2 on all routers, I'll just add a default route on the Corp router to our ISP, as I would normally. I'll then add another command to advertise my network to the other routers in the AS as the default route to show them where to send packets destined for the Internet.

Here's my new Corp configuration:

```
Corp(config)#ip route 0.0.0.0 0.0.0.0 fa0/0
Corp(config)#router rip
Corp(config-router)#default-information originate
```

Now, let's take a look at the last entry found in the Corp routing table:

```
S* 0.0.0.0/0 is directly connected, FastEthernet0/0
```

Let's see if the LA router can see this same entry:

```
LA#sh ip route
Gateway of last resort is 172.16.10.5 to network 0.0.0.0
R 192.168.10.0/24 [120/2] via 172.16.10.5, 00:00:04, Serial0/0/1
172.16.0.0/30 is subnetted, 2 subnets
C 172.16.10.4 is directly connected, Serial0/0/1
L 172.16.10.5/32 is directly connected, Serial0/0/1
R 172.16.10.0 [120/1] via 172.16.10.5, 00:00:04, Serial0/0/1
C 192.168.20.0/24 is directly connected, FastEthernet0/0
L 192.168.20.1/32 is directly connected, FastEthernet0/0
10.0.0.0/24 is subnetted, 1 subnets
R 10.10.10.0 [120/1] via 172.16.10.5, 00:00:04, Serial0/0/1
R 192.168.218.0/24 [120/3] via 172.16.10.5, 00:00:04, Serial0/0/1
R 192.168.118.0/24 [120/2] via 172.16.10.5, 00:00:05, Serial0/0/1
R* 0.0.0.0/0 [120/1] via 172.16.10.5, 00:00:05, Serial0/0/1
```

Can you see that last entry? It screams that it's an RIP injected route, but it's also a default route, so our default-information originate command is working! Last, notice that the gateway of last resort is now set as well.

Summary

This chapter covered IP routing in detail. Again, it's extremely important to fully understand the basics we covered in this chapter because everything that's done on a Cisco router will typically have some kind of IP routing configured and running.

You learned how IP routing uses frames to transport packets between routers and to the destination host. From there, we configured static routing on our routers and discussed the administrative distance used by IP to determine the best route to a destination network. You found out that if you have a stub network, you can configure default routing, which sets the gateway of last resort on a router.

We then discussed dynamic routing, specifically RIPv2 and how it works on an internetwork, which is not very well!

Chapter 10

Wide Area Networks

The Cisco IOS supports a ton of different wide area network (WAN) protocols that help you extend your local LANs to other LANs at remote sites. And all of us know just how essential information exchange between disparate sites is these days! But it wouldn't be cost effective or efficient to install your own cable and connect all of your company's remote locations yourself, would it? A much better way to get this done is to just lease the existing installations that service providers already have in place.

This is exactly why I'm going to devote most of this chapter to covering the various types of connections, technologies, and devices used in today's WANs.

We'll also delve into how to implement and configure High-Level Data-Link Control (HDLC), and Point-to-Point Protocol (PPP). I'll describe Point-to-Point Protocol over Ethernet (PPPoE), cable, digital subscriber line (DSL), MultiProtocol Label Switching (MPLS), Metro Ethernet, plus last mile and long-range WAN technologies.

To find your included bonus material, as well as Todd Lammle videos. practice questions and hands-on labs, please see www.lammle.com/ccna.

Introduction to Wide Area Networks

Let's begin exploring WAN basics by asking, what's the difference between a wide area network (WAN) and a local area network (LAN)? Clearly there's the distance factor, but modern wireless LANs can cover some serious turf, so there's more to it than that. What about bandwidth? Here again, really big pipes can be had for a price in many places, so that's not it either. What's the answer we're looking for?

A major distinction between a WAN and a LAN is that while you generally own a LAN infrastructure, you usually lease a WAN infrastructure from a service provider. Modern technologies sometimes blur this characteristic somewhat, but this factor still fits neatly into the context of Cisco's exam objectives.

I've already talked about the Data Link that you usually own back when we covered Ethernet, so now, I'm going to focus on the type you typically lease from a service provider.

There are several reasons why WANs are necessary in corporate environments today.

LAN technologies provide solid speeds—10/40/100Gbps is now common— at great prices, but these solutions can only work well in relatively small geographic areas. We still need WANs in a communications environment because some business needs require connections to remote sites for many reasons, including the following:

- People in the regional or branch offices of an organization need to be able to communicate and share data.

- Organizations often want to share information with other organizations across large distances.

- Employees who travel on company business frequently need to access information that resides on their corporate networks.

Here are three major characteristics of WANs:

- WANs generally connect devices that are separated by a broader geographic area than a LAN can serve.

- WANs use the services of carriers such as telcos, cable companies, satellite systems, and network providers.

- WANs use serial connections of various types to provide access to bandwidth over large geographic areas.

The first key to understanding WAN technologies is to be familiar with the different WAN topologies, terms, and connection types commonly used by service providers to join your LAN networks together. We'll begin covering these topics now.

WAN Topology Options

A physical topology describes the physical layout of the network, in contrast to logical topologies, which describe the path a signal takes through the physical topology. There are three basic topologies for a WAN design.

Star or hub-and-spoke topology   This topology features a single hub (central router) that provides access from remote networks to a core router. Figure 10.1 illustrates a hub-and-spoke topology:

FIGURE 10.1   Hub-and-spoke

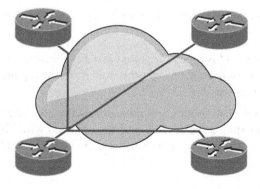

All communication among the networks travels through the core router. The advantages of a star physical topology are less cost and easier administration, but the disadvantages are pretty significant:

- The central router (hub) represents a single point of failure.
- The central router limits the overall performance for access to centralized resources. It is a single pipe that manages all traffic intended either for the centralized resources or for the other regional routers.

Fully meshed topology   In this topology, each routing node on the edge of a given packet-switching network has a direct path to every other node on the cloud. Figure 10.2 shows a fully meshed topology:

FIGURE 10.2   Fully Meshed Topology

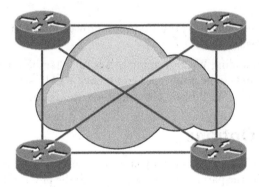

This configuration clearly provides a high level of redundancy, but the costs are the highest. So a fully meshed topology really isn't viable in large packet-switched networks. Some issues you'll contend with using a fully meshed topology include:

- Many virtual circuits are required—one for every connection between routers, which brings up the cost.
- Configuration is more complex for routers without multicast support in non-broadcast environments.

Partially Meshed Topology   This type of topology reduces the number of routers within a network that have direct connections to all other routers in the topology. Figure 10.3 depicts a partial meshed topology

Unlike the full mesh network, all routers are not connected to all other routers, yet it still provides more redundancy than a typical hub-and-spoke design will. This is actually considered the most balanced design because it provides more virtual circuits, plus redundancy and performance.

FIGURE 10.3   Partially Meshed

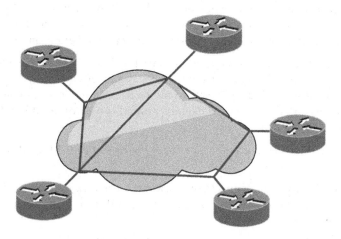

Defining WAN Terms

Before you run out and order a WAN service type from a provider, you really need to understand the following terms that service providers typically use. Here they are in Figure 10.4:

FIGURE 10.4   WAN terms

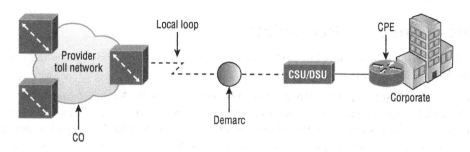

Customer premises equipment (CPE)   *Customer premises equipment (CPE)* is equipment that's typically owned by the subscriber and located on the subscriber's premises.

CSU/DSU   A CSU/DSU is a device that is used to connect a DTE to a digital circuit, such as a T1/T3 line. A device is considered DTE if it's either a source or destination for digital data—for example, PCs, servers and routers. In Figure 10.4, the router is considered DTE because it is passing data to the CSU/DSU, which will forward the data to the service provider. Although the CSU/DSU connects to the service provider's infrastructure using a telephone or coaxial cable, such as a T1 or E1 line, it connects to the router with a serial cable. The most important aspect to remember for the CCNA objectives, is the CSU/DSU provides clocking of the line to the router. You really need to understand this completely, which is why I'll cover it in depth later in the serial interface configuration section.

Demarcation point   The *demarcation point* (demarc for short) is the precise spot where the service provider's responsibility ends and the CPE begins. It's generally a device in a telecommunications closet owned and installed by the telecommunications company (telco). It's your responsibility to cable (extended demarc) from this box to the CPE, which is usually a connection to a CSU/DSU.

Local loop   The *local loop* connects the demarc to the closest switching office, referred to as the central office.

Central office (CO)   This point connects the customer's network to the provider's switching network. Make a mental note that a *central office (CO)* is sometimes also referred to as a *point of presence (POP)*.

Toll network   The *toll network* is a trunk line inside a WAN provider's network. This network is a collection of switches and facilities owned by the Internet service provider (ISP).

Optical fiber converters: Even though I'm not employing this device in Figure 10.1, optical fiber converters are used where a fiber-optic link terminates to convert optical signals into electrical signals and vice versa. You can also implement the converter as a router or switch module.

Make sure you're comfortable with these terms, what they represent, and where they're located, as shown in Figure 10.4, because they're key to understanding WAN technologies.

WAN Connection Bandwidth

Next, I want you to know these basic but very important bandwidth terms used when referring to WAN connections:

Digital Signal 0 (DS0)   This is the basic digital signaling rate of 64 Kbps, equivalent to one channel. Europe uses the E0 and Japan uses the J0 to reference the same channel speed. Typical to T-carrier transmission, this is the generic term used by several multiplexed digital carrier systems and is also the smallest-capacity digital circuit. 1 DS0 = 1 voice/data line.

T1   Also referred to as a DS1, a T1 comprises 24 DS0 circuits bundled together for a total bandwidth of 1.544 Mbps.

E1   This is the European equivalent of a T1 and comprises 30 DS0 circuits bundled together for a bandwidth of 2.048 Mbps.

T3   Referred to as a DS3, a T3 comprises 28 DS1s bundled together, or 672 DS0s, for a bandwidth of 44.736 Mbps.

OC-3   Optical Carrier (OC) 3 uses fiber and is made up of three DS3s bundled together. It's made up of 2,016 DS0s and avails a total bandwidth of 155.52 Mbps.

OC-12 Optical Carrier 12 is made up of four OC-3s bundled together and contains 8,064 DS0s for a total bandwidth of 622.08 Mbps.

OC-48 Optical Carrier 48 is made up of four OC-12s bundled together and contains 32,256 DS0s for a total bandwidth of 2488.32 Mbps.

WAN Connection Types

A WAN can use a number of the different connection types available today. Figure 10.5 shows these different types used to connect your LANs together, which are made up of data terminal equipment, (DTE) over the data communication equipment (DCE) network.

FIGURE 10.5 WAN connection types

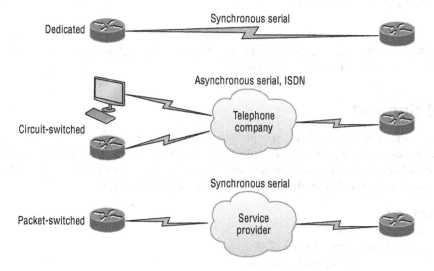

Let's go over the different WAN connection types in detail now:

Dedicated (leased lines) These are usually referred to as a *point-to-point* or dedicated connections. A *leased line* is a pre-established WAN communications path that goes from the CPE through the DCE switch, then over to the CPE of the remote site. The CPE enables DTE networks to communicate at any time with no cumbersome setup procedures to muddle through before transmitting data. When you've got plenty of cash, this is definitely the way to go because it uses synchronous serial lines up to 45 Mbps. HDLC and PPP encapsulations are frequently used on leased lines, which I'll go over with you soon.

Circuit switching When you hear the term *circuit switching*, think phone call. The big advantage is cost; most plain old telephone service (POTS) and ISDN dial-up connections are not flat rate, which is their advantage over dedicated lines. No data can transfer before an end-to-end connection is established. Circuit switching uses dial-up modems or ISDN and is used for low-bandwidth data transfers. I know what you're thinking: "Modems? Did he say modems? Aren't those only in museums now?" After all, with all the wireless technologies available, who would use a modem these days? Well, some people do have ISDN; it's still viable and there are a few who still use a modem now and then. Circuit switching can be used in some of the newer WAN technologies as well.

Packet switching   This is a WAN switching method that allows you to share bandwidth with other companies to save money. *Packet switching* can be thought of as a network that's designed to look like a leased line, but it charges you more, like circuit switching does. There's definitely a serious downside to this technology. If you need to transfer data constantly, just forget about this option and go with a leased line instead! Packet switching will only really work for you if your data transfers are bursty, not continuous—think of a busy highway, where you can only go as fast as the traffic—packet switching is the same thing. Frame Relay and X.25 are packet-switching technologies with speeds that can range from 56 Kbps up to T3 (45 Mbps).

> MultiProtocol Label Switching (MPLS) uses a combination of both circuit switching and packet switching.

WAN Support

Cisco supports many layer 2 WAN encapsulations on its serial interfaces, including HDLC, PPP, and Frame Relay, which all map to the Cisco exam objectives. You can view them via the encapsulation ? command from any serial interface, but understand that the output you'll get can vary based upon the specific IOS version you're running:

```
Corp#config t
Corp(config)#int s0/0/0
Corp(config-if)#encapsulation ?
  atm-dxi       ATM-DXI encapsulation
  frame-relay   Frame Relay networks
  hdlc          Serial HDLC synchronous
  lapb          LAPB (X.25 Level 2)
  ppp           Point-to-Point protocol
  smds          Switched Megabit Data Service (SMDS)
  x25           X.25
```

I want to point out that if I had other types of interfaces on my router, I would have a different set of encapsulation options. Never forget that you can't configure an Ethernet encapsulation on a serial interface or vice versa!

Next, I'm going to define the most prominently known WAN protocols used in the latest Cisco exam objectives: Frame Relay, ISDN, HDLC, PPP, PPPoE, cable, DSL, MPLS, ATM,

3G/4G/5G, VSAT, and Metro Ethernet. Just so you know, the only WAN protocols you'll usually find configured on a serial interface are HDLC, PPP, and Frame Relay, but who said you're stuck with using only serial interfaces for wide area connections? There are fewer serial connections today because they're not as scalable or cost effective as an Ethernet connection to your ISP.

Frame Relay   A packet-switched technology that made its debut in the early 1990s, *Frame Relay* is a high-performance Data Link and Physical layer specification. It's pretty much a successor to X.25, except that much of the technology in X.25 that's there to compensate for physical errors like noisy lines has been eliminated. An upside to Frame Relay is that it can be more cost effective than point-to-point links, plus it typically runs at speeds of 64 Kbps up to 45 Mbps (T3). Another Frame Relay benefit is that it provides features for dynamic bandwidth allocation and congestion control.

ISDN   *Integrated Services Digital Network (ISDN)* is a set of digital services that transmit voice and data over existing phone lines. ISDN offers a cost-effective solution for remote users who need a higher-speed connection than analog POTS dial-up links can give them. It's also a good choice to use as a backup link for other types of links, such as Frame Relay or T1 connections.

HDLC   *High-Level Data-Link Control (HDLC)* was derived from Synchronous Data Link Control (SDLC), which was created by IBM as a Data Link connection protocol. HDLC works at the Data Link layer and creates very little overhead compared to Link Access Procedure, Balanced (LAPB).

Generic HDLC wasn't intended to encapsulate multiple Network layer protocols across the same link—the HDLC header doesn't contain any identification about the type of protocol being carried inside the HDLC encapsulation. Because of this, each vendor that uses HDLC has its own way of identifying the Network layer protocol, meaning each vendor's HDLC is proprietary with regard to its specific equipment.

PPP   *Point-to-Point Protocol (PPP)* is a pretty famous, industry-standard protocol. Because all multiprotocol versions of HDLC are proprietary, PPP can be used to create point-to-point links between different vendors' equipment. It uses a Network Control Protocol field in the Data Link header to identify the Network layer protocol being carried and allows authentication and multilink connections to be run over asynchronous and synchronous links.

PPPoE   *Point-to-Point Protocol over Ethernet* encapsulates PPP frames in Ethernet frames and is usually used in conjunction with xDSL services. It gives you a lot of the familiar PPP features like authentication, encryption, and compression, but there's a downside—it has a lower maximum transmission unit (MTU) than standard Ethernet does. If your firewall isn't solidly configured, this factor can really cause some grief!

Still somewhat popular in the United States, PPPoE's main feature is that it adds a direct connection to Ethernet interfaces while also providing DSL support. It's often used by many hosts on a shared Ethernet interface for opening PPP sessions to various destinations via at least one bridging modem.

Cable   In a modern *hybrid fiber-coaxial (HFC)* network, typically 500 to 2,000 active data subscribers are connected to a particular cable network segment, all sharing the upstream and downstream bandwidth. HFC is a telecommunications industry term for a network that incorporates both optical fiber and coaxial cables to create a broadband network. The actual bandwidth for Internet service over a cable TV (CATV) line can be up to about 27 Mbps on the download path to the subscriber, with about 2.5 Mbps of bandwidth on the upload path. Typically users get an access speed from 256 Kbps to 6 Mbps. This data rate varies greatly throughout the United States and is usually much, much higher today!

DSL   Digital subscriber line is a technology used by traditional telephone companies to deliver advanced services such as high-speed data and sometimes video over twisted-pair copper telephone wires. It typically offers lower data-carrying capacity than HFC networks, and data speeds can be limited in range by line lengths and quality. Digital subscriber line is not a complete end-to-end solution but rather a Physical layer transmission technology like dial-up, cable, or wireless. DSL connections are deployed in the last mile of a local telephone network—the local loop. The connection is set up between a pair of DSL modems on either end of a copper wire located between the customer premises equipment (CPE) and the Digital Subscriber Line Access Multiplexer (DSLAM). A DSLAM is the device located at the provider's central office (CO) and concentrates connections from multiple DSL subscribers.

MPLS   *MultiProtocol Label Switching (MPLS)* is a data-carrying mechanism that emulates some properties of a circuit-switched network over a packet-switched network. MPLS is a switching mechanism that imposes labels (numbers) to packets and then uses them to forward packets. The labels are assigned on the edge of the MPLS network, and forwarding inside the MPLS network is carried out solely based on the labels. The labels usually correspond to a path to layer 3 destination addresses, which is on par with IP destination-based routing. MPLS was designed to support the forwarding of protocols other than TCP/IP. Because of this, label switching within the network is achieved the same way irrespective of the layer 3 protocol. In larger networks, the result of MPLS labeling is that only the edge routers perform a routing lookup. All the core routers forward packets based on the labels, which makes forwarding the packets through the service provider network faster. This is a big reason most companies have replaced their Frame Relay networks with MPLS service today. Last, you can use Ethernet with MPLS to connect a WAN, and this is called Ethernet over MPLS, or EoMPLS.

ATM   Asynchronous Transfer Mode (ATM) was created for time-sensitive traffic, providing simultaneous transmission of voice, video, and data. ATM uses cells that are a fixed 53-bytes long instead of packets. It also can use isochronous clocking (external clocking) to help the data move faster. Typically, if you're running Frame Relay today, you will be running Frame Relay over ATM.

Cellular 3G/4G   Having a wireless hot spot in your pocket is pretty normal these days. If you have a pretty current cellular phone, then you can probably gain access through your phone to the Internet. You can even get a 3G/4G card for an ISR router that's useful for a small remote office that's in the coverage area.

VSAT   Very Small Aperture Terminal (VSAT) can be used if you have many locations geographically spread out in a large area. VSAT uses a two-way satellite ground station with dishes available through many companies like Dish Network or Hughes and connects to satellites in geosynchronous orbit. A good example of where VSATs are a useful, cost-effective solution would be companies that use satellite communications to VSATs, like gasoline stations that have hundreds or thousands of locations spread out over the entire country. How could you connect them otherwise? Using leased lines would be cost prohibitive and dial-ups would be way too slow and hard to manage. Instead, the signal from the satellite connects to many remote locations at once, which is much more cost effective and efficient! It's a lot faster than a modem (about 10x faster), but the upload speeds only come in at about 10 percent of their download speeds.

Metro Ethernet   Metropolitan-area Ethernet is a metropolitan area network (MAN) that's based on Ethernet standards and can connect a customer to a larger network and the Internet. If available, businesses can use Metro Ethernet to connect their own offices together, which is another very cost-effective connection option. MPLS-based Metro Ethernet networks use MPLS in the ISP by providing an Ethernet or fiber cable to the customer as a connection. From the customer, it leaves the Ethernet cable, jumps onto MPLS, and then onto Ethernet again on the remote side. This is a smart and thrifty solution that's very popular if you can get it in your area.

Cabling the Serial Wide Area Network

There are definitely a few things that you need to know before connecting your WAN to ensure success. For starters, you need to understand the kind of WAN Physical layer implementation that Cisco provides and be familiar with the various types of WAN serial connectors involved.

The good news is that Cisco serial connections support almost any type of WAN service. Your typical WAN connection is a dedicated leased line using HDLC, PPP, and Frame Relay with speeds that can kick it up to 45 Mbps (T3).

HDLC, PPP, and Frame Relay can use the same Physical layer specifications. I'll go over the various types of connections and then we'll move on to the WAN protocols specified in the CCNA R/S objectives.

Serial Transmission

WAN serial connectors use *serial transmission*, which takes place 1 bit at a time over a single channel.

Older Cisco routers have used a proprietary 60-pin serial connector that you have to get from Cisco or a provider of Cisco equipment. Cisco also has a new, smaller proprietary serial connection that's about one-tenth the size of the 60-pin basic serial cable called the *smart-serial*, but you'll need to verify you have the right type of interface on your router before using it.

The type of connector you have on the other end of the cable depends on your service provider and its particular end-device requirements. There are several different types of ends you'll run into:

- EIA/TIA-232—Allowed speed up to 64 Kbps on 24-pin connector

- EIA/TIA-449

- V.35—Standard used to connect to a CSU/DSU, with speeds up to 2.048 Mbps using a 34-pin rectangular connector

- EIA-530

Make sure you're clear that serial links are described in frequency, or cycles per second (hertz). The amount of data that can be carried within these frequencies is called *bandwidth*. Bandwidth is the amount of data in bits per second that the serial channel can carry.

Data Terminal Equipment and Data Communication Equipment

By default, router interfaces are typically *data terminal equipment (DTE)*, and they connect into *data communication equipment (DCE)* like a *channel service unit/data service unit (CSU/DSU)* using a V.35 connector. CSU/DSU then plugs into a demarcation location (demarc) and is the service provider's last responsibility. Most of the time, the demarc is a jack that has an RJ45 (8-pin modular) female connector located in a telecommunications closet.

Actually, you may already have heard of demarcs. If you've ever had the glorious experience of reporting a problem to your service provider, they'll usually tell you everything tests out fine up to the demarc, so the problem must be the CPE, or customer premises equipment. In other words, it's your problem, not theirs!

Figure 10.6 shows a typical DTE-DCE-DTE connection and the devices used in the network.

FIGURE 10.6 DTE-DCE-DTE WAN connection: Clocking is typically provided by the DCE network to routers. In nonproduction environments, a DCE network is not always present.

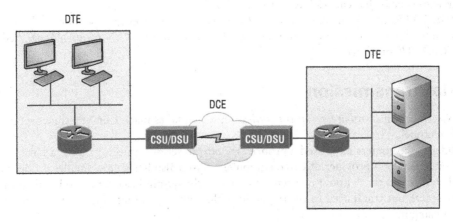

The idea behind a WAN is to be able to connect two DTE networks through a DCE network. The DCE network includes the CSU/DSU, through the provider's wiring and switches, all the way to the CSU/DSU at the other end. The network's DCE device (CSU/DSU) provides clocking to the DTE-connected interface (the router's serial interface).

As mentioned, the DCE network provides clocking to the router; this is the CSU/DSU. If you have a nonproduction network and you're using a WAN crossover type of cable and do not have a CSU/DSU, then you need to provide clocking on the DCE end of the cable by using the clock rate command. To find out which interface needs the clock rate command, use the show controllers *int* command:

```
Corp#sh controllers s0/0/0
Interface Serial0/0/0
Hardware is PowerQUICC MPC860
DCE V.35, clock rate 2000000
```

The preceding output shows a DCE interface that has the clock rate set to 2000000, which is the default for ISR routers. This next output shows a DTE connector, so you don't need to enter the clock rate command on this interface:

```
SF#sh controllers s0/0/0
Interface Serial0/0/0
Hardware is PowerQUICC MPC860
DTE V.35 TX and RX clocks detected
```

Terms such as *EIA/TIA-232, V.35, X.21,* and *HSSI (High-Speed Serial Interface)* describe the Physical layer between the DTE (router) and DCE device (CSU/DSU).

High-Level Data-Link Control (HDLC) Protocol

The High-Level Data-Link Control (HDLC) protocol is a popular ISO-standard, bit-oriented, Data Link layer protocol. It specifies an encapsulation method for data on synchronous serial data links using frame characters and checksums. HDLC is a point-to-point protocol used on leased lines. No authentication is provided by HDLC.

In byte-oriented protocols, control information is encoded using entire bytes. On the other hand, bit-oriented protocols use single bits to represent the control information. Some common bit-oriented protocols are SDLC and HDLC. TCP and IP are byte-oriented protocols.

HDLC is the default encapsulation used by Cisco routers over synchronous serial links. And Cisco's HDLC is proprietary, meaning it won't communicate with any other vendor's HDLC implementation. But don't give Cisco grief for it—*everyone's* HDLC implementation is proprietary. Figure 10.7 shows the Cisco HDLC format.

FIGURE 10.7   Cisco's HDLC frame format: Each vendor's HDLC has a proprietary data field to support multiprotocol environments.

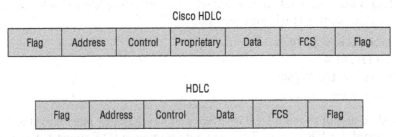

Supports only single-protocol environments

The reason every vendor has a proprietary HDLC encapsulation method is that each vendor has a different way for the HDLC protocol to encapsulate multiple Network layer protocols. If the vendors didn't have a way for HDLC to communicate the different layer 3 protocols, then HDLC would be able to operate in only a single layer 3 protocol environment. This proprietary header is placed in the data field of the HDLC encapsulation.

It's pretty simple to configure a serial interface if you're just going to connect two Cisco routers across a T1. Figure 10.8 shows a point-to-point connection between two cities.

FIGURE 10.8   Configuring Cisco's HDLC proprietary WAN encapsulation

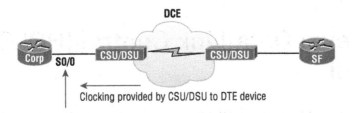

Clocking provided by CSU/DSU to DTE device

We can easily configure the routers with a basic IP address and then enable the interface. Assuming the link to the ISP is up, the routers will start communicaing using the default HDLC encapsulation. Let's take a look at the Corp router configuration so you can see just how easy this can be:

```
Corp(config)#int s0/0
Corp(config-if)#ip address 172.16.10.1 255.255.255.252
Corp(config-if)#no shut
```

```
Corp#sh int s0/0
Serial0/0 is up, line protocol is up
  Hardware is PowerQUICC Serial
  Internet address is 172.16.10.1/30
  MTU 1500 bytes, BW 1544 Kbit, DLY 20000 usec,
     reliability 255/255, txload 1/255, rxload 1/255
  Encapsulation HDLC, loopback not set
  Keepalive set (10 sec)

Corp#sh run | begin interface Serial0/0
interface Serial0/0
 ip address 172.16.10.1 255.255.255.252
!
```

So all I did was add an IP address before I then enabled the interface—pretty simple! As long as the SF router is running the default serial encapsulation, this link will come right up. In the preceding output, notice that the show interface command does show the encapsulation type of HDLC, but the output of show running-config does not. This is important—remember that if you don't see an encapsulation type listed under a serial interface in the active configuration file, you know it's running the default encapsulation of HDLC.

So let's say you have only one Cisco router and you need to connect to a non-Cisco router because your new Cisco router is on order... What would you do? You couldn't use the default HDLC serial encapsulation because it wouldn't work. Instead, you would need to go with an option like PPP, an ISO-standard way of identifying the upper-layer protocols. Now is a great time to get into more detail about PPP as well as how to connect to routers using the PPP encapsulation. You can check out RFC 1661 for more information on the origins and standards of PPP.

Point-to-Point Protocol (PPP)

Point-to-Point Protocol (PPP) is a Data Link layer protocol that can be used over either asynchronous serial (dial-up) or synchronous serial (ISDN) media. It relies on Link Control Protocol (LCP) to build and maintain data-link connections. Network Control Protocol (NCP) enables multiple Network layer protocols (routed protocols) to be used on a point-to-point connection.

Because HDLC is the default serial encapsulation on Cisco serial links and it works great, why in the world would you choose to use PPP? Well, the basic purpose of PPP is to transport layer 3 packets across a Data Link layer point-to-point link, and it's nonproprietary. So unless you have only Cisco routers, you need PPP on your serial interfaces because the HDLC encapsulation is Cisco proprietary, right? Plus, since PPP can encapsulate several layer 3 routed protocols and provide authentication, dynamic addressing, and callback, PPP could actually be the best encapsulation solution for you over HDLC anyway.

Figure 10.9 shows the PPP protocol stack compared to the OSI reference model.

FIGURE 10.9 Point-to-Point Protocol stack

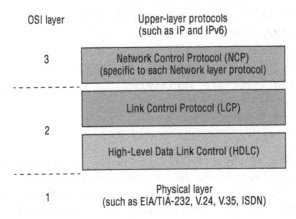

PPP contains four main components:

EIA/TIA-232-C, V.24, V.35, and ISDN   A Physical layer international standard for serial communication.

HDLC   A method for encapsulating datagrams over serial links.

LCP   A method of establishing, configuring, maintaining, and terminating the point-to-point connection. It also provides features such as authentication. I'll give you a complete list of these features soon.

NCP   NCP is a method of establishing and configuring different Network layer protocols for transport across the PPP link. NCP is designed to allow the simultaneous use of multiple Network layer protocols. Two examples of protocols here are Internet Protocol Control Protocol (IPCP) and Cisco Discovery Protocol Control Protocol (CDPCP).

Burn it into your mind that the PPP protocol stack is specified at the Physical and Data Link layers only. NCP is used to allow communication of multiple Network layer protocols by identifying and encapsulating the protocols across a PPP data link.

Remember that if you have a Cisco router and a non-Cisco router connected with a serial connection, you must configure PPP or another encapsulation method like Frame Relay because the HDLC default just won't work!

Next, we'll cover the options for LCP and PPP session establishment.

Link Control Protocol (LCP) Configuration Options

Link Control Protocol (LCP) offers different PPP encapsulation options, including the following:

Authentication This option tells the calling side of the link to send information that can identify the user. The two methods for this task are PAP and CHAP.

Compression This is used to increase the throughput of PPP connections by compressing the data or payload prior to transmission. PPP decompresses the data frame on the receiving end.

Error detection PPP uses Quality and Magic Number options to ensure a reliable, loop-free data link.

Multilink PPP (MLP) Starting with IOS version 11.1, multilink is supported on PPP links with Cisco routers. This option makes several separate physical paths appear to be one logical path at layer 3. For example, two T1s running multilink PPP would show up as a single 3 Mbps path to a layer 3 routing protocol.

PPP callback On a dial-up connection, PPP can be configured to call back after successful authentication. *PPP callback* can be great because it allows us to keep track of usage based upon access charges for accounting records, plus a bunch of other reasons. With callback enabled, a calling router (client) will contact a remote router (server) and authenticate. Predictably, both routers have to be configured for the callback feature for this to work. Once authentication is completed, the remote router will terminate the connection and then reinitiate a connection to the calling router from the remote router.

PPP Session Establishment

When PPP connections are started, the links go through three phases of session establishment, as shown in Figure 10.10:

FIGURE 10.10   PPP session establishment

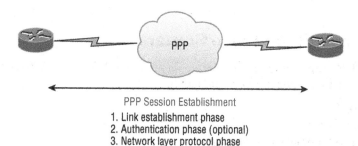

PPP Session Establishment
1. Link establishment phase
2. Authentication phase (optional)
3. Network layer protocol phase

Link-establishment phase LCP packets are sent by each PPP device to configure and test the link. These packets contain a field called Configuration Option that allows each device to see the size of the data, the compression, and authentication. If no Configuration Option field is present, then the default configurations will be used.

Authentication phase If required, either CHAP or PAP can be used to authenticate a link. Authentication takes place before Network layer protocol information is read, and it's also possible that link-quality determination will occur simultaneously.

Network layer protocol phase PPP uses the *Network Control Protocol (NCP)* to allow multiple Network layer protocols to be encapsulated and sent over a PPP data link. Each Network layer protocol (e.g., IP, IPv6, which are routed protocols) establishes a service with NCP.

PPP Authentication Methods

There are two methods of authentication that can be used with PPP links:

Password Authentication Protocol (PAP) The *Password Authentication Protocol (PAP)* is the less secure of the two methods. Passwords are sent in clear text and PAP is performed only upon the initial link establishment. When the PPP link is first established, the remote node sends the username and password back to the originating target router until authentication is acknowledged. Not exactly Fort Knox!

Challenge Handshake Authentication Protocol (CHAP) The *Challenge Handshake Authentication Protocol (CHAP)* is used at the initial startup of a link and at periodic checkups on the link to ensure that the router is still communicating with the same host.

After PPP finishes its initial link-establishment phase, the local router sends a challenge request to the remote device. The remote device sends a value calculated using a one-way hash function called MD5. The local router checks this hash value to make sure it matches. If the values don't match, the link is immediately terminated.

CHAP authenticates at the beginning of the session and periodically throughout the session.

Configuring PPP on Cisco Routers

Configuring PPP encapsulation on an interface is pretty straightforward. To configure it from the CLI, use these simple router commands:

```
Router#config t
Router(config)#int s0
Router(config-if)#encapsulation ppp
Router(config-if)#^Z
Router#
```

Of course, PPP encapsulation has to be enabled on both interfaces connected to a serial line in order to work and there are several additional configuration options available to you via the ppp ? command.

Configuring PPP Authentication

After you configure your serial interface to support PPP encapsulation, you can then configure authentication using PPP between routers. But first, you must set the hostname of the router if it hasn't been set already. After that, you set the username and password for the remote router that will be connecting to your router, like this:

```
Router#config t
Router(config)#hostname RouterA
RouterA(config)#username RouterB password cisco
```

When using the username command, remember that the username is the hostname of the remote router that's connecting to your router. It's case sensitive too. Also, the password on both routers must be the same. It's a plain-text password that you can see with a show run command, and you can encrypt the password by using the command service password-encryption. You must have a username and password configured for each remote system you plan to connect to. The remote routers must also be similarly configured with usernames and passwords.

Now, after you've set the hostname, usernames, and passwords, choose either CHAP or PAP as the authentication method:

```
RouterA#config t
RouterA(config)#int s0
RouterA(config-if)#ppp authentication chap pap
RouterA(config-if)#^Z
RouterA#
```

If both methods are configured on the same line as I've demonstrated here, then only the first method will be used during link negotiation. The second acts as a backup just in case the first method fails.

There is yet another command you can use if you're using PAP authentication… The ppp pap sent-username <*username*> password <*password*> command enables outbound PAP authentication. The local router uses the username and password that the *ppp pap sent-username* command specifies to authenticate itself to a remote device. The other router must have this same username/password configured as well.

Verifying and Troubleshooting Serial Links

Okay—now that PPP encapsulation is enabled, you need to verify that it's up and running. First, let's take a look at a figure of a sample nonproduction network serial link. Figure 10.11 shows two routers connected with a point-to-point serial connection, with the DCE side on the Pod1R1 router.

FIGURE 10.11   PPP authentication example

Pod1R1   Pod1R2

hostname Pod1R1   hostname Pod1R2
username Pod1R2 password cisco   username Pod1R1 password cisco
interface serial 0   interface serial 0
ip address 10.0.1.1 255.255.255.0   ip address 10.0.1.2 255.255.255.0
encapsulation ppp   encapsulation ppp
clock rate 64000   bandwidth 512
bandwidth 512   ppp authentication chap
ppp authentication chap

You can start verifying the configuration with the show interface command like this:

```
Pod1R1#sh int s0/0
Serial0/0 is up, line protocol is up
  Hardware is PowerQUICC Serial
  Internet address is 10.0.1.1/24
  MTU 1500 bytes, BW 1544 Kbit, DLY 20000 usec,
     reliability 239/255, txload 1/255, rxload 1/255
  Encapsulation PPP
  loopback not set
  Keepalive set (10 sec)
  LCP Open
  Open: IPCP, CDPCP
[output cut]
```

The first line of output is important because it tells us that serial 0/0 is up/up. Notice that the interface encapsulation is PPP and that LCP is open. This means that it has negotiated the session establishment and all is well. The last line tells us that NCP is listening for the protocols IP and CDP, shown with the NCP headers IPCP and CDPCP.

But what would you see if everything isn't so perfect? I'm going to type in the configuration shown in Figure 10.12 to find out.

FIGURE 10.12   Failed PPP authentication

Pod1R1   Pod1R2

hostname Pod1R1   hostname Pod1R2
username Pod1R2 password Cisco   username Pod1R1 password cisco
interface serial 0   interface serial 0
ip address 10.0.1.1 255.255.255.0   ip address 10.0.1.2 255.255.255.0
clock rate 64000   bandwidth 512
bandwidth 512   encapsulation ppp
encapsulation ppp   ppp authentication chap
ppp authentication chap

So what's wrong here? Take a look at the usernames and passwords. Do you see the problem now? That's right, the C is capitalized on the Pod1R2 username command found in the configuration of router Pod1R1. This is wrong because the usernames and passwords are case sensitive. Now let's take a look at the show interface command and see what happens:

```
Pod1R1#sh int s0/0
Serial0/0 is up, line protocol is down
  Hardware is PowerQUICC Serial
  Internet address is 10.0.1.1/24
  MTU 1500 bytes, BW 1544 Kbit, DLY 20000 usec,
     reliability 243/255, txload 1/255, rxload 1/255
  Encapsulation PPP, loopback not set
  Keepalive set (10 sec)
  LCP Closed
   Closed: IPCP, CDPCP
```

First, notice that the first line of output shows us that Serial0/0 is up and line protocol is down. This is because there are no keepalives coming from the remote router. The next thing I want you to see is that the LCP and NCP are closed because the authentication failed.

Debugging PPP Authentication

To display the CHAP authentication process as it occurs between two routers in the network, just use the command debug ppp authentication.

If your PPP encapsulation and authentication are set up correctly on both routers and your usernames and passwords are all good, then the debug ppp authentication command will display an output that looks like the following output, which is called the three-way handshake:

```
d16h: Se0/0 PPP: Using default call direction
1d16h: Se0/0 PPP: Treating connection as a dedicated line
1d16h: Se0/0 CHAP: O CHALLENGE id 219 len 27 from "Pod1R1"
1d16h: Se0/0 CHAP: I CHALLENGE id 208 len 27 from "Pod1R2"
1d16h: Se0/0 CHAP: O RESPONSE id 208 len 27 from "Pod1R1"
1d16h: Se0/0 CHAP: I RESPONSE id 219 len 27 from "Pod1R2"
1d16h: Se0/0 CHAP: O SUCCESS id 219 len 4
1d16h: Se0/0 CHAP: I SUCCESS id 208 len 4
```

But if you have the password wrong as they were previously in the PPP authentication failure example back in Figure 10.12 the output would look something like this:

```
1d16h: Se0/0 PPP: Using default call direction
1d16h: Se0/0 PPP: Treating connection as a dedicated line
1d16h: %SYS-5-CONFIG_I: Configured from console by console
```

```
1d16h: Se0/0 CHAP: O CHALLENGE id 220 len 27 from "Pod1R1"
1d16h: Se0/0 CHAP: I CHALLENGE id 209 len 27 from "Pod1R2"
1d16h: Se0/0 CHAP: O RESPONSE id 209 len 27 from "Pod1R1"
1d16h: Se0/0 CHAP: I RESPONSE id 220 len 27 from "Pod1R2"
1d16h: Se0/0 CHAP: O FAILURE id 220 len 25 msg is "MD/DES compare failed"
```

PPP with CHAP authentication is a three-way authentication, and if the username and passwords aren't configured exactly the way they should be, then the authentication will fail and the link will go down.

Mismatched WAN Encapsulations

If you have a point-to-point link but the encapsulations aren't the same, the link will never come up. Figure 10.13 shows one link with PPP and one with HDLC.

FIGURE 10.13 Mismatched WAN encapsulations

Pod1R1   Pod1R2

```
hostname Pod1R1                         hostname Pod1R2
username Pod1R2 password cisco          username Pod1R1 password cisco
interface serial 0                      interface serial 0
ip address 10.0.1.1 255.255.255.0       ip address 10.0.1.2 255.255.255.0
clock rate 64000                        bandwidth 512
bandwidth 512                           encapsulation hdlc
encapsulation ppp
```

Look at router Pod1R1 in this output:

```
Pod1R1#sh int s0/0
Serial0/0 is up, line protocol is down
  Hardware is PowerQUICC Serial
  Internet address is 10.0.1.1/24
  MTU 1500 bytes, BW 1544 Kbit, DLY 20000 usec,
    reliability 254/255, txload 1/255, rxload 1/255
  Encapsulation PPP, loopback not set
  Keepalive set (10 sec)
  LCP REQsent
Closed: IPCP, CDPCP
```

The serial interface is up/down and LCP is sending requests but will never receive any responses because router Pod1R2 is using the HDLC encapsulation. To fix this problem, you would have to go to router Pod1R2 and configure the PPP encapsulation on the serial interface. One more thing: Even though the usernames are configured incorrectly, it doesn't matter because the command ppp authentication chap isn't used under the serial interface configuration. This means that the username command isn't relevant in this example.

You can set a Cisco serial interface back to the default of HDLC with the no encapsulation command like this:

```
Router(config)#int s0/0
Router(config-if)#no encapsulation
*Feb 7 16:00:18.678:%LINEPROTO-5-UPDOWN: Line protocol on Interface Serial0/0,
changed state to up
```

Notice the link came up because it now matches the encapsulation on the other end of the link!

> Always remember that you just can't have PPP on one side and HDLC on the other—they don't get along!

Mismatched IP Addresses

A tricky problem to spot is if you have HDLC or PPP configured on your serial interface but your IP addresses are wrong. Things seem to be just fine because the interfaces will show that they are up. Take a look at Figure 10.14 and see if you can see what I mean—the two routers are connected with different subnets—router Pod1R1 with 10.0.1.1/24 and router Pod1R2 with 10.2.1.2/24.

FIGURE 10.14   Mismatched IP addresses

Pod1R1   Pod1R2

```
hostname Pod1R1                         hostname Pod1R2
username Pod1R2 password cisco          username Pod1R1 password cisco
interface serial 0                      interface serial 0
ip address 10.0.1.1 255.255.255.0       ip address 10.2.1.2 255.255.255.0
clock rate 64000                        bandwidth 512
bandwidth 512                           encapsulation ppp
encapsulation ppp                       ppp authentication chap
ppp authentication chap
```

This will never work! Let's take a look at the output:

```
Pod1R1#sh int s0/0
Serial0/0 is up, line protocol is up
  Hardware is PowerQUICC Serial
  Internet address is 10.0.1.1/24
  MTU 1500 bytes, BW 1544 Kbit, DLY 20000 usec,
    reliability 255/255, txload 1/255, rxload 1/255
```

```
Encapsulation PPP, loopback not set
Keepalive set (10 sec)
LCP Open
Open: IPCP, CDPCP
```

See that? The IP addresses between the routers are wrong but the link appears to be working just fine. This is because PPP, like HDLC and Frame Relay, is a layer 2 WAN encapsulation, so it doesn't care about IP addresses at all. So yes, the link is up, but you can't use IP across this link since it's misconfigured, or can you? Well, yes and no. If you try to ping you'll see that this actually works! This is a feature of PPP, but not HDLC or Frame Relay. But just because you can ping to an IP address that's not in the same subnet doesn't mean your network traffic and routing protocols will work. So be careful with this issue, especially when troubleshooting PPP links!

Take a look at the routing table of Pod1R1 and see if you can find the mismatched IP address problem:

```
[output cut]
   10.0.0.0/8 is variably subnetted, 2 subnets, 2 masks
C      10.2.1.2/32 is directly connected, Serial0/0
C      10.0.1.0/24 is directly connected, Serial0/0
```

Interesting! We can see our serial interface S0/0 address of 10.0.1.0/24, but what is that other address on interface S0/0— 10.2.1.2/32? That's our remote router's interface IP address! PPP determines and places the neighbor's IP address in the routing table as a connected interface, which then allows you to ping it even though it's actually configured on a separate IP subnet.

 For the Cisco objectives, you need to be able to troubleshoot PPP from the routing table as I just described.

To find and fix this problem, you can also use the show running-config, show interfaces, or show ip interfaces brief commands on each router, or you can use the show cdp neighbors detail command:

```
Pod1R1#sh cdp neighbors detail
-------------------------
Device ID: Pod1R2
Entry address(es):
  IP address: 10.2.1.2
```

Since the layer 1 Physical and layer 2 Data Link is up/up, you can view and verify the directly connected neighbor's IP address and then solve your problem.

Multilink PPP (MLP)

There are many load balancing mechanisms available, but this one is free for use on serial WAN links! It provides multivendor support and is specified in RFC 1990, which details the fragmentation and packet sequencing specifications.

You can use MLP to connect your home network to an Internet Service Provider using two traditional modems or to connect a company via two leased lines.

The MLP feature provides a load-balancing functionality over multiple WAN links while allowing for multivendor interoperability. It offers support for packet fragmentation, proper sequencing and load calculation on both inbound and outbound traffic.

MLP allows packets to be fragmented and then sent simultaneously over multiple point-to-point links to the same remote address. It can work over synchronous and asynchronous serial types.

MLP combines multiple physical links into a logical link called an MLP bundle, which is essentially a single, virtual interface that connects to the remote router. None of the links inside the bundle have any knowledge about the traffic on the other links.

The MLP over serial interfaces feature provides us with the following benefits:

Load balancing   MLP provides bandwidth on demand, utilizing load balancing on up to ten links and can even calculate the load on traffic between specific sites. You don't actually need to make all links the same bandwidth but doing so is recommended. Another key MLP advantage is that it splits packets and fragments across all links, which reduces latency across the WAN.

Increased redundancy   This one is pretty straightforward… If a link fails, the others will still transmit and receive.

Link fragmentation and interleaving   The fragmentation mechanism in MLP works by fragmenting large packets, then sending the packet fragments over the multiple point-to-point links. Smaller real-time packets are not fragmented. So interleaving basically means real time packets can be sent in between sending the fragmented, non-real time packets, which helps reduce delay on the lines.

So let's configure MLP now to get a good feel for how it actually works.

Configuring MLP

We're going to use Figure 10.15 to demonstrate how to configure MLP between two routers:

FIGURE 10.15   MLP between Corp and SF Routers

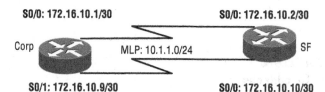

S0/0: 172.16.10.1/30   S0/0: 172.16.10.2/30

Corp   MLP: 10.1.1.0/24   SF

S0/1: 172.16.10.9/30   S0/0: 172.16.10.10/30

But first, I want you to study the configuration of the two serial interfaces on the Corp router that we're gong to use for making our bundle:

```
Corp# show interfaces Serial0/0
Serial0/0 is up, line protocol is up
  Hardware is M4T
  Internet address is 172.16.10.1/30
  MTU 1500 bytes, BW 1544 Kbit/sec, DLY 20000 usec,
     reliability 255/255, txload 1/255, rxload 1/255
  Encapsulation PPP, LCP Open
  Open: IPCP, CDPCP, crc 16, loopback not set

Corp# show interfaces Serial1/1
Serial1/1 is up, line protocol is up
  Hardware is M4T
  Internet address is 172.16.10.9/30
  MTU 1500 bytes, BW 1544 Kbit/sec, DLY 20000 usec,
     reliability 255/255, txload 1/255, rxload 1/255
  Encapsulation PPP, LCP Open
  Open: IPCP, CDPCP, crc 16, loopback not set
```

Did you notice that each serial connection is on a different subnet (they have to be) and that the encapsulation is PPP?

When you configure MLP, you must first remove your IP addresses off your physical interface. Then, you configure a multilink bundle by creating a multilink interface on both sides of the link. After that, you assign an IP address to this multilink interface, which effectively restricts a physical link so that it can only join the designated multilink group interface.

So first I'm going to remove the IP addresses from the physical interfaces that I'm going to include in my PPP bundle.

```
Corp# config t
Corp(config)# int Serial0/0
Corp(config-if)# no ip address
Corp(config-if)# int Serial1/1
Corp(config-if)# no ip address
Corp(config-if)# end
Corp#

SF# config t
SF(config)# int Serial0/0
SF(config-if)# no ip address
SF(config-if)# int Serial0/1
```

```
SF(config-if)# no ip address
SF(config-if)# end
SF#
```

Now we create the multilink interface on each side of the link and add the MLP commands to enable the bundle.

```
Corp#config t
Corp(config)# interface Multilink1
Corp(config-if)# ip address 10.1.1.1 255.255.255.0
Corp(config-if)# ppp multilink
Corp(config-if)# ppp multilink group 1
Corp(config-if)# end

SF#config t
SF(config)# interface Multilink1
SF(config-if)# ip address 10.1.1.2 255.255.255.0
SF(config-if)# ppp multilink
SF(config-if)# ppp multilink group 1
SF(config-if)# exit
```

You can see that a link joins an MLP bundle only if it negotiates to use the bundle when a connection is established and the identification information that has been exchanged matches the info for an existing bundle.

When you configure the ppp multilink group command on a link, that link won't be allowed to join any bundle other than the indicated group interface.

Verifying MLP

To verify that your bundle is up and running, just use the show ppp multilink and show interfaces multilink1 commands:

```
Corp# show ppp multilink

Multilink1
  Bundle name: Corp
  Remote Endpoint Discriminator: [1] SF
  Local Endpoint Discriminator: [1] Corp
  Bundle up for 02:12:05, total bandwidth 4188, load 1/255
  Receive buffer limit 24000 bytes, frag timeout 1000 ms
    0/0 fragments/bytes in reassembly list
    0 lost fragments, 53 reordered
    0/0 discarded fragments/bytes, 0 lost received
    0x56E received sequence, 0x572 sent sequence
```

```
   Member links: 2 active, 0 inactive (max 255, min not set)
     Se0/1, since 01:32:05
     Se1/2, since 01:31:31
No inactive multilink interfaces
```

So great—the physical interfaces, Se0/1 and Se1/1, are members of the logical interface bundle Multilink 1. Now we'll verify the status of the interface Multilink1 on the Corp router:

```
Corp# show int Multilink1
Multilink1 is up, line protocol is up
  Hardware is multilink group interface
  Internet address is 10.1.1.1/24
  MTU 1500 bytes, BW 1544 Kbit/sec, DLY 20000 usec,
     reliability 255/255, txload 1/255, rxload 1/255
Encapsulation PPP, LCP Open, multilink Open
Open: IPCP, CDPCP, loopback not set
 Keepalive set (10 sec)
[output cut]
```

Let's move on to configure a PPPoE client on a Cisco router.

PPP Client (PPPoE)

Used with ADSL services, PPPoE (Point-to-Point Protocol over Ethernet) encapsulates PPP frames in Ethernet frames and uses common PPP features like authentication, encryption, and compression. But as I said earlier, it can be trouble, which is especially true if you've got a badly configured firewall!

Basically, PPPoE is a tunneling protocol that layers IP and other protocols running over PPP with the attributes of a PPP link. This is done so protocols can then be used to contact other Ethernet devices and initiate a point-to-point connection to transport IP packets.

Figure 10.16 displays typical usage of PPPoE over ADSL. As you can see, a PPP session is connected from the PC of the end user to the router. Subsequently, the subscriber PC IP address is assigned by the router via IPCP.

FIGURE 10.16 PPPoE with ADSL

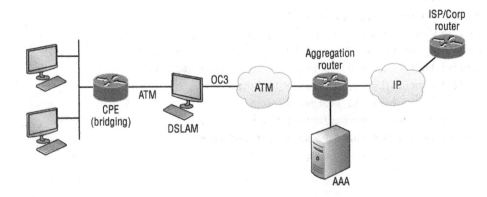

Your ISP will typically provide you with a DSL line and this will act as a bridge if your line doesn't provided enhanced features. This means only one host will connect using PPPoE. By using a Cisco router, you can run the PPPoE client IOS feature on the Cisco router, which will connect multiple PCs on the Ethernet segment that is connected to the router.

Configuring a PPPoE Client

The PPPoE client configuration is simple and straightforward. First, you need to create a dialer interface and then tie it to a physical interface.

Here are the easy steps:

1. Create a dialer interface using the `interface dialer` *number* command.

2. Instruct the client to use an IP address provided by the PPPoE server with the `ip address negotiated` command.

3. Set the encapsulation type to PPP.

4. Configure the dialer pool and number.

5. Under the physical interface, use the `pppoe-client dial-pool number` *number* command.

On your PPPoE client router, enter the following commands:

```
R1# conf t
R1(config)# int dialer1
R1(config-if)# ip address negotiated
R1(config-if)# encapsulation ppp
R1(config-if)# dialer pool 1
R1(config-if)# interface f0/1
R1(config-if)# no ip address
R1(config-if)# pppoe-client dial-pool-number 1
*May 1 1:09:07.540: %DIALER-6-BIND: Interface Vi2 bound to profile Di1
*May 1 1:09:07.541: %LINK-3-UPDOWN: Interface Virtual-Access2, changed state to up
```

That's it! Now let's verify the interface with the `show ip interface brief` and the `show pppoe session` commands:

```
R1# show ip int brief
Interface              IP-Address      OK? Method Status        Protocol
FastEthernet0/1        unassigned      YES manual up                up
<output cut
Dialer1                10.10.10.3      YES IPCP   up                up
Loopback0              192.168.1.1     YES NVRAM  up                up
Loopback1              172.16.1.1      YES NVRAM  up                up
Virtual-Access1        unassigned      YES unset  up                up
Virtual-Access2        unassigned      YES unset  up                up
```

```
R1#show pppoe session
    1 client session

Uniq ID  PPPoE  RemMAC          Port            VT  VA       State
         SID    LocMAC                              VA-st    Type
   N/A    4     aacb.cc00.1419  FEt0/1          Di1 Vi2      UP
                aacb.cc00.1f01                      UP
```

All is well...Our connection using a PPPoE client is up and running!

Summary

In this chapter, you learned the difference between the following WAN services: cable, DSL, HDLC, PPP, and PPPoE. You also found out that you can use a VPN once any of those services are up and running, as well as create and verify a tunnel interface.

It's so important for you to understand High-Level Data-Link Control (HDLC) and how to verify with the show interface command that HDLC is enabled! You've been provided with really vital HDLC information as well as information on how the Point-to-Point Protocol (PPP) is used if you need more features than HDLC offers—also true if you're using two different brands of routers. You now know that this is because various versions of HDLC are proprietary and won't work between two different vendors' routers.

When we went through the section on PPP, I discussed the various LCP options as well as the two types of authentication that can be used: PAP and CHAP.

Glossary

10BaseT   An implementation of Ethernet that specifies a 10Mbps signaling rate, baseband signaling, and twisted-pair cabling.

100BaseT   Based on the IEEE 802.3u standard, 100BaseT is the Fast Ethernet specification of 100Mbps baseband that uses UTP wiring. 100BaseT sends link pulses (containing more information than those used in 10BaseT) over the network when no traffic is present. *See also* 10BaseT, Fast Ethernet, IEEE 802.3 CSMA/CD Networking.

100BaseTX   Based on the IEEE 802.3u standard, 100BaseTX is the 100Mbps baseband Fast Ethernet specification that uses two pairs of UTP or STP wiring. The first pair of wires receives data; the second pair sends data. To ensure correct signal timing, a 100BaseTX segment cannot be longer than 100 meters.

A

access control list (ACL)   A list of rights that an object has to resources in the network. Also can be referred to as a type of firewall. In this case, the lists reside on a router and determine which machines can use the router and in what direction.

access link   Switch port assigned to only one VLAN.

ACK   *See* acknowledgment (ACK).

acknowledgment (ACK)   A message confirming that the data packet was received. This occurs at the Transport layer of the OSI model.

ACL   *See* access control list (ACL).

Active Directory   A directory service developed by Microsoft for Windows domain networks. It is included in most Windows Server operating systems as a set of processes and services.

active hub   A hub that is powered and actively regenerates any signal that is received. *See also* hub.

ad hoc RF network   A network created when two RF-capable devices are brought within transmission range of each other. A common example is handheld PDAs beaming data to each other.

adapter   Technically, the peripheral hardware that installs into your computer or the software that defines how the computer talks to that hardware.

address   Designation to allow PCs to be known by a name or number to other PCs. Addressing allows a PC to transmit data directly to another PC by using its address (IP or MAC).

address learning   The process by which switches/bridges receive a frame and place the source address of the frame in the content addressable memory (CAM) table.

address mask   A bit combination descriptor identifying which portion of an address refers to the network or subnet and which part refers to the host. Sometimes simply called the mask. *See also* subnet mask.

address record   Part of a DNS table that maps an IP address to a domain name. Also known as an A (or host) record.

address resolution   The process used for resolving differences between computer addressing schemes. Address resolution typically defines a method for tracing Network layer (Layer 3) addresses to Data Link layer (Layer 2) addresses.

Address Resolution Protocol (ARP)   The Network layer protocol that IP uses to ascertain the MAC address of a known IP address when IP determines that the destination is on the local subnet and communication with the destination must therefore occur at the Data Link layer.

administrative distance (AD)   A number that is used by routing protocols to determine the trustworthiness of a route. If two route updates are received on a router with different ADs, the router will accept only the one with the lower AD and discard the other route update.

ADSL   *See* asymmetrical digital subscriber line (ADSL).

Advanced Encryption Standard (AES)   A block-cipher adapted form of encryption that was created by Vincent Rinjndael and standardized by the US government. It is now used worldwide. Before we used AES, the Data Encryption Standard (DES) was widely used.

alias record   *See* CNAME record.

antivirus   A category of software that uses various methods to eliminate viruses in a computer. It typically also protects against future infection. *See also* virus.

Application layer   The seventh layer of the OSI model, which deals with how applications access the network and describes application functionality, such as file transfer, messaging, and so on.

application-specific integrated circuit (ASIC)   An integrated circuit (IC) customized for a particular use rather than intended for general-purpose use. For example, a chip designed solely to run a LAN switch is an ASIC.

ARP table   A table that is used by the Address Resolution Protocol (ARP) and contains a list of known TCP/IP addresses and their associated MAC addresses. The table is cached in memory so that ARP lookups do not have to be performed for frequently accessed TCP/IP addresses but are aged out so that associations do not become stagnant. *See also* Address Resolution Protocol (ARP), Media Access Control (MAC), Transmission Control Protocol/Internet Protocol (TCP/IP).

asymmetrical digital subscriber line (ADSL)   An implementation of DSL where the upload and download speeds are different. *See also* Digital Subscriber Line (DSL).

Asynchronous Transfer Mode (ATM)   A connection-oriented network architecture based on broadband ISDN technology that uses constant-size 53-byte cells instead of packets. Because cells don't change size, they are switched much faster and more efficiently than packets across a network.

ATM   *See* Asynchronous Transfer Mode (ATM).

Attachment Unit Interface (AUI) port   Port on some NICs that lets you connect the NIC to different media types by using an external transceiver.

attenuation   Attenuation is the degradation of a signal and affects the propagation of waves and signals in electrical circuits and in optical fibers as well as in air (radio waves).

auto-detect mechanism   A means by which network devices can auto-detect options such as speed and duplex, just to name two. A LAN switch is a good example of how a port can auto-detect 10Mbps or 100Mbps or full- and half-duplex operation with the network card that is attached to the port via cable.

B

B channel   *See* bearer channel (B channel).

backbone   The part of most networks that connects multiple segments together to form a LAN. The backbone usually has a higher speed than the segments. *See also* local area network (LAN), segment.

bandwidth   In network communications, the amount of data that can be sent across a wire or circuit in a given time in a given time. Each communication that passes along the wire decreases the amount of available bandwidth.

bandwidth throttling   A method of ensuring that a bandwidth-intensive device, such as a server or your ISP's router/server, will limit (throttle) the quantity of data it transmits and/ or accepts within a specified period of time. For servers, bandwidth throttling helps limit network congestion and server crashes. For ISPs, bandwidth throttling can be used to limit users' speeds across certain applications or limit upload speeds.

baseband   A transmission technique in which the signal uses the entire bandwidth of a transmission medium.

baseline   A category of network documentation that indicates how the network normally runs. It includes such information as network statistics, server-utilization trends, and processor performance statistics.

bearer channel (B channel)   A channel in an ISDN line that carries data. Each bearer channel typically has a bandwidth of 64Kbps.

best-effort transmission   Transmission that occurs between devices without any form of connection establishment or acknowledgment of received data. Best-effort transmission is performed by protocols that are both connectionless and unreliable, such as UDP, IP, and Ethernet.

binding   *See* bonding.

bit   A binary digit that takes a value of either 0 or 1 and that is the basic unit of information storage and communication in digital computing and digital information theory. Four bits equal a nibble. Eight bits equal a byte.

bonding   A procedure where two ISDN B channels are joined together to provide greater bandwidth. *BONDING* stands for Bandwidth ON Demand Interoperability Group, but it's often seen written in lowercase as a more generalized term referring to inverse multiplexing. *Bonding* can also refer to binding multiple Ethernet segments together to gain greater bandwidth and throughput.

boot sector virus   An especially nasty virus that hides in the boot sector and is loaded with the operating system. A boot sector (sometimes called a bootblock) is a sector of a hard disk that contains code for booting programs.

Border Gateway Protocol (BGP)   The core routing protocol of the Internet. It is a very advanced routing protocol and it can be used to make multiple connections to the Internet and perform load balancing. It works by maintaining a table of IP networks or prefixes that designate network reachability among autonomous systems. It is described as a path or distance vector protocol.

bottleneck   A location in the network that creates congestion because it cannot handle the load. A router interface or server can be a bottleneck.

bounded media   Network media used at the Physical layer, where the signal travels over a cable of some kind.

bridge   A network device, operating at the Data Link layer, that logically separates a single network into segments but lets the two segments appear to be one network to higher-layer protocols.

broadband   A network-transmission method in which a single transmission medium is divided so that multiple signals can travel across the same medium simultaneously.

broadcast address   A special network address that refers to all nodes on the network. For example, the TCP/IP address 255.255.255.255 is the broadcast address for Layer 3 and FF.FF.FF.FF.FF.FF is the broadcast address for Layer 2. Any packets and frames sent to that address will be sent to everyone on that LAN.

broadcast domain The collection of all devices that will receive each other's broadcast frames. Each interface on a router terminates a broadcast domain. Routers will not forward broadcasts to other interfaces. They can be made to turn certain broadcasts into unicasts to specific devices, but they will not propagate broadcasts. VLANs created on LAN switches are broadcast domains. Any broadcast created by a device attached to a switch port assigned to a VLAN will be received only by those devices attached to switch ports assigned to the same VLAN.

broadcast storm Broadcast storms are typically created by network loops or a bad NIC. Because of the loop or bad NIC, worthless broadcasts can be sent in the millions and this can create an extreme amount of broadcast and multicast traffic on a computer network and render the network unable to transport normal traffic.

buffer A place in memory to store incoming packets. All computers have buffers.

burned-in address (BIA) Usually, a MAC address that has been burned into an EEPROM on a networking device, becoming a permanent physical address for the device.

bus A pathway in a PC that allows data and signals to be transmitted between the PC components. Types of buses include ISA and PCI.

bus topology A topology where the cable and signals run in a straight line from one end of the network to the other.

butt set A special type of telephone used by technicians for installing and testing local-loop telephone lines.

byte A basic unit of measurement of information storage in a computer. It is considered to be a unit of memory addressing. A byte most often consists of 8 bits.

C

cable A physical transmission medium that has a central conductor of wire or fiber surrounded by a plastic jacket.

cable map General network documentation indicating each cable's source and destination as well as where each network cable runs.

cable modem A device used to interconnect computing and networking equipment, via Ethernet, with a television cable company's data network through the same cable circuit used to deliver television programming. The standard for data communications over the cable television network is known as the data over cable service interface specification (DOCSIS).

cable tester A special instrument that is used to test the integrity of LAN cables. *See also* time-domain reflectometer (TDR).

call setup   The overall length of time required to establish a circuit-switched call between users.

carrier   A signal at a frequency that is chosen to carry data. The addition of data to the frequency is called modulation, and the removal of data from the frequency is called demodulation. This is used on analog devices like modems.

Carrier Sense Multiple Access with Collision Avoidance (CSMA/CA)   A media access method that sends a Request to Send (RTS) packet and waits to receive a Clear to Send (CTS) packet before sending. Once the CTS is received, the sender sends the packet of information.

Carrier Sense Multiple Access with Collision Detection (CSMA/CD)   A media access method that first senses whether there is a signal on the wire, indicating that someone is transmitting currently. If no one else is transmitting, it attempts a transmission and listens for someone else trying to transmit at the same time. If this happens, both senders back off and don't transmit again until some specified period of time has passed. *See also* collision.

categories   Different grades of cables that determine how much protection is offered against interference from outside the cable. Category 1 allows voice data only. Category 2 allows data transmissions up to 4Mbps. Category 3 allows data transmissions up to 10Mbps. Category 4 allows data transmissions up to 16Mbps. Category 5 allows data transmissions up to 100Mbps. The only cables we use now are Cat 5 and Cat 6, which provide up to 1Gbps.

central office (CO)   The office in any metropolitan or rural area that contains the telephone switching equipment for that area. The CO connects all users in that area to each other as well as to the rest of the PSTN. *See also* Public Switched Telephone Network (PSTN).

centralized computing   Computing done at a central location using terminals that are attached to a central computer. The computer itself may control all the peripherals directly, or they may be attached via a terminal server.

certificate authority (CA)   An entity that issues digital certificates for use by other companies or institutions. A CA is a characteristic of many Public Key Infrastructure (PKI) schemes.

Challenge Handshake Authentication Protocol (CHAP)   A client-server authentication method that uses MD5 encryption and a random value to authenticate a client. The authentication server "challenges" the client to come up with the same value based on the random value and the secret shared between client and server.

channel service unit (CSU)   Generally used with a T1 Internet line, it is used to terminate the connection from the T1 provider. The CSU is usually part of a CSU/DSU unit. It also provides diagnostics and testing if necessary.

CHAP   *See* Challenge Handshake Authentication Protocol (CHAP).

checksum A hexadecimal value computed from transmitted data that is used in error-checking routines.

circuit switching A switching method where a dedicated connection between the sender and receiver is maintained throughout the conversation. POTS and ISDN, for example, establish circuit-switched connections through dialed numbers. *See also* packet switching.

Class A network Part of the Internet Protocol hierarchical addressing scheme. Class A networks have only 8 bits for defining networks and 24 bits for defining hosts and subnets on each network.

Class B network Part of the Internet Protocol hierarchical addressing scheme. Class B networks have 16 bits for defining networks and 16 bits for defining hosts and subnets on each network.

Class C network Part of the Internet Protocol hierarchical addressing scheme. Class C networks have 24 bits for defining networks and only 8 bits for defining hosts and subnets on each network.

classful Relates to the default characteristics of and constraints placed on an IP address based on the class of address in question. For example, a Class C address, by default, has 24 network bits and 8 host bits, limiting it to no more than 254 hosts per network. Classful defaults are considered in the absence of detailed configuration information, such as a non-default subnet mask.

classful routing The use of routing protocols that do not send subnet mask information when a route update is sent out.

Classless Inter-Domain Routing (CIDR) The new routing method used by InterNIC to assign IP addresses. CIDR can be described as a "slash *x*" network. The *x* represents the number of bits in the network that InterNIC controls.

classless routing Routing that sends subnet-mask information in the routing updates. Classless routing allows Variable-Length Subnet Masks (VLSMs) and supernetting. Routing protocols that support classless routing are RIP version 2, EIGRP, and OSPF.

client The part of a client-server network where the computing is usually done. In a typical setting, a client will use the server for remote storage, backups, or security such as a firewall.

client-server network A server-centric network in which all resources are stored on a file server and processing power is distributed among workstations and the file server.

clustering A computing technology where many servers work together so that they appear to be one high-powered server. If one server fails, the others in the cluster take over the services provided by the failed server.

CNAME record A DNS record type that specifies other names for existing hosts. This allows a DNS administrator to assign multiple DNS hostnames to a single DNS host. Also known as an *alias record*.

coaxial cable   Often referred to as coax. A type of cable used in network wiring. Typical coaxial cable connector types include RG-58 and RG-62. 10Base2 Ethernet networks use coaxial cable. Coaxial cable is usually shielded, which means that it is more immune to interference than unshielded cables.

collision   The error condition that occurs when two stations on a CSMA/CD network transmit data (at the Data Link layer) at the same time. *See also* Carrier Sense Multiple Access with Collision Detection (CSMA/CD).

collision domain   The group of devices whose frames could potentially collide with one another. Each interface on a bridge, switch, or router terminates a collision domain. These devices become responsible for recovering from collisions that occur due to their forwarding of frames out other interfaces.

collision light   An LED on a NIC or hub that indicates when a collision has occurred.

concentrator   *See* hub.

connectionless   A type of communication between two hosts where no session is established for synchronizing sent data. If the service is also unreliable, the data is not acknowledged at the receiving end. This can allow for data loss.

connectionless services   *See* connectionless, connectionless transport protocol.

connectionless transport protocol   A transport protocol, such as UDP, that does not create a virtual connection between sending and receiving stations before transmitting user data between them. *See also* User Datagram Protocol (UDP).

connection-oriented   A type of communication between two hosts that establishes a session for synchronizing sent data. If the service is also reliable, the data is acknowledged by the receiving device. This allows for guaranteed delivery of data between PCs.

connection-oriented transport protocol   A transport protocol that establishes a virtual connection between sending and receiving stations before any user data is transmitted between them. TCP is a connection-oriented protocol. *See also* Transmission Control Protocol (TCP).

Control Panel   A special window inside Microsoft Windows operating systems (Windows 95 and above) that has icons for all of the configurable options for the system.

controller   Part of a PC that allows connectivity to peripheral devices. A disk controller allows the PC to be connected to a hard disk. A network controller allows a PC to be connected to a network. A keyboard controller is used to connect a keyboard to the PC.

convergence   The process required for all routers in an internetwork to update their routing tables and create a consistent view of the network using the best possible paths, also referred to as steady state. When all routers have converged, they are said to be in a steady state.

cost   A value given to a route between PCs or subnets to determine which route may be best. Cost is used in OSPF to determine the metric to a neighbor or network. The word *hop* is sometimes used to refer to the number of routers between two PCs or subnets. *See also* hop.

country codes   The two-letter abbreviations for countries used in the DNS hierarchy. *See also* Domain Name Service (DNS).

CRC   *See* cyclic redundancy check (CRC).

crossover cable   The troubleshooting tool used in Ethernet UTP installations to test communications between two stations, bypassing the hub. Crossover cables can also be used to interconnect two DTE devices, such as PCs and routers, or two DCE devices, such as hubs and switches. *See also* unshielded twisted-pair (UTP) cable, medium dependent interface (MDI), medium dependent interface-crossover (MDI-X).

crosstalk   A type of interference that occurs when two LAN cables run close to each other. If one cable is carrying a signal and the other isn't, the one carrying a signal will induce a "ghost" signal (crosstalk) in the other cable.

CSMA/CA   *See* Carrier Sense Multiple Access with Collision Avoidance (CSMA/CA).

CSMA/CD   *See* Carrier Sense Multiple Access with Collision Detection (CSMA/CD).

customer premises equipment (CPE)   Items such as telephones, modems, and terminals installed at customer locations and connected to the service provider network.

cyclic redundancy check (CRC)   An error-checking method in data communications that runs a formula against data before transmissions. The sending station then appends the resultant value (called a checksum) to the data and sends it. The receiving station uses the same formula on the data. If the receiving station doesn't get the same checksum result for the calculation, it considers the transmission invalid, rejects the frame, and asks for a retransmission.

D

D channel   *See* delta channel (D channel).

daemon   Pronounced "demon," is a kernal process in Linux, and is like a terminate-and-stay-resident (TSR) application by loading into memory and lurking there for any trigger that calls on its services.

data communication equipment (DCE)   Equipment that provides clocking to DTE equipment. DCE equipment starts at the CSU/DSU and is defined as a connection all the way to the provider's network.

Data Encryption Standard (DES)   A deprecated cryptographic block cipher that falls to brute-force attacks due to its short 56-bit key. Triple DES (3DES), which was widely used before AES became a standard, is a block cipher formed from the DES cipher by using it three times.

data frame   A frame is the Protocol Data Unit encapsulation at the Data Link layer of the OSI reference model. A data frame encapsulates packets from the Network layer and prepares the data for transmission on a network medium.

Data Link Connection Identifiers (DLCIs)   Used to identify virtual circuits in a Frame Relay network.

Data Link layer   The second layer of the OSI model. It describes the logical topology of a network, which is the way that packets move throughout a network. It also describes the method of media access. *See also* Open Systems Interconnect (OSI).

data over cable service interface specification (DOCSIS)   *See* cable modem.

data packet   A unit of data sent over a network. A packet includes a header, addressing information, and the data itself. A packet is treated as a single unit as it is sent from device to device. Also known as a *datagram*.

data terminal equipment (DTE)   Any device that is located at the user end of a user-network interface and serves as a destination, a source, or both. DTE includes devices such as multiplexers, routers, protocol translators, and computers. The connection to a data network is made through data communication equipment (DCE) such as a modem, using the cloaking signals generated by that device. *See also* data communication equipment (DCE).

datagram   A logical collection of information transmitted as a Network layer unit over a medium without a previously established virtual circuit. IP datagrams have become the primary information unit of the Internet. At various layers of the OSI reference model, the terms *cell*, *frame*, *message*, *packet*, and *segment* also define these logical information groupings.

de-encapsulation   The technique used by layered protocols in which a layer removes header information from the Protocol Data Unit (PDU) from the layer below. *See also* encapsulation.

default gateway   The router that all packets are sent to when the workstation doesn't know where the destination station is or when it can't find the destination station on the local segment.

delta channel (D channel)   A channel on an ISDN line used for link management. For Basic Rate Interface (BRI) circuits, the D channel is 16Kbps. For the Primary Rate Interface (PRI), the D channel is 64Kbps. *See also* Integrated Services Digital Network (ISDN).

demarcation point (demarc)   The point on any telephone installation where the telephone lines from the central office enter the customer's premises.

demilitarized zone (DMZ) A physical or logical subnetwork that contains and exposes an organization's external services to a larger, untrusted network, usually the Internet. Named after the military usage of the term; also known as a demarcation zone or perimeter network.

denial of service (DoS) attack Type of hack that prevents any users—even legitimate ones—from using the system.

destination port number The Transport layer address of the PC to which data is being sent from a sending PC. The port portion allows for the demultiplexing of data to be sent to a specific application.

DHCP *See* Dynamic Host Configuration Protocol (DHCP).

Digital Subscriber Line (DSL) A digital WAN technology that brings high-speed digital networking to homes and businesses over POTS. There are many types, including HDSL (high bit-rate DSL) and VDSL (very high bit-rate DSL). *See also* plain old telephone service (POTS), asymmetrical digital subscriber line (ADSL).

Direct Sequence Spread Spectrum (DSSS) A modulation technique used by the original IEEE 802.11 standard, as well as by the 802.11b standard, that creates a redundant bit pattern for each bit that is transmitted. This way, if one or more bits in the bit pattern are damaged in transmission, the original data may be recoverable from the redundant bits. *See also* Frequency Hopping Spread Spectrum (FHSS), Orthogonal Frequency Division Multiplexing (OFDM).

directional antenna (Yagi) A point-to-point antenna that, when used as a wireless access point, is not suitable for general client access but rather for point-to-point bridging of access points. *See also* omnidirectional antenna (Omni).

directory A network database that contains a listing of all network resources, such as users, printers, groups, and so on.

directory service A network service that provides access to a central database of information, which contains detailed information about the resources available on a network.

Discretionary Access Control (DAC) Defined by the Trusted Computer System Evaluation Criteria as a means of restricting access to objects based on the identity of subjects and/ or groups to which they belong.

distance vector routing protocol A route discovery method in which each router, using broadcasts, tells every other router what networks and routes it knows about and the distance to them.

distributed denial of service (DDos) attacks *See* denial of service (DoS) attack.

distributed WAN An approach used by companies to provide WAN optimization by accelerating a broad range of applications accessed by distributed enterprise users via eliminating redundant transmissions, staging data in local caches, compressing and prioritizing data, and streamlining chatty protocols.

DIX   Another name for a 15-pin AUI connector or a DB-15 connector.

DNS   *See* Domain Name Service (DNS).

DNS server   Any server that performs address resolution by translating DNS hostnames to IP addresses. *See also* Domain Name Service (DNS), Internet Protocol (IP).

DNS zone   An area in the DNS hierarchy that is managed as a single unit. *See also* Domain Name Service (DNS).

DOCSIS   *See* cable modem.

DoD Networking Model   A four-layer conceptual model describing how communications should take place between computer systems. The four layers are Process/Application, Host-to-Host, Internet, and Network Access.

domain   A group of networked Windows computers that share a single Active Directory or NTDS database.

Domain Name Service (DNS)   The network service used in TCP/IP networks that translates hostnames to IP addresses. *See also* Transmission Control Protocol/Internet Protocol (TCP/IP).

dotted decimal   Notation used by TCP/IP to designate an IP address. The notation is made up of 32 bits (4 bytes), each byte separated by a decimal. The range of numbers for each octet is 0 to 255. The leftmost octet contains the high-order bits, and the rightmost octet contains the low-order bits.

DSL   *See* Digital Subscriber Line (DSL).

DSSS   *See* Direct Sequence Spread Spectrum (DSSS).

dumb terminal   A keyboard and monitor that send keystrokes to a central processing computer (typically a mainframe or minicomputer) that returns screen displays to the monitor. The unit has no processing power of its own, hence the moniker "dumb."

duplicate servers   Two servers that are identical for use in clustering.

dynamic ARP table entries   *See* dynamic entry.

dynamic entry   An entry made in the ARP table whenever an ARP request is made by the Windows TCP/IP stack and the MAC address is not found in the ARP table. The ARP request is broadcast on the local segment. When the MAC address of the requested IP address is found, that information is added to the ARP table. *See also* Internet Protocol (IP), Media Access Control (MAC), Transmission Control Protocol/Internet Protocol (TCP/IP).

Dynamic Host Configuration Protocol (DHCP)   A protocol used on a TCP/IP network to send configuration data, including TCP/IP address, default gateway, subnet mask, and DNS configuration, to clients. *See also* default gateway, Domain Name Service (DNS), subnet mask, Transmission Control Protocol/Internet Protocol (TCP/IP).

dynamic packet filtering   A type of firewall used to accept or reject packets based on the contents of the packets.

dynamic ports   *See* dynamic VLAN.

dynamic routing   The use of route-discovery protocols to talk to other routers and find out what networks they are attached to. Routers that use dynamic routing send out special packets to request updates of the other routers on the network as well as send their own updates.

dynamic VLAN   An administrator will create an entry in a special server with the hardware addresses of all devices on the internetwork. The server will then report the associated VLAN to a switch that requests it, based on the new device's hardware address.

dynamically allocated port   A TCP/IP port used by an application when needed. The port is not constantly used.

E

EEPROM   *See* electrically erasable programmable read-only memory (EEPROM).

electrically erasable programmable read-only memory (EEPROM)   A special integrated circuit on expansion cards that allows data to be stored on the chip. If necessary, the data can be erased by a special configuration program. Typically used to store hardware configuration data for expansion cards.

electromagnetic interference (EMI)   The interference that can occur during transmissions over copper cable because of electromagnetic energy outside the cable. The result is degradation of the signal.

electronic mail (email) software   An application that allows people to send messages via their computers on the same network or over the Internet.

EMI   *See* electromagnetic interference (EMI).

encapsulation   The technique used by layered protocols in which a layer adds header information to the Protocol Data Unit (PDU) from the layer above. As an example, in Internet terminology, a packet contains a header from the Data Link layer, followed by a header from the Network layer (IP), followed by a header from the Transport layer (TCP), followed by the application protocol data.

encoding   The process of translating data into signals that can be transmitted on a transmission medium.

encryption key   The string of alphanumeric characters used to encrypt and decrypt data.

endpoint   The two ends of a connection for transmitting data. One end is the receiver, and the other is the sender.

Enhanced Interior Gateway Routing Protocol (EIGRP)   An advanced routing protocol created by Cisco, combining the advantages of link state and distance vector protocols. EIGRP has superior convergence attributes, including high operating efficiency. *See also* Interior Gateway Protocol (IGP), Open Shortest Path First (OSPF), and Routing Information Protocol (RIP) and Routing Information Protocol version 2 (RIPv2).

Ethernet   A shared-media network architecture. It operates at the Physical and Data Link layers of the OSI model. As a media-access method, it uses baseband signaling over either a bus or a star topology with CSMA/CD. The cabling used in Ethernet networks can be coax, twisted-pair, or fiber-optic. *See also* Carrier Sense Multiple Access with Collision Detection (CSMA/CD), Open Systems Interconnect (OSI).

Ethernet address   *See* MAC address.

expansion slot   A slot on the computer's bus into which expansion cards are plugged to expand the functionality of the computer (for example, using a NIC to add the computer to a network). *See also* Network Interface Card (NIC).

Extensible Authentication Protocol (EAP)   An extension to PPP that supports multiple authentication methods, including Kerberos, passwords, certificates, smart cards, and so on. IEEE 802.1x is the standard that dictates how EAP is used within Ethernet frames.

Exterior Gateway Protocol (EGP)   Protocols used to connect autonomous systems (ASs) together. An example is BGP.

extranet   An intranet interconnected and intercommunicating with networks that are under separate administrative control by way of an arrangement between the administrative entities. *See also* internetwork, intranet.

extranet VPN   A VPN in which the various sites are owned by different enterprises. If all the sites in a VPN are owned by the same enterprise, the VPN is a corporate intranet.

F

Fast Ethernet   The general category name given to 100Mbps Ethernet technologies.

FHSS   *See* Frequency Hopping Spread Spectrum (FHSS).

Fiber Channel   A type of server-to-storage system connection that uses fiber-optic connectors.

fiber-optic   A type of network cable that uses a central glass or plastic core surrounded by a plastic coating.

file server   A server specialized in holding and distributing files.

File Transfer Protocol (FTP)   A TCP/IP protocol and software that permit the transferring of files between computer systems. Because FTP has been implemented on numerous types of computer systems, files can be transferred between disparate computer systems (for example, a personal computer and a minicomputer). *See also* Transmission Control Protocol/Internet Protocol (TCP/IP).

file virus   *See* virus.

firewall   A combination of hardware and software that protects a network from attack by hackers who could gain access through public networks, including the Internet.

flat network   A network that is one large collision domain and one large broadcast domain.

flow control   A methodology used to ensure that receiving units are not overwhelmed with data from sending devices. Pacing, as it is called in IBM networks, means that when buffers at a receiving unit are full, a message is transmitted to the sending unit to temporarily halt transmissions until all the data in the receiving buffer has been processed and the buffer is again ready for action.

forward/filter decision   Process in which a frame is received on an interface and the switch then looks at the destination hardware address and finds the exit interface in the MAC database. The frame is forwarded only out the specified destination port.

FQDN   *See* fully qualified domain name (FQDN).

frame   A logical unit of information sent by the Data Link layer over a transmission medium. The term often refers to the header and trailer, employed for synchronization and error control, that surround the data contained in the unit.

frame filtering   Process in which a switch reads the destination hardware address of a frame and then looks for this address in the filter table built by the switch. It then sends the frame out only to the port where the hardware address is located; the other ports do not see the frame. Frame filtering is used on Layer 2 switches to provide more bandwidth.

Frame Relay   A WAN technology that transmits packets over a WAN using packet switching. *See also* packet switching.

frame tagging   Process by which switches within a VLAN that spans multiple connected switches (which Cisco calls a switch fabric) keep track of frames as they are received on the switch ports and also keep track of the VLAN they belong to as the frames traverse this switch fabric. Switches can then direct frames to the appropriate port.

frequency-division multiplexing (FDM)   A multiplexing technique whereby different signals are sent across multiple frequencies.

Frequency Hopping Spread Spectrum (FHSS)   A modulation technique specified by the original IEEE 802.11 standard but not supported by manufacturers. DSSS is the modulation technique of choice of 802.11 equipment makers. FHSS modulates the data signal with a carrier signal that hops through a random, yet predictable, sequence of frequencies. A hopping code determines the transmission frequencies. The receiver is set to the same code, allowing it to listen to the incoming signal at the right time and frequency to properly receive the signal. *See also* Direct Sequence Spread Spectrum (DSSS), Orthogonal Frequency Division Multiplexing (OFDM).

FTP   *See* File Transfer Protocol (FTP).

FTP proxy   A server that uploads files to and downloads files from another server on behalf of a workstation.

full backup   A backup that copies all data to the archive medium.

full duplex   The capacity to transmit information between a sending station and a receiving unit at the same time. *See also* half duplex.

fully qualified domain name (FQDN)   An address that uses both the hostname (workstation name) and the domain name.

G

gateway   The hardware and software needed to connect two disparate network environments so that communications can occur.

H

half duplex   The capacity to transfer data in only one direction at a time between a sending unit and receiving unit. *See also* full duplex.

hardware address   A Data Link layer address assigned to every NIC at the MAC sublayer. The address is in the format $xx:xx:xx:xx:xx:xx$. Each xx is a two-digit hexadecimal number. *See also* Media Access Control (MAC), Network Interface Card (NIC).

hardware loopback   A small plug used in a NIC that connects the transmission pins directly to the receiving pins, allowing diagnostic software to test whether a NIC can successfully transmit and receive. *See also* Network Interface Card (NIC).

heartbeat   The data transmission between two servers in a cluster to detect when one fails. When the standby server detects no heartbeats from the main server, it comes online and takes control of the responsibilities of the main server. This allows for all services to remain online and accessible.

hierarchical addressing   Any addressing plan employing a logical chain of command to determine location. IP addresses are made up of a hierarchy of network numbers, subnet numbers, and host numbers to direct packets to the appropriate destination.

high bit-rate digital subscriber line (HDSL)   The first DSL technology to use a higher-frequency spectrum of copper twisted-pair cables.

honeypot   A trap set to detect, deflect, or in some manner counteract attempts at unauthorized use of information systems. This can be a wired or wireless trap to collect information about the attacker.

hop   One pass through a router. *See also* cost, router.

hop count   A means of limiting the number of routers a packet can cross on the way to its destination. As a packet travels over a network through multiple routers, each router will increment the hop-count field in the packet by one as it crosses the router.

host   Any network device with a TCP/IP network address. *See also* Transmission Control Protocol/Internet Protocol (TCP/IP).

host address   A logical address configured by an administrator or server on a device. It logically identifies this device on an internetwork.

Host-to-Host layer   A layer in the DoD model that corresponds to the Transport layer of the OSI model. *See also* DoD Networking Model, Open Systems Interconnect (OSI).

HTML   *See* Hypertext Markup Language.

HTTP   *See* Hypertext Transfer Protocol.

hub   A Physical layer device that serves as a central connection point for several network devices. A hub repeats the signals it receives on one port to all other ports. *See also* active hub.

hybrid routing protocol   A routing protocol that uses the attributes of both distance vector and link state. Enhanced Interior Gateway Routing Protocol (Enhanced IGRP) is an example of a hybrid routing protocol.

Hypertext Markup Language (HTML)   A set of codes used to format text and graphics that will be displayed in a browser. The codes define how data will be displayed.

Hypertext Transfer Protocol (HTTP)   The protocol used for communication between a web server and a web browser.

Hypertext Transfer Protocol over SSL/TLS (HTTPS)   A Uniform Resource Identifier (URI) scheme used to indicate a secure communication such as payment transactions and corporate information systems.

I

ICMP   *See* Internet Control Message Protocol (ICMP).

IEEE   *See* Institute of Electrical and Electronics Engineers (IEEE).

IEEE 802.x standards   Standards for LAN and MAN networking.

IEEE 802.1 LAN/MAN Management   Standard that specifies LAN/MAN network management and internetworking.

IEEE 802.2 Logical Link Control   Standard that specifies the operation of the Logical Link Control (LLC) sublayer of the Data Link layer of the OSI model. The LLC sublayer provides an interface between the MAC sublayer and the Network layer. *See also* Media Access Control (MAC), Open Systems Interconnect (OSI).

IEEE 802.3 CSMA/CD Networking   Standard that specifies a network that uses Ethernet technology and a CSMA/CD network access method. *See also* Carrier Sense Multiple Access with Collision Detection (CSMA/CD).

IEEE 802.5 Token Ring   Specifies a logical ring, physical star, and token-passing media access method based on IBM's Token Ring.

IEEE 802.10 LAN/MAN Security   A series of guidelines dealing with various aspects of network security.

IEEE 802.11 Wireless LAN   Standards for implementing wireless technologies such as infrared and spread-spectrum radio.

IETF   *See* Internet Engineering Task Force (IETP).

implicit deny   A default test statement found at the end of each access list.

Independent Computing Architecture (ICA)   A proprietary protocol for an application server system, designed by Citrix Systems. ICA lays down a specification for passing data between server and clients but is not bound to any one platform.

Institute of Electrical and Electronics Engineers (IEEE)   An international organization that sets standards for various electrical and electronics issues.

Integrated Services Digital Network (ISDN)   A telecommunications standard that is used to digitally send voice, data, and video signals over the same lines. *See also* delta channel (D channel).

Interior Gateway Protocol (IGP)   A routing protocol used within an autonomous system to update the routing table on all the routers. Examples of IGPs are RIP, EIGRP, OSPF, and IS-IS.

internal bridge   A bridge created by placing two NICs in a computer.

internal modem   A modem that is a regular PC card and is inserted into the bus slot. These modems are inside the PC.

International Organization for Standardization (ISO)   The standards organization that developed the OSI model. This model provides a guideline for how communications occur between computers.

Internet   A global network made up of a large number of individual networks interconnected through the use of data circuits and TCP/IP protocols. *See also* Transmission Control Protocol/Internet Protocol (TCP/IP).

Internet Architecture Board (IAB)   The committee that oversees management of the Internet. It is made up of two subcommittees: the Internet Engineering Task Force (IETF) and the Internet Research Task Force (IRTF). *See also* Internet Engineering Task Force (IETF), Internet Research Task Force (IRTF).

Internet Control Message Protocol (ICMP)   A message and management protocol for TCP/IP. The **ping** utility uses ICMP. *See also* ping, Transmission Control Protocol/Internet Protocol (TCP/IP).

Internet Engineering Task Force (IETF)   An international organization that works under the Internet Architecture Board to establish standards and protocols relating to the Internet. *See also* Internet Architecture Board (IAB).

Internet layer   Layer in the Internet Protocol suite of protocols that provides network addressing and routing through an internetwork.

Internet Protocol (IP)   The protocol in the TCP/IP protocol suite responsible for network addressing and routing. *See also* Transmission Control Protocol/Internet Protocol (TCP/IP).

Internet Research Task Force (IRTF)   An international organization that works under the Internet Architecture Board to research new Internet technologies. *See also* Internet Architecture Board (IAB).

Internet service provider (ISP)   A company that provides direct access to the Internet for home and business computer users.

internetwork   Also known as an internet, for short, the interconnection and intercommunication between autonomous networks. *See also* intranet, extranet.

Inter-Switch Link (ISL) routing   A Cisco-proprietary method of frame tagging in a switched internetwork. Frame tagging is a way to identify the VLAN membership of a frame as it traverses a switched internetwork.

intranet   Often an internetwork encompassing only networks under a single administrative domain; very often used to refer to a large corporation's internal internetwork. *See also* internetwork, extranet.

intrusion detection system (IDS)   Software and/or hardware designed to detect unwanted attempts at accessing, manipulating, and/or disabling computer systems, mainly through a network such as the Internet. This detects problems but does not solve them. *See* intrusion prevention system (IPS).

intrusion prevention system (IPS)   A network security device that monitors network and/or system activities for malicious or unwanted behavior and can react, in real time, to block or prevent those activities. Unlike IDS, IPS can stop a network attack. *See* intrusion detection system (IDS).

inverse multiplexing   The network technology that allows one signal to be split across multiple transmission lines at the transmission source and combined at the receiving end.

IP   *See* Internet Protocol (IP).

IP address   An address that is used by the Internet Protocol and identifies a device's location on the network.

IP proxy   A server technology that protects your network. With an IP proxy, all communications look as if they originated from a proxy server because the IP address of the user making a request is hidden. IP proxies use a technology known as NAT. *See also* Network Address Translation (NAT).

IP spoofing   An attack in which a hacker tries to gain access to a network by pretending their machine has the same network address as the internal network.

ipconfig   A Windows utility used to display a machine's current configuration.

IPv4   A protocol that provides logical addressing and routing through an internetwork. Has an address field of 32 bits.

IPv6   A protocol that provides logical addressing and routing through an internetwork. Has an address field of 128 bits.

IS-IS   An Interior gateway routing protocol that is typically only used within ISPs.

ISDN   *See* Integrated Services Digital Network (ISDN).

ISDN terminal adapter   The device used to connect a local network (or single machine) to an ISDN network. It provides power to the line as well as translates data from the LAN or individual computer for transmission on the ISDN line. *See also* Integrated Services Digital Network (ISDN).

ISP   *See* Internet service provider (ISP).

J

Java   A programming language developed by Sun Microsystems that is used to write programs that will run on any platform that has a Java Virtual Machine installed.

Java Virtual Machine (JVM)   Software developed by Sun Microsystems that creates a virtual Java computer on which Java programs can run. A programmer writes a program once without having to recompile or rewrite the program for all platforms.

jumper   A small connector (cap or plug) that connects pins. This creates a circuit that indicates a setting to a device.

JVM   *See* Java Virtual Machine (JVM).

K

Kerberos   An authentication and encryption method that can be used by Cisco routers to ensure that data cannot be "sniffed" off the network. Kerberos was developed at MIT and was designed to provide strong security using the Data Encryption Standard (DES) cryptographic algorithm.

kernel   The core component of any operating system. Handles the functions of memory management, hardware interaction, and program execution.

key   A folder in the Windows Registry that contains subkeys and values or a value with an algorithm to encrypt and decrypt data.

L

LAN   *See* local area network (LAN).

LAN driver   The interface between the NetWare kernel and the NIC installed in the server. Also a general category of drivers used to enable communications between an operating system and a NIC. *See also* Network Interface Card (NIC).

laser printer   A printer that uses a laser to form an image on a photo-sensitive drum. The image is then developed with toner and transferred to paper. Finally, a heated drum fuses toner particles onto the paper.

latency sensitivity   Broadly, the time it takes a data packet to get from one location to another. In specific networking contexts, it can mean either (1) the time elapsed (delay) between the execution of a request for access to a network by a device and the time the mechanism actually is permitted transmission or (2) the time elapsed between when a mechanism receives a frame and the time that frame is forwarded out of the destination port. The sensitivity of a connection is defined by the extent to which an application can tolerate latency without requiring a new socket.

Layer 2 switch   A switching hub that operates at the Data Link layer and builds a table of the MAC addresses of all the connected stations. *See also* Media Access Control (MAC).

Layer 3 switch   Functioning at the Network layer, a switch that performs the multiport, virtual LAN, data-pipelining functions of a standard Layer 2 switch but can also perform basic routing functions between virtual LANs.

layered architecture   An industry-standard way of creating applications to work on a network, which allows the application developer to make changes in only one layer instead of the whole program.

layers   Term used in networking to define how the OSI model works to encapsulate data for transmission on the network.

LCP   *See* Link Control Protocol (LCP).

lease   In DHCP, the duration of time for which a client is allowed to use the parameters assigned to it by the server. *See also* Dynamic Host Configuration Protocol (DHCP).

leased line   A permanent connection between two points. These connections are leased from telephone companies.

Link Control Protocol (LCP)   The protocol used to establish, configure, and test the link between a client and PPP host. *See also* Point-to-Point Protocol (PPP).

link light   A small light-emitting diode (LED) that is found on both the NIC and the hub. It is usually green and labeled Link or something similar. A link light indicates that the NIC and the hub are making a Data Link layer connection. *See also* hub, Network Interface Card (NIC).

link state route discovery   A route discovery method that transmits special packets (link state packets, or LSPs) that contain information about the networks to which the router is connected.

link state routing   A type of routing that advertises a router's entire routing table only at startup and possibly at infrequently scheduled intervals. Aside from that, the router sends updates to other routers only when changes occur in the advertiser's routing table.

link state routing protocol   A routing protocol whereby the router sends out incremental information only, such as updates to its own routing table. Examples of link state routing protocols are OSPF and IS-IS.

Linux   A version of Unix, developed by Linus Torvalds. It runs on Intel-based PCs and is generally free. *See also* Unix.

load balancing The act of balancing packet load over multiple links to the same remote network.

local area network (LAN) A network that is restricted to a single building, a group of buildings, or even a single room. A LAN can have one or more servers. LANs are defined by the Data Link protocols they run. For example, Ethernet networks are LANs, but PPP networks are not. They are WAN links.

Local Connector (LC) A type of optical fiber connector that terminates the end of an optical fiber and enables quicker connection and disconnection than splicing. The connectors mechanically couple and align the cores of fibers so that light can pass.

local groups Groups created on individual servers. Rights can be assigned only to local resources.

local loop The part of the PSTN that goes from the central office to the demarcation point at the customer's premises. *See also* central office (CO), demarcation point (demarc), Public Switched Telephone Network (PSTN).

log file A file that keeps a running list of all errors and notices, the time and date they occurred, and any other pertinent information.

logical address A Network layer address that defines how data is sent from one network to another. Examples of logical addresses are IP and IPv6.

logical bus topology A type of topology in which the signal appears to travel the distance of the cable and is received by all stations on the backbone. Compare to a physical bus topology, in which this is actually the case. Logical bus topologies are most often implemented as physical star topologies. *See also* backbone.

Logical Link Control (LLC) A sublayer of the Data Link layer that provides an interface between the MAC sublayer and the Network layer. *See also* Media Access Control (MAC), topology.

logical network addressing The addressing scheme used by protocols at the Network layer. An example of logical network addressing (also called routed protocols) is IP and IPv6.

logical network diagram A network design that is placed on top of a physical network design. A logical network diagram or design is an example of an IP or IPv6 logical addressing scheme. Before you can create the logical network diagram, you must first have a physical network diagram.

logical parallel port A port used by the **CAPTURE** command to redirect a workstation printer port to a network print queue. The logical port has no relation to the port to which the printer is actually attached or to the physical port. *See also* physical parallel port.

logical port address A value that is used at the Transport layer to differentiate between the upper-layer services.

logical ring topology   A network topology in which all network signals travel from one station to another, being read and forwarded by each station.

logical topology   A way that information can flow. The same as a physical topology except that the flow of information, rather than the physical arrangement, specifies the type of topology.

loop avoidance   Term that typically refers to the Spanning Tree Protocol (STP) to stop loops in a switched network. Routing protocols, such as RIP and EIGRP, have Layer 3 loop avoidance schemes as well.

M

MAC   *See* Media Access Control (MAC).

MAC address   The address that is either assigned to a network card or burned into the NIC. This is how PCs keep track of one another and keep each other separate.

macro virus   *See* virus.

magnetic flux   This is represented by the Greek letter ϕ (phi) and is a measure of the quantity of magnetism using the strength and the extent of a magnetic field.

mail exchanger (MX) record   A DNS record type that specifies the DNS hostname of the mail server for a particular domain name.

managed objects   Devices managed by SNMP.

Management Information Base (MIB)   Software on hosts used by Simple Network Management Protocol (SNMP) to manage devices.

mechanical transfer registered jack (MT-RJ)   A jack used to connect pairs of optical fibers together. It uses a form factor and latch like the RJ-45 connectors, supports full duplex, costs less than ST or SC connectors, and is easier to terminate and install than ST or SC connectors.

media access   The process of vying for transmission time on the network media.

Media Access Control (MAC)   A sublayer of the Data Link layer that controls the way multiple devices use the same media channel. It controls which devices can transmit and when they can transmit.

media converter   A networking device that converts from one network media type to another—for example, from an AUI port to an RJ-45 connector for 10BaseT.

medium dependent interface (MDI)   The standard pin configuration for a wiring specification. The transmit and receive pairs of an MDI port are crossed with respect to those of an MDI-X port. MDI is generally considered to be the pin configuration used on the device acting as data terminal equipment (DTE). There is generally one port on Ethernet hubs or switches that can be switched between MDI and MDI-X. Hub or switch ports set for MDI allow the hub or switch to be connected to the standard MDI-X port of another hub or switch without the use of a crossover cable. *See also* medium dependent interface-crossover (MDI-X).

medium dependent interface-crossover (MDI-X)   A nonstandard pin configuration for a wiring specification, characterized by reversing the transmit and receive channels with respect to the MDI specification. MDI-X is generally considered to be the pin configuration used on the device acting as data communication equipment (DCE). There is generally one port on Ethernet hubs or switches that can be switched between MDI and MDI-X. Hub or switch ports set for MDI allow the hub or switch to be connected to the standard MDI-X port of another hub or switch without the use of a crossover cable. If the switchable port is set for MDI-X, it can be used with a straight-through cable for connection to an end device, such as a PC or router. *See also* medium dependent interface (MDI).

mesh topology   A network topology in which there is a connection from each station to every other station in the network.

Microsoft Challenge Handshake Authentication Protocol (MS-CHAP)   Microsoft's version of CHAP, designed for authentication communications between Windows clients and servers. *See also* Challenge Handshake Authentication Protocol (CHAP).

misuse-detection IDS (MD-IDS)   *See* intrusion detection system (IDS).

modem   A communication device that converts digital computer signals into analog tones for transmission over the PSTN and converts them back to digital on reception. The word *modem* is an acronym for *modulator/demodulator.*

MS-CHAP   *See* Microsoft Challenge Handshake Authentication Protocol (MS-CHAP).

MultiProtocol Label Switching (MPLS)   A data-carrying mechanism that belongs to the family of packet-switched networks, like Frame Relay and ATM, but is an upgrade from those protocols. MPLS operates at an OSI model layer of 2.5.

multicast   Broadly, any communication between a single sender and multiple receivers. Unlike broadcast messages, which are sent to all addresses on a network, multicast messages are sent to a defined subset of the network addresses; this subset has a group multicast address, which is specified in the packet's destination address field. *See also* broadcast address.

multicast group   A defined set of users or hosts that are allowed to read or view data sent via multicast. Multicast works by sending messages or data to IP multicast group addresses.

multipartite virus   *See* virus.

multiple input, multiple output (MIMO)   Protocol used by 802.11n to provide full-duplex wireless communication.

multiplexing   A technology that combines multiple signals into one signal for transmission over a slow medium. *See also* frequency-division multiplexing (FDM), inverse multiplexing.

multipoint RF network   A radio frequency (RF) network consisting of multiple stations, each with transmitters and receivers. This type of network also requires an RF bridge as a central sending and receiving point.

N

name resolution   The process of translating (resolving) logical hostnames to network addresses.

NAT   *See* Network Address Translation (NAT).

National Computing Security Center (NCSC)   The agency that developed the Trusted Computer System Evaluation Criteria (TCSEC) and the Trusted Network Interpretation Environmental Guideline (TNIEG).

National Security Agency (NSA)   The US government agency responsible for protecting US communications and producing foreign intelligence information. It was established by presidential directive in 1952 as a separately organized agency within the Department of Defense (DoD).

nbtstat (NetBIOS over TCP/IP statistics)   The Windows TCP/IP utility that is used to display NetBIOS over TCP/IP statistics. See also Network Basic Input/Output System (NetBIOS), Transmission Control Protocol/Internet Protocol (TCP/IP).

NCSC   *See* National Computing Security Center (NCSC).

NetBEUI   *See* NetBIOS Extended User Interface (NetBEUI).

NetBIOS   *See* Network Basic Input/Output System (NetBIOS).

NetBIOS Extended User Interface (NetBEUI)   A transport protocol that is based on the NetBIOS protocol and has datagram support and support for connectionless transmission. NetBEUI is native to Microsoft networks and is mainly for use by small businesses. It is a nonroutable protocol that cannot pass over a router but does pass over a bridge because it operates at the Data Link layer. *See also* Network Basic Input/Output System (NetBIOS).

NetBIOS name   The unique name used to identify and address a computer using NetBEUI.

netstat   A utility used to determine which TCP/IP connections—inbound or outbound—the computer has. It also allows the user to view packet statistics, such as how many packets have been sent and received. See also Transmission Control Protocol/Internet Protocol (TCP/IP).

network A group of devices connected by some means for the purpose of sharing information or resources.

Network Access layer The bottom layer in the Internet Protocol suite that provides media access to packets.

network address An address that is used with the logical network addresses to identify the host addresses in an internetwork. Logical addresses are hierarchical in nature and have at least two parts: network and host. An example of a hierarchical address is 172.16.10.5, where 172.16 is the network address and 10.5 is the host address.

Network Address Translation (NAT) A TCP/IP service that many routers, firewalls, and IP proxies can provide. NAT translates addresses that are legal for an inside network but illegal for a corresponding outside network into addresses that are legal for the outside network. NAT also resolves the outside addresses back to the inside addresses as return traffic for the originating device comes back from the outside network. *See also* IP proxy.

network-attached storage Storage, such as hard drives, attached to a network for the purpose of storing data for clients on the network. Network-attached storage is commonly used for backing up data.

Network Basic Input/Output System (NetBIOS) A Session layer protocol that opens communication sessions for applications that want to communicate on a network.

Network File System (NFS) A protocol that enables users to access files on remote computers as if the files were local.

Network Interface Card (NIC) A physical device that connects computers and other network equipment to the transmission medium.

Network layer The third layer of the OSI model. It is responsible for logical addressing and translating logical names into physical addresses. This layer also controls the routing of data from source to destination as well as the building and dismantling of packets. *See also* Open Systems Interconnect (OSI).

Network Management System (NMS) Software that works with SNMP to monitor and control network elements such as hosts, gateways, and terminal servers. These network elements use a management agent to perform the network management functions requested by the network management stations.

network media The physical cables that link computers in a network; also known as *physical media*.

network operating system (NOS) The software that runs on a network server and offers file, print, application, and other services to clients.

network segmentation The process of breaking up a large network into smaller networks. Routers, switches, and bridges are used to create network segmentation.

network software diagnostics   Software tools, either protocol analyzers or performance monitoring tools, used to troubleshoot network problems.

network-centric   A description of network operating systems that use directory services to maintain information about the entire network.

NFS   *See* Network File System (NFS).

nibble   A unit of information storage made up of 4 bits.

NIC   *See* Network Interface Card (NIC).

NIC diagnostics   Software utilities that verify that the NIC is functioning correctly and test every aspect of NIC operation. *See also* Network Interface Card (NIC).

NIC driver   *See* LAN driver.

node address   An address that identifies a specific device in an internetwork. It can be a hardware address, which is burned into the NIC, or a logical network address, which an administrator or server assigns to the node.

nonce   A nonce is an arbitrary number used only once to sign a cryptographic communication.

non-unicast packet   A packet that is not sent directly from one workstation to another.

NOS   *See* network operating system (NOS).

NSA   *See* National Security Agency (NSA).

N-series connector   A male/female screw-and-barrel connector used with thinnet and thicknet cabling.

nslookup   A utility that allows you to query a name server to see which IP address a name resolves to.

O

octet   Refers to 8 bits; one-fourth of an IP address.

OFDM   *See* Orthogonal Frequency Division Multiplexing (OFDM).

offline   The general name for the condition when some piece of electronic or computer equipment is unavailable or inoperable.

Omni   *See* omnidirectional antenna (Omni).

omnidirectional antenna (Omni)   A point-to-multipoint antenna that provides equal power dispersion in almost all directions. Omni is the primary antenna type used with a wireless access point that is designed to offer service to clients in any direction simultaneously. Contrast with directional Yagi antennas. *See also* directional antenna (Yagi).

Open Shortest Path First (OSPF)   A link state, hierarchical routing algorithm derived from an earlier version of the IS-IS protocol, whose features include multipath routing, load balancing, and least-cost routing. OSPF is the suggested successor to RIP in the corporate environment. *See also* Enhanced Interior Gateway Routing Protocol (EIGRP), Interior Gateway Protocol (IGP), and Internet Protocol (IP).

Open Systems Interconnect (OSI)   A model defined by the ISO to categorize the process of communication between computers in terms of seven layers. The seven layers are Application, Presentation, Session, Transport, Network, Data Link, and Physical. *See also* International Organization for Standardization (ISO).

OpenLinux   A version of the Linux network operating system developed by Caldera.

operator error (OE)   A problem with the user not knowing how to operate software or hardware. An OE problem can be a serious one.

organizationally unique identifier (OUI)   The first 24 bits of a 48-bit MAC address. Each OUI is assigned by the IEEE to a single manufacturer of devices that have MAC addresses assigned to them. As long as the manufacturer does not duplicate the last 24 bits of the MAC address, the assumption is that the entire MAC address will be unique worldwide. However, renegade manufacturers and manufacturing mistakes can result in duplicate MAC addresses. As long as the devices with duplicate addresses do not make it onto the same local network segment (the same IP subnet, for example), this conflict will never be an issue.

Orthogonal Frequency Division Multiplexing (OFDM)   A modulation technique used by 802.11g/a that is implemented with a system of 52 subcarriers. OFDM's spread-spectrum technique distributes the data over these 52 subcarriers, which are spaced apart at precise frequencies. This spacing helps prevent demodulators from seeing frequencies other than their own. *See also* Direct Sequence Spread Spectrum (DSSS), Frequency Hopping Spread Spectrum (FHSS).

OSI   *See* Open Systems Interconnect (OSI).

P

packet   The basic division of data sent over a network.

packet filtering   A firewall technology that accepts or rejects packets based on their content.

packet sniffer   Software run on a host that gathers packets and analyzes them. Can also be referred to as a packet analyzer.

packet switching   A method of switching that sends information as potentially smaller discrete packets, each one independently addressed for the intended recipient. Intermediate devices, such as switches and routers, can send these packets along one or more different paths to the same destination, making the autonomy of each packet imperative. A packet-switched connection is virtual, and the physical paths are shared, in contrast to the concept of the dedicated paths of circuit switching. *See also* Frame Relay, circuit switching.

passive detection   A type of intruder detection that logs all network events to a file for an administrator to view later.

passive hub   A hub that makes physical and electrical connections between all connected stations. Generally speaking, these hubs are not powered.

PAT   See Port Address Translation (PAT).

patch   Software that fixes a problem with an existing program or operating system.

patch cable   A cable used to electrically connect jacks together on a patch panel from a wall jack to a host. *See also* unshielded twisted-pair (UTP) cable.

patch panel   A central wiring point for multiple devices on a UTP network. The patch panel itself contains no electronic circuits. Generally, patch panels are in server rooms or located near switches or hubs to provide an easy means of patching over wall jacks or hardware.

PDU   *See* Protocol Data Unit (PDU).

peer communication   The use of headers to allow corresponding protocol processes in two devices to communicate with one another as if there were a direct connection between the devices at the protocol's layer.

peer-to-peer network   Computers that are hooked together and have no centralized authority. Each computer is equal and can act as both a server and a workstation.

peripheral   Any device that can be attached to a computer to expand its capabilities.

permanent virtual circuit (PVC)   A technology used by Frame Relay that allows virtual data communications (circuits) to be set up between sender and receiver over a packet-switched network.

PGP   *See* Pretty Good Privacy (PGP).

phishing   The criminally fraudulent process of attempting to acquire sensitive information such as usernames, passwords, and credit card details by masquerading as a trustworthy entity in an electronic communication.

physical address   *See* MAC address.

physical bus topology   A network that uses one network cable that runs from one end of the network to the other. Workstations connect at various points along this cable.

Physical layer   The first layer of the OSI model. This layer controls the functional interface. *See also* Open Systems Interconnect (OSI).

physical media   *See* network media.

physical mesh topology   A network configuration in which each device has multiple connections. These multiple connections provide redundancy in the form of backup connections.

physical network diagram   A network drawing that details the physical network layout, including routers, switches, and sometimes servers. After the physical network is designed and a diagram is created, a logical network diagram can be designed as a second layer to the physical network diagram.

physical parallel port   A port that is on the back of a computer and allows a printer to be connected with a parallel cable.

physical port   An opening on a network device that allows a cable of some kind to be connected. Ports allow devices to be connected to each other with cables.

physical ring topology   A network topology that is set up in a circular fashion. Data travels around the ring in one direction, and each device on the ring acts as a repeater to keep the signal strong as it travels. Each device incorporates a receiver for the incoming signal and a transmitter to send the data on to the next device in the ring. The network is dependent on the ability of the signal to travel around the ring.

physical star topology   A network in which a cable runs from each network entity to a central device called a hub. The hub allows all devices to communicate as if they were directly connected. *See also* hub.

physical topology   The physical layout of a network, such as a bus, star, ring, or mesh.

ping   A TCP/IP utility used to test whether another host is reachable. An ICMP request is sent to the host, which responds with a reply if it is reachable. The request times out if the host is not reachable.

Ping of Death attack   Type of attack in which a large ICMP packet is sent to overflow the remote host's buffer. This usually causes the remote host to reboot or hang.

plain old telephone service (POTS)   The classic analog circuit commonly used to connect to the Public Switched Telephone Network (PSTN) to make voice calls for conversations and modem and facsimile sessions. *See* asymmetrical digital subscriber line (ADSL), Digital Subscriber Line (DSL), Public Switched Telephone Network (PSTN).

plenum-rated coating   A coaxial cable coating that does not produce toxic gas when burned.

point of presence (POP)   The physical location where an interexchange carrier has placed equipment to interconnect with a local exchange carrier.

point-to-point   Network communication in which two devices have exclusive access to a network medium. For example, a printer connected to only one workstation would be using a point-to-point connection.

Point-to-Point Protocol (PPP)   The protocol used with serial interfaces, DSL and dial-up connections to the Internet. Its functions include error control, security, dynamic IP addressing, and support for multiple protocols.

Point-to-Point Protocol over Ethernet (PPPoE)   A PPP protocol that can be used over Ethernet for authentication purposes.

Point-to-Point Tunneling Protocol (PPTP)   A protocol that allows the creation of virtual private networks (VPNs), which allow users to access a server on a corporate network over a secure, direct connection via the Internet. *See also* virtual private network (VPN).

POP3   *See* Post Office Protocol version 3 (POP3).

port   A numerical value used in the headers of such protocols as TCP and UDP to signify the identity of the next-highest-layer protocol responsible for control of information that follows the header containing the port number. Using this value, the protocol is able to hand its payload to the appropriate protocol at the next, higher layer, creating the appearance of simultaneously multiplexing the PDUs of multiple higher-layer protocols.

Port Address Translation (PAT)   A process that allows a single IP address to represent multiple resources by recording the source TCP or UDP port number.

port numbers   Used at the transport layer with TCP and UDP to keep track of host-to-host virtual circuits.

positive acknowledgment with retransmission   A connection-oriented session that provides acknowledgment and retransmission of the data if it is not acknowledged by the receiving host within a certain time frame.

positive forward acknowledgment   A term used to describe acknowledgment schemes, such as the one used by TCP, that acknowledge only properly received PDUs (no negative acknowledgments to indicate errors in reception) and do so by specifying the next PDU identifier (the sequence number in TCP) the recipient expects to receive, not previously received identifiers.

Post Office Protocol version 3 (POP3)   The protocol used to download email from an SMTP email server to a network client. *See also* Simple Mail Transfer Protocol (SMTP).

POTS   *See* plain old telephone service (POTS).

Power over Ethernet (PoE)   A protocol that allows power to be sent over unused wires in an Ethernet cable to provide power to devices like access points and phones.

PPP   *See* Point-to-Point Protocol (PPP).

PPTP   *See* Point-to-Point Tunneling Protocol (PPTP).

prefix routing   A method of defining how many bits are used in a subnet and how this information is sent in a routing update. For example, RIP version 1 does not send subnet mask information in the route updates. However, RIP version 2 does. This means that RIP v2 updates will send /24, /25, /26, and so on with a route update, which RIP v1 will not.

Presentation layer   The sixth layer of the OSI model; responsible for formatting data exchange such as graphic commands and conversion of character sets. Also responsible for data compression, data encryption, and data stream redirection. *See also* Open Systems Interconnect (OSI).

Pretty Good Privacy (PGP)   A shareware implementation of RSA encryption. *See also* RSA Data Security, Inc.

print server   A centralized device that controls and manages all network printers. The print server can be hardware, software, or a combination of both. Some print servers are actually built into the network printer NICs. *See also* Network Interface Card (NIC).

print services   The network services that manage and control printing on a network, allowing multiple and simultaneous access to printers.

private key   A technology in which both the sender and the receiver have the same key. A single key is used to encrypt and decrypt all messages. *See also* public key.

Process/Application layer   Upper layer in the Internet Protocol stack that is responsible for network services.

protocol   A predefined set of rules that dictates how computers or devices communicate and exchange data on the network.

protocol address   A generic term for Network layer addresses, such as IP or IPv6 addresses, that alludes to the protocol dependency of the address.

protocol analyzer   A software and hardware troubleshooting tool that is used to decode protocol information to try to determine the source of a network problem and to establish baselines.

Protocol Data Unit (PDU)   A generic term used to describe the end product of a protocol. It can be thought of as the entire data structure handed down by a protocol to the protocol at the next lowest layer or the information placed on the network media by the Physical layer. A PDU will consist of the original user data and any upper-layer control information (headers and trailers) imposed by upper-layer protocols encapsulated by the control information of the protocol creating the PDU.

protocol suite   The set of rules a computer uses to communicate with other computers.

protocol switching   A process in which a packet, as it arrives on a router to be forwarded, is copied to the router's process buffer, and the router performs a lookup on the Layer 3 address. Using the route table, an exit interface is associated with the destination address.

The processor forwards the packet with the added new information to the exit interface, while the router initializes the fast-switching cache. Subsequent packets bound for the same destination address follow the same path as the first packet.

proxy   A type of firewall that prevents direct communication between a client and a host by acting as an intermediary. *See also* firewall.

proxy cache server   An implementation of a web proxy. The server receives an HTTP request from a web browser and makes the request on behalf of the sending workstation. When the response comes, the proxy cache server caches a copy of the response locally. The next time someone makes a request for the same web page or Internet information, the proxy cache server can fulfill the request out of the cache instead of having to retrieve the resource from the Web.

proxy server   A type of server that makes a single Internet connection and services requests on behalf of many users.

PSTN   *See* Public Switched Telephone Network (PSTN).

public   For use by everyone. Also a popular name for certain Unix and FTP folders.

public key   A technology that uses two keys to facilitate communication: a public key and a private key. The public key is used to encrypt a message to a receiver. *See also* private key.

Public Key Infrastructure (PKI)   A cryptography arrangement that binds public keys with respective user identities by means of a certificate authority (CA) server.

public network   The part of a network that is on the outside of a firewall and is exposed to the public. *See also* firewall.

Public Switched Telephone Network (PSTN)   The US public telephone network. It is also called the plain old telephone service (POTS). *See also* central office (CO).

punch-down tool   A hand tool used to terminate twisted-pair wires on a wall jack or patch panel.

PVC   *See* permanent virtual circuit (PVC).

Q

QoS   *See* quality of service (QoS).

quad decimal   Four sets of octets separated by a decimal point; an IP address.

quality of service (QoS)   Data prioritization at the Network layer of the OSI model. It results in guaranteed throughput rates. *See also* Open Systems Interconnect (OSI).

R

radio frequency interference (RFI) Interference on copper cabling systems caused by radio frequencies.

README file A file that the manufacturer includes with software to give the installer information that came too late to make it into the software manuals. It's usually a last-minute addition that includes tips on installing the software, possible incompatibilities, and any known installation problems that might have been found right before the product was shipped.

reference model *See* Open Systems Interconnect (OSI).

regeneration process A process in which signals are read, amplified, and repeated on the network to reduce signal degradation. This signal regeneration results in a longer overall possible length of the network.

registered jack (RJ) connector A modular connection mechanism that allows for as many as eight copper wires (four pairs). RJ connectors are most commonly used for telephone (such as the RJ-11) and network adaptors (such as RJ-45).

reliable The quality of a protocol that uses acknowledgments to allow the recipient to confirm error-free receipt of data from a source device. *See also* unreliable.

remote-access protocol Any networking protocol that is used to gain access to a network over public communication links.

remote-access server A computer that has one or more modems installed to enable remote connections to the network.

remote-access VPN A type of VPN that allows remote users like telecommuters to securely access the corporate network wherever and whenever they need to.

Remote Authentication Dial-In User Service (RADIUS) A protocol that is used to communicate between the remote-access device and an authentication server. Sometimes an authentication server running RADIUS is called a RADIUS server.

remote copy (rcp) An old Unix command to perform a remote copy. It is not secure.

Remote Desktop Protocol (RDP) A multichannel protocol that allows a user to connect to a computer running Microsoft Remote Desktop Services. The server listens by default on TCP port 3389.

remote shell (rsh) A command-line computer program that can execute shell commands on another computer across a network. The remote system on which rsh executes the command needs to be running the rshd daemon.

Rendezvous   An IP-based ZeroConf open-service discovery protocol that allows devices to be added to and removed from networks without configuration.

repeater   A Physical layer device that amplifies the signals it receives on one port and resends or repeats them on another. A repeater is used to extend the maximum length of a network segment.

replication   The process of copying directory information to other servers to keep them all synchronized.

RFI   *See* radio frequency interference (RFI).

RG-58   The type designation for the coaxial cable used in Thin Ethernet (10Base2). It has a 50 ohm impedance rating and uses BNC connectors.

RG-62   The type designation for the coaxial cable used in ARCnet networks. It has a 93 ohm impedance and uses BNC connectors.

ring topology   A network topology in which each computer in the network is connected to exactly two other computers. With ring topology, a single break in the ring brings down the entire network.

RIP, RIPv2   *See* Routing Information Protocol (RIP) and Routing Information Protocol version 2 (RIPv2).

RJ (registered jack) connector   *See* registered jack (RJ) connector.

roaming profiles   Profiles downloaded from a server at each login. When a user logs out at the end of the session, changes made are remembered for the next time the user logs in.

rogue access point   An access point not authorized to be up and running by the corporate office by the WLAN administrators of the office. A very large security issue, and expensive software can find these APs and shut them down.

rollover   Used to connect an RS-232 from your PC to a console connection on a router or switch.

route   The path to get to the destination from a source.

route cost   The number of router hops, bandwidth, or delay between source and destination in an internetwork. *See also* hop, router.

routed protocol   A protocol (such as IP or IPv6) used to transmit user data through an internetwork. By contrast, routing protocols (such as RIP, IGRP, and OSPF) are used to update routing tables between routers.

router   A device that connects two networks and allows packets to be transmitted and received between them. A router determines the best path for data packets from source to destination. *See also* hop and cost.

routing   A function of the Network layer that involves moving data throughout a network. Data passes through several network segments using routers that can select the path the data takes. *See also* router.

Routing Information Protocol (RIP) and Routing Information Protocol version 2 (RIPv2)   Distance vector routing protocols used by IP and IPv6. They use hops or ticks to determine the cost for a particular route.

routing protocol   One of a collection of protocols designed to allow routers to dynamically learn routes from one another, reducing or eliminating the need for manual configuration of routes. Examples of routing protocols are RIP, IGRP and EIGRP, OSPF, IS-IS, BGP, NLSP, and ATM's Private Network-to-Network Interface (PNNI).

routing table   A table that contains information about the locations of other routers on the network and their distance from the current router.

RS-232   A connection on your PC that is typically 9 pins. This is being phased out by a USB connection.

RSA Data Security, Inc.   A commercial company that produces encryption software. RSA stands for Rivest, Shamir, and Adleman, the founders of the company.

S

Secure Copy Protocol (SCP)   A protocol to securely transfer files between devices on a network.

Secure Hypertext Transfer Protocol (HTTPS or S-HTTP)   A protocol used for secure communications between a web server and a web browser. This is an alternative mechanism to the HTTPS URI scheme for encrypting web communications carried over HTTP.

Secure Shell (SSH)   A network protocol that allows data to be exchanged using a secure channel between two networked devices.

security log   A log file used in Windows Event Viewer to keep track of security events specified by the domain's Audit policy.

security policy   A rule set in place by a company to help ensure the security of a network. This may include how often a password must be changed or how many characters a password should be.

segment   A unit of data smaller than a packet. Also refers to a portion of a larger network (a network can consist of multiple network segments). *See also* backbone.

sequence number   A number used to determine the order in which parts of a packet are to be reassembled after the packet has been split into sections.

server   A computer that provides resources to the clients on the network.

server and client configuration   A network configuration in which the resources are located on a server for use by the clients.

server-centric   A network design model that uses a central server to contain all data as well as control security.

service accounts   Accounts created on a server for users to perform special services. Examples are local system, backup operators, account operators, and server operators.

Session layer   The fifth layer of the OSI model, which determines how two computers establish, use, and end a session. Security authentication and network-naming functions required for applications occur here. The Session layer establishes, maintains, and breaks dialogs between two stations. *See also* Open Systems Interconnect (OSI).

shared key   A password or other object shared by two devices communicating across a link, often used to create a one-way hash that is transmitted and compared by the recipient to a one-way hash it creates using the same shared key. The shared key is generally not sent across the link.

share-level security   Form of network security where, instead of users being assigned rights to network resources, passwords are assigned to individual files or other network resources (such as printers). The passwords are then given to all users who need access to these resources. All resources are visible from anywhere in the network, and any user who knows the password for a particular network resource can make changes to it.

shell   A Unix interface based solely on command prompts. There is no graphical interface.

shielded   Term that describes cabling that has extra wrapping to protect it from stray electrical or radio signals. Shielded cabling is more expensive than unshielded.

shielded twisted-pair cable (STP)   A type of cabling that includes pairs of copper conductors twisted around each other inside a metal or foil shield. This type of medium can support faster speeds than unshielded wiring because of less crosstalk.

shortest-path-first protocols   *See* Open Shortest Path First (OSPF).

S-HTTP   *See* Secure Hypertext Transfer Protocol (HTTPS or S-HTTP).

signal   A transmission from one PC to another. This could be a notification to start a session or end a session.

signal encoding   The process whereby a protocol at the Physical layer receives information from the upper layers and translates all the data into signals that can be transmitted on a transmission medium.

signaling method   A method of transmitting data across the medium. Two types of signaling are digital and analog.

Simple Mail Transfer Protocol (SMTP) A program that looks for mail on SMTP servers and sends it along the network to its destination at another SMTP server.

Simple Network Management Protocol (SNMP) The management protocol created for sending information about the health of the network to network-management consoles.

SMTP *See* Simple Mail Transfer Protocol (SMTP).

Smurf attack An attack that generates a lot of computer network traffic to a victim host.

SNMP *See* Simple Network Management Protocol (SNMP).

social engineering The art of manipulating people into performing actions that divulge confidential information and compromise security.

socket A combination of a port address and an IP address.

software address *See* logical address.

source address The address of the station that sent a packet, usually found in the source area of a packet header.

source port number The Layer 4 address of the PC that is sending data to a receiving PC. The port portion allows for multiplexing of data to be sent from a specific application.

Spanning Tree Protocol (STP) The bridge protocol (IEEE 802.1D) that enables a learning bridge to dynamically avoid loops in a layer-2 switched network by creating a spanning tree using the spanning-tree algorithm. Spanning-tree frames called Bridge Protocol Data Units (BPDUs) are sent and received by all switches in the network at regular intervals. The switches participating in the spanning tree don't forward the BPDUs; instead, they're processed to determine the spanning-tree topology itself.

SSH File Transfer Protocol (SFTP) A network protocol that provides file transfer over any reliable data stream. It is typically used with SSHv2 (TCP port 22) to provide secure file transfer but is intended to be usable with other protocols as well.

star topology A network topology in which all devices on the network have a direct connection to a single device on the network. These networks are the typical physical networks we use today.

state table A firewall security method that monitors the state of all connections through the firewall.

state transition Digital signaling scheme that reads the "state" of the digital signal in the middle of the bit cell. If it is five volts, the cell is read as a one. If the state of the digital signal is zero volts, the bit cell is read as a zero.

static ARP table entry Entry in the ARP table that is manually added by a user when a PC will be accessed often. This speeds up the process of communicating with the PC because the IP-to-MAC address does not have to be resolved.

static routing   A method of routing packets in which the router's routing table is updated manually by the network administrator instead of automatically by a route-discovery protocol.

static VLAN   A VLAN that is manually configured port by port. This is the method typically used in production networks.

straight tip (ST)   A type of fiber-optic cable connector that uses a mechanism similar to the BNC connectors used by thinnet. This is the most popular fiber-optic connector currently in use.

subnet mask   A group of selected bits that identify a subnetwork within a TCP/IP network. *See also* Transmission Control Protocol/Internet Protocol (TCP/IP).

subnetting   The process of dividing a single IP address range into multiple address ranges.

subnetwork   A network that is part of another network. Also referred to as a subnet. The connection is made through a gateway, bridge, or router.

subnetwork address   A part of the 32-bit IPv4 address that designates the address of the subnetwork. Also referred to as a subnet address.

subscriber connector (SC)   A type of fiber-optic connector. These connectors are square shaped and have release mechanisms to prevent the cable from accidentally being unplugged.

supernetting   The process of combining multiple IP address ranges into a single IP network.

switch   In networking, a device responsible for multiple functions such as filtering, flooding, and sending frames. It works using the destination addresses of individual frames. Switches operate at the Data Link layer of the OSI model.

switched   Term used to describe a network that has multiple routes to get from a source to a destination. This allows for higher speeds.

symmetric digital subscriber line (SDSL)   Type of DSL that provides the same speeds upstream and downstream. It is the opposite of ADSL. See also asymmetrical digital subscriber line (ADSL).

symmetrical keys   Keys that are used to both encrypt and decrypt data.

SYN flood   A denial of service attack in which the hacker sends a barrage of SYN packets. The receiving station tries to respond to each SYN request for a connection, thereby tying up all the resources. All incoming connections are rejected until all current connections can be established.

Synchronous Optical Network (SONET)   A standard in the United States that defines a base data rate of 51.84Mbps. Multiples of this rate are known as optical carrier (OC) levels, such as OC-3, OC-12, and so on.

T

TA   *See* Terminal Adapter (TA).

TCP   *See* Transmission Control Protocol (TCP).

TCP/IP   *See* Transmission Control Protocol/Internet Protocol (TCP/IP).

TDMA   *See* Time Division Multiple Access (TDMA).

TDR   *See* time-domain reflectometer (TDR).

telephony server   A computer that functions as a smart answering machine for the network. It can also perform call-center and call-routing functions.

Telnet   A protocol that functions at the Application layer of the OSI model, providing terminal-emulation capabilities. *See also* Open Systems Interconnect (OSI).

template   A set of guidelines that you can apply to every new user account created.

Terminal Access Controller Access-Control System Plus (TACACS+)   An enhanced version of TACACS, similar to RADIUS. *See also* Remote Authentication Dial-In User Service (RADIUS).

Terminal Adapter (TA)   In ISDN, the device (often erroneously referred to as an ISDN modem) that is used to interconnect ISDN-incompatible devices, such as PC serial ports or Ethernet interfaces and POTS phones, to an ISDN network for eventual connection to an ISDN circuit.

terminal emulator   A program that enables a PC to act as a terminal for a mainframe or a Unix system.

TFTP   *See* Trivial File Transfer Protocol (TFTP).

Thick Ethernet (thicknet)   A type of Ethernet that uses thick coaxial cable and supports a maximum transmission distance of 500 meters. Also called 10Base5.

Thin Ethernet (thinnet)   A type of Ethernet that uses RG-58 cable and 10Base2.

three-way handshake   Term used in a TCP session to define how a virtual circuit is set up. It is called this because it uses three data segments.

Time Division Multiple Access (TDMA)   A method to divide individual channels in broadband communications into separate time slots, allowing more data to be carried at the same time. It is also possible to use TDMA in baseband communications.

Time-to-Live (TTL)   A field in IP packets that indicates how many routers the packet can still cross (hops it can still make) before it is discarded. TTL is also used in ARP tables to indicate how long an entry should remain in the table.

time-domain reflectometer (TDR)   A tool that sends out a signal and measures how much time it takes to return. It is used to find short or open circuits. Also called a *cable tester*.

tone generator   A small electronic device that is used to test network cables for breaks and other problems by sending an electronic signal down one set of UTP wires. Used with a tone locator. *See also* tone locator, unshielded twisted-pair (UTP) cable.

tone locator   A device used to test network cables for breaks and other problems. It senses the signal sent by the tone generator and emits a tone when the signal is detected in a particular set of wires.

toner probe   A device that allows telephone and cable technicians to find and test cables. The probe listens for the tone coming from a tone generator.

topology   The physical and/or logical layout of the transmission media specified in the Physical and Logical layers of the OSI model. *See also* Open Systems Interconnect (OSI).

Traceroute   *See* tracert.

tracert   A Microsoft-based TCP/IP command-line utility that shows the user every router interface a TCP/IP packet passes through on its way to a destination. The command **traceroute** is used in such environments as the Cisco IOS CLI. *See also* Transmission Control Protocol/Internet Protocol (TCP/IP).

trailer   A section of a data packet that contains error-checking information.

transceiver   The part of any network interface that transmits and receives network signals.

transmission   The sending of packets from the PC to the network cable.

Transmission Control Protocol (TCP)   The protocol found at the Host-to-Host layer of the DoD model. This protocol breaks data packets into segments, numbers them, and sends them in random order. The receiving computer reassembles the data so that the information is readable for the user. In the process, the sender and the receiver confirm that all data has been received; if not, it is resent. This is a connection-oriented protocol. *See also* connection-oriented transport protocol.

Transmission Control Protocol/Internet Protocol (TCP/IP)   The protocol suite developed by the DoD as an internetworking protocol suite that could route information around network failures. Today it is the de facto standard for communications on the Internet.

transmission media   Physical cables and/or wireless technology across which computers are able to communicate.

transparent bridging   The bridging scheme that is used in Ethernet and IEEE 802.3 networks and passes frames along one hop at a time, using bridging information stored in tables that associate end-node MAC addresses with bridge ports. This type of bridging is considered transparent because the source node does not know it has been bridged because the destination frames are addressed directly to the end node.

Transport layer   The fourth layer of the OSI model, which is responsible for checking that data packets created in the Session layer were received error free. If necessary, it also changes the length of messages for transport up or down the remaining layers. *See also* Open Systems Interconnect (OSI).

Triple Data Encryption Standard (3DES)   *See* Data Encryption Standard (DES).

Trivial File Transfer Protocol (TFTP)   A protocol similar to FTP that does not provide the security or error-checking features of FTP. *See also* File Transfer Protocol (FTP).

Trojan horse   A virus or other malicious process that hides within another, possibly trusted, program that the user executes without knowing the Trojan horse is embedded. Execution of the host program generally launches the Trojan horse.

trunk lines   The telephone lines that form the backbone of a telephone network for a company. These lines connect the telephone(s) to the telephone company and to the PSTN. *See also* Public Switched Telephone Network (PSTN).

trunk link   A link used between switches and from some servers to the switches. Trunk links carry traffic for many VLANs. Access links are used to connect host devices to a switch and carry only VLAN information for the VLAN of which the device is a member.

T-series connections   A series of digital connections leased from the telephone company. Each T-series connection is rated with a number based on speed. T1 and T3 are the most popular.

TTL   *See* Time-to-Live (TTL).

tunneling   A method of avoiding protocol restrictions by wrapping packets from one protocol in another protocol's frame and transmitting this encapsulated packet over a network that supports the wrapper protocol. *See also* encapsulation.

twisted-pair cable   A network transmission medium that contains one or more pairs of color-coded, insulated copper wires that are twisted around each other in a common jacket.

type   A DOS command that displays the contents of a file. Also short for *data type*.

U

UDP   *See* User Datagram Protocol (UDP).

Uniform Resource Locator (URL)   One way of identifying a document on the Internet. Consists of the protocol that is used to access the document and the domain name or IP address of the host that holds the document. For example, `http://www.sybex.com`.

uninterruptible power supply (UPS)   A natural-line conditioner that uses a battery and power inverter to run the computer equipment that plugs into it. The battery charger continuously charges the battery. The battery charger is the only thing that runs off line voltage.

During a power problem, the battery charger stops operating and the equipment continues to run off the battery.

Universal Serial Bus (USB)   A versatile, chainable serial-bus technology that connects up to 127 devices at speeds of 1.5Mbps and 12Mbps (versions 1.0 and 1.1; 1.5Mbps is the sub-channel rate) as well as 480Mbps (version 2.0, Hi-Speed USB).

Unix   A 32-bit, multitasking operating system developed in the 1960s for use on mainframes and minicomputers.

unreliable   The quality of a protocol that does not use acknowledgments to allow a receiving device to inform the source that it received its transmitted data without error. *See also* reliable.

unshielded   Term that describes cabling that has little or no wrapping to protect it from stray electrical or radio signals. Unshielded cabling is less expensive than shielded.

unshielded twisted-pair (UTP) cable   Twisted-pair cable consisting of a number of twisted pairs of copper wire with a simple plastic casing. Because no shielding is used in this cable, it is very susceptible to EMI, RFI, and other types of interference. *See also* crossover cable, electromagnetic interference (EMI), radio frequency interference (RFI).

upgrade   To increase an aspect of a PC by, for example, adding more RAM, changing to a faster CPU, and so on.

UPS   *See* uninterruptible power supply (UPS).

URL   *See* Uniform Resource Locator (URL).

user   The person who is using a computer or network.

User Datagram Protocol (UDP)   A protocol at the Host-to-Host layer of the DoD model that corresponds to the Transport layer of the OSI model. Data segments are divided, sent randomly, and put back together at the receiving end. This is a connectionless protocol. *See also* connectionless transport protocol, Open Systems Interconnect (OSI).

user-level security   A type of network security in which user accounts can read, write, change, and take ownership of files. Rights are assigned to user accounts, and each user knows only their own username and password, which makes this the preferred method for securing files.

V

very high bit-rate digital subscriber line (VDSL)   A DSL technology that provides faster data transmission over a single flat untwisted or twisted pair of copper wires. VDSL is capable of supporting high-bandwidth applications such as HDTV as well as telephone services (Voice over IP) and general Internet access over a single connection.

virtual circuit   A logical circuit devised to ensure reliable communication between two devices on a network. Defined by a virtual path identifier/virtual channel (really the only time *channel* is used) identifier (VPI/VCI) pair, a virtual circuit can be permanent (PVC) or switched (SVC). Virtual circuits are used in Frame Relay and X.25. Known as virtual channel in ATM. *See also* permanent virtual circuit (PVC).

virtual COM port   A logical port that is used as if it were a serial port when the actual serial-port interface does not exist.

virtual LAN (VLAN)   A technology that allows users on different switch ports to participate in their own network separate from, but still connected to, the other stations on the same or a connected switch.

virtual private network (VPN)   A network that uses the public Internet as a backbone for a private interconnection (network) between locations.

virus   A program intended to damage a computer system. Sophisticated viruses are encrypted and hide in a computer and may not appear until the user performs a certain action or until a certain date. *See also* antivirus.

virus engine   The core program that runs the virus-scanning process.

VLAN   *See* virtual LAN (VLAN).

Voice over Internet Protocol (VoIP)   A general term for a family of transmission technologies for delivery of voice communications over the Internet or other packet-switched networks.

VPN   *See* virtual private network (VPN).

VPN concentrator   A device that can terminate multiple VPN connections. Typically found at a corporate office to which remote offices connect.

W

WAN   *See* wide area network (WAN).

web proxy   A type of proxy that is used to act on behalf of a web client or web server.

web server   A server that holds and delivers web pages and other web content using the HTTP protocol. *See also* Hypertext Transfer Protocol (HTTP).

wide area network (WAN)   A network that crosses local, regional, or international boundaries.

wire crimper   Used for attaching ends onto different types of network cables by a process known as crimping. Crimping involves using pressure to press some kind of metal teeth into the inner conductors of a cable.

Wired Equivalent Privacy (WEP)   A security protocol for 802.11b wireless LANs that gets its name from the fact that it is designed to provide a security level roughly equivalent to a wired LAN. This is done by encrypting the data that is transmitted wirelessly.

wireless (I know—duh!)   An 802.11 specification that allows data transmission over unbounded media.

wireless access point (WAP)   A wireless bridge used in a multipoint RF network.

wireless bridge   A bridge that performs all the functions of a regular bridge but uses RF instead of cables to transmit signals.

workgroup   A specific group of users or network devices organized by job function or proximity to shared resources.

workstation   A computer that is not a server but is on a network. Generally, it is used to do work, whereas a server is used to store data or perform a network function. In the simplest terms, a workstation is a computer that is not a server.

World Wide Web (WWW)   A collection of HTTP servers running on the Internet. They support the use of documents formatted with HTML. *See also* Hypertext Markup Language (HTML), Hypertext Transfer Protocol (HTTP).

worm   A program that is similar to a virus but that propagates over a network. *See also* virus.

WWW   *See* World Wide Web (WWW).

X

X Windows   A graphical user interface (GUI) developed for use with the various flavors of Unix.

xDSL   A family of technologies that provides digital data transmission over the wires of a local telephone network. Collectively called Digital Subscriber Line (DSL), the family includes ADSL, VDSL, and SDSL.

Y

Yagi   *See* directional antenna (Yagi).

Index